US History Study Guide: A Targeted & Thematic Approach for the AP and SAT II Tests

Paul Pinto

American History Tutoring Guide   Paul Pinto

Table of Contents

HOW TO USE THIS GUIDE 5

PART ONE: WHAT TO STUDY 6

    DIAGNOSTIC TEST 13

    TOPIC 1: FOREIGN POLICY AND WESTWARD EXPANSION 38

    TOPIC 2: THE AFRICAN-AMERICAN POLITICAL EXPERIENCE 62

    TOPIC 3: THE ECONOMIC ROLE OF GOVERNMENT 82

    TOPIC 4: THE CONSTITUTION 101

    TOPIC 5: BUSINESS AND ECONOMY 114

    TOPIC 6: THE PATH TO INDEPENDENCE 138

    TOPIC 7: POLITICAL PARTIES 145

    TOPIC 8: FOUNDING COLONIES 154

    TOPIC 9: THE RIGHTS OF WOMEN 160

    TOPIC 10: AMERICAN LITERATURE AND PHILOSOPHY 168

    TOPIC 11: THE PRESIDENCY 177

    TOPIC 12: NATIVE AMERICANS 185

    TOPIC 13: THE LABOR MOVEMENT 193

    TOPIC 14: IMMIGRATION 199

    TOPIC 15: THE PROGRESSIVE MOVEMENT 205

    TOPIC 16: RELIGION IN AMERICAN HISTORY 211

    TOPIC 17: SOCIAL AND DEMOGRAPHIC TRENDS 222

    TOPIC 18: THE CIVIL WAR 228

PART TWO: HOW TO STUDY 240

    LESSON ONE: HOW TO READ THE TEXTBOOK 240

    LESSON TWO: ESSAY WRITING 242

    LESSON THREE: THE DBQ 246

    LESSON FOUR: MULTIPLE CHOICE 260

    LESSON FIVE: HOW TO INTERPRET POLITICAL CARTOONS 263

    LESSON SIX: HOW TO READ AND INTERPRET CHARTS, GRAPHS AND TABLES 267

    LESSON SEVEN: FREQUENTLY TESTED ESSAY TOPICS 270

    LESSON EIGHT: LINKING GENERAL THEMES TO SPECIFIC QUESTIONS 272

    LESSON NINE: HISTORICAL TIMELINES 278

PART THREE: REFERENCE MATERIALS **281**
   KEY RESOURCES 281
   SAMPLE FREE-RESPONSE ESSAY PROMPTS 282
   WORKS OF AMERICAN FICTION AND NONFICTION 288
   BIOGRAPHICAL SKETCHES OF MAJOR FIGURES IN AMERICAN HISTORY 296

American History Tutoring Guide

INTRODUCTION

Dear Student,

Welcome to your friendly guide to American history! This guide is designed to help you efficiently prepare for the AP and SAT II US history tests by showing you what to study and how to study it. My analysis and categorization of thousands of test questions reveals one central fact: *the content of both tests is concentrated among a manageable set of historical topics*. It turns out that over half of the SAT II/AP multiple choice questions are captured by just four historical categories: foreign policy, the African-American political experience, the government's role in the economy, and the Constitution. Over *ninety-five* percent of the questions on these tests are covered by a total of eighteen historical topics, all of which are reviewed here with original summaries that provide both a broad analysis of the topic and an array of specific facts arranged in a logical way to help you retain them. You may customize your test preparation further by taking and scoring an included diagnostic practice test which will help you focus your study time on an optimal combination of the most important topics and the topics that you need the most practice on.

In my experience from years of tutoring US history, success on tests does not come from trying to cram as many individual facts in your memory as possible. Rather, you should aim to cultivate an understanding of the patterns that structure each historical topic. These patterns will help you organize a range of facts and events into a coherent framework and will even help you fill in the blanks by process of elimination when you come across an unfamiliar fact. This is where the first part of the guide comes in: it contains topic summaries that provide an explanation of the pattern underpinning a given topic before presenting the specific facts relevant to that topic. As you read the summaries, think carefully about the overarching framework and try to attach specific facts, events, or people to the framework in a way that makes the most sense to you.

The second part of the guide reviews best practices, including lessons on reading the textbook critically and efficiently, writing essays and DBQs, answering multiple choice questions, analyzing political cartoons and data tables, and much more.

Finally, for those times when you are looking for a specific fact, an individual biography, or a relevant quote, the third section of the guide – the reference materials – contains comprehensive information including biographical sketches of prominent individuals and a list of major works of American fiction and nonfiction.

A good student of history cultivates his or her ability to organize a set of specific facts into a broader explanation of historical events. This guide is organized around helping you learn the patterns that will help you connect facts together in meaningful ways.

As you work to prepare for the tests, be mindful of the broader value of what you are doing. According to the American Historical Association, the study of history is both useful – knowing the past is indispensable for understanding the present – and beautiful – understanding the human condition is a beautiful thing. Good luck and thanks for reading.

Paul Pinto

American History Tutoring Guide   Paul Pinto

HOW TO USE THIS GUIDE

The guide contains three main sections:

1. *What to study: the diagnostic test and topic summaries*
   AP and the SAT II US History test questions are concentrated around a number of key topics. Your preparation for the test should be centered around these topics. Prioritize the most commonly occurring topics, as well as the topics that you need the most work on. This guide lays out the basic pattern or framework governing each historical topic, accompanied by specific facts in the form of timelines, data tables, and charts. The goal is to be able to understand and explain the topic at a high level in order to properly fit specific facts, people, events and dates into a coherent framework.

2. *How to study: lesson guides*
   Scoring well on the tests requires you to master a number of key skills, from learning how to read the textbook efficiently to writing DBQ essays or answering multiple choice questions. Each "how to" lesson provides step-by-step guidance and draws from actual test content.

3. *Finding information: reference materials*
   The reference materials include biographical sketches of major figures in America history, a dictionary of quotes, and a list of key works of American fiction and nonfiction. Use this information to build up your database of historical knowledge slowly but surely during the year. It will serve you well during test time. Students taking the SAT II test in particular should first read the topic covering American Literature and Philosophy and subsequently familiarize themselves with the list of works of American fiction and nonfiction found in the reference materials.

ABOUT THE AUTHOR:
Paul Pinto is currently a PhD candidate in Political Science at Yale University who has worked as a private tutor of US, European and World history for several years. He may be contacted at pinto.paul@gmail.com.

PART ONE: WHAT TO STUDY

One of the best and most commonly taught US history textbooks – *America: Past and Present*, written by Robert Divine, T.H. Breen, and four other colleagues – weighs in at a hefty one thousand pages spread across two volumes (Divine et al. 2007). Covering five centuries of history from Columbus to the inauguration of Barack Obama, the textbook contains an immense variety and quantity of historical narratives; political, economic and demographic trends; and social and cultural themes. Small wonder that producing all of this information required a collaborative effort from no fewer than five master historians! The good news is that neither the AP nor the SAT II requires students to demonstrate a comprehensive and balanced mastery over all or even most of the textbook material. Both tests instead concentrate their test questions on eighteen or so important historical topics. Some of these topics cover specific historical events or processes, such as the movement towards independence, while others deal with long-term general trends such as the evolving rights of women. In other words, some topics can be reviewed by simply going to a specific chapter or section in the textbook, while others will require you to trace the story (such as women's rights) over the course of multiple centuries and book chapters. Your preparation for the AP US History and SAT II tests should be organized around the systematic study of the eighteen main topics – *this is the most efficient and targeted way to raise your score.*

You may be wondering why the tests focus on such a comparatively limited list of topics. One reason is that certain events or processes occurred during a "critical juncture" or key moment that shaped the nature of the country and its people for many years to come; contrast the founding of New England from that of Virginia, for instance: the differing imperatives of Puritan religion and tobacco planting led to divergent social and economic systems that produced substantially different types of colonies. Other processes tend to be tested frequently because they tap directly into the main narratives of American history: the long battle of African-Americans to obtain freedom and civil rights, for example, illustrates the broader nature of democracy and liberty in overall American history.

To prove the case that the content of the AP and SAT II tests draws primarily from a relatively limited set of major topics, I conducted a large-scale content analysis by examining a sample of 1,000 AP US history multiple choice questions and 1,000 SAT II US history multiple choice questions. I used the specific content of each question to assign it to a broader historical category. For example, a question about Supreme Court's decision in *Marbury v. Madison* that laid down the principle of judicial review belongs to the broader category of the Constitution. The charts below display the distribution of questions organized by category:

Figure 1: Distribution of SAT II/AP US History Test Questions by Content Area

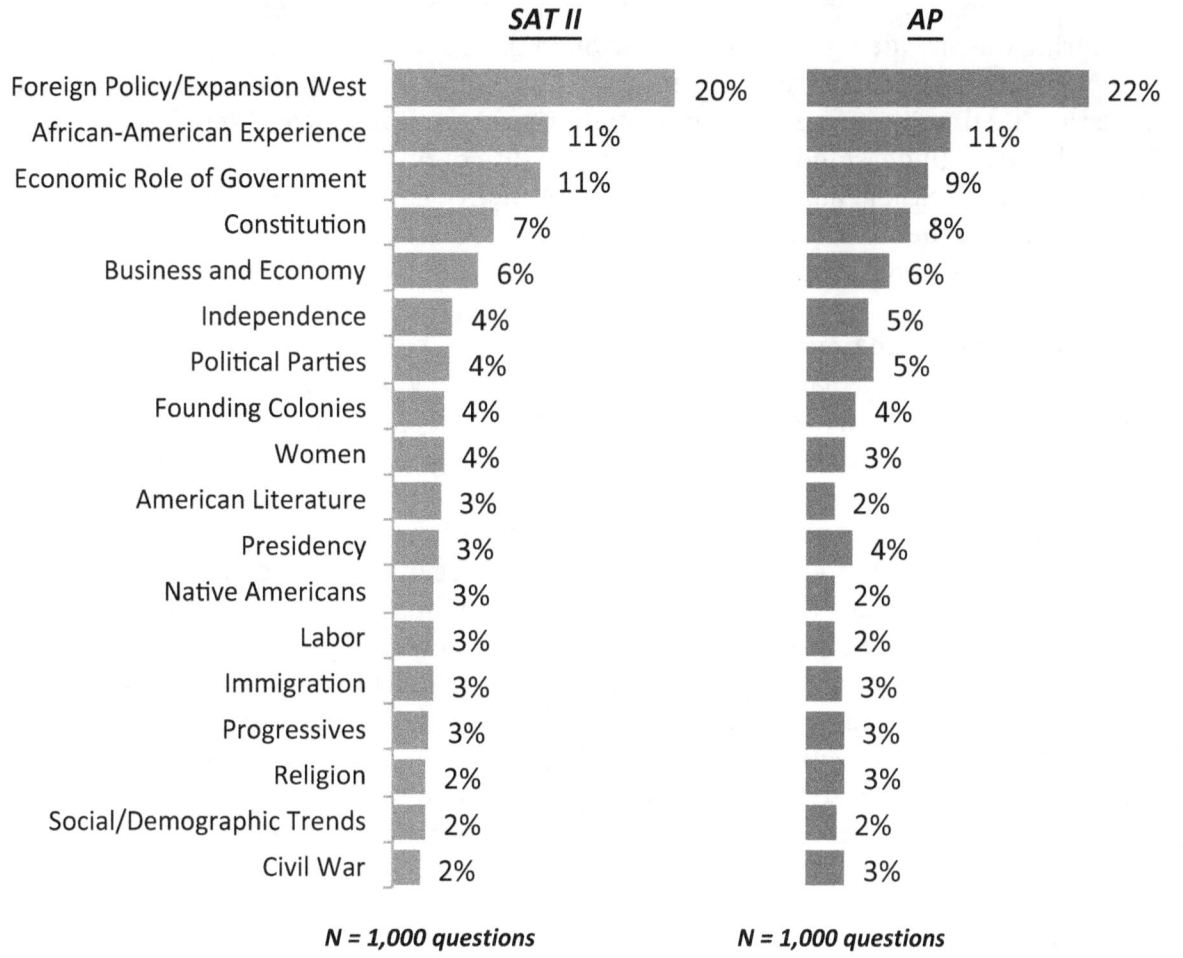

The data are highly concentrated by topic area: on the SAT II, just four topics – foreign policy/westward expansion, the African-American experience, the government's role in the economy, and the Constitution – account for half (49%) of all the questions. Overall, the eighteen topic areas account for 95% of all the questions on the test. The AP test has a remarkably similar distribution of questions by topic area – the corresponding figures are 50% and 96%, respectively. The overall lesson is clear: *preparation for the test is most efficient when it is organized around these eighteen topics.* One simple and optimal path is to start at the beginning with Topic #1 (Foreign Policy & Expansion West) and work your way through the topics one after the other. To further customize your test preparation, take the practice diagnostic test, calculate your success rate by topic area using the answer key, and go through the topics in order of the difficulty you have with each topic.

The concentration of topics suggests that the best way to review for the AP or SAT II tests is not to flip chronologically through the textbook in the hopes of finding crucial nuggets of information but rather to work thematically because the themes are already arranged in order of the most likely test content. Reviewing the content thematically will also help you gain mastery over important historical topics by drawing together various strands of information – which may be scattered across historical time periods – into a coherent and meaningful whole. For example, Americans since the founding of the Republic have been arguing over the proper role of the federal government in the economy: this debate dominated the first dozen years of the early Republic (Hamilton vs. Jefferson) and gained steam during the presidency of Andrew Jackson in the 1830s; it reemerged during the Gilded Age and era of Progressive reforms, rose to a high point during the Great Depression and the New Deal, and returned once more with rise of the Republican "New Right" in the 1970s and 1980s. Understanding the recurring nature of this topic allows you to assign historical actors to either "limited government" or "active government" sides and then quickly determine their perspective on a specific economic issue of their time (and answer the associated question(s) correctly!)

The diagnostic test and developing a study plan
This section begins with a diagnostic test that will provide you with an assessment of your current strengths and weaknesses relative to the eighteen main topics. If you are using this guidebook to prepare for the AP test, complete the first 80 questions; for the SAT, complete all 90 questions. Grade your results using the grading template, which will calculate your overall score and as well as your accuracy rate on each of the eighteen topics. The template multiplies your accuracy rate by the weighted importance of each topic to provide you with a ranking of the order in which you should review the eighteen topics. The section then continues with the content summaries for each of the eighteen topic areas. Each summary includes an introductory overview; charts or tables that describe the main events, people and facts relevant to the topic; and some concluding thoughts to pull the material together. The content summaries are designed not only to provide the information covered by multiple choice tests but also to present the arguments and evidence needed to produce quality essays. Each topic area section concludes with practice multiple choice and essay questions.

Differences between the AP and SAT II tests
A common question posed by many students is how the multiple-choice section of the AP US history test differs from the SAT II US history test. The short answer is that they are not very different at all. Both tests are created by the same organization, the College Board. The purpose of the AP test is to examine how well a student has mastered the material presented in a year-long college-level history course; the purpose of the SAT II is not terribly dissimilar – to demonstrate to colleges mastery over US history content. My experience in tutoring a large number of students for both tests is that scores tend to be highly correlated: students who perform well on the AP test perform well on the SAT II and vice versa. Figure 1 provides data that supports this claim: it shows that the distribution of test questions by content area is remarkably similar. Perhaps the main difference between the two tests is that SAT II questions tend to be somewhat more specific than AP questions. This increase in specificity, however, is no reason to change our preparation plan: the most efficient and effective preparation still relies on first mastering the overall themes that structure the most important topics and then working our way toward the specific facts that rest on these themes. SAT II questions are also something of a lagging indicator relative to the more progressive AP Test; that is to say, the AP test has been swifter to give relatively less weight to traditional categories like American Literature and relatively more weight to social history topics like religion, African-American history, and Native American

history. In other words, it is increasingly likely that the SAT II will move closer and closer in form and content to the multiple-choice section of the AP test.

How have the tests changed over the years, and what changes can we expect this year?

Another common question deals the evolution of the tests over the past decade and the implications of these changes for the future. Both tests blend an older tradition of narrative political history with newer approaches focused economic and social history. Narrative political history in its classical form is primarily concerned with the sayings and doings of the leaders of society, particularly during crucial moments such as revolutions or wars. Narrative American political history pays particular attention to events like the path to independence, the Constitution, the Civil War, and World War II; it emphasizes the role of leaders of society such as George Washington, Thomas Jefferson, Abraham Lincoln and Franklin Roosevelt. Since the 1960s, academic historians have expanded the borders of American history by placing an increasing emphasis on social history, which examines the lives of ordinary Americans as well as their leaders. Social history has highlighted the important role played by minorities, women, and other marginalized groups and used the experience of these groups to illuminate the nature of American society in general. Historians have also made an effort to incorporate the important role played by economics in shaping social and political outcomes, particularly during times of rapid economic change such as the Industrial Revolution. Economic and social history have together helped broaden our historical perspective by highlighting data and other forms of evidence that shows us how society as a whole has changed or developed. We may directly examine the way in which the content on the tests has changed by comparing the content distribution of a test from 1977 with one from 2012. The results are illuminating:

Figure 2: Distribution of AP US History Test Questions by Content Area

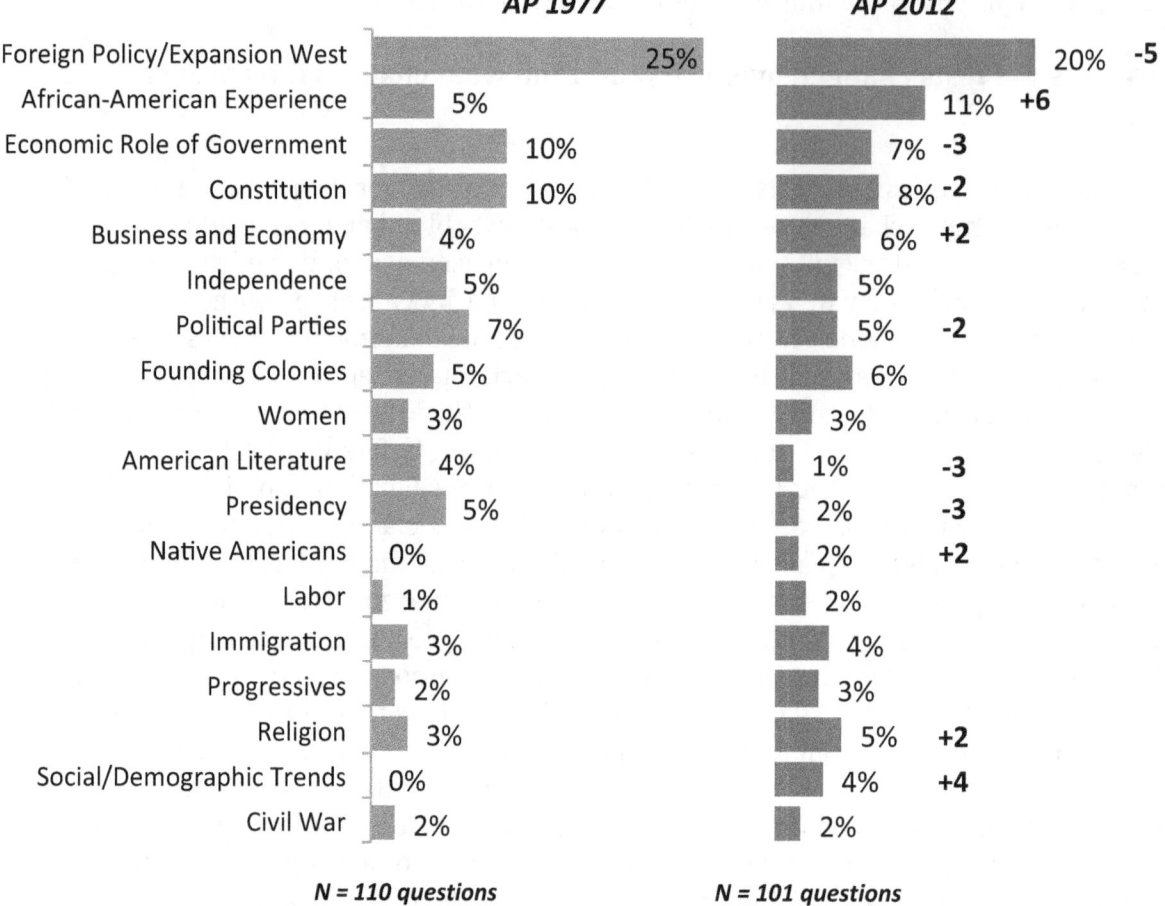

The bedrock topics in narrative political history – foreign policy, the presidency, the Constitution, political parties – have all declined as a share of the overall questions (while remaining important). Traditional topics like American Literature have also declined sharply in relative importance. Picking up the slack are topics like social and demographic trends, which track large-scale population, family, and cultural changes; African-American history, with a renewed focus on Reconstruction and its connection to the Civil Rights Movement; Native American history; and religion, which previously focused mostly on the Puritans and is now broadened to include topics like religion's connection to social movements and relationships between Protestants and other religious groups.

What specific topics should I make sure to study?

This guide is designed around the premise of working from the general to specific for each of the eighteen topics. However, the content analysis of 2,000 questions allows for the categorization of each question by its specific rather than general content (e.g., the First Amendment specifically rather than the Constitution more generally). A list of the one hundred most frequently tested topics is shown on the next page. You should make sure that you have at least a high-level knowledge of each of these topics prior to taking the test.

Concluding Thoughts

This guide contains a great deal of information and analysis of the eighteen major historical topics that together supply the vast majority of the questions on the test. Try to own each historical topic by reading it carefully, taking notes or highlighting text as necessary, and organizing information in your own way using your own charts, timelines, or tables. Controlling your own process of organizing and reorganizing information in a way that makes the most sense to you is often what gets specific facts to stick, and is a process that I cannot recommend highly enough.

Good luck and enjoy learning about US history – it will make you a more informed citizen as well as a better student!

Figure 3: Most Frequently Tested Individual Topics (N=2,000 questions)

#	Topic	Likelihood	#	Topic	Likelihood
1	Slavery	2.4%	51	Korean War	0.5%
2	New Deal	2.2%	52	Northwest Ordinance	0.5%
3	Labor Unions	2.1%	53	Open Door	0.5%
4	World War II	2.0%	54	Presidency	0.5%
5	Reconstruction	1.9%	55	Reform Movements	0.5%
6	Civil Rights	1.8%	56	Stamp Act	0.5%
7	Women's Rights	1.7%	57	American System	0.5%
8	American Literature	1.6%	58	Bank of the United States	0.5%
9	Native Americans	1.4%	59	Immigration	0.5%
10	Puritans	1.3%	60	Industrialism	0.5%
11	Civil War	1.2%	61	Louisiana Purchase	0.5%
12	Vietnam War	1.2%	62	Nixon Administration	0.5%
13	Cold War	1.1%	63	Transcendentalism	0.5%
14	Supreme Court	1.1%	64	Women's Suffrage	0.5%
15	Articles of Confederation	1.0%	65	Bill of Rights	0.4%
16	European Immigration	1.0%	66	Dawes Act	0.4%
17	Nativism	1.0%	67	Federal Reserve	0.4%
18	Farmers	0.9%	68	Free Silver	0.4%
19	Abolitionism	0.9%	69	Indentured Servitude	0.4%
20	Political Parties	0.9%	70	Popular Sovereignty	0.4%
21	Popular Culture	0.9%	71	Segregation	0.4%
22	Progressives	0.9%	72	Urbanization	0.4%
23	Railroads	0.9%	73	Colonial Virginia	0.4%
24	War of 1812	0.9%	74	Dred Scott v. Sanford	0.4%
25	World War I	0.9%	75	Emancipation Proclamation	0.4%
26	Revolutionary War	0.8%	76	First Amendment	0.4%
27	Territorial Expansion	0.8%	77	Mexican-American War	0.4%
28	Diplomacy	0.8%	78	Oil	0.4%
29	Ratification of Constitution	0.8%	79	Populist Party	0.4%
30	Spanish-American War	0.8%	80	Prohibition	0.4%
31	Tariff/Taxes	0.8%	81	Roosevelt Corollary	0.4%
32	Education	0.7%	82	Sherman Antitrust Act	0.4%
33	Founding Colonies	0.7%	83	Social Darwinism	0.4%
34	French and Indian War	0.7%	84	Tobacco Plantations	0.4%
35	Great Society	0.7%	85	Compromise of 1850	0.3%
36	Monroe Doctrine	0.7%	86	Early Explorers	0.3%
37	Great Depression	0.6%	87	Eisenhower Administration	0.3%
38	Hamilton	0.6%	88	Election of 1824	0.3%
39	Imperialism	0.6%	89	Japanese Internment	0.3%
40	Jackson Administration	0.6%	90	Marshall Plan	0.3%
41	Manifest Destiny	0.6%	91	Missouri Compromise	0.3%
42	Reagan Administration	0.6%	92	Muckraking	0.3%
43	Women Workers	0.6%	93	NAACP	0.3%
44	Great Awakening	0.6%	94	Oregon Territory	0.3%
45	Isolationism	0.6%	95	Republican Party	0.3%
46	League of Nations	0.6%	96	Roosevelt Administration	0.3%
47	McCarthyism	0.6%	97	Sectional Differences	0.3%
48	Mercantilism	0.6%	98	Urban Politics	0.3%
49	Nullification	0.6%	99	Virtual Representation	0.3%
50	Declaration of Independence	0.5%	100	Carter Administration	0.3%

American History Tutoring Guide Paul Pinto

DIAGNOSTIC TEST

The diagnostic test will help you determine which of the eighteen sections you will benefit most from reviewing. The score template below will help you calculate your performance by topic area. Good luck!

Time: AP Test: 55 minutes for the first 80 questions
       SAT II Test: 60 minutes for all 90 questions

1. Why did America lose the Vietnam War?
   A. American policymakers focused on the threat of communism failed to consider the importance of nationalism among the Vietnamese people
   B. The US Army failed to win any major battles against the North Vietnamese
   C. The Tet Offensive demonstrated the superiority of Vietnamese military forces
   D. American public opinion forced the United States to draw its military forces down by 1966
   E. The Soviet Union provided a great deal of direct military assistance to the North Vietnamese Army

2. Which philosopher's work had the most influence on the political theory informing the Declaration of Independence?
   A. John Locke
   B. Thomas Hobbs
   C. Baron de Montesquieu
   D. John Cotton
   E. Alexis de Tocqueville

3. Which of the following battles/campaigns of the Civil War split the territory of the Confederacy in 1863?
   A. Antietam
   B. Gettysburg
   C. First Battle of Bull Run
   D. Vicksburg
   E. Sherman's March to the Sea

4. "It is a proposition too plain to be contested, that the constitution controls any legislative act repugnant to it..."
   Marbury v. Madison (1803)

   The above quotation from John Marshall refers to which of the following concepts?
   A. separation of powers
   B. judicial review
   C. popular sovereignty
   D. manifest destiny
   E. anti-federalism

5. Which of the following products was NOT included in the Townshend Acts of 1767?
   A. Tea
   B. Glass
   C. Paper
   D. Stamps
   E. Coffee

6. What theory or concept did the British government appeal to in order to justify its taxation of the American colonies from 1763-1776?
   A. Virtual representation
   B. Divide-and-rule
   C. Natural law
   D. Direct representation
   E. Royal prerogative

7. Which of the following individuals championed religious liberty in the seventeenth century?
   A. Thomas Jefferson
   B. John Adams
   C. Roger Williams
   D. William Bradford
   E. Jonathan Edwards

8. Which of the following is NOT a Progressive-era constitutional amendment?
   A. The Fourteenth Amendment
   B. The Eighteenth Amendment
   C. The Seventeenth Amendment
   D. The Nineteenth Amendment
   E. The Sixteenth Amendment

9. Which of the following freedoms is NOT protected by the Bill of Rights?
   A. Freedom of speech
   B. Freedom of the press
   C. The right to bear arms
   D. The right against self-incrimination
   E. The right to vote

10. Which union is INCORRECTLY aligned with a strike in which it played a significant role?
    A. American Railway Union - Pullman Strike of 1894
    B. United Mine Workers - Anthracite Coal Strike of 1902
    C. Amalgamated Association of Iron and Steel Workers - Homestead Strike of 1892
    D. United Mine Workers - Coal Strike of 1919
    E. Knights of Labor - Steel Strike of 1952

11. Which nineteenth-century president issued more vetoes than all his predecessors combined?
    A. Theodore Roosevelt
    B. Andrew Jackson
    C. Andrew Johnson
    D. Millard Fillmore
    E. James K. Polk

12. The Monroe Doctrine received unexpected and unrequested enforcement assistance from which European nation?
    A. Great Britain
    B. France
    C. The Netherlands
    D. Portugal
    E. None of the above

13. The Monroe Doctrine stated or implied the opposition of the United States to all of the following EXCEPT
    A. European recolonization of Latin America
    B. Coups instigated at the behest of European powers in the Western Hemisphere
    C. European trade with the Western Hemisphere
    D. The recreation of Latin American monarchies
    E. The assassination of Latin American political leaders by European mercenaries

14. The Embargo Act of 1807 was
    A. A political success that ushered in a second term for John Adams
    B. A political disaster for the Federalists that led directly to the Hartford Convention
    C. A political success for Thomas Jefferson that led to the "Era of Good Feelings"
    D. A political disaster for Thomas Jefferson that resulted in a dramatic decline of US foreign trade
    E. A political success for Thomas Jefferson that persuaded Britain to stop its practice of impressment

15. Which of the following documents directly cited text from the Declaration of Independence to make a political point?
    A. The Declaration of Sentiments
    B. The Communist Manifesto
    C. The Wilmot Proviso
    D. The Roosevelt Corollary
    E. The Open Door Policy

16. Republicans in Congress impeached President Andrew Johnson for all the following political and legal reasons EXCEPT
    A. Johnson fired Secretary of War Edward Stanton and violated the Tenure of Office Act
    B. Johnson favored Presidential Reconstruction over Congressional Reconstruction
    C. Johnson opposed the mission of the Freedmen's Bureau
    D. Johnson opposed the Thirteenth Amendment
    E. Johnson aimed to reconstitute the political coalition of the Democratic Party in order to maintain white supremacy in the South

17. Andrew Jackson initiated the "Bank War" to prevent the rechartering of the Second Bank of the United States for all of the following reasons EXCEPT
    A. His belief in limited government
    B. His view that the Bank was corrupting politics
    C. Strong opposition to the Bank from his constituents like small farmers
    D. His rivalry with Nicholas Biddle, head of the Bank of the United States
    E. His desire to humiliate Martin Van Buren

18. The Know-Nothing Party of the 1850s won over a million votes in the election of 1854 primarily due to its opposition to
    A. Immigrants
    B. African-Americans
    C. Native Americans
    D. The Republican Party
    E. Slavery

19. John C. Calhoun served as an intellectual advocate for which political concept?
    A. Nullification
    B. Manifest Destiny
    C. Congregationalism
    D. Popular Sovereignty
    E. Nativism

20. All of the following postwar social trends are paired with one of their main causes EXCEPT
    A. The rise of the youth culture of the 1960s - Baby Boom
    B. Opposition to social and political authority - Vietnam War
    C. Rise in the number of lower and middle-income college students - GI Bill
    D. Migration to the Sunbelt – construction of Army camps in the South and West
    E. Increase in non-European immigration - Four Freedoms

21. Executive Order 9066 (1942) refers to which of the following?
    A. The wartime internment of American citizens/residents of Japanese ancestry
    B. The sale of Native American lands to encourage private property ownership
    C. The exclusion of Chinese immigrants
    D. The execution of Nazi saboteurs without a jury trial
    E. Approval for a military plan to assassinate Adolf Hitler

22. Which of the following scientists led the development of the atomic bomb but later fell afoul of the "Second Red Scare" of the 1950s and suffered the loss of his security clearance as a consequence?
    A. Robert Oppenheimer
    B. Albert Einstein
    C. Niels Bohr
    D. Julius Rosenberg
    E. Robert Welch

23. Why did Senator Joseph McCarthy's effort to identify and prosecute alleged communists in the American government end in 1952?
    A. McCarthy accused President Eisenhower of being a communist, earning the scorn of the nation
    B. McCarthy was censured by the Senate after accusing the Army of harboring communists without significant evidence
    C. McCarthy decided to run for president
    D. McCarthy decided that civil rights was a more important cause
    E. McCarthy wanted to return to his earlier work on economic affairs

24. All of the following were political principles or social programs of the Progressive Movement EXCEPT:
    A. Desegregation of public facilities
    B. Committees of experts to improve city governance
    C. Settlement houses
    D. Prohibition
    E. Women's suffrage

25. Each of the following presidents is correctly associated with an advance in civil rights during his presidency EXCEPT:
    A. Lyndon Johnson –Civil Rights Act of 1964
    B. Harry Truman – Desegregation of the armed forces in 1948
    C. Ulysses S. Grant –Civil Rights Act of 1875
    D. Franklin D. Roosevelt –Fair Employment Act of 1941
    E. Richard Nixon –Voting Rights Act of 1965

26. "The compact which exists between the North and the South is 'a covenant with death and an agreement with hell.'"

    Which of the following social reformers made this statement?
    A. Horace Mann
    B. William Lloyd Garrison
    C. Dorothea Dix
    D. John Dewey
    E. John Marshall

27. "I did not write it. God wrote it. I merely did His dictation."
    Uncle Tom's Cabin introduction

    Which of the following women wrote *Uncle Tom's Cabin*?
    A. Dorothea Dix
    B. Elizabeth Cady Stanton
    C. Margaret Sanger
    D. Jane Addams
    E. Harriet Beecher Stowe

28. Which of the following schools of thought emphasized the importance of self-reliance, independent thinking, and interaction with nature?
    A. Transcendentalism
    B. Pragmatism
    C. Social Darwinism
    D. Naturalism
    E. Romanticism

29. Congress under the Articles of Confederation had the power to perform all of the following functions except:
    A. Borrow money
    B. Impose taxes
    C. Conduct diplomacy
    D. Arrange foreign trade relations
    E. Organize settlement in the West

30. The Northwest Ordinance (1785) provided for
    A. The settlement and organization of Western territories and their eventual incorporation on an equal basis with existing states
    B. The extension of existing state borders further west
    C. Peace with Native American tribes including the Algonquin and Sioux
    D. Friendship with Great Britain through the establishment of a free trade area with Canada
    E. The acquisition of New Orleans

31. The territory of Florida served Spain strategically because of
    A. its warm-water fisheries
    B. the presence of powerful Native American allies
    C. its role as the religious headquarters of the Dominican monks
    D. its role as a buffer against the southward expansion of British North America
    E. its role as a haven for escaped slaves ('Maroons')

32. Jefferson agreed to the Louisiana Purchase despite his reservations about its constitutional propriety because
    A. The territory included the Mississippi, a crucial waterway for western farmers to bring their goods to market
    B. The territory allowed the United States to achieve its aim of Manifest Destiny by expanding to the Pacific
    C. The deal included a treaty of friendship and protection from Napoleonic France
    D. The British were threatening to acquire the territory
    E. He thought it was the mission of the United States to civilize the Native Americans in the Louisiana territory

33. Which of the following innovations came from Thomas Edison's laboratory at Menlo Park, New Jersey?
    A. Direct current electrification
    B. The assembly line
    C. The automobile
    D. The mechanical reaper
    E. The fluorescent light bulb

34. Why did many small and medium-sized farmers find themselves in economic trouble from 1890-1920?
    A. Reduced interest rates on loans offered by banks
    B. Overproduction caused by mechanization and improved farming techniques
    C. An influx of agricultural exports from industrial agribusinesses in Europe
    D. A switch to a bimetallic system based on gold and silver
    E. All of the above

35. Which of the following were part of Alexander Hamilton's economic program?
    A. A national bank to help finance infrastructure and trade
    B. Excise taxes to fund the federal government
    C. A national debt to bind the economic interests of the wealthy classes to the new republic
    D. The acquisition of state war debts by the federal government
    E. All of the above

36. Which of the following incidents illustrated the weakness of the government under the Articles of Confederation?
    A. The Whiskey Rebellion
    B. Bacon's Rebellion
    C. Shays's Rebellion
    D. The Boston Tea Party
    E. Pontiac's Rebellion

37. The cartoon above shows Theodore Roosevelt guiding the policies of his protégé William Howard Taft. What happened to the relationship between Roosevelt and Taft by 1912?
    A. Roosevelt supported Taft's bid for reelection with grateful thanks for Taft's loyal work in completing Roosevelt's political program
    B. Roosevelt supported Woodrow Wilson for president against Taft because he thought Wilson's politics were more progressive
    C. Roosevelt himself ran for President on a third party Progressive ticket
    D. Roosevelt believed that Taft would be better suited for the Supreme Court than the Presidency
    E. Roosevelt defeated Taft for the Republican party nomination

38. Bacon's rebellion (1676) was caused by all of the following EXCEPT
    A. The poor treatment of indentured servants
    B. The use of the public treasury to reward friends of the leading planters
    C. The rivalry between Bacon and Virginia governor William Berkeley
    D. Bacon's ambition to destroy the power of local Native American tribes
    E. Bacon's desire to win religious freedom for the people of Virginia

39. Which of the following presidential administrations suffered a foreign policy setback with the failed invasion at the Bay of Pigs?
    A. Truman
    B. Eisenhower
    C. Kennedy
    D. Johnson
    E. Nixon

40. Which president presided over the acquisition of the Philippines?
    A. William McKinley
    B. Theodore Roosevelt
    C. James K. Polk
    D. Woodrow Wilson
    E. Franklin D. Roosevelt

41. The Open Door policy (1900) was designed to
    A. Increase immigration to the United States from Asia
    B. Provide education and civic training for urban immigrants
    C. Maintain a neutral trading environment for all foreign powers in China
    D. Divide Africa among Western powers
    E. Provide education to Filipinos

42. The Black Codes (1865-66)
    A. prevented freedmen from voting
    B. restricted the rights of African-Americans to work in occupations of their choice
    C. included anti-vagrancy provisions that limited freedom of movement for freedmen
    D. signaled the intention of those in South to maintain a racial hierarchy
    E. all of the above

43. Which political party adopted the motto and platform of the Free Soil party: "Free Soil, Free Speech, Free Labor and Free Men"?
    A. The Democratic-Republican Party
    B. The Populist Party
    C. The Republican Party
    D. The Whig Party
    E. The Know-Nothing Party

44. Which of the following reformers were NOT devout Christians whose religion motivated their efforts to improve society?
    A. Harriet Beecher Stowe
    B. Theodore Dwight Weld
    C. Elijah P. Lovejoy
    D. Martin Luther King, Jr.
    E. Margaret Sanger

45. Which of the following Indian tribes or confederations adopted institutions of white Southern society such as an economy based on agriculture, republican government, literacy, and slavery in the eighteenth century in an attempt to win legal and political recognition from their white neighbors?
    A. Cherokee
    B. Wampanoag
    C. Iroquois
    D. Sioux
    E. Tillamook

46. Which of the following rebellions illustrated the futility of armed resistance by slaves in the South?
    A. Bacon's Rebellion
    B. Pontiac's Rebellion
    C. Nat Turner's Rebellion
    D. Shay's Rebellion
    E. The Whiskey Rebellion

47. Which of the following administration's economic policy was confounded by stagflation?
    A. Carter
    B. Reagan
    C. Bush
    D. Clinton
    E. Kennedy

48. The Federal Reserve Bank can increase the money supply of the economy by taking which of the following actions?
    A. Reducing taxes
    B. Imposing tariffs on foreign economies
    C. Shifting to the gold standard
    D. Reducing the interest rate charged to banks affiliated with the Federal Reserve System
    E. Selling large quantities of mortgage-backed securities

49. Which of the following explorers did not sail to the Americas?
    A. Ferdinand Magellan
    B. Jacques Cartier
    C. Christopher Columbus
    D. Vasco da Gama
    E. John Cabot

50. Which of the following presidents signed into law the Civil Rights Act, Voting Rights Act, Economic Opportunity Act, Elementary and Secondary Education Act, and Medicare?
    A. John F. Kennedy
    B. Dwight D. Eisenhower
    C. Lyndon B. Johnson

D. Harry S. Truman
E. Franklin D. Roosevelt

51. During his Farewell Address, which president cautioned about the dangers to democracy and peace posed by the "military-industrial" complex?
    A. George Washington
    B. Ulysses S. Grant
    C. Theodore Roosevelt
    D. Woodrow Wilson
    E. Dwight Eisenhower

52. Which of the following labor unions excluded both women and minorities from its membership?
    A. American Railway Union
    B. American Federation of Labor
    C. Women's Trade Union League
    D. Knights of Labor
    E. Congress of Industrial Organizations

53. The First Great Awakening produced
    A. a reinvigorated church hierarchy in North America
    B. the expulsion of meddling British ministers such as George Whitefield and John Wesley
    C. an emotional democratization of Protestantism
    D. equal rights for women in church
    E. the separation of church and state in colonial Virginia

54. Which of the following groups opposed the Louisiana Purchase?
    A. Jefferson's allies in Congress
    B. Federalists from New England
    C. The French government
    D. The Jacksonian Democrats
    E. Small farmers in the West

55. Which of the following reasons help explain why labor unions struggled to achieve legal and political recognition from 1880 to 1930?
    A. Many Americans feared that organized labor was linked to communism
    B. Laissez-faire philosophy dominated Republican Party thinking in the 1880s and 1890s d
    C. Anti-union businesses enjoyed significant political influence during the Gilded Age
    D. The Supreme Court consistently acted in favor of business over labor
    E. All of the above

56. What was one primary purpose of the Alien & Sedition Acts?
    A. To weaken the Democratic-Republican party
    B. To provide procedures for the swift naturalization of immigrants
    C. To censor Federalist printers who were taking advantage of freedom of the press
    D. To supply propaganda against the British
    E. To push America into alliance with France

57. By the 1930s, European immigrants living in cities voted in large majorities for which party?
    A. The Democratic Party
    B. The Republican Party
    C. The Greenback Party
    D. The Populist Party
    E. The Progressive Party

58. The Embargo Act produced all of the following results EXCEPT
    A. A steep reduction in America's foreign trade
    B. A rise in smuggling in New England
    C. A halt to British practices of impressment
    D. A decline in immigration from Asia
    E. A decline in popular support for Thomas Jefferson

59. Which of the following individuals opposed the arguments presented in *The Federalist* and argued instead that the federal government proposed by the Constitution was dangerous to the liberties of the people and the states?
    A. Patrick Henry
    B. George Washington
    C. Alexander Hamilton
    D. John Jay
    E. James Madison

60. The War of 1812 resulted in
    A. the death of Tecumseh
    B. a victory at the Battle of New Orleans that made Andrew Jackson's reputation
    C. a substantial loss of support for the Federalist party
    D. a rise in national patriotism
    E. All of the above

61. The cartoon above depicts a strategic situation that encouraged American policymakers to develop which policy or set of policies?
   A. Détente
   B. The Marshall Plan
   C. The Fair Deal
   D. The Taft-Hartley Plan
   E. All of the above

62. The Erie Canal helped which city grow into the economic center of the United States?
   A. New York
   B. Philadelphia
   C. Cleveland
   D. Chicago
   E. Boston

63. Which of the following factors helped make the Deep South the world's greatest producer of cotton in the nineteenth century?
    I. The cotton gin
    II. Demand from British textile manufacturers
    III. High-quality land in Alabama, Mississippi and Louisiana
    IV. Slavery

    A. I only
    B. I and II only
    C. I and IV only
    D. I, II and III
    E. I, II, III and IV

64. Henry Clay's American System was based in large part on the economic principles of which of the following statesmen?
    A. James Madison
    B. George Washington
    C. Daniel Webster
    D. Alexander Hamilton
    E. Andrew Jackson

65. Why did Southern states insist on an equal balance between the number of free and slave states in the discussion leading to the Missouri Compromise of 1820? The South hoped
    A. to draw even with the North in population, thereby obtaining an advantage in the popular vote thanks to the Three-Fifths Compromise
    B. to eventually persuade Northern states to reinstate slavery in the North
    C. that equal balance would create the coalition necessary to reopen the international slave trade
    D. to maintain balance in the Senate, thereby ensuring that laws restricting slavery could not be passed
    E. to create a winning coalition in the Electoral College for the foreseeable future

66. Manifest Destiny refers to which of the following propositions?
    A. That the United States and her people are ordained by God with the duty to expand into a continental republic
    B. That all of the Americas should be converted to Protestant Christianity
    C. That the Native Americans tribes must be transferred to Canada
    D. That European powers must be removed from Latin America
    E. That the seas must be made safe for neutral shipping

67. Which of the following increased the power of the federal government?
    I. The New Deal
    II. The Great Society
    III. *McCulloch v. Maryland*
    IV. World War II

    A. I only
    B. I and II only
    C. I, II and III
    D. I, II and IV
    E. I, II, III and IV

68. "If ever America undergoes great revolutions, they will be brought about by the presence of the black race on the soil of the United States; that is to say, they will owe their origin, not to the equality, but to the inequality of condition."

    Which astute foreign observer wrote these words in the 1830s?
    A. Alexis de Tocqueville
    B. Edmund Burke
    C. Charles Dickens
    D. the Marquis de Lafayette
    E. Montesquieu

69. "No government ever voluntarily reduces itself in size. Government programs, once launched, never disappear. Actually, a government bureau is the nearest thing to eternal life we'll ever see on this earth!"

    The author of this statement was first elected to the presidency in
    A. 1972
    B. 1976
    C. 1980
    D. 1984
    E. 1988

70. "That's our motto. We want freedom by any means necessary. We want justice by any means necessary. We want equality by any means necessary."
    Which African-American leader of the 1960s made this statement?
    A. Martin Luther King, Jr.
    B. Malcolm X
    C. W.E.B. Du Bois
    D. A. Philip Randolph
    E. Booker T. Washington

71. Which of the following presidents did NOT expand US territorial possessions during his administration?
    A. James K. Polk
    B. Thomas Jefferson
    C. William McKinley
    D. James Monroe
    E. Ulysses S. Grant

72. Who put Ralph Waldo Emerson's ideas on self-reliance, independent thinking and connection with nature into practice?
    A. Henry David Thoreau
    B. Harriet Beecher Stowe
    C. Mark Twain
    D. Walt Whitman
    E. Ernest Hemingway

73. Why did American settlers in Texas seek independence from Mexico?
    A. Mexican law required the emancipation of slaves
    B. The Mexican government required the settlers to pay import duties on goods from the United States
    C. Mexico did not grant the settlers a sufficient measure of self-government
    D. Mexican law required all settlers to convert to Catholicism
    E. All of the above

74. Which of the following women reformers ran a settlement house for immigrants and members of the urban poor in Chicago?
    A. Jane Addams
    B. Dorothea Dix
    C. Harriet Beecher Stowe
    D. Elizabeth Cady Stanton
    E. Carrie Chapman Catt

75. The rallying cry "Fifty-four forty or fight" refers to disputes over which territory?
    A. Louisiana
    B. The Ohio River Valley
    C. Oregon
    D. Texas
    E. California

76. Under which of the following treaties did Mexico cede California and New Mexico to the United States?
    A. Webster-Ashburton
    B. Guadalupe Hidalgo
    C. Paris
    D. Adams-Onís
    E. Hay-Bunau-Varilla

77. Immigration from 1820-40 derived mostly from
    A. The British Isles and Germany
    B. Poland
    C. Italy
    D. China and Japan
    E. Mexico

78. The Republican Party's position on slavery in the election of 1860 was:
    A. Slavery should be banned from the territories in the West
    B. Slavery should be banned in the United States by constitutional amendment
    C. Congress should buy and free slaves from the South
    D. The Missouri Compromise should be recreated and the line dividing free from slave states extended to the Pacific
    E. Slavery should be restricted to only those states in the South that possessed at the time of the ratification of the Constitution

79. What argument did female reformers like Jane Addams successfully make in order to win the right to vote?
    A. Women have the natural right to vote
    B. The Declaration of Independence guarantees women the right to vote
    C. Men are ready for female leadership in all spheres of society
    D. Women can improve the nature of politics by applying their knowledge of child rearing and home making to the betterment of society
    E. All of the above

80. The Compromise of 1850
    A. Brought California into the Union as a free state
    B. Allowed popular sovereignty to determine whether Utah and New Mexico territories were to be free or slave states
    C. Banned slave auctions in Washington, DC
    D. Created a more powerful federal Fugitive Slave Law
    E. All of the above

**STOP HERE IF YOU ARE TAKING THE AP DIAGNOSTIC;
CONTINUE IF TAKING THE SAT II DIAGNOSTIC**

81. The Kansas-Nebraska Act aroused strong opposition in the North because
    A. It repealed the Missouri Compromise
    B. It violated the principle of popular sovereignty
    C. It betrayed the Southern states by providing for the gradual emancipation of slaves in the Deep South
    D. It banned the publication of abolitionist literature in the South
    E. It violated the Compromise of 1850

82. Nativist sentiments have been directed against which of the following groups in American history?
    I. Catholics
    II. Latinos
    III. Chinese
    IV. Anglo-Saxon Protestants

    A. I only
    B. II only
    C. III only
    D. I, II and III
    E. I, II, III and IV

83. Which of the following presidents was NOT able to carry out a broad realignment of American politics? (A realignment refers to the winning of an election in a way that causes the reordering of political coalitions).
    A. Abraham Lincoln
    B. Franklin D. Roosevelt
    C. Thomas Jefferson
    D. Ronald Reagan
    E. Woodrow Wilson

84. Which of the following domestic social changes were caused by World War II?
    A. Women and African-Americans gained the opportunity to work in much larger numbers in factories
    B. Army camps in the South and West created a foundation for future migration to the Sunbelt
    C. Many Japanese Americans living on the West Coast were forced to sell their property at a loss
    D. Full employment was restored to the nation
    E. All of the above

85. Immigration from which country was limited under Theodore Roosevelt's "Gentleman's Agreement?"
    A. Japan
    B. South Korea
    C. The Philippines
    D. Italy
    E. Ireland

86. Which of the following strategic advantages did the South have in the Civil War?
    A. The benefits of defending its own territory
    B. Recognition from Great Britain
    C. A strong industrial base
    D. More firearms than the North
    E. A navy capable of breaking the northern blockade

87. Which of the following advantages did Jefferson Davis enjoy compared to his northern counterpart Abraham Lincoln?
    A. A disciplined party apparatus that maintained public support for the war
    B. A strong bureaucracy capable of overriding state governors
    C. A powerful navy
    D. A top-notch military leadership
    E. None of the above

88. The British declined to recognize and support the Confederacy for all of the following reasons EXCEPT
    A. The inability of the Confederacy to win a clear victory at Antietam
    B. The sympathy of the majority of the British people with abolitionism
    C. Ample supplies of cotton from the surplus harvest of 1860
    D. The desire of the British government to avoid a long and costly war with the United States
    E. The desire of elements of the British government, including aristocrats and textile manufacturers, for an independent Confederacy

89. Which book served as a rallying cry for the women's movement of the 1960s?
    A. *On the Road*
    B. *The Catcher in the Rye*
    C. *The Feminine Mystique*
    D. *Silent Spring*
    E. *Lady Chatterley's Lover*

90. African-American soldiers served in which of the following wars?
    A. The Revolutionary War
    B. The Civil War
    C. The Spanish-American War
    D. World War I
    E. All of the above

END OF DIAGNOSTIC TEST

American History Tutoring Guide — Paul Pinto

#	Question	Answer Text	Answer	Your Ans.	Topic Category
1	Why did America lose the Vietnam War?	American policymakers fixated on the threat of communism failed to consider the importance of nationalism among the Vietnamese people	A		Foreign Policy and Expansion West
2	Which philosopher's work had the most influence on the political theory informing the Declaration of Independence?	John Locke	A		Independence
3	Which of the following battles/campaigns of the Civil War split the Confederacy in half?	Vicksburg	D		Civil War
4	"It is a proposition too plain to be contested, that the constitution controls any legislative act repugnant to it…" Marbury v. Madison (1803) The above quotation from John Marshall refers to which of the following concepts?	judicial review	B		Constitution
5	Which of the following products were NOT covered by the Townshend Acts of 1767?	Stamps	D		Independence
6	What theory or concept did the British government appeal to in order to justify its taxation of the American colonies?	Virtual representation	A		Independence
7	Which of the following individuals championed religious liberty in seventeenth century?	Roger Williams	C		Religion
8	Which of the following is NOT a Progressive-era constitutional amendment?	The Fourteenth Amendment	A		Progressives
9	Which of the following freedoms is NOT protected by the Bill of Rights?	The right to vote	E		Constitution
10	Which union is INCORRECTLY aligned with a strike in which it played a significant role?	Knights of Labor - Steel Strike of 1952	E		Labor
11	Which nineteenth-century president issued more vetoes than all his predecessors combined?	Andrew Jackson	B		Presidency
12	The Monroe Doctrine received unexpected and unrequested enforcement cooperation from which European nation?	Great Britain	A		Foreign Policy and Expansion West
13	The Monroe Doctrine opposed all of the following EXCEPT	European trade with the Western Hemisphere	C		Foreign Policy and Expansion West
14	The Embargo Act of 1807 was	A political disaster for Thomas Jefferson that resulted in the decimation of US foreign trade	D		Foreign Policy and Expansion West
15	Which of the following documents deliberately drew from the Declaration of Independence?	The Declaration of Sentiments	A		Independence
16	Republicans in Congress impeached President Andrew Johnson for all the following political and legal reasons EXCEPT	Johnson opposed the Thirteenth Amendment	D		African-American Experience
17	Andrew Jackson initiated the "Bank War" to prevent the rechartering of the Second Bank of the United States for all of the following reasons EXCEPT	His desire to humiliate Martin Van Buren	E		Economic Role of Government

American History Tutoring Guide — Paul Pinto

#	Question	Answer	Key	Category
18	The Know-Nothing Party of the 1850s won over a million votes in the election of 1854 primarily due to its opposition to	Immigrants	A	Immigration
19	John C. Calhoun served as an intellectual advocate for which political concept?	Nullification	A	Constitution
20	All of the following postwar social trends are paired with one of their main causes EXCEPT	Increase in non-European immigration - Four Freedoms	E	Social/Demographic Trends
21	Executive Order 9066 (1942) refers to which of the following:	The wartime internment of American citizens/residents of Japanese ancestry	A	Foreign Policy and Expansion West
22	Which of the following scientists, responsible in part for the development of the atomic bomb, fell afoul of the "Second Red Scare" of the 1950s and suffered the loss of his security clearance as a consequence?	Robert Oppenheimer	A	Foreign Policy and Expansion West
23	Why did Senator Joseph McCarthy's effort to identify and prosecute alleged communists in the US government end in 1952?	McCarthy was censured by the Senate after accusing the Army of harboring communists without evidence	B	Foreign Policy and Expansion West
24	All of the following were political principles or social programs of the Progressive Movement EXCEPT:	The desegregation of public facilities	A	Progressives
25	Each of the following presidents is correctly associated with an advance in civil rights during his presidency EXCEPT:	Richard Nixon – the Voting Rights Act of 1965	E	African-American Experience
26	"The compact which exists between the North and the South is 'a covenant with death and an agreement with hell.'" Which of the following social reformers made this statement?	William Lloyd Garrison	B	African-American Experience
27	"I did not write it. God wrote it. I merely did His dictation." Uncle Tom's Cabin introduction. Which of the following women wrote Uncle Tom's Cabin?	Harriet Beecher Stowe	E	African-American Experience
28	Which of the following schools of thought emphasized the importance of self-reliance, independent thinking, and interaction with nature?	Transcendentalism	A	American Literature & Philosophy
29	Congress under the Articles of Confederation had the power to perform all of the following functions except:	Impose taxes	B	Constitution
30	The Northwest Ordinance (1785) provided for	The settlement and organization of Western territories and their eventual incorporation on an equal basis with existing states	A	Constitution
31	The territory of Florida served Spain strategically because of	its role as a buffer against the southward expansion of British North America	D	Founding Colonies
32	Jefferson agreed to the Louisiana Purchase despite his reservations about its constitutional propriety because	The territory included the Mississippi, a crucial waterway for western farmers to bring their goods to market	A	Economic Role of Government

#	Question	Answer		Category
33	Which of the following innovations came from Thomas Edison's laboratory at Menlo Park, New Jersey?	Direct current electrification	A	Business and Economy
34	Why did many small and medium-sized farmers find themselves in economic trouble from 1890-1920?	Overproduction caused by mechanization and improved farming techniques	B	Business and Economy
35	Which of the following were part of Alexander Hamilton's economic program?	All of the above	E	Economic Role of Government
36	Which of the following incidents illustrated the weakness of the government under the Articles of Confederation?	Shays's Rebellion	C	Constitution
37	The cartoon above shows Theodore Roosevelt guiding the policies of his protégé William Howard Taft. What happened to the relationship between Roosevelt and Taft by 1912?	Roosevelt himself ran for President on a third party Progressive ticket	C	Political Parties
38	Bacon's rebellion (1676) was caused by all of the following EXCEPT	Bacon's desire to win religious freedom for the people of Virginia	E	Founding Colonies
39	Which of the following presidential administrations suffered a foreign policy setback with the failed invasion at the Bay of Pigs?	Kennedy	C	Foreign Policy and Expansion West
40	Which president presided over the acquisition of the Philippines?	William McKinley	A	Foreign Policy and Expansion West
41	The Open Door policy (1900) was designed to	Maintain a neutral trading environment for all foreign powers in China	C	Foreign Policy and Expansion West
42	The Black Codes (1865-66)	all of the above	E	African-American Experience
43	Which political party adopted the motto and platform of the Free Soil party: "Free Soil, Free Speech, Free Labor and Free Men"?	The Republican Party	C	Political Parties
44	Which of the following reformers were NOT devout Christians whose religion motivated their efforts to improve society?	Margaret Sanger	E	Religion
45	Which of the following Indian tribes or confederations adopted institutions of white Southern society such as an economy based on agriculture, republican government, literacy, and slavery in the eighteenth century in an attempt to win legal and political recognition from their white neighbors?	Cherokee	A	Native Americans
46	Which of the following rebellions illustrated the futility of armed resistance by slaves in the South?	Nat Turner's Rebellion	C	African-American Experience
47	Which of the following administration's economic policy was confounded by stagflation?	Carter	A	Business and Economy
48	The Federal Reserve Bank can increase the money supply of the economy by taking which of the following actions?	Reducing the interest rate charged to banks affiliated with the Federal Reserve System	D	Economic Role of Government
49	Which of the following explorers did not sail to the Americas?	Vasco da Gama	D	Early Explorers

#	Question	Answer	Key	Topic
50	Which of the following presidents signed into law the Civil Rights Act, Voting Rights Act, Economic Opportunity Act, Elementary and Secondary Education Act, and Medicare?	Lyndon B. Johnson	C	Economic Role of Government
51	During his Farewell Address, which president cautioned about the dangers to democracy and peace posed by the "military-industrial" complex?	Dwight Eisenhower	E	Presidency
52	Which of the following labor unions excluded women and minorities from its membership?	American Federation of Labor	B	Labor
53	The First Great Awakening produced	an emotional democratization of Protestantism	C	Religion
54	Which of the following groups opposed the Louisiana Purchase?	Federalists from New England	B	Political Parties
55	Which of the following reasons help explain why labor unions struggled to achieve legal and political recognition from 1880 to 1930?	All of the above	E	Labor
56	What was one primary purpose of the Alien & Sedition Acts?	To weaken the Democratic-Republican party	A	Constitution
57	By the 1930s, European immigrants living in cities voted in large majorities for which party?	The Democratic Party	A	Political Parties
58	The Embargo Act produced all of the following results EXCEPT	A halt to British practices of impressment	C	Foreign Policy and Expansion West
59	Which of the following individuals opposed the arguments presented in The Federalist and argued instead that the federal government proposed by the Constitution was dangerous to the liberties of the people and the states?	Patrick Henry	A	Constitution
60	The War of 1812 resulted in	All of the above	E	Foreign Policy and Expansion West
61	The cartoon above depicts a strategic situation that encouraged American policymakers to develop which policy or set of policies?	The Marshall Plan	B	Foreign Policy and Expansion West
62	The Erie Canal helped which city grow into the economic center of the United States?	New York	A	Economic Role of Government
63	Which of the following factors helped make the Deep South the world's greatest producer of cotton in the nineteenth century? I. The cotton gin II. Demand from British textile manufacturers III. High-quality land in Alabama, Mississippi and Louisiana IV. Slavery	I, II, III and IV	E	Business and Economy
64	Henry Clay's American System was based in large part on the economic principles of which of the following statesmen?	Alexander Hamilton	D	Economic Role of Government
65	Why did Southern states insist on an equal balance between the number of free and slave states in the discussion leading to the Missouri Compromise of 1820? The South hoped	to maintain balance in the Senate, thereby ensuring that laws restricting slavery could not be passed	D	African-American Experience
66	Manifest Destiny refers to which of the following propositions?	That the United States and her people are ordained by God with the duty to expand into a	A	Foreign Policy and Expansion West

		continental republic		
67	Which of the following increased the power of the federal government? I. The New Deal II. The Great Society III. McCulloch v. Maryland IV. World War II	I, II and IV	E	Economic Role of Government
68	"If ever America undergoes great revolutions, they will be brought about by the presence of the black race on the soil of the United States; that is to say, they will owe their origin, not to the equality, but to the inequality of condition." Which astute foreign observer wrote these words in the 1830s?	Alexis de Tocqueville	A	American Literature & Philosophy
69	"No government ever voluntarily reduces itself in size. Government programs, once launched, never disappear. Actually, a government bureau is the nearest thing to eternal life we'll ever see on this earth!" The author of this statement was first elected to the presidency in	1980	C	Economic Role of Government
70	"That's our motto. We want freedom by any means necessary. We want justice by any means necessary. We want equality by any means necessary." Which African-American leader of the 1960s made this statement?	Malcolm X	B	African-American Experience
71	Which of the following presidents did NOT expand US territorial possessions during his administration?	Ulysses S. Grant	E	Presidency
72	Who put Ralph Waldo Emerson's ideas on self-reliance, independent thinking and connection with nature into practice?	Henry David Thoreau	A	American Literature & Philosophy
73	Why did American settlers in Texas seek independence from Mexico?	All of the above	E	Foreign Policy and Expansion West
74	Which of the following women reformers ran a settlement house for immigrants and members of the urban poor in Chicago?	Jane Addams	A	Women
75	The rallying cry "Fifty-four forty or fight" refers to disputes over which territory?	Oregon	C	Foreign Policy and Expansion West
76	Under which of the following treaties did Mexico cede California and New Mexico to the United States?	Guadalupe Hidalgo	B	Foreign Policy and Expansion West
77	Immigration from 1820-40 derived mostly from	The British Isles and Germany	A	Immigration
78	The Republican Party's position on slavery in the election of 1860 was:	Slavery should be banned from the territories in the West	A	African-American Experience
79	What argument did female reformers like Jane Addams successfully make in order to win the right to vote?	Women can improve the nature of politics by applying their knowledge of child rearing and home making to the betterment of society	D	Women
80	The Compromise of 1850	All of the above	E	Civil War

81	The Kansas-Nebraska Act aroused strong opposition in the North because	It repealed the Missouri Compromise	A		Civil War
82	Nativist sentiments have been directed against which of the following groups in American history? I. Catholics II. Latinos III. Chinese IV. Anglo-Saxon Protestants	I, II and III	D		Immigration
83	Which of the following presidents was NOT able to carry out a broad realignment of American politics? (A realignment refers to the winning of an election in a way that causes the reordering of political coalitions).	Woodrow Wilson	E		Presidency
84	Which of the following domestic social changes were caused by World War II?	All of the above	E		Social/Demographic Trends
85	Immigration from which country was limited under Theodore Roosevelt's "Gentleman's Agreement?"	Japan	A		Immigration
86	Which of the following strategic advantages did the South have in the Civil War?	The benefits of defending its own territory	A		Civil War
87	Which of the following advantages did Jefferson Davis enjoy compared to his northern counterpart Abraham Lincoln?	A top-notch military leadership	D		Civil War
88	The British declined to recognize and support the Confederacy for all of the following reasons EXCEPT	The desire of elements of the British government, including aristocrats and textile manufacturers, for an independent Confederacy	E		Foreign Policy and Expansion West
89	Which book served as a rallying cry for the women's movement of the 1960s?	The Feminine Mystique	C		Women
90	African-American soldiers served in which of the following wars?	All of the above	E		African-American Experience

TOPIC 1: FOREIGN POLICY AND WESTWARD EXPANSION

Foreign policy refers to the diplomatic, economic, and military relations of a given country with the rest of the world. As generations of international relations scholars have pointed out, there is no world government with the power to force nations to live in peace with one another; countries must therefore rely on their own military, economic, and cultural strength, along with their ability to form alliances with other nations, in order to preserve the security and welfare of their people. For most of human history, the conduct of international politics has followed the law of the jungle: strong countries dominate weaker ones. The United States, to its good fortune, avoided the worst ramifications of the law of the jungle by entering into independence as a middle-rank power already capable of dealing on an equal basis with many other countries. Nevertheless, the young republic fared poorly when its foreign policies conflicted with the global strategies of France and Britain, the dominant world powers. Through careful policy and a measure of good luck, the United States was generally able to avoid major conflicts with these world powers in the nineteenth century. Factors such as the geographic space afforded by the Atlantic and Pacific oceans, the relative weakness of the Latin America republics, and a strong record of industrial growth allowed America to build up its own power and increasingly dictate foreign policy to allies and enemies alike. By the late nineteenth century, the United States was a match for the leading European powers; under the pressures of World War II, it became a superpower, a status it has retained to the present day.

To accurately answer test questions dealing with foreign policy, combine the fact that the United States passed through different foreign policy phases, each with a specific level of relative power, with the fact that foreign policy works like the law of the jungle (big powers dominate smaller ones). In the early periods, the United States had to follow the lead of the great powers; in the middle periods, it found itself able to deal with these powers on even terms; and in the last half-century or so it found itself responsible for the leadership of a large portion of the world while balanced against a strong foe in the Soviet Union. To take a specific example, during the period 1788-1810, the United States was a middle-rank power compared to great powers like Britain and France and was therefore could not bend these nations to her will on matters like control of the seas. Specific questions from this period (e.g., the Embargo Act of 1807) should be approached with the general perspective that the United States was operating from a position of relative weakness versus the European powers. President Jefferson's attempt to punish Britain and France by restraining trade with an embargo failed because the United States simply did not have sufficient power to enforce its will in this matter. Consider the following question:

> The Jay Treaty of 1794 received criticism from the American public because it
> A. compelled the British to remove remaining troops from the Northwest
> B. severed all diplomatic links with Britain
> **C. failed to resolve the impressment of American seamen**
> D. forced Britain to pay a large war indemnity
> E. allowed Native American tribes free rights of passage between the United States and Canada

American History Tutoring Guide Paul Pinto

The correct answer, (B), uses the verb "failed" to signify a position of relative US weakness, rather than verbs like "compelled," "forced," or "severed," which are verbs more indicative of the aggressiveness that characterizes the actions of great powers. Its weak navy allowed the United States no opportunity to dictate shipping policy to the European powers, which meant that America could only respond with the self-damaging "protest" of the embargo. As a general rule, understanding the basic power relationship in a foreign policy conflict (ask yourself who has power and who has less) goes a long way towards helping you identify the right answer to a foreign policy question.

The twin tools of foreign policy are diplomacy, or the use of negotiation and discussion to settle political differences, and war, the application of military force. The job of political leaders is to select the best mix of these two strategies. Countries with strong militaries are unsurprisingly more willing to resort to force, but weaker countries will on occasion determine that they have no choice but to take up arms (e.g., the American Revolution). Remember that war is not just about fighting; it is also a political process. A country can win all the battles but lose the war if the politics are not aligned correctly (as the United States did in Vietnam).

The table below summarizes the seven major historical periods during which the United States developed from a relatively weak set of colonies to a middle-rank independent nation to a great power and ultimately to the superpower status it occupies today.

Period	US Power Level	Great Powers	Middle Powers	Weak States	Description
Colonial Shelter (1600-1776)	Weak → Middle Power	Britain, France	Spain	Native American tribes	American colonies protected by the power of the British government
Independence and Early Republic (1776-1823)	Middle Power	Britain, France	Spain, Barbary States	Native American tribes, Latin America	US strong enough to deal with Spain, Latin America and Native American tribes but struggles with Britain/France in the Atlantic; negotiates Louisiana Purchase which solidifies expansion west
Westward Expansion (1819-1890)	Great Power	Britain, France, US, Germany	Russia, Japan	Native American tribes, Mexico, Spain	US moves westward, defeating Native American tribes and Mexico and negotiating with Britain and Russia
Imperialism (1890-1914)	Great Power	Britain, US, Germany	France, Russia, Japan	Spain, Cuba, China, Philippines	United States establishes an overseas empire by defeating Spain and taking the Philippines

Period	US Power Level	Great Powers	Middle Powers	Weak States	Description
World War I (1914-1918)	Great Power	Britain, US, Germany	France, Russia, Japan	Austria-Hungary,	The United States stays out of the total war in Europe until 1917, and then joins the war. President Wilson attempts to shape postwar future through Versailles Treaty but fails to pass it through the Senate
World War II (1939-1945)	Super-power	Soviet Union, US, Germany	Britain, France, Japan, Italy	China	The United States again stays out of total war in Europe but is pulled in by Pearl Harbor. The United States wins the war in Asia and plays a major role in the war in Europe
Cold War (1945-1989)	Super-power	Soviet Union, United States	Europe, China	"Third World" nations	The Soviet Union and the United States compete in a battle of political systems, which is only concluded with the fall of the Berlin Wall and the subsequent collapse of the Soviet Union

We are now prepared to analyze each period in some detail. During the period of **Colonial Shelter (1600-1776)**, the thirteen colonies of North America benefitted from the protection of the British Army and Navy, which sheltered the colonies from competing European powers such as Spain and France. Part of the price of imperial protection was the participation of the colonies in a mercantilist system of trade that privileged England, the mother country. For example, many valuable American products could be shipped to Europe only after going through British Empire ports; failure to do so was punished with a tax. However, due to the British policy of **salutary neglect** (lax British regulation and monitoring), American colonists were often able to evade British mercantilist policies. On a local level, American colonists fought their own battles against Native American tribes; at the cost of much bloodshed, the colonists defeated the tribes and forced them to migrate west. American troops also assisted the British Army during the French & Indian War (1756-63), a long and expensive conflict for the British empire that resulted in the taxation of the colonies by Parliament and the colonial protests that led to independence.

In the table below, the column marked "Foreign Relationship" lists a country and its relationship to the American colonies. Countries at war with America are designated as "enemies"; countries competing economically or politically as "rivals"; and countries with cooperative alliances "partners." Note that the boundary between rivals and enemies is often blurry: countries shift from rivals to enemies and back depending on their strategic priorities and whether they choose to resolve their differences with force. The second column states the relative power of the American colonies compared to other countries. The American colonies during the period of Colonial Shelter were stronger than neighboring Native American tribes, for example, but weaker than either England or France. The third column lists specific historical events, issues, or incidents, while the fourth column describes the outcome of these incidents.

Colonial Shelter (1600s-1776)

Foreign Relation	US Relative Power	Issue/ Incident	Outcome
Britain (colonial parent)	Weaker	Navigation Acts (1660s)	Colonies required to defer to the economic interests of the mother country by sending important products like sugar and tobacco through British Empire ports or pay a tax; however, the British policy of **salutary neglect** allows some enterprising Americans to evade these mercantilist taxes
		Establishment of the Dominion of New England (1684-88)	King James II attempts to establish greater royal control; he replaces the self-governing charters of Massachusetts and other New England colonies with a single Dominion of New England, run by an royal governor with autocratic powers; this experiment fails and the colonies regain their charters when James II is deposed in the Glorious Revolution (1688)
		Proclamation of 1763	Decree limiting settlement in the Ohio River Valley to ease tensions with Native Americans
France (enemy)	Weaker (but sheltered by British power)	French & Indian War (1756-63)	British Army with colonial support defeats French army and their Indian allies; the war costs a great deal of money which Parliament tries to recoup with colonial taxes; American soldiers and civilians often treated with disdain by British 'regulars' (professional soldiers)
Native American Tribes (enemies)	Stronger	King Philip's War (1675-78)	A confederation of Indian tribes led by a chief named Metacom (aka King Philip) tries to expel English colonists from the New England area; hundreds of colonists and thousands of Indians are killed during the three-year war, which ends with the capture of Metacom and the displacement of the tribes west to Appalachia

During the period of **Independence and the Early Republic (1776-1823)**, American bravery, military skill and commitment to the Revolutionary cause was amply demonstrated and (with assistance from the French) resulted in the defeat of the previously dominant British Empire and independence for the thirteen colonies. Despite the grand victory, the newly independent nation was financially troubled, politically divided, and buffeted by a series of major foreign policy challenges. The British retained their dominance of the seas, and the generation-long global war between Britain and Revolutionary France (commonly called the Napoleonic Wars) constantly threatened to draw in the United States. The British practice of capturing American sailors and using them as forced labor (impressment) badly damaged American commerce, and Jefferson's response in the form of a trade embargo (1807) only made matters worse. Despite these troubles, the United States generally managed to avoid getting pulled into the Napoleonic Wars (with the exception of the relatively short War of 1812 against England) and actually benefitted from them in the form of the Louisiana Purchase from France (1803), which doubled the territory of the nation for a modest financial price. The Monroe Doctrine (1823) concluded the era with a bold declaration warning European powers to keep their political designs out of the Western Hemisphere.

Independence and Early Republic (1776-1823)

Foreign Relation	US Relative Power	Issue/ Incident	Outcome
BRITAIN (enemy)	Equal	Battle of Saratoga (1777)	American victory demonstrates the staying power of George Washington's Continental Army; British army fails to divide colonies
(enemy)	Equal	Battle of Yorktown (1781)	Allied French and American army defeats the British army in a decisive battle; forces the British to begin negotiations to end the war
(enemy)	Equal	Treaty of Paris (1783)	Ends the American Revolutionary war as Britain concedes independence and gives up claims to lands east of the Mississippi and south of Canada
(rival)	Weaker (at sea)	Impressment at sea (1790-1816)	Conflicts with Revolutionary France cause Britain to exert maximum power on the seas, which includes capturing American sailors and forcing them to serve in the British Navy (impressment)
(rival)	Weaker	Jay Treaty (1794)	American diplomat John Jay attempts to negotiate removal of British troops from the Northwest and solve the impressment issue; British agree to removal but refuse to halt impressment, angering American public
(rival)	Weaker	Embargo Act	Jefferson imposes a trade embargo (ban on trade) against all nations in order to punish

		(1807)	Britain and France for their aggressive actions at sea; embargo fails to achieve desired purpose and deeply damages the American economy
(enemy)	Equal	War of 1812	Short-lived conflict over tensions caused by British navy; ends quickly in a tie with Britain burning the White House but America winning battles on land and sea (Battle of New Orleans)
FRANCE (rival)	Weaker	Citizen Gênet Affair (1793)	Democratic goals of French Revolution create sympathy in the United States; French ambassador Gênet attempts to rally American sentiment by calling on Americans to help the French capture British ships; Gênet rebuked by Washington, who prefers to maintain neutrality
(rival)	Weaker	XYZ Affair (1798-1800)	American diplomats in Paris negotiating neutrality of the seas are asked to pay bribe by Minister Talleyrand; US refuses in disgust, leading to undeclared war at sea
(partner)	Equal	Louisiana Purchase (1803)	US sends negotiators to Paris to inquire about obtaining control of the port of New Orleans; Napoleon instead offers the entire Louisiana territory for $15Mdollars
GENERAL	--	Proclamation of Neutrality (1793)	Declaration by Washington administration that the United States would not choose sides in the conflict between France and Britain
	--	Farewell Address (1796)	Warns future administrations to avoid making permanent alliances with European powers
	--	Monroe Doctrine (1823)	Declaration that US would not tolerate European interference in the Western Hemisphere and is willing to use force to prevent efforts to recolonize Latin America: "...As a principle in which the rights and interests of the United States are involved, that the American continents, by the free and independent condition which they have assumed and maintain, are henceforth not to be considered as subjects for future colonization by any European powers."

Foreign policy for the next 65 years remained focused on issues closer to home, as the United States engaged in a period of **Westward Expansion (1819-1890)**, defeating and displacing Native American tribes and the government of Mexico to build a continental republic. During this period of expansion, the United States was generally able to dictate to neighboring nations intimidated or impressed by its rapidly growing economic, demographic and political power. This dominance over foreign powers was a significant change from the relatively weak power position of the United States in the previous historical period. In fact, the greatest single obstacle to the settlement of the West was neither the presence of foreign powers nor Native Americans but rather the sectional dispute over slavery. Conflict over how and where slavery might be extended to the western territories was settled for thirty years by the **Missouri Compromise** (1820), which banned slavery north of the parallel 36° 30' north (think of a straight line running west to the Pacific and just touching the top of Texas) except for the state of Missouri, which was brought into a union as a slave state (Part of northern Massachusetts was split off and brought into the union as the free state of Maine in order to maintain slave-free balance).

Two ideas about the process of American expansion to the West are worthy of further description. **Manifest Destiny** refers to the belief that God or Providence had favored America by blessing the nation with ideal religious, economic and political institutions, and that it was the duty of Americans so blessed to expand the United States westward to the Pacific, regardless of the opposition of less favored peoples. The other idea is historian Frederick Jackson Turner's "**frontier thesis**" (1893), which argued that the existence of a western frontier played a crucial role in American history by providing a zone of liberty and democracy for people trying to shake off social hierarchies and improve their economic condition. As the pioneers built the west, argues Jackson, they furthered the cause of liberty, democracy and political equality.

Westward Expansion (1819-1890)

Foreign Relation	US Relative Power	Issue/ Incident	Outcome
SPAIN (rival)	Stronger	Cession of Florida (1819)	After the loss of most of its Latin American empire in 1808, Spain abandons its desire to control Florida and cedes the territory to the United States
NATIVE AMERICAN TRIBES (rivals)	Stronger	Indian Removal Act (1830)	Mandatory removal of Indian tribes from the southeast (Georgia) to Oklahoma; many Native Americans die along the way ("the Trail of Tears")
MEXICO (rival)	Stronger	Texas Convention (1832)	American settlers in Texas (then part of Mexico) organize themselves to oppose the Mexican government's upcoming decision to ban slavery in Texas

(enemy)	Stronger	Independence of Texas (1836)	American settlers in Texas take up arms; defeat Mexican army despite losing the battle of the Alamo (1836); Treaty of Velasco ends the conflict and recognizes Texas as an independent country
(rival)	Stronger	Annexation of Texas (1845)	Congress passes a bill to incorporate Texas as part of the United States and sends troops to defend Texas from Mexico, which vehemently opposed the annexation; Texas gains statehood in 1845
(enemy)	Stronger	Mexican-American War (1846-48)	War precipitated by US-Mexico rivalry over Texas and desire of President James Polk to obtain California (then part of Mexico); American troops comprehensively defeat Mexico
(rival)	Stronger	Treaty of Guadalupe-Hidalgo (1848)	Ends the war and forces Mexico to give up the territories of California and New Mexico; US pays $18M to Mexico in return
BRITAIN (partner)	Equal	Webster-Ashburton Treaty (1842)	Peacefully establishes firm northeastern border with Canada
(rival/ partner)	Equal	Division of Oregon Territory (1846)	Negotiations to divide the vast Oregon territory between British-controlled Canada and the United States come close to war ("54° 40' or fight!") but eventually were peacefully settled through negotiation at the 49th parallel
MORMON SETTLERS IN UTAH*	Stronger	Conflict over governance of Utah (1857)	Mormons fleeing religious persecution settle in what is now Utah, arranging a theocratic form of government and practicing polygamy (marriage with multiple wives). The United States army is sent by President Buchanan in 1857 to force the Mormons to give up polygamy; bad weather and negotiations prevent the issue from being settled with armed force. The decision of the Mormon church to give up polygamy in 1890 paved the way for Utah to become a state

Note*: Mormon settlers, of course, are Americans; they are placed in this table given the efforts of Mormon leaders in the mid-19th century to set up an independent nation in what is now Utah

American History Tutoring Guide Paul Pinto

With the settlement of the West completed by 1890, America began to dip its toes into international waters (the period of **Imperialism and Dollar Diplomacy, 1890-1914**), defeating the decrepit Spanish Empire in 1898 and acquiring control over the Philippines and de facto control over newly independent Cuba. American financial power was deployed to maintain friendly governments in Latin America, and American diplomats and naval officers used a mix of force and persuasion to keep markets such as China open to American products.

Imperialism and Dollar Diplomacy (1890-1914)

Foreign Relation	US Relative Power	Issue/ Incident	Outcome
SPAIN (enemy)	Stronger	Spanish-American War (1898)	Cubans unhappy with Spanish rule rebel and look to the United States for support. After the failure of negotiations, the United States declares war on Spain in April 1898 and wins a decisive victory in Cuba in a matter of weeks. The American navy also defeats a Spanish fleet in southeast Asia and occupies the Philippines (a Spanish colony)
		Treaty of Paris (1898)	Treaty ending the Spanish-American War grants independence to Cuba and transfers control of Puerto Rico, Guam, and the Philippines to the US
PHILIPPINES (colony)	Stronger	Philippine-American War (1898-1902)	After the Spanish defeat, Filipinos hoped that America would grant them independence; when the US refuses to do so, Filipinos revolt and fight a bloody guerrilla war. They are defeated when the American army adopts brutal but successful tactics such as burning whole villages and torturing people for information; the Philippines remain under American control until 1946
HAWAII (colony)	Stronger	Annexation of Hawaii (1898)	Annexation of Hawaii is justified on security (seize it before the Japanese) and cultural (Christianize the local population) grounds
CHINA (quasi-colony)	Stronger	Open Door Policy (1899)	Policy of keeping trade in China open to all world powers. China itself has little say in the matter – the US mostly negotiates with Great Britain, France and Russia, all of whom control their own spheres of influence in China

PANAMA (quasi-colony)	Stronger	Hay-Bunau-Varilla Treaty (Panama Canal, 1903)	Roosevelt administration encourages Panama to rebel from Colombia; supports the subsequent revolt, and in return is rewarded with control of the canal zone		
GENERAL		**Roosevelt Corollary (1904)**	Declares that the United States reserves the right to intervene in the government of any Latin American countries that fail to properly manage their own political and economic affairs		
		Dollar Diplomacy	Government policy of using American financial and industrial power to achieve diplomatic goals and to benefit American businesses and banks		

The US Census Bureau's *Historical Statistics of the United States* (1949) provides a helpful table that shows the full extent of the expansion of America, on the continent and overseas, from the founding of the Republic to the close of World War II. As practice for learning to read data tables, the format of the table has been preserved as organized by the bureau; each column should be read from bottom to top rather than vice versa. The left column focused on contiguous territories, or territories physically connected to territory of the United States; the right column focused on noncontiguous territories.

Territorial Expansion of the United States: 1790-1945

Accession	Date	Gross area (sq. mi.)	Accession	Date	Gross area (sq. mi.)
Total	1945	3,734,644	Territories and possessions	1945	712,257
Continental US	1945	3,022,387	US Virgin Islands	1917	133
Gadsden Purchase	1853	29,640	Panama Central Zone	1904	553
Mexican Cession	1848	529,017	American Samoa	1900	76
Oregon	1846	285,580	Philippines	1899	115,000
Texas	1845	390,144	Guam	1899	206
Florida	1819	58,560	Puerto Rico	1899	3,435
Other areas from Spain	1819	13,448	Hawaii/Pacific Islands	1898	6,454
Louisiana Purchase	1803	827,192	Alaska	1867	586,400
Territory in 1790	-	888,811			

Source: US Census Bureau. *Historical Statistics of the United States, 1790-1946.* Series B 24-25.

World War I (1914-1918) confirmed the status of America as a great world power; her reluctant entry in the latter stages of the war tipped the balance against Germany and produced a victory for the Western democracies (USA, Britain, France). The efforts of President Woodrow Wilson to embed the United States in a new global order coordinated by the League of Nations failed due to a wave of isolationism led by Americans disappointed by the war and tired of the grubby and dangerous conduct of European power politics. World War I set two crucial events into motion: the Russian Revolution (1917), which led to the founding of the Soviet Union, a global superpower antagonistic to the capitalist and democratic West; and the humiliation and defeat of Germany, which produced massive economic chaos and a desire for revenge in Europe's largest economy, leading eventually to the rise of Hitler and World War II.

World War I and the Treaty of Versailles (1914-1920)

Foreign Relation	US Relative Power	Issue/ Incident	Outcome
GERMANY (enemy)	Equal	World War I (1914-18)	Germany's effort to conquer Europe and obtain a global empire unites Britain, France, and Tsarist Russia against it in 1914. German unrestricted submarine warfare in the Atlantic (U-boats) and the inflammatory Zimmerman Telegram, which promised the restoration of US territory to Mexico in return for Mexican aid, provoked the United States, which finally entered the war in 1917 on the side of the allies, tipping the balance and compelling Germany to surrender in 1918
BRITAIN & FRANCE (allies)	Equal	World War I (1914-18)	Britain and especially France suffer grievous physical and human damage during the war; strong desire to blame Germany and demand reparations
RUSSIA (SOVIET UNION) (emerging enemy)	Stronger	Russian Revolution (1917)	German invasion of Russia precipitates the collapse of the Tsarist monarchy. A Bolshevik (Communist) revolution follows months later and results in the execution of the Tsar, a bloody civil war, and the founding of the Soviet Union (USSR). A coalition of Western powers, including 15,000 American soldiers, sends troops to guard Western interests in Russia and place pressure on the Communist government; this action damages future relations
GENERAL		Treaty of Versailles (1919)	A compromise between the British and French, who wanted to punish Germany for the war, and the USA, which prioritized a durable peace settlement. Germany is forced to accept responsibility for the war, give up its overseas colonies, and pay huge financial reparations. President Wilson lobbies for the creation of a **League of Nations** to manage international conflict. However, constitutional concerns among Republicans cause the treaty to be rejected by the United States Senate

		Palmer Raids (1919-20)	The successful communist revolution in the Soviet Union produces a period of public panic about the rise of communism in the US (the 'Red Scare'); Attorney General A. Mitchell Palmer attempts to identify and deport hundreds of foreign citizens who were suspected communists, trampling on civil liberties

The rapid growth of the American economy in the 1920s contrasted sharply with poor economic performance in Britain, France, and particularly Germany, all of which struggled to overcome dislocations caused by the war. The Great Depression, which ended the economic boom of the United States, pushed the European economies into outright depression. The result was the rise to power of fascism (political dictatorship while maintaining a capitalist economy) in Germany, Japan and Italy. The expansionist drive of all three countries led directly to **World War II (1939-1945)**, the economic and social costs of which removed Germany, Japan, Britain and France from the ranks of the great powers and upgraded the United States and the Soviet Union to the status of global superpowers. The war ended with the unconditional victory of the Allies (the USA, the Soviet Union, and a weakened Britain) over Germany and Japan.

World War II (1939-45)

Foreign Relation	US Relative Power	Issue/ Incident	Outcome
GERMANY (enemy)	Weaker	Rise of the Nazi Party and war in Europe (1930s)	Expansionist policies of the Nazi Party lead to war with Britain and France after Hitler invades Poland in 1939. Isolationist sentiment in Congress keeps America out of the war even after France surrenders in six weeks.
	Stronger	Defeat and partition of Germany (1945)	Germany is ultimately defeated by a Soviet army in the east and a joint Anglo-American force in the West. Hitler's suicide and unconditional surrender lead to the partition of Germany into East and West Germany, a division made permanent by the tensions of the Cold War
JAPAN (enemy)	Equal	Japan builds empire in the Far East (1930s-40s)	Japan conquers parts of Manchuria (northern China) in 1931; invades China en masse in 1937. Also conquers Taiwan and Korea, and defeats the British in Singapore (1942)
	Equal	Pearl Harbor (1941)	Forms an alliance with Germany (the Axis) and then brings the United States into the war with a surprise attack on the US Navy in Hawaii. US

			declares war on Japan on Dec. 9, 1941
	Stronger	Internment of Japanese civilians (1942)	All Japanese-Americans living on West Coast moved inland to internment camps and kept under armed guard (forced to sell property)
	Stronger	Atomic bombs and surrender (1945)	After years of naval fighting in the Pacific ('island-hopping'), the United States obtains an unconditional surrender from Japan by using atomic bombs on Hiroshima and Nagasaki. The United States occupies Japan until 1951, rewriting its constitution and making Japan a strong ally
BRITAIN (strong ally)	Stronger	War in Europe (1939-1945)	Britain stands alone against Germany in 1940. Hemmed in by strong isolationist opinion, FDR nudges the US towards supporting Britain
	Stronger	Cash & Carry (1939)	FDR persuades Congress to pass a Cash and Carry policy that allows countries to buy war equipment from the United States, but only if they could transport the goods themselves (this favored Britain).
	Stronger	Transfer of destroyers (1940)	FDR trades 50 battleships to England in return for valuable island bases. This probably violated US neutrality but helped the British and benefitted the strategic position of the United States
	Stronger	Lend-Lease (1941)	The US donates supplies/war material to England on an almost unlimited basis, with the goal being to keep England in the war (defeat would have ceded control of the Atlantic to Germany)
	Stronger	D-Day (1944)	Britain and the United States form a close military and political partnership on the Western front, culminating in the 1944 D-Day invasion at Normandy. After the war, the United States takes Britain's customary role as the leading power in the West
SOVIET UNION (uneasy	Equal	War in Europe (1941-45)	Surprised by German invasion in 1941, the Soviet Union is very nearly defeated before the German war machine gets bogged down by the

ally)			Russian winter. The Soviet Union, helped by equipment and material sent by the United States Lend-Lease program, ends up carrying the bulk of the military burden in the war – the majority of casualties in World War II are taken on the Eastern Front.
		Yalta Conference (Feb 1945)	Meeting of Britain, America and the Soviet Union to discuss the postwar reorganization of Europe. Stalin hints that the Soviet Union will seek to establish a sphere of influence in Eastern Europe but also promises free elections in Poland
		Potsdam Conference (July 1945)	Stalin makes it clear that the Soviet Union is going to establish puppet communist governments in Eastern Europe
LATIN AMERICA (from quasi-colonies to partners)	Stronger	Good Neighbor Policy (1933)	Hoover administration retracts the Roosevelt Corollary; Roosevelt extends this with a pledge of goodwill to Latin America and a promise that the United States would not be so quick to treat Latin American nations as colonies

Mutual suspicion about the intent of the other side pushed the United States and Soviet Union into the **Cold War (1945-1989)**, a half-century long political conflict between democratic capitalism and communist dictatorship. The nuclear arsenals of both sides fortunately ruled out the prospect of all-out war, so the Cold War was instead fought through proxy conflicts in Korea (1950-53), Cuba (1962), Vietnam (1965-76), and Afghanistan (1979). Fears of the threat posed by communism led many American policymakers to conclude that communism was a virus whose spread had to be confronted wherever it sought to expand. Anti-communist feelings were a major contributor to the creation of what historians call an American "garrison state" which maintained the massive war machine built in World War II and indeed sought to extend its reach to various bases and host countries around the world. What ideology had created, financial interests sought to preserve: President Eisenhower criticized in his Farewell Address the rise of a "military-industrial" complex in which the profits of defense corporations depended on the maintenance of a large military presence. The combination of anti-communism and the military-industrial complex led the United States into the Vietnam War, a difficult and dispiriting conflict which involved denying the Vietnamese the very rights of independence and freedom so dear to American ideals. Although Vietnam ended badly, as the 1970s proceeded it became increasingly clear that the battle of economic and political models epitomized by the United States and the Soviet Union had been decided firmly in the favor of democratic capitalism. The end of the Cold War due to the economic exhaustion and political bankruptcy of the Soviet Union left the United States as the sole remaining superpower, but this supremacy was soon challenged –fittingly, given the law of the jungle that prevails in international relations – by Islamic terrorism and the rise of China as a superpower-in-waiting.

The Cold War (1945-1989)

Foreign Relation	US Relative Power	Issue/ Incident	Outcome
SOVIET UNION (enemy)	Equal	The Cold War (1945-89)	Stalin wants to create communist buffer states in Eastern Europe for protection against further invasions. He also wants to extend communism as a political system around the world.
	Equal	Strategy of Containment (1946-7)	George Kennan, a State Department officer in Moscow, articulates the principle of containment, in which American money and force were to be used to contain Soviet expansionism
	Equal	Truman Doctrine (1947)	Commits the US to support self-determination (the right of the people in a country to determine its form of government) overseas, particularly in areas like Greece where Communists were attempting to take control of the government
	Equal	Marshall Plan (1948-52)	Large program of American economic aid given to Western European countries to revive their economies and reduce the popularity of domestic communist parties (particularly in France & Italy)
	Equal	Berlin Airlift (1948)	Berlin, located in the Soviet portion of conquered Germany, is itself divided into Soviet and American sections; the Soviets attempt to take over the American section with a blockade, but American air supplies relieve the section until the Soviets give up the effort. Significant because it almost led to war and also because it demonstrates the resolve of the United States
CHINA (ally then enemy)	Stronger	Establishment of the People's Republic of China (1949)	The People's Liberation Army (PLA) under Chairman Mao Tse-tung defeats the Chinese Nationalists of Chiang Kai-shek (American ally) and establishes a communist government in China allied to the Soviet Union. Major

			domestic fallout in the United States ("Who lost China?" accuse Republicans)
(enemy)	Stronger	Korean War (1950-53)	Korea divided after World War II into a pro-Communist North and pro-Western South. North Korea under Kim Il Sung invades the South. Truman goes to the United Nations and the US leads a coalition force allied to the South Koreans. Succeeds in pushing North Koreans back but then China enters the war. 50,000 US and hundreds of thousands of Chinese troops killed before an armistice agreed that divides Korea in half at the 38th parallel
(partner)	Stronger	Nixon goes to China	Richard Nixon, known as a strong Cold Warrior, surprises the world by traveling to China in order to formally recognize its government and open up economic relations; this move made possible by China's unwillingness to follow the lead of the Soviet Union
CUBA (enemy)	Stronger	Cuba Revolution (1959)	Guerillas under the control of Fidel Castro overthrow Cuban government. Castro tries to obtain support from the US, but this proves impossible given his administration's desire to expropriate the property of US corporations as part of a broader land reform; Eisenhower responds to the expropriation by placing an embargo on trade with Cuba. Castro responds by allying with the Soviet Union
(enemy)	Stronger	Bay of Pigs (1961)	Cuban exiles trained and supported by the CIA are supposed to overthrow Castro's government; the invasion is a miserable failure and President Kennedy is forced to take public responsibility
(enemy)	Equal (w/Soviet support)	Cuban Missile Crisis (1962)	The Soviet Union starts to place weapons in Cuba, including nuclear missiles. President Kennedy forms a naval blockade around Cuba, precipitating a nuclear standoff that almost escalates into war. Shaken by the threat of nuclear war, both the US and the USSR make initial steps to reduce tensions

VIETNAM (enemy)	Equal	Vietnam War (1965-1976)	Like Korea, Vietnam is divided between a Communist North and a pro-Western South. The Communists under Ho Chi Minh succeed in combining nationalism and independence from foreign powers with their ideology and therefore only grow stronger as the United States tries to intervene. In 1965, America sends in combat troops but despite raising troop levels to 500,000 soldiers and never losing a battle, the US is unable to win the war for the hearts and minds of the Vietnamese people. The war becomes a divisive political issue, and President Johnson drops his reelection bid in 1968
HOME FRONT		McCarthyism (1952-53)	Efforts by Senator Joseph McCarthy to identify and prosecute suspected Communists in the United States. Despite slim evidence, McCarthy succeeds in ruining many innocent people's lives. He is finally stopped after accusing the Army of harboring suspected communists. The emptiness of this charge ruins his political name and he is censured by the Senate
		Vietnam Protests (1966-76)	Students and young people take to the streets, protesting both the military draft and the injustice of the war
		Pentagon Papers (1971)	Leak of classified Pentagon documents published in *The New York Times* reveals to the public how badly the Vietnam War was going
END OF THE COLD WAR		Prague Spring (1968)	Uprising of Czechoslovakia against Soviet control and communist government. Soviets stop the uprising with military force
		Reforms of Gorbachev (1980s)	Russian Premier Mikhail Gorbachev institutes both political and economic reforms; signals that he will not prevent Eastern European countries from leaving Soviet control; Berlin Wall torn down by Germany (1989)

Concluding Thoughts

America's foreign policy journey parallels its history as a country: small British colonies gave birth to a large but vulnerable young republic; westward expansion to the Pacific led to overseas expansion and colonial acquisitions; industrial growth underpinned an emerging world power in World War I and a global superpower in World War II. After World War II the United States did not, for the first time in its history, demobilize the vast majority of its armed forces but created instead what historians call the National Security State – a set of permanent military and political institutions, supported by a network of defense corporations – that kept the nation at high military alertness. This 'garrison state' succeeded in keeping the nation safe throughout the Cold War, but at some cost to democracy and freedom. The presidency, responsible for the army and foreign relations, gained a great deal of power, and not surprisingly, sometimes exceeded its mandate as during the Iran-Contra scandal, where senior members of the Reagan administration defied Congress to illegally fund a secret war in Nicaragua.

American desires to battle communism overseas with military force achieved mixed outcomes: South Korea was spared a lifetime of Stalinist tyranny thanks to the US Army, but millions of Vietnamese died in a similar effort fifteen years later. The United States Army generally performed brilliantly on the battlefield, and proved to be an engine of social transformation domestically. Millions of army soldiers went to college under the GI Bill, and the desegregation of the Army in 1948 provided a pathway for millions of African-Americans into the middle class.

The United States remains what many commentators call the 'indispensable power' of international relations: it cannot dictate terms to other nations, but major international deals typically cannot be arranged without American cooperation and coordination. The period after September 11th illustrates both the tremendous power of the United States and its failure to effectively use this power to achieve a number of important foreign policy goals: the American military was extremely effective in quickly eliminating both the Taliban regime in Afghanistan and Saddam Hussein's government in Iraq, but the inability of the army to fight a shadowy and changing insurgency in both nations is a strong reminder of the danger of confusing wars, which contain both military and political elements, with battles, which are mostly military in nature.

American History Tutoring Guide Paul Pinto

QUESTIONS

Multiple Choice

1. Which process describes efforts by American and Soviet statesmen to achieve a modus vivendi; that is, a willingness to live together despite major differences?
   A. Détente
   B. The Strategic Defense Initiative (SDI)
   C. McCarthyism
   D. The race to the moon
   E. None of the above

2. Which of the following countries emerged from World War I in the strongest economic position?
   A. The United States
   B. Germany
   C. Britain
   D. France
   E. Russia

3. Which of the following Native American leaders was known as King Philip to New England colonists in the seventeenth century?
   A. Metacom
   B. Tecumseh
   C. Pontiac
   D. Geronimo
   E. Tasaquantum (Squanto)

Territorial Expansion of the United States: 1790-1945

Accession	Date	Gross area (sq. mi.)	Accession	Date	Gross area (sq. mi.)
Total	1945	3,734,644	Territories and possessions	1945	712,257
Continental US	1945	3,022,687	US Virgin Islands	1917	133
Gadsden Purchase	1853	29,640	Panama Central Zone	1904	553
QUESTION 4	1848	529,017	American Samoa	1900	76
Oregon	1846	285,580	QUESTION 6	1899	115,000
Texas	1845	390,144	Guam	1899	206
Florida	1819	58,560	Puerto Rico	1899	3,435
Other areas from Spain	1819	13,448	Hawaii/Pacific Islands	1898	6,454
QUESTION 5	1803	827,192	Alaska	1867	586,400
Territory in 1790	-	888,811			

Source: US Census Bureau, *Historical Statistics of the United States 1789-1945*

Questions 4-6 are based on the chart above, which shows the domestic and foreign territorial acquisitions of the United States since 1803.

4. Which of the following territories was acquired by the United States in 1848?
   A. Alaska
   B. West Virginia
   C. The Mexican Cession
   D. Cuba
   E. The Philippines

5. Which of the following territories was acquired by the United States in 1803?
   A. The Louisiana Purchase
   B. The port of New Orleans
   C. New Canada
   D. Nova Scotia
   E. Spanish Florida

6. Which of the following territories was acquired by the United States in 1899?
   A. The Philippines
   B. Haiti
   C. Hawaii
   D. The Panama Canal Zone
   E. Columbia

7. The Cold War ended in part thanks to the reforming efforts of Russian premier
   A. Leonid Brezhnev
   B. Joseph Stalin
   C. Mikhail Gorbachev
   D. Yuri Andropov
   E. Nikita Khrushchev

8. President Lyndon Johnson used which authorization from Congress to scale up the US military presence in Vietnam?
   A. The Gulf of Tonkin Resolution
   B. The War Powers Act
   C. Authorization of Use of Military Force
   D. United Nations Coalition Agreement
   E. None of the above

9. From 1620-1640, tens of thousands of English Puritans migrated to North America. Why did this flow decline markedly in the 1640s?
   A. The English Civil War brought Oliver Cromwell and his pro-Puritan New Model Army to power
   B. Climactic conditions in New England worsened, resulting in poor crops and famines
   C. King Philip's War in New England scared off prospective migrants
   D. King Charles I promised to convert to Protestantism
   E. All of the above

10. Senator Joseph McCarthy's demagogic campaign to identify and prosecute suspected Communists in the United States government was halted when he held hearings investigating
    A. Famous Hollywood directors and actors
    B. Members of Congress
    C. President Eisenhower
    D. The Army
    E. The State Department

11. Whose revolution in the Caribbean in 1958 led to the failed US invasion at the Bay of Pigs?
    A. Manuel Noriega
    B. Pablo Escobar
    C. Fidel Castro
    D. Simon Bolivar
    E. Toussaint Louverture

12. The Korean War (1950-53) concluded with
    A. A victory for the North and the voluntary exile of Syngman Rhee's government
    B. The division of the country into Communist and Western portions above and below the 38th parallel
    C. A durable peace treaty negotiated under the auspices of the United Nations
    D. The election of President Dwight D. Eisenhower
    E. None of the above

13. The Hay-Bunau-Varilla Treaty provided for
    A. US acquisition of the Panama Canal Zone in perpetuity
    B. The opening of Hong Kong to US trade
    C. Peace with Colombia
    D. The acquisition of the Hawaiian islands
    E. The Gadsden Purchase

14. Woodrow Wilson placed great importance on obtaining Senate approval of the Treaty of Versailles primarily because of
    A. financial reparations due from Germany
    B. it recognized American leadership in world politics
    C. The League of Nations
    D. His desire for an independent Yugoslavia governed by self-determination
    E. All of the above

15. Why did President McKinley not grant independence to the Philippines in 1899?
    A. He believed that European powers or Japan would recolonize the Philippines
    B. He did not believe that the Filipino people were ready for independence
    C. He thought it would be desirable to "Christianize and civilize" the Philippines
    D. He did not want to give the Philippines back to Spain
    E. All of the above

16. The Open Door treaty announced by Secretary of State John Hay in 1899 was most acceptable to which of the following nations?
    A. Great Britain
    B. France
    C. Germany
    D. Japan
    E. Russia

17. Dollar diplomacy refers to
    A. The efforts of the United States to invest money in Western Europe
    B. the alliance of American financial and diplomatic power to increase economic ties and support US businesses overseas
    C. The use of Treasury money to keep farm prices high
    D. An effort by the United States to purchase the Hawaiian Islands
    E. None of the above

18. World War I and World War II are similar in that
    A. Both greatly increased federal government spending
    B. Both resulted in mass mobilizations of economy and society as well as the military
    C. Both required the construction of vast amounts of arms and armaments
    D. Both involved the close coordination of industry with government
    E. All of the above

19. The successful launch of *Sputnik* in 1957 caused which of the following?
    A. Doubt among the American public that their society remained ahead of Russia in science and technology
    B. Renewed resources and effort dedicated to the US space program
    C. Approval in Congress of the National Defense Education Act (NDEA) to help schools invest further in math and science education
    D. An increase in the Pentagon's budget
    E. All of the above

20. Which of the following Presidents initiated American involvement in Vietnam?
    A. John F. Kennedy
    B. Lyndon Johnson
    C. Dwight D. Eisenhower
    D. Richard Nixon
    E. Harry Truman

American History Tutoring Guide Paul Pinto

Practice Essay Questions

1. Analyze the main factors that contributed to the formation of the American National Security State after World War II.

2. Compare and contrast the ways in which violations of the neutrality of the Atlantic contributed to America's involvement in the following wars:
   A. The War of 1812
   B. World War I
   C. World War II

3. How did World War II transform America at home? In your answer, focus on two or three of the many major social, economic, and demographic changes caused by the war.

4. How did American expansion westwards from 1819-1890 serve as a model for American imperial expansion in the late 19th century?

5. Select TWO of the following events and discuss how it marked a turning point in American foreign policy.
   A. The Spanish-American War
   B. World War II
   C. The Vietnam War

6. Use the example of America's evolving relationship with China from the 1880s to 1976 to illustrate the changing position of the United States in the world.

7. How did the Franco-American alliance help the United States win independence?

8. How did foreign policy shape domestic politics during TWO of the following time periods:
   1788 – 1808
   1880 – 1905
   1914 – 1920

9. Compare and contrast the role of the United States in shaping the League of Nations and the United Nations.

10. How did the foreign policy successes or failures of Franklin Roosevelt (1932-1945) and Lyndon Johnson (1963-68) affect prospects for the American welfare state at home?

American History Tutoring Guide

Answers to Multiple Choice Questions
1. A
2. A
3. A
4. C
5. A
6. A
7. C
8. A
9. A
10. D
11. C
12. B
13. A
14. C
15. E
16. A
17. B
18. E
19. E
20. A

American History Tutoring Guide   Paul Pinto

TOPIC 2: THE AFRICAN-AMERICAN POLITICAL EXPERIENCE

The long and frequently painful struggle of African-Americans to obtain equal rights in America is an important story that illuminates not only the history of a specific community but also the whole fabric of democracy and liberty in America. Both the AP and SAT II tests focus heavily on the African-American experience with multiple questions on slavery, the Civil War, Reconstruction, migration to the North, and the Civil Rights Movement. Reading this section will help you master the general themes that define the African-American historical narrative: segregation from the broader political community; discriminatory treatment in economic, political and social spheres; and periodic countermovements to claim freedom, equality, and citizenship. Develop a strong understanding of these central themes and you will be able to answer questions whose historical specifics you may not be perfectly familiar with.

Demography, the study of population movements and changes, often underpins historical analysis because the large-scale movement of people and groups frequently sets the course of subsequent historical events. One of the most powerful examples of demographic change shaping history is the international slave trade and the rapid domestic growth of slavery in the American South; by 1790, the year of the first US Census, African-Americans – the vast majority enslaved – represented thirty-five percent of the South's total population. This substantial percentage made southern society both economically dependent on and politically deeply alarmed by their slave population. Rather than finding ways to emancipate and live with their slaves in peace, slaveowners and politicians in the South worked to deprive slaves of virtually all political and social rights and negotiated protections in the Constitution that leveraged the very presence of their slaves to inflate slave state political representation in Congress (the **Three-Fifths Compromise**). In something of a bitter irony, rapid democratization of the United States in the early nineteenth century acted as an additional barrier restraining liberty and citizenship for black slaves: whites (slaveowning or not) living in majority black congressional districts in states like Alabama or South Carolina were keenly aware of the demographic and democratic consequences of freeing their slaves and giving them the right to vote. In other words, readiness to give ordinary white citizens the right to vote – the hallmark of Jacksonian democracy – was married to an equal determination to prevent African-Americans from gaining the same benefits: democracy, in this case, blocked further democratization because of racial tensions.

For the purposes of the test, we may organize the African-American political experience into three phases:
- Slavery and the battle for emancipation (1600s-1865)
- Reconstruction – a noble, failed attempt to create multiracial democracy (1865-1877)
- The Civil Rights Movement: a successful movement in which African-Americans and Northern leaders united to pass legislation guaranteeing equal rights (1954-1965)

The growth of slavery polarized existing racial views among white Americans. The majority of white Americans in the early nineteenth century agreed that whites and blacks were at best inherently different and believed that blacks should not have the right to participate in American democracy on an equal footing. In other words, despite the universal rhetoric of the Declaration of Independence ('all men are created equal') and the refusal of the Constitution to link slavery to race, politics in most of the United States operated along separate and certainly unequal racial lines. In New England, where slavery was significantly less entrenched than the South, states motivated by the ongoing American Revolution took measures to provide for the immediate or gradual abolition of slavery. Vermont's constitution, approved in 1777, banned slavery outright, as did Massachusetts and New Hampshire in 1783 and 1784. Pennsylvania, Rhode Island and Connecticut initiated reforms in the 1780s designed to gradually eliminate slavery over a period of years (Horton 2012). Finally, the Northwest Ordinance, passed by Congress under the Articles of Confederation in the 1780s, banned slavery in the Northwest Territory. The northern and soon-to-be midwestern states thus set themselves on a path away from the distorting effect of slavery on society, economy and politics, and their efforts to abolish slavery were made simpler by the fact that slaves represented relatively small or nonexistent proportions of their populations. However, it is important to note that emancipation did not lead to full equality and political participation, because northern states usually prevented freedmen from voting, serving on juries, and participating in state militias and also denied freedmen equal access to education. This racist and discriminatory treatment was mild only when compared to the ruthlessness of the southern states, which were determined to maintain and strengthen slavery despite growing recognition of the cruelty and injustice of the system. First and foremost, slavery formed the economic foundation of the economy of the South, as South Carolina delegate to the Constitutional Convention Rawlins Lowndes made clear in 1788: "Without [slaves], this state is one of the most contemptible in the Union...[they are] our only natural resource" (Ibid). Southern leaders also feared that emancipation of large slave populations (slaves represented nearly a majority of Americans in states like South Carolina and Georgia) would destabilize the political structure as freed African-Americans might leverage their numbers to demand full political rights in addition to freedom. The southern states therefore refused to ratify any version of the Constitution that did not provide robust protection for their cherished 'peculiar institution'. They lobbied successfully for a number of provisions in support of slavery, including:

- The Three Fifths Compromise (described above), which increased Southern political representation in Congress and in the Electoral College (Article I, Section 2)
- A fugitive slave clause that required either the states or the federal government to return escaped slaves to their place of origin upon request of the slave owner (Article IV, Sec. 2)[1]
- A clause restricting the ability of Congress to ban the international slave trade for 20 years (until 1807/8; Article I, Sec. 9)

The third provision may be viewed as a compromise in that it conceded to Congress the power to eventually regulate the slave trade, which implied that Congress also had the power to regulate slavery itself. Note that Congress abolished the slave trade on schedule in 1807, an act that southerners did not resist given that slave populations had risen by that point to proportions considered dangerous to public order by southern state leaders.

---

[1] "No Person held to Service or Labour in one State, under the Laws thereof, escaping into another, shall, in Consequence of any Law or Regulation therein, be discharged from such Service or Labour, But shall be delivered up on Claim of the Party to whom such Service or Labour may be due." US Constitution: Article IV, Sec. 2.

The **Missouri Compromise of 1820** continued the tradition of using political compromise to placate the South and maintain the stability of the federal union. The Compromise was negotiated during congressional debates over the impending entry of Missouri into the union as a slave state. New York Senator James Tallmadge commenced the debate from a moderate abolitionist perspective by proposing the **Tallmadge Amendment** (1819), which provided for the gradual emancipation of slavery in the territory (all children born into slavery would be freed at the age of twenty-five and no new slaves could be introduced into the territory). The Tallmadge amendment passed the House but failed in the Senate. Instead of the abolishing slavery, the Missouri Compromise incorporated Missouri into the union as a slave state, balancing the number of slave and free states with the entry of Maine as a free state, and drew a line at the 36° 30' parallel (a straight line from the east to the west at a latitude crossing over the top of the Texas panhandle).

The tradition of political compromise to paper over fundamental differences in the societies and economies of the northern and southern states began to falter with the rise of a robust abolitionist movement in the 1820s. This movement, which spanned the Atlantic, resulted in the abolition of slavery in the British Empire in 1833, an event which gave further confidence to American abolitionists centered in and around New England, which was currently in the midst of a Second Great Awakening that stressed the common salvation potential and humanity of all people, regardless of race.

The abolitionist movement remained a minority even in the North, however, and was generally outflanked politically by solid Southern support for slavery. Over the next twenty years, however, southern intransigence on slavery and the rising popularity of a free-labor movement in the West started to produce anti-slavery majorities in the North. Politics from the late 1840s until the Civil War was then consumed by slavery, as the fearful South attempted to reach for increasingly harsh measures that would guarantee the political security of slavery. A watershed arrived with the Supreme Court's *Dred Scott* (1857) decision, which ruled that Americans of African descent could not be considered American citizens simply because of their race. The Court ruled further that Congress had no power to ban slavery from the territories, which legally invalidated the main political principle of the new Republican Party. *Dred Scott* rejected the main idea of the Declaration of Independence and created a racial test for political participation.

The timeline below tracks the events leading to emancipation and notes the impact of each event on abolitionists, compromisers and stalwart defenders of slavery:

American History Tutoring Guide Paul Pinto

Event	Abolitionists	Compromisers	Slavery Stalwarts
The Missouri Compromise (1820) Slavery banned above the 36° 30' parallel and Missouri and Maine brought into the Union as slave and free states	• Northern congressmen try but fail to pass law gradually extinguishing slavery (**Tallmadge Amendment**)	• The key to the compromise is balance in the Senate between free and slave states	• The deal pacifies the South until further expansion west raises the slavery issue again
Nat Turner's Rebellion (1831) Turner, a preacher and slave in Virginia, organizes a bloody revolt, killing dozens	• Suppression of the rebellion confirms views among abolitionists that slavery requires physical brutality	• Moderate whites in the South panic, approving a new series of restrictive laws protecting slavery	• Slaveowners and police in the South put down the rebellion with great violence, killing hundreds of slaves
Founding of the *Liberator* (1831) Journal founded by NY abolitionist William Lloyd Garrison	• Calling slavery an abomination, Garrison demands immediate emancipation		• Slaveowners demand the suppression of abolitionist publications in the South
Abolitionist Revivals (1835-7) Northern evangelicals preach and publish for abolition	• Theodore Dwight Weld, an evangelical Protestant, tours Ohio and NY with revival meetings preaching abolitionism	• Angry mobs in the North confront and criticize Weld and fellow abolitionists	• Abolitionist printer Elijah Lovejoy murdered by pro-slavery crowd in Illinois
Founding of the *North Star* (1847) Journal founded by Frederick Douglas to give African-Americans a voice	• Douglas, a former slave, pushes white abolitionists to give African-Americans a role		• Challenges the racist message of slaveowners that African-Americans are incapable of self-governance

Event	Abolitionists	Compromisers	Slavery Stalwarts
Compromise of 1850 — Congressional deal on slavery in the west that aims to reduce tensions by allowing the issue to be settled by popular sovereignty	• California enters the Union as a free state • Abolition of slave auctions and depots in Washington, DC	• Henry Clay and Stephen Douglas arrange for New Mexico and Utah to decide slavery via **popular sovereignty**, or vote by the people of each	• Strengthening of the Fugitive Slave Law; suspension of right to jury trial for suspected fugitives
Kansas-Nebraska Act (1854) — Bill authorizing popular sovereignty for Western territories in the North; repeals Missouri Compromise	• Pushes many Northerners into abolitionist camp • Political realignment leads to formation of the Republican Party	• Designed by Douglas as a democratic compromise to solve the slavery issue, popular sovereignty only sharpens divisions	• Pro and anti-slavery advocates move to Kansas and engage in political competition and military conflict ('Bleeding
***Dred Scott v. Sanford* (1857)** — African-Americans have no right to citizenship; Congress has no power to regulate slavery in the Western territories	• Further expands the ranks of abolitionists in the North	• Makes the popular sovereignty position of Stephen Douglas far more difficult to maintain	• Fails to convince the South that slavery will be protected
Lecompton Constitution (1858) — Pro-slavery Kansas state constitution initially accepted and then rejected by Congress; Kansas enters as a free state	• Outraged by President Buchanan's initial decision to accept the Lecompton Constitution	• No room for compromise on the issue of Kansas: either the pro-slavery or the anti-slavery	• Delighted by Buchanan's decision to accept the Lecompton Constitution

American History Tutoring Guide   Paul Pinto

Event	Abolitionists	Compromisers	Slavery Stalwarts
Raid on Harper's Ferry (1858) Abolitionist John Brown leads men on a failed raid on the federal arsenal in VA to start a war to eradicate slavery; Brown tried for treason and hanged	• Great sympathy for Brown's goals if not his violent tactics; he becomes a Northern symbol for the cause of abolition	• Radicals like Brown shrink the space for compromise, as both the North and South begin to consider the possibility of war	• Most Southerners interpret Northern sympathy for Brown's demise as majority support for abolition
Election of 1860 Republican nominee Abraham Lincoln wins as Democratic Party splits between Northern and Southern wings	• Lincoln wins 40% of the national popular vote and 180 out of 267 electoral votes • Lincoln wins zero electoral votes and very few popular votes in the South	• Democratic Party wins 48% of the popular vote and 84 electoral votes but votes split between Stephen Douglas (30% and 12 EVs) and Southerner John C. Breckinridge	• The South views Lincoln's victory as a de facto declaration of war against slavery and South Carolina moves toward secession
Emancipation Proclamation (1863) Wartime measure that frees all the slaves located in states currently at war with the Union	• Abolitionists greet proclamation with praise but look beyond to the liberation of all the slaves • Some abolitionists begin to plan for civil and voting rights for slaves	• The Proclamation is carefully calibrated so as not to alienate loyal border states such as Tennessee and Maryland; it does not ban slavery in these states	• Rules out any negotiated peace with the South, which recognizes that victory for the Union means the end of slavery
Thirteenth Amendment (1865) Abolishes slavery throughout the United States	• Many abolitionists see the amendment as the first step in a longer process of providing equal rights to slaves		• Southern states are expected to approve the amendment as a condition for readmission to the Union

The following table places a number of important historical actors according to their position on slavery:

Strong Abolitionists	Abolitionist Allies	Unionists	Conciliators	Southern Moderates	Southern Stalwarts
• Frederick Douglass (black leader, freed slave) • Harriet Tubman (underground railroad) • William Lloyd Garrison (newspaper publisher) • Harriet Beecher Stowe (*Uncle Tom's Cabin*)	• Charles Sumner • William Seward • Daniel Webster (all Northern Senators) • Thaddeus Stevens (Northern congress-man)	• Abraham Lincoln (later moves to abolitionist position)	• Stephen Douglas (Senator, champion of popular sovereignty)	• Andrew Johnson (Senator, later President) • Roger B. Taney, Chief Justice of the Supreme Court (authored *Dred Scott* decision)	• Jefferson Davis (leader of the Confederacy) • John C. Calhoun (SC Senator, godfather of states' rights)

The Civil War destroyed slavery (Thirteenth Amendment, 1865) but left unresolved the issue of whether African-Americans should be allowed to participate in a true multiracial democracy, a problem made even more difficult by the fact that large black populations were located in the very places where racism was most virulent. Reconstruction may thus be interpreted as a competition between a coalition of African Americans and white liberals (Radical Republicans) versus Southern whites, with less-committed Northern whites as a "swing vote." This "swing vote" found itself closely allied to the Radical Republicans during the last years of the war and the beginning of Reconstruction due to its desire to punish the South for the carnage and treason of the Civil War. This desire, of course, was temporary and faded with the end of the war. Although Reconstruction resulted in a number of profound legal and political achievements, culminating in the Fourteenth and Fifteenth Amendments, which guaranteed the citizenship and voting rights of African Americans, the ability of Southern whites to resist implementation of the amendments eventually resulted in the reassertion of white domination in the South. Reconstruction failed because Northern politicians had little hope of persuading Southern whites to try multiracial democracy; they could only force them to do so through the might of the occupying Union Army. The strength of racial feeling in the North as well as the South and the natural desire of many in the Union Army to return home made the situation untenable in the long term. The "swing vote" of Northern whites swung away from Reconstruction and towards the national project of rebuilding the nation and settling the west. The price of this agenda was the abandonment of African Americans, whose civil and political rights were restricted until the Civil Rights Movement.

American History Tutoring Guide Paul Pinto

The main historical actors in Reconstruction can be charted as follows:

African American Leaders	Radical Republicans	Moderate Republicans	Unionists	Southern Stalwarts
• Frederick Douglass (black leader, freed slave) • Blanche K. Bruce (Senator from Mississippi)	• Charles Sumner (Senator) • Thaddeus Stevens (Congressman) • Gen. Otis Howard (head of Freedmen's Bureau)	• William Seward • Ulysses S. Grant	• Andrew Johnson	• Nathan Forrest (leader of the KKK) • Alexander Stephens (former VP of Confederacy)

During the Civil War, Lincoln suggested a trial policy by which the southern states might be restored to the Union. This policy was generous: the **Ten Percent Plan (1863)** required only ten percent of a rebellious state's citizens to swear a loyalty oath after which the state would be permitted to set up a loyal government and rejoin the Union. He tested this approach on Louisiana and Arkansas after these states were conquered by the Union army in 1864. The rest of the Republican party took a rather dim view of Lincoln's policy and refused to allow the Louisiana and Arkansas representatives to be seated in Congress. The Radical Republicans rejected Lincoln's plan because they wanted to provide full political rights to African-Americans, while other Republicans cared more about punishing the treason committed by the Confederacy. Both groups of Republicans wanted to reform the South root-and-branch. After rejecting the Ten Percent Plan, Republicans in Congress passed the **Wade-Davis Bill (1864)**, which required 50% of the voters in a state to take an oath of loyalty. Lincoln, trying to keep his options open, refused to sign the bill, preferring to defer the process of returning rebellious states to the union until the end of the war.

The assassination of Abraham Lincoln in 1865 brought little-known Andrew Johnson to the presidency. Johnson had been selected as vice-president precisely because of his standing as a moderate southerner from Tennessee, someone who could understand both the North and South. As President, he followed Lincoln and pursued a conciliatory policy with the South (Presidential Reconstruction), which enraged Radical Republicans, who believed that Johnson was throwing away much of what they had fought for during the war. Taking quasi-revolutionary action, they impeached Johnson, who escaped conviction in the Senate by a single vote. The Radical Republicans then took over the project of Reconstruction (Congressional Reconstruction). Here is a summary of the policies of Presidential and Congressional Reconstruction:

PRESIDENTIAL RECONSTRUCTION (1865-6)

- Southern states assign provisional governors and call constitutional conventions; Confederate leaders are excluded
- To rejoin the Union, state conventions are required to (1) redefine their secession in 1860 as illegal; (2) cancel the state debts incurred under the Confederacy (meaning that the southern owners of these debts were left with nothing); and (3) ratify the Thirteenth Amendment, which banned slavery
- Although most southern states find these terms acceptable if distasteful, northern politicians are disappointed when the southern states take active measures to ban freed slaves from voting and pass laws known as the **Black Codes (1865-66)** which force freedmen into a form of indentured servitude
- Adding insult to injury, southern states proceed to elect many leading ex-Confederate political and military leaders to office
- President Johnson vetoes two high-priority bills of the Republicans: (1) extension of the **Freedman's Bureau**, an organization dedicated to educating freed slaves and finding them employment; and (2) the Civil Rights Bill of 1866, which sought to cancel the Black Codes
- The Republicans overcome Johnson's veto of the Civil Rights Bill with a two-thirds majority (first time in history Congress had overturned a presidential veto)
- Congress responds by passing the **Fourteenth Amendment**, which requires the federal government to guarantee the citizenship and equal rights of all Americans, regardless of race. Radical Republicans signal to the southern states that their readmission to the Union depends on their ratification of the Fourteenth Amendment.
- President Johnson advises southern states to reject the Fourteenth Amendment, a de facto declaration of war against Congressional Republicans
- In the election of 1866, the Republicans increase their representation in the House and Senate with two-thirds of each body

Source: (Divine et al. 2007)

CONGRESSIONAL RECONSTRUCTION (1866-1872)

- Congressional Reconstruction plan a far-reaching reorganization of Southern society and politics
- **First Reconstruction Act** (1867) places the South under military rule, with five Union generals each in charge of a military district
- Generals use military rule to prevent anti-Reconstruction partisans from suppressing the rights of African-Americans
- Johnson's efforts to hinder Congressional Reconstruction led to impeachment crisis (1868). The specific incident that set impeachment proceedings was Johnson's removal from office of Secretary of War Edwin Stanton, the only Radical Republican in the Cabinet. Johnson escapes impeachment by a single vote in the Senate. His political near-death experience convinces him to refrain from challenging further measures of Congressional Reconstruction.
- Congress declines to provide compensation to freed slaves in the form of "forty acres and a mule." African-Americans are instead pushed into a sharecropping system in which they must work as tenant farmers to obtain a modest share of the harvest
- In addition to the right to vote, African-Americans enjoy new rights such as the right to be married, the right to found and run their own churches and schools, and the right to organize politically
- The **Fourteenth Amendment** guaranteeing equal protection and due process is ratified (1868)
- The **Fifteenth Amendment** guaranteeing African-Americans the right to vote is ratified (1870)
- The Ku Klux Klan, a white supremacist organization founded by Confederate veterans, uses violence to prevent African-Americans from voting (1868-1870). President Grant passes the **Force Act**, which made voting suppression a federal crime and restored black participation in southern elections
- However, Northern willingness to continue to provide troops to defend black voting rights declined through the 1870s. By 1876, black voter suppression was well under way
- The presidential election of 1876, in which Republican Rutherford B. Hayes lost the popular vote and the electoral college votes were disputed, resulted in a political deal in which Hayes was granted the presidency but Reconstruction was ended in the South (**Compromise of 1877**)
- White **Redeemers** of the South used poll taxes, educational criteria and other discriminatory measures to suppress black voting and put into place a system of social and political segregation known as **Jim Crow**, designed to keep African-Americans subservient to whites
- An average of 187 African-Americans lynched every year from 1889-1899
- Although a powerful Civil Rights Act, the last gasp of Reconstruction, was passed in 1875, it was overturned by the Supreme Court in 1883. The Reconstruction Amendments were also gutted by the Supreme Court, lingering as magnificent but empty ornaments in the Constitution

Source: (Divine et al. 2007)

African-Americans in the South were sentenced by Jim Crow segregation to the systematic limitation of their rights and opportunities: they could not meaningfully participate in politics, own or run large commercial enterprises, or use the same public or transport facilities as whites. As the industrial economy in the North boomed, many African-Americans decided that their only hope for a better life lay in migrating from the South to the North.

Abandoned by white politicians in the North and South, African-Americans were forced to look to their own leaders for a way forward. Booker T. Washington emphasized a policy of nonconfrontation and economic advancement. His Tuskegee Institute (opened in 1881) taught agricultural and industrial sciences to men and women. Washington believed that if African-Americans worked their way up through sheer hard work, whites would respect them and racial peace could be achieved. This policy is known as the **Atlanta Compromise** (1895). An alternative approach was championed by W.E.B. DuBois, a Harvard-trained African-American sociologist. DuBois, one of the founders of the **National Association for the Advancement of Colored People (NAACP, 1909)**, argued that African-Americans, despite all their hard work, would never advance to a position of equality in society without equal voting rights and economic opportunities. He therefore encouraged African-Americans to push both themselves and the broader society they were a part of, encouraging wealthier and intellectually able African-Americans (the 'Talented Tenth') to help their less fortunate brethren. DuBois and his fellow leaders' rejection of Booker T. Washington's go-slowly strategy is known as the **Niagara Movement**, and can be seen as the model for the civil rights movement that emerged a half-century later.

The Second World War, the Cold War, and the movement of many African-Americans from the South to the cities of the North eventually resulted in favorable conditions for a movement for civil rights. The purpose of this movement was not to win over white Southerners, who remained almost uniformly reluctant to grant African-Americans civil rights, but rather to prod the federal government to push the South into treating African-Americans equally. The **Civil Rights Movement** combined a range of strengths – nonviolent protest, links to northern Congressmen of both parties, adroit use of the media, international support – to give African Americans the rights and liberties they had long sought, rights enjoyed by most other Americans. The following table outlines some of the major historical figures:

African American Leaders	Democratic Party Leaders	Dixiecrats
• Martin Luther King, Jr. (preacher, movement leader) • John L. Lewis (student, movement leader) • Thurgood Marshall (lawyer for NAACP, later Supreme Court Justice) • Malcolm X (minister, Nation of Islam), pushed for black separation	• John F. Kennedy (President) • Lyndon Johnson (President) • William Fulbright (Senator from Arkansas)	• Orval Faubus (Governor of Arkansas) • George Wallace (Governor of Alabama) • Police Commissioner Eugene "Bull" Connor (Birmingham, AL)

In addition to achieving its great aims of political and social equality for African-Americans, the Civil Rights Movement also distinguished itself by the way it achieved its goals – nonviolent civil disobedience – and the fact that its leadership was almost uniformly African-American. Nonviolent civil disobedience was a concept articulated by Henry David Thoreau that had been used to great effect by Gandhi in India. It consisted of protest marches, boycotts, and demonstrations but never the use of force.

KEY EVENTS IN THE CIVIL RIGHTS MOVEMENT (1948-65)

- **1948:** Harry Truman desegregates the armed services by executive order
- **1954:** Supreme Court unanimously declares in *Brown v. Board of Education* that "separate educational facilities are inherently unequal"; orders the desegregation of schools, but on a slow schedule that allows Southern state and local governments to evade compliance with the ruling. NAACP attorney Thurgood Marshall served as the lead counsel in arguing this case before the Court: he would later be named the first African-American Supreme Court justice (in 1967).
- **1955:** Rosa Parks, an NAACP activist and seamstress, refuses to give up her seat on the bus to a white passenger and is jailed. This sparks a mass protest involving bus boycotts (**Montgomery Bus Boycotts**), led by a young minister from Atlanta named Martin Luther King, Jr.
- **1957: Southern Christian Leadership Conference (SCLC)** founded by King to coordinate a mass campaign of nonviolent resistance to segregation and Jim Crow laws. King's peaceful but persistent strategy to win over the South with Christian love had the advantage of also appealing to white Americans in the North
- **1957:** President Eisenhower uses federal troops to integrate a high school in Arkansas over the objection of Governor Orval Faubus
- **1960:** Students in North Carolina stage a sit-in at a whites-only diner in Greensboro
- **1960:** The Students' Nonviolent Coordinating Committee (SNCC) is founded; also committed to peaceful resistance
- **1962:** James Meredith, an African-American student, attempts to attend the University of Mississippi; does so with the help of federal marshals but sets of a mass riot
- **1963**: King and other civil rights leaders hold the **March on Washington,** where King delivers his "**I Have a Dream**" speech calling for racial equality and friendship
- **1964**: **Civil Rights Act** passed by the Johnson administration. The Act made segregation of public facilities illegal and created an Equal Employment Opportunity Commission to address racial discrimination by corporations and businesses. Because all the Democratic Senators from the South opposed the bill, it required support from Northern Republicans in order to pass. As Strom Thurmond, the segregationist Democratic Senator from South Carolina, put it: "This is the worst civil-rights package ever presented to the Congress and is reminiscent of the Reconstruction proposals and actions of the radical Republican Congress."[2]

    The Bill passed with the following levels of support by Party and region (US Senate):
    Southern Democrats: 1 –20 (1 in favor, 20 opposed)
    Southern Republicans: 0 – 1
    Northern Democrats: 45 – 1
    Northern Republicans: 27 – 5
    Overall: 73 - 27
- **1965**: **Voting Rights Act** passed by the Johnson administration. The Act banned literacy tests in southern states and installed federal election monitors

---

[2] United Press International, 1963.
http://www.upi.com/Audio/Year_in_Review/Events-of-1963/Civil-Rights-Bill/12295509434394-8/

Backlash Against Civil Rights

Although the Civil Rights Act transformed America by placing the weight of the federal government behind equal rights for African-Americans, it is important to remember that conservative forces opposed to the law did not completely abandon their efforts to oppose it or at least limit its scope. First, the new law produced a realignment in American politics, as virtually all Southern congressmen and senators abandoned the Democratic Party to first form a third party and then to join the Republican party, which slowly transformed itself from the party of the urban and business North and West to a party rooted in the South and the rural West. Second, urban riots caused by clashes between poor African-Americans seeking to challenge their subordinate position and the police caused many whites and wealthy African-Americans to leave the cities for the suburbs. Finally, the rise of the "War on Drugs" and the disproportionate targeting of black men as drug criminals led to what sociologists call a "carceral state" (a prison population so vast that it is like a mini-nation of itself) in the United States with about 2.3 million people in jail in 2009, 900,000 of which are African-Americans.

The rise of the conservative limited-government movement led by Ronald Reagan often took aim at federal policies and programs designed to address racial disparities, and has sought to reduce, reform or eliminate many of these policies.

Concluding Thoughts

America in many ways has transformed itself for the better with regard to race, as evidenced by the progress of the African-American middle class and powerful symbols like the election of Barack Obama in 2008. Yet the poverty and criminality in which many African-Americans find themselves today suggests that America still has a long road to travel before race ceases to be a crucial element in American politics.

American History Tutoring Guide Paul Pinto

QUESTIONS

Multiple Choice
1. Republicans in Congress used which specific incident as a pretext to impeach President Andrew Johnson?
    A. Dismissal of Secretary of War Edwin Stanton in 1868, which violated the Tenure of Office Act
    B. Naming of Salmon P. Chase to the Supreme Court of the United States
    C. Refusal to use military force to suppress the Ku Klux Klan
    D. Refusal to redistribute land confiscated from slaveowners to freed slaves
    E. All of the above

2. Republicans in Congress impeached Andrew Johnson because
    A. Johnson supported the redistribution of land owned by former Confederate leaders to freed slaves
    B. Johnson was using his powers as Commander-in-Chief of the armed forces in a way that threatened the Constitution
    C. Johnson opposed the Radical Republican project to remake the South into a multiracial democracy based on equal rights for blacks and whites
    D. Johnson opposed the Thirteenth Amendment
    E. All of the above

3. To obtain a filibuster-proof majority for passage of the Civil Rights in the Senate, the Democratic party leadership relied on votes from:
    I. Democratic Senators in the South
    II. Republican Senators in the South
    III. Republican Senators in the North

    A. I only
    B. II only
    C. III only
    D. II and III
    E. I, II and III

4. Which of the following African-American leaders advocated black separatism from whites?
    A. Malcolm X
    B. Martin Luther King, Jr.
    C. W.E.B. Du Bois
    D. A. Philip Randolph
    E. James Weldon Johnson

5. Which of the following factors help to explain why the Civil Rights Movement succeeded while Reconstruction failed?
   A. The federal government in the 1960s remained consistently dedicated to the task of enforcing the civil and voting rights of African-Americans
   B. Soviet criticism of American racial policies during the height of the Cold War spurred American policymakers to take action in favor of civil rights
   C. The nonviolent Civil Rights Movement helped persuade many whites in the north and some in the south of the justice of equal rights for African-Americans
   D. The Supreme Court defended the cause of civil rights in the 1950s and 1960s
   E. All of the above

Population, Decennial Summary – Race: 1790-1860

Year	Total	Total White	%	Total Black	%	Free Black	%	Slaves	%
1790	3,929,214	3,172,006	80.7%	757,208	19.3%	59,527	1.5%	697,681	17.8%
1800	5,308,483	4,306,446	81.1%	1,002,037	18.9%	108,435	2.0%	893,602	16.8%
1810	7,239,881	5,862,073	81.0%	1,377,808	19.0%	186,446	2.6%	1,191,362	16.5%
1820	9,638,453	7,866,797	81.6%	1,771,656	18.4%	233,634	2.4%	1,538,022	16.0%
1830	12,866,020	10,537,378	81.9%	2,328,642	18.1%	319,599	2.5%	2,009,043	15.6%
1840	17,069,458	14,195,805	83.2%	2,873,648	16.8%	386,293	2.3%	2,487,355	14.6%
1850	23,191,876	19,553,068	84.3%	3,638,808	15.7%	434,495	1.9%	3,204,313	13.8%
1860	31,443,321	26,922,587	85.6%	4,441,830	14.1%	488,070	1.6%	3,953,760	12.6%

Source: US Census Bureau, *Historical Statistics of the United States 1789-1945*

6. Which of the following statements is most consistent with the data table above?
   A. Slaves did not constitute a majority of the total African-American population
   B. The white population grew more slowly than the African-American population from 1790 to 1860
   C. The proportion of free African-Americans as a percentage of the total population rose from 1790-1810 and subsequently declined
   D. Slaves were mistreated in the South and therefore did not grow rapidly in population in the first half of the nineteenth century
   E. The total slave population was an insignificant share of a rising American population bolstered by immigration

7. Slaves in the south during the antebellum period took advantage of which of the following institutions to create some degree of autonomy and control in their lives?
   A. Religion
   B. Local politics
   C. Gender
   D. Loyal service in auxiliary roles in the southern state militias
   E. All of the above

8. Nat Turner, who in 1831 led the largest rebellion of slaves in the antebellum period, served in what public role in addition to being a slave?
   A. Justice of the peace
   B. Local town hall official
   C. Baptist preacher
   D. Plantation overseer
   E. None of the above

9. Lincoln was reluctant to commit to immediate emancipation in the early years of the Civil War because
   A. He wanted to maintain the loyalty of border states like Kentucky and Missouri
   B. He realized that white racial prejudice would make it difficult to create a stable multiracial democracy
   C. He preferred a policy of voluntary "colonization" of freedmen to Africa
   D. He preferred a policy of gradual and compensated emancipation
   E. All of the above

10. The Supreme Court's decision in *Dred Scott v. Sanford*
    A. Made political compromise over slavery significantly more difficult
    B. Denied citizenship to African-Americans, whether slave or free
    C. Denied Congress the power to regulate slavery in the territories
    D. Declared the Missouri Compromise unconstitutional
    E. All of the above

11. Which of the following Supreme Court cases expanded civil rights for minorities?
    A. *Dred Scott v. Sanford*
    B. *Plessy v. Ferguson*
    C. *Cherokee Nation v. Georgia*
    D. *Brown v. Board of Education*
    E. the "Slaughter-House" Cases

12. Which of the following abolitionists was executed for treason in 1859 for his violent raid on the federal arsenal at Harpers Ferry, Virginia?
    A. Frederick Douglas
    B. William Lloyd Garrison
    C. Horace Greeley
    D. Elijah Lovejoy
    E. John Brown

13. How many electoral votes did Abraham Lincoln win in the South in the election of 1860?
    A. Zero
    B. One
    C. Three
    D. Four
    E. Ten

14. Which leader's Atlanta Compromise approach to race relations argued that African-Americans should focus on property acquisition and demonstrating their work ethic rather than on equal rights?
    A. Marcus Garvey
    B. W.E.B. Du Bois
    C. A. Philip Randolph
    D. Booker T. Washington
    E. James Weldon Johnson

15. Which of the following factors helped the Civil Rights Movement gain critical mass in the late 1950s and 1960s?
    I. A nationwide network of African-American churches that supplied the movement with leaders and funding
    II. The growing responsiveness of the federal government to Soviet Cold War critiques of American racial policies
    III. President Eisenhower's willingness to pass a Civil Rights Law that banned segregation in all public places and placed the power of the federal government behind its enforcement

    A. I only
    B. II only
    C. I and II
    D. II and III
    E. I, II and III

16. Martin Luther King's strategy of nonviolent civil disobedience drew from which nineteenth-century American thinker?
    A. James Madison
    B. Dorothea Dix
    C. John Cotton
    D. Andrew Carnegie
    E. Henry David Thoreau

17. How did Southern states respond to the efforts of the Civil Rights Movement to win equal civil and voting rights for African-Americans from 1960-63?
    A. Some states accepted the goals of the civil rights movement, while others remained recalcitrant
    B. Almost all of the states except for holdouts like Alabama and Mississippi accepted the goals of the movement
    C. All of the southern states resisted virtually every effort and policy espoused by the Civil Rights movement
    D. The Southern states appealed to the Supreme Court for protection against what they saw as the legal overreaching of the Civil Rights movement
    E. The Southern states set up a system of local popular sovereignty in which individuals cities and towns like Birmingham could determine whether or not they wanted segregation

18. Which of the following African-American leaders who served as lead counsel in *Brown v. Board of Education* was named to the Supreme Court in the 1960s?
    A. Thurgood Marshall
    B. W.E.B. Du Bois
    C. A. Philip Randolph
    D. Marcus Garvey
    E. Booker T. Washington

19. Reconstruction was formally ended after
    A. The defeat of the Ku Klux Klan in 1872
    B. The disputed election of 1876, in which Republican Rutherford B. Hayes was awarded the presidency despite seemingly winning fewer electoral votes than Democrat Samuel J. Tilden
    C. The impeachment of President Grant
    D. The "great migration" of African-American laborers to the North
    E. The death of Radical Republican Thaddeus Stevens in 1868

20. Which of the following African-American groups reversed its previous commitment to nonviolence in the late 1960s?
    A. The Southern Christian Leadership Conference (SCLC)
    B. The National Association for the Advancement of Colored People (NAACP)
    C. The Student Nonviolent Coordinating Committee (SNCC)
    D. The Black Panthers
    E. All of the above

American History Tutoring Guide   Paul Pinto

Practice Essay Questions
1. Why did the Civil Rights Movement succeed where Reconstruction failed? In your answer, discuss at least TWO of the following factors:
   A. The size and scope of the federal government
   B. The Cold War
   C. The size, wealth and geographical distribution of the African-American population
   D. Racial attitudes among the American people

2. Compare and contrast the goals, strategies and approaches adopted by Martin Luther King and by Malcolm X.

3. How well did the political system of the United States deal with the challenge of extending slavery into the West from 1820-1860?

4. Assess the ways in which the practice of popular sovereignty exacerbated the sectional crisis from 1850-1860.

5. Why did the vast majority of Union Army troops consider John Brown to be a hero? Do you think Brown was a hero?

6. What factors are most responsible for the formalization and growth of the slave system of the American South from 1650-1850?

7. Compare and contrast the leadership strategies of W.E.B. Du Bois and Booker T. Washington. Which leader was more successful?

8. Slaves in the South lived lives dominated by the economic and social dictates of their masters. What social and cultural institutions and practices did slaves draw on to assert a small but significant degree of autonomy?

Answers to Multiple Choice Questions

1. A	11. D
2. C	12. E
3. C	13. A
4. A	14. D
5. E	15. C
6. C	16. E
7. A	17. C
8. C	18. A
9. E	19. B
10. E	20. C

American History Tutoring Guide　　　　　　　　　　　　　　　　Paul Pinto

TOPIC 3: THE ECONOMIC ROLE OF GOVERNMENT

The proper role of the government in the economy has been contested throughout American history, from the passage of the Navigation Acts by Parliament in the 1660s to the passage of the Affordable Care Act ('Obamacare') in 2010. Since the ratification of the Constitution in 1788, the main issue has been the power, or lack thereof, of the federal government to regulate various parts of the economy.

The Constitution clearly provides Congress with the power to regulate interstate commerce and international trade (Section 1, Article 8). It does not state clearly, however, whether Congress has the power to carry out important economic functions such as:
- The creation of a national bank
- Regulation of labor conditions – working hours, worker safety, etc – and recognition and protection of labor unions
- Power to coordinate and regulate industries like farming, banking, and manufacturing

At the time of the founding, there were two main competing perspectives on the proper role of the federal government in the economy. Alexander Hamilton, the first Secretary of the Treasury, led a group of Federalists who championed active government support for and intervention in the economy. Pitted against this group were Thomas Jefferson's Democratic Republicans, who preferred a much more limited approach based on their suspicion of the corruption inherent in close government involvement with finance and commerce.

PERSPECTIVE	HAMILTONIAN	JEFFERSONIAN
On the extent of the power granted to Congress by the Constitution to regulate the economy	• *Broad construction*: Congress may do whatever is implied in its general economic powers	• *Narrow construction*: Congress may do only what is clearly specified in the text of the Constitution
Role of the federal government in encouraging commerce and manufacturing	• *Active:* Government should fund roads, canals and other internal improvements; use tariffs to protect young manufacturing companies	• *Passive:* Government should stay out of the way of the private economy; no tariffs should be used as they hurt farmers
National Debt	• Seen as a useful tool to invest in the nation and bind the different states together	• Distrusted as a magnet for financial speculators
National Bank	• In favor of a national bank as a way to develop trade and industry	• Feared political and financial corruption inherent in a national bank

The Hamiltonian viewpoint originally enjoyed the ascendancy: as Secretary of the Treasury, Hamilton consolidated the state war debts into a single national debt and set up the First National Bank of the United States. The Bank was a public-private initiative that collected and channeled money from investors and the federal government to finance investment in large-scale agriculture, manufacturing, trade and internal improvements. The Bank primarily served members of what we might call the commercial classes: merchants, bankers, manufacturers, and plantation owners. The tendency of some individuals with political links to the Bank to use its political connections and financial power to shape politics and line their pockets convinced many Jeffersonians, who already doubted its constitutionality, that the Bank was a source of corruption and must be eliminated. After a mighty struggle, Jefferson's political heir Andrew Jackson managed to prevent the renewal of the Bank's charter in 1832, and upon winning reelection that same year, he closed down the Bank by pulling out federal government funds. Another issue that separated northern Hamiltonians from southern Jeffersonians was the **tariff**, a tax on imported manufactured goods. The tariff had two purposes: to raise money for the federal government and to protect American manufacturing by raising the price of international goods. Although the Constitution clearly assigns Congress the authority to levy tariffs, Jeffersonians saw the tax as a tool for boosting northern manufacturing interests and increasing the power of the federal government.

The battle over the Bank spurred the creation of the Whig Party, which took up the idea of federal government funding for internal improvements such as roads, bridges and canals. Following in Hamilton's footsteps, Whig leaders such as Henry Clay believed that the government could and should play an important role in helping businesses prosper through protective taxes or the provision of subsidies (Clay's program of protective tariffs for manufacturing and roads for transportation is known as the **American System**). The Democrat Party – led by Andrew Jackson – believed that direct federal government investment in the economy was unconstitutional and would only lead to inefficiency and corruption. The Whigs and Democrats fought to a political standstill on the issue of federal involvement in the economy in the years before the Civil War, with the Whigs securing some internal improvements and the Democrats successfully vetoing others (such as the Maysville Road Veto of 1830, in which Jackson rejected the construction of a road through Kentucky that relied on federal funds).

The rise of industrial capitalism in the 19th century accelerated the debate over the proper role of the government in the economy. Mega-corporations like Standard Oil, United States Steel, and Northern Securities (a railway company) were formed from the combination of a large number of smaller firms. These companies used a range of tactics – fair and foul – to establish monopolies, which gave them the market power to raise prices to a level above that obtaining in a competitive market. The move towards an industrial economy occurred at a time when the ideology of free markets, or *laissez-faire* ("let it be", or, from the perspective of industrialists speaking to government, "leave us alone") was at its peak. Laissez-faire theorists argued that government intervention in the market would produce suboptimal outcomes by interfering with the laws of supply and demand, making everyone worse off. When free-market ideology was not sufficient to win the argument, industrial company owners used their money to elect politicians who would protect their rights and privileges. Efforts by workers to organize and form unions in order to bargain for better conditions and pay were unsurprisingly rejected by a government heavily influenced by corporate money. In places where state governments were controlled by progressive reformers, initiatives to regulate working hours for women and children were rejected by a Supreme Court fully committed to *laissez-faire* philosophy. The result was a Gilded Age politics in which industrialism created great disparities in wealth, and those with great amounts of wealth used their financial power to tilt the system further in their favor. Over time, it became increasingly clear to many Americans that only the coordinated power of the federal government was capable of channeling and regulating the industrial market in order to ameliorate economic inequalities and restrain the boom-and-bust tendencies of industrialism that threatened the stability of the economic (and political) system. Two main waves of political reform – the Progressive movement and the New Deal – built on a tentative set of initial policies dating back to the 19th century in order to construct an economic system which blended free market capitalism with government regulation and a moderate degree of income redistribution.

- **Late 19th Century:** Starting in the 1880s, Congress took some initial steps to manage the power of large industrial firms, passing the Sherman Antitrust Act (1887) to regulate monopolies and the Interstate Commerce Act (1887), which created an Interstate Commerce Commission (ICC) to regulate railroad price fixing and other abusive practices. Although these items of legislation were powerful in theory, they were written in relatively vague terms and neither Congress nor the President applied them with great vigor; these measures generally failed to fix market abuses.
- **The Progressive Movement:** The Progressive movement was a middle-class reform effort that aimed to improve but not systematically transform the prevailing free-market system. Progressive Presidents like Theodore Roosevelt put teeth into the Sherman Antitrust Act (but not to the point of breaking up all monopolies), and Woodrow Wilson's Clayton Antitrust Act went part of the way towards recognizing unions and legitimizing their activities without creating laws to allow all unions the ability to organize and collectively bargain.
- **The New Deal:** The Great Depression transformed many long-held certainties about the economy. Although the Republican President Herbert Hoover attempted a range of policy initiatives to encourage businesses to boost demand and hire workers, a horrifying downward spiral of bank failures and layoffs continued until the unemployment rate reached 25% in 1932. The country was therefore politically prepared for the incoming Roosevelt Administration, which promised major government intervention to boost the economy. Like the Progressives, Roosevelt sought to preserve rather than destroy the essence of American free-market capitalism. To do so, he installed a range of new laws, policies, and federal agencies intended to stabilize and balance the system. In the process, the government's power to shape the economy expanded to an unprecedented degree, and federal power as a whole grew. World War II cemented this expansion of government power, and America moved into a new era: the era of the regulatory welfare state. In many ways, the economic transformation wrought by the New Deal should be considered as an unwritten constitutional amendment, because it gave Congress the power to regulate virtually all aspects of economic life. The Supreme Court, composed of men committed to the nineteenth-century *laissez-faire* viewpoint, declared many of Roosevelt's signature

programs unconstitutional, arguing that the federal government had no right to intervene so forcefully in the national economy. Roosevelt considered proposing a constitutional amendment but elected instead for his court-packing scheme (1937), which reputedly intimidated the justices to the point that justice changed his vote on a crucial case involving the New Deal and a number of other justices retired in short order. The Court subsequently confirmed some of the signature economic legislation of the New Deal, including Social Security (government pensions paid for with employee payroll taxes) and the Wagner Act (recognizing labor unions). The New Deal saved capitalism by reforming it through regulation and reducing its boom-and-bust tendencies through the operation of welfare state programs like Social Security. Although Roosevelt earned the bitter enmity of many capitalists who believed that his programs were changing the American system of free enterprise, the New Deal was far more moderate than the "Share the Wealth" program proposed by socialist Louisiana Senator Huey Long, whose recommendations of economic socialism were quite popular before his assassination in 1934.

GOVT. REGULATION	PROGRESSIVES (1900-1920)	NEW DEAL (1932-1940)
Trusts (Monopolies)	• Dept. of Labor and Commerce created to monitor trusts (1903) • Hepburn Act (1906) strengthens ICC's powers to set railroad prices • Clayton Antitrust Act (1914) makes corporate officers responsible for antitrust violations	
Labor Conditions	• Federal Workmen's Compensation Act (1916) provides compensation for government workers hurt on the job • Owens-Keating Act (1916) prohibits shipment of products made w/child labor (reversed by Supreme Court)	• Fair Labor Standards Act (1938) sets minimum wage and maximum hours of work per week standards
Labor Unions	• Teddy Roosevelt serves as neutral umpire during United Mine Workers' strike (1903) but declines to offer unions full legal recognition • Clayton Antitrust Act (1914) approves peaceful union activities	• **Wagner Act** (1935) creates a **National Labor Relations Board**, which guarantees the right of unions to form and collectively bargain with employers; major increase in the power of unions
Factory conditions	• Meat Inspection Act (1906) requires sanitary meatpacking	
Banks	• **Federal Reserve Act** (1913) creates the first central bank system since Jackson administration	• **Glass-Stegall Act** (1933) stabilizes banking system by separating commercial from investment banks and insuring

		the former (Federal Deposit Insurance Corp, **FDIC**)
Business Regulation	• Federal Trade Commission (1914) created with power to investigate business practices	• **National Recovery Act** (NRA, 1933) coordinates wages and production levels (overturned by the Court) • **Agricultural Adjustment Administration** (AAA, 1933) provides subsidies to farmers in exchange for reduced production
Social Welfare Programs		• **Social Security Act** (1935) provides welfare system to aid the aged, unemployed, and disabled • **Works Progress Administration** (WPA) and **Civilian Conservation Corps** (CCC) provide government work for the unemployed

With the **Great Society** set of social programs, President Lyndon Johnson set out to complete the work of Franklin Roosevelt. The idea behind the Great Society was that the federal government would develop a range of policies and programs to provide opportunities and economic assistance to those groups – minorities, the poor, the sick, the elderly – who were struggling to achieve the American dream. Johnson leveraged his experience as Senate Majority Leader to pass an impressive range of social legislation. Great Society policies and programs are described below:

PROGRAM	SECTOR	DESCRIPTION
Civil Rights Act (1964)	Civil Rights	• Banned racial job discrimination and the segregation in public facilities. Followed by the Civil Rights Act of 1968 that banned housing discrimination and extended constitutional rights of due process, equal protection of the law and civil rights to Native Americans living on reservations (the Civil Rights Act revived and enforced the Fourteenth Amendment)
Voting Rights Act (1965)	Voting/ Civil Rights	• Provided strong federal government support to ensure that racial minorities in the South were guaranteed the right to vote (revived and enforced the Fifteenth Amendment)
Economic Opportunity Act (1964)	Poverty	• Authorized a federal Office of Economic Opportunity (OEO) to run the "War on Poverty." Included programs like Head Start (early childhood education, healthcare, nutrition and parental assistance for poor children) and a Job Corps for

			high school dropouts
Medicare	Healthcare	•	Government-provided health insurance for Americans over 65. After Social Security, Medicare is the most expensive federal government program ($560B out of a total budget of $3.6T)
Medicaid	Healthcare	•	A joint federal-state program that provides healthcare for poor individuals, families and people with disabilities
Elementary/ Secondary Education Act (ESEA, 1965)	Education	•	Provides federal aid to schools, particularly low-income schools (schools are primarily funded by local taxes with additional state support)
National Endowment for Arts(NEA, 1965)	Arts	•	Federal support for art, music, drama, etc.
Transportation Reforms	Transport	• • •	Urban Mass Transport Act (1964) provided federal matching funds for public transit projects Highway safety a priority due to the efforts of consumer and seatbelt advocate Ralph Nader Creation of the Department of Transportation in 1966
Other	Consumer protection, environ-ment	• • •	Cigarette Labeling Act requires warning labels Wholesome Meat Act improved meat quality standards Clean Air and Water Acts

Analyzing the Federal Budget

The previous tables may give the impression that the federal government's budget has grown with the rise of the welfare state. However, this is not quite true: the welfare state, in the form of programs like Social Security and Medicare, certainly represents a healthy portion of the budget *during peacetime*. However, as the chart of federal government expenditures and revenues from 1792-2011 shows, by far the largest expansions of federal spending are those caused by the involvement of the United States in major wars such as the Civil War, World War I and World War II.

The federal government of the early Republic was tiny and remained so once Jefferson's program of limited government won a broad majority of political support.

The Federal Government Budget, 1792-1835 (millions of dollars)

Year	Receipts	Outlays	Balance	Commentary
1792	3.7	5.1	-1.4	In 1789 Congress passes a 10% tax on imported goods (a tariff) that
1793	4.7	4.5	0.2	covers salt, sugar, tea, coffee, manufactured goods, etc. The tariff
1794	5.4	7.0	-1.6	is designed to produce revenue for the federal govt. but also to
1795	6.1	7.5	-1.4	support domestic manufacturing by making imported products
1796	8.4	5.7	2.7	more expensive. The tariff is increased in 1790, 1792, and 1794
1797	8.7	6.1	2.6	
1798	7.9	7.7	0.2	
1799	7.5	9.7	-2.1	
1800	10.8	10.8	0.1	Jefferson elected, pledges to reduce size of govt.
1801	12.9	9.4	3.5	
1802	15.0	7.9	7.1	
1803	11.1	7.9	3.2	
1804	11.8	8.7	3.1	Although Jefferson succeeds in running a surplus every year...
1805	13.6	10.5	3.1	
1806	15.6	9.8	5.7	
1807	16.4	8.4	8.0	
1808	17.1	9.9	7.1	...the Embargo Act of 1807 eventually produces a decline in
1809	7.8	10.3	-2.5	commerce and in federal tariff revenue, pushing the govt. into deficit
1810	9.4	8.2	1.2	
1811	14.4	8.1	6.4	
1812	9.8	20.3	-10.5	War of 1812 pushes federal government further into deficit
1813	14.3	31.7	-17.3	
1814	11.2	34.7	-23.5	
1815	15.7	32.7	-17.0	
1816	47.7	30.6	17.1	
1817	33.1	21.8	11.3	
1818	21.6	19.8	1.8	
1819	24.6	21.5	3.1	
1820	17.9	18.3	-0.4	
1821	14.6	15.8	-1.2	
1822	20.2	15.0	5.2	
1823	20.5	14.7	5.8	
1824	19.4	20.3	-0.9	
1825	21.8	15.9	6.0	
1826	25.3	17.0	8.2	
1827	23.0	16.1	6.8	
1828	24.8	16.4	8.4	Jackson elected; pledges to limit size of federal government
1829	24.8	15.2	9.6	
1830	24.8	15.1	9.7	
1831	28.5	15.2	13.3	
1832	31.9	17.3	14.6	South Carolina issues nullification threat over high federal tariff
1833	33.9	23.0	10.9	
1834	21.8	18.6	3.2	
1835	35.4	17.6	17.9	Jackson runs a strong surplus throughout his administration

The federal government remained of modest size throughout the nineteenth century, with only the Civil War providing a sharp and temporary rise in government spending.

The Federal Government Budget, 1836-1879 (millions of dollars)

Year	Receipts	Outlays	Balance	Commentary
1836	50.8	30.9	20.0	
1837	25.0	37.2	-12.3	Panic of 1837, fueled by lack of gold and silver backing much of
1838	26.3	33.9	-7.6	the paper money in circulation, causes and economic recession
1839	31.5	26.9	4.6	
1840	19.5	24.3	-4.8	
1841	16.9	26.6	-9.7	
1842	20.0	25.2	-5.2	
1843	8.3	11.9	-3.6	
1844	29.3	22.3	7.0	
1845	30.0	22.9	7.0	
1846	29.7	27.8	1.9	Mexican-American War begins
1847	26.5	57.3	-30.8	
1848	35.7	45.4	-9.6	
1849	31.2	45.1	-13.8	
1850	43.6	39.5	4.1	
1851	52.6	47.7	4.9	
1852	49.8	44.2	5.7	
1853	61.6	48.2	13.4	
1854	78.8	58.0	20.8	
1855	65.4	59.7	5.6	
1856	74.1	69.6	4.5	
1857	69.0	67.8	1.2	Collapse of Ohio Life Insurance and Trust Company causes a banking
1858	46.7	74.2	-27.5	panic that causes 5,000 businesses to fail
1859	53.5	69.1	-15.6	
1860	56.1	63.1	-7.1	
1861	41.5	66.5	-25.0	Civil War begins
1862	52.0	474.8	-422.8	Federal expenditures increase by a factor of 7
1863	112.7	714.7	-602.0	
1864	264.6	865.3	-600.7	Federal expenditures peak at $1.3B. The $3 billion spent on the
1865	333.7	1,297.6	-963.8	war is approximately double all federal spending from 1792-1861
1866	558.0	520.8	37.2	
1867	490.6	357.5	133.1	
1868	405.6	377.3	28.3	
1869	370.9	322.9	48.1	
1870	411.3	309.7	101.6	Small federal government: spending just 4% of estimated GDP of $7.4B
1871	383.3	292.2	91.1	
1872	374.1	277.5	96.6	
1873	333.7	290.3	43.4	Panic of 1873, caused by the collapse of banking house J. Cooke & Co.,
1874	305.0	302.6	2.3	reduces government revenues steeply. Like many other large banks,
1875	288.0	274.6	13.4	Cooke was involved in railroad financial speculation
1876	294.1	265.1	29.0	
1877	281.4	241.3	40.1	
1878	257.8	237.0	20.8	
1879	273.8	266.9	6.9	

Despite the progress of the Industrial Revolution, the federal government remains of modest size until the imposition of the federal income tax and the massive spending of World War I.

The Federal Government Budget, 1880-1923 (millions of dollars)

Year	Receipts	Outlays	Balance	Commentary
1880	333.5	267.6	65.9	
1881	360.8	260.7	100.1	Industrial Revolution produces rapid economic growth and
1882	403.5	258.0	145.5	rising federal revenues, while expenditures remain stable.
1883	398.3	265.4	132.9	The result is a 28 consecutive years of surpluses from 1866-1893
1884	348.5	244.1	104.4	
1885	323.7	260.2	63.5	
1886	336.4	242.5	94.0	
1887	371.4	267.9	103.5	
1888	379.3	267.9	111.3	
1889	387.1	299.3	87.8	
1890	403.1	318.0	85.0	
1891	392.6	365.8	26.8	
1892	354.9	345.0	9.9	
1893	385.8	383.5	2.3	The Panic of 1893, caused by a run on the banks, results in diminished
1894	306.4	367.5	-61.2	government revenues, pushing the federal budget into deficit
1895	324.7	356.2	-31.5	
1896	338.1	352.2	-14.0	
1897	347.7	365.8	-18.1	
1898	405.3	443.4	-38.0	
1899	516.0	605.1	-89.1	
1900	567.2	520.9	46.4	Economic recovery again leads to balanced budgets in most years
1901	587.7	524.6	63.1	
1902	562.5	485.2	77.2	
1903	561.9	517.0	44.9	
1904	541.1	583.7	-42.6	
1905	544.3	567.3	-23.0	
1906	595.0	570.2	24.8	
1907	665.9	579.1	86.7	Failure of Knickerbocker Trust Company leads to a general panic
1908	601.9	659.2	-57.3	and run on trust companies, which is only halted when J.P. Morgan
1909	604.3	693.7	-89.4	and a private syndicate of bankers steps in with ready capital
1910	675.5	693.6	-18.1	
1911	701.8	691.2	10.6	
1912	692.6	689.9	2.7	
1913	724.1	724.5	-0.4	Sixteenth Amendment passed (Federal Income Tax); Creation of
1914	734.7	735.1	-0.4	the Federal Reserve national banking system
1915	697.9	760.6	-62.7	
1916	782.5	734.1	48.5	
1917	1,124.3	1,977.7	-853.4	World War I explodes the federal budget
1918	3,664.6	12,696.7	-9,032.1	
1919	5,152.3	18,514.9	-13,362.6	
1920	6,694.6	6,403.3	291.2	
1921	5,624.9	5,115.9	509.0	
1922	4,109.1	3,372.6	736.5	
1923	4,007.1	3,294.6	712.5	The economic growth of the Roaring Twenties creates large surpluses

American History Tutoring Guide   Paul Pinto

The federal government runs a series of budget surpluses in the 1920s until the Great Depression greatly reduces federal revenues while compelling a large increase in federal spending:

The Federal Government Budget, 1924-1967 (millions of dollars)

Year	Receipts	Outlays	Balance	Commentary
1924	4,012	3,049	963.4	
1925	3,780	3,063	717.0	
1926	3,963	3,098	865.1	
1927	4,129	2,974	1,155.4	
1928	4,042	3,103	939.1	
1929	4,033	3,299	734.4	
1930	4,178	3,440	737.7	
1931	3,116	3,577	-462.0	The Great Depression results in a massive drop in revenues from
1932	1,924	4,659	-2,735.0	$4.2B in 1930 to just $1.9B in 1932
1933	1,997	4,598	-2,602.0	
1934	2,955	6,541	-3,586.0	
1935	3,609	6,412	-2,803.0	Social Security Act passed
1936	3,923	8,228	-4,304.0	
1937	5,387	7,580	-2,193.0	Roosevelt, responding to criticism from the Republicans and the
1938	6,751	6,840	-89.0	public, attempts to balance, the budget, pushing the economy
1939	6,295	9,141	-2,846.0	back into a deep recession
1940	6,548	9,468	-2,920.0	
1941	8,712	13,653	-4,941.0	World War II restores full employment and produces strong GDP
1942	14,634	35,137	-20,503.0	growth, resulting in booming federal receipts. However, the
1943	24,001	78,555	-54,554.0	massive cost of mobilization creates enormous deficits
1944	43,747	91,304	-47,557.0	
1945	45,159	92,712	-47,553.0	
1946	39,296	55,232	-15,936.0	
1947	38,514	34,496	4,018.0	
1948	41,560	29,764	11,796.0	
1949	39,415	38,835	580.0	
1950	39,443	42,562	-3,119.0	The Korean War pushes the federal government back into
1951	51,616	45,514	6,102.0	deficit after three years of postwar surplus
1952	66,167	67,686	-1,519.0	
1953	69,608	76,101	-6,493.0	
1954	69,701	70,855	-1,154.0	
1955	65,451	68,444	-2,993.0	
1956	74,587	70,640	3,947.0	
1957	79,990	76,578	3,412.0	
1958	79,636	82,405	-2,769.0	
1959	79,249	92,098	-12,849.0	
1960	92,492	92,191	301.0	
1961	94,388	97,723	-3,335.0	John F. Kennedy passes a large tax cut that does not reduce
1962	99,676	106,821	-7,146.0	government revenues due to strong economic growth
1963	106,560	111,316	-4,756.0	
1964	112,613	118,528	-5,915.0	
1965	116,817	118,228	-1,411.0	
1966	130,835	134,532	-3,698.0	Vietnam War expenditures balloon
1967	148,822	157,464	-8,643.0	

American History Tutoring Guide

The rise of the anti-tax, small-government Republican party in the late 1970s and its disagreements with the pro-welfare state Democrats lead to a situation in which the federal government continues to spend lots of money while not raising sufficient taxes, causing chronic budget deficits.

The Federal Government Budget, 1968-2011 (millions of dollars)

Year	Receipts	Outlays	Balance	Commentary
1968	152,973	178,134	-25,161	
1969	186,882	183,640	3,242	
1970	192,807	195,649	-2,842	
1971	187,139	210,172	-23,033	Recession caused by oil crisis and rising foreign competition
1972	207,309	230,681	-23,373	push the United States into a "structural" deficit
1973	230,799	245,707	-14,908	
1974	263,224	269,359	-6,135	
1975	279,090	332,332	-53,242	
1976	298,060	371,792	-73,732	
1977	81,232	95,975	-14,744	
1978	355,559	409,218	-53,659	
1979	399,561	458,746	-59,185	
1980	463,302	504,028	-40,726	Reagan elected to the presidency on a policy of tax cuts and
1981	517,112	590,941	-73,830	reductions in government spending
1982	599,272	678,241	-78,968	
1983	617,766	745,743	-127,977	
1984	600,562	808,364	-207,802	
1985	666,438	851,805	-185,367	
1986	734,037	946,344	-212,308	
1987	769,155	990,382	-221,227	
1988	854,288	1,004,017	-149,730	Reagan succeeds with tax cuts but not in reducing government
1989	909,238	1,064,416	-155,178	spending; the result is a larger permanent deficit
1990	991,105	1,143,744	-152,639	
1991	1,031,958	1,252,994	-221,036	
1992	1,054,988	1,324,226	-269,238	Clinton elected, passes deficit reduction plan which includes
1993	1,091,208	1,381,529	-290,321	raising of taxes
1994	1,154,335	1,409,386	-255,051	
1995	1,258,566	1,461,753	-203,186	
1996	1,351,790	1,515,742	-163,952	
1997	1,453,053	1,560,484	-107,431	
1998	1,579,232	1,601,116	-21,884	
1999	1,721,728	1,652,458	69,270	Rapid economic growth produces Clinton budget surpluses, the
2000	1,827,452	1,701,842	125,610	first large surpluses in a generation
2001	2,025,191	1,788,950	236,241	Bush passes large tax cuts
2002	1,991,082	1,862,846	128,236	
2003	1,853,136	2,010,894	-157,758	Iraq war begins
2004	1,782,314	2,159,899	-377,585	Bush reelected; passes additional tax cuts
2005	1,880,114	2,292,841	-412,727	
2006	2,153,611	2,471,957	-318,346	
2007	2,406,869	2,655,050	-248,181	
2008	2,567,985	2,728,686	-160,701	
2009	2,523,991	2,982,544	-458,553	
2010	2,104,989	3,517,677	-1,412,688	
2011	2,162,724	3,456,213	-1,293,489	

Sources: US Census Bureau, *Historical Statistics of the United States 1789-1945*; Philadelphia Regional Bank of the Federal Reserve, Office of Management and Budget Historical Tables (http://www.whitehouse.gov/omb/budget/Historicals)

The chart below, which tracks the number of civilian federal employees from 1816-2010, reinforces the point about wars being the strongest factor behind the rise in size of the federal government. The size of government begins to rise around 1913 or so, with the installation of the federal income tax, but increases far more rapidly with World War I and especially World War II. Note that although the number of federal government workers rises substantially during the New Deal (from 583,000 workers in 1932 to 921,000 in 1939), this increase is dwarfed by the effect of World War II, when the number of federal (civilian) workers rose to 3.8 million. After World War II, the number of workers drops but only down to about 2 million; it then rises back over 3 million during the high tide of Vietnam and the Great Society, and begins to decline again the 1980s with the rise of the conservative right under Reagan.

Sources: US Census Bureau *Historical Statistics of the United States 1789-1945*; *Historical Statistics of the United States: Colonial Times to 1970*; US Office of Personnel Management

Concluding thoughts

Americans since the beginning of the Republic have battled over the proper economic role of the federal government. In the early years, Hamilton articulated an active role for the federal government that was opposed by Jefferson, whose vision of limited federal government was generally triumphant throughout the first half of the nineteenth century despite the efforts of statesmen like Henry Clay. During the first century and a half of United States history, federal government spending only accounted for a major portion of GDP during times of war.

The Industrial Revolution and the Great Depression changed the terms of the debate, with the first massively increasing the productivity and wealth of society and the second demonstrating the dangerous political consequences of the booms and busts produced by industrial capitalism. FDR's New Deal created a system in which the federal government took new and major responsibility for smoothing the boom-and-bust cycle with regulation of business and welfare programs to provide independent sources of income to citizens.

By 1975, the regulatory welfare state created by the New Deal and strengthened by Lyndon Johnson's Great Society achieved the highest accolade in American politics: it was accepted and acknowledged by the other party. Republican presidents like Eisenhower and Nixon accepted the general structure of the New Deal, and focused only on trimming it at the edges. However, this was not the end of the story: just five years later, Ronald Reagan led a broad-based conservative movement to roll back the government's role in the economy, arguing that federal intervention and regulation of the economy had reached the point of being counterproductive: government was not the solution, but was itself the problem. Cutting back the regulatory state and reducing taxes, Reagan argued, would revive the entrepreneurial spirit of the country and reignite economic growth. The success of Reagan's program created a durable conservative movement that has sought to deregulate the economy and reduce taxes at every opportunity. By the 1990s, the tables had been completely turned: even the Democratic Party, the party of the New Deal, was working to trim the government's role in the economy. Although the financial crisis of 2008 halted this momentum, the conservative movement to reduce the role of the state in the economy remains alive and well, as does the age-old debate over the proper role of the federal government in the economy.

American History Tutoring Guide   Paul Pinto

QUESTIONS

Multiple Choice

1. "He smote the rock of the national resources, and abundant streams of revenue gushed forth. He touched the dead corpse of the Public Credit, and it sprung upon its feet. The fabled birth of Minerva, from the brain of Jove, was hardly more sudden or more perfect than the financial system of the United States, as it burst forth from the conceptions of _____."
Speech by Daniel Webster, New York, N.Y., 10 Mar. 1831

    Who is Webster referring to?
    A. John Jay
    B. Robert Morris
    C. Thomas Jefferson
    D. George Washington
    E. Alexander Hamilton

2. Prior to the Sixteenth Amendment (federal income tax), how did the federal government primarily fund its operations?
    A. The sale of lands in the West
    B. Confiscation of foreign contraband
    C. A tariff on imported goods
    D. Requisitions from state governments
    E. A tax on federal employees' salaries

3. Why did Andrew Jackson engage in the famous Bank War?
    I. He believed that the Bank served the interests of the rich and powerful at the expense of farmers and laborers
    II. He had a philosophical objection to a strong role for the federal government in coordinating the economy
    III. He was angry about the Peggy Eaton affair
    IV. He believed that the Bank was developing a mechanism to finance the long-term emancipation and African colonization of the slaves

    A. I only
    B. II only
    C. I and II only
    D. I, II and III
    E. I, II, III and IV

4. Which president sought to complete the work of Franklin D. Roosevelt in building a welfare state?
    A. Richard Nixon
    B. Dwight Eisenhower
    C. Theodore Roosevelt
    D. Lyndon Johnson
    E. George H.W. Bush

5. Which of the following are examples of Great Society programs created by Lyndon Johnson?
   I. Medicare
   II. Medicaid
   III. Voting Rights Act
   IV. National Endowment for the Arts

   A. I only
   B. II only
   C. III only
   D. I, II, and III
   E. I, II, III, and IV

6. Whose "Share the Wealth" program of the early 1930s placed pressure from the left on FDR's New Deal?
   A. Huey Long
   B. Herbert Hoover
   C. Harry Truman
   D. Sinclair Lewis
   E. Charles Lindbergh

Federal Government Budget, 1800-1807

Year	Receipts	Outlays	Balance
1800	$10.8M	$10.8M	$0.1M
1801	12.9	9.4	3.5
1802	15.0	7.9	7.1
1803	11.1	7.9	3.2
1804	11.8	8.7	3.1
1805	13.6	10.5	3.1
1806	15.6	9.8	5.7
1807	16.4	8.4	8.0

7. The chart above provides data that specifically support which of the following political programs?
   A. Jefferson's program of limited federal government and low budgets
   B. Hamilton's promise of the utility of a national bank
   C. Adam's program of neutrality
   D. Robert Morris' role as the Financier of the Revolution
   E. None of the above

8. Which of the following New Deal programs recognized labor unions and provided an organized role of the federal government in negotiations between business and labor?
   A. The AAA
   B. The WPA
   C. The Wagner Act
   D. The CCC
   E. The Hepburn Act

9. Which of the following policy areas were NOT addressed by Progressive reforms?
   A. Railroad price gouging
   B. Urban corruption
   C. Federal income tax
   D. Healthcare for the elderly
   E. Interstate commerce

10. Which of the following policy areas or programs was NOT part of the New Deal?
    A. Agricultural price reform
    B. Civilian Conservation Corps
    C. Civil Rights
    D. Social Security
    E. Labor relations

11. Which of the following programs and policy areas are jointly funded and/or administered by the states and the federal government?
    A. Public education
    B. Healthcare for the poor or disabled
    C. Transportation infrastructure
    D. Child Nutrition
    E. All of the above

12. Which president started the War on Poverty?
    A. Franklin D. Roosevelt
    B. Harry S. Truman
    C. John F. Kennedy
    D. Dwight D. Eisenhower
    E. Lyndon B. Johnson

13. Which of the following factors were most responsible for pushing the federal government into large budget deficits during the nineteenth century?
    A. Wars
    B. Trade embargoes
    C. Poor relief
    D. Ill-advised land sales
    E. Poor crop harvests

14. Which of the following events provided the political impetus for the creation of a national banking system in 1913?
    A. The Civil War
    B. The Bank War
    C. The Great Depression
    D. The Sherman Anti-Trust Act
    E. The Panic of 1907

15. Who coordinated the raising of capital that calmed the financial system in 1907?
    A. J.P. Morgan
    B. John D. Rockefeller
    C. Cornelius Vanderbilt
    D. President Woodrow Wilson
    E. Secretary of the Treasury Andrew Mellon

16. According to the chart above, what event or period was most responsible for the growth of the federal government in terms of the number of its civilian employees?
    A. The Civil War
    B. The New Deal
    C. The Progressive Era
    D. World War II
    E. The Era of Good Feelings

17. "A national debt if it is not excessive will be to us a national blessing."
    Letter to Robert Morris, 30 Apr. 1781

    Who expressed the sentiment above?
    A. John Quincy Adams
    B. Henry Clay
    C. George Washington
    D. James Madison
    E. Alexander Hamilton

18. Which of the following interventions into the economy was Theodore Roosevelt NOT involved in?
    A. The Pure Food and Drug Act
    B. Conservation of natural resources through the creation of National Parks and Forests
    C. Renewed enforcement of trusts through the Clayton Anti-Trust Act
    D. The resolution of the anthracite coal strike of 1903
    E. Increased enforcement authority for the Interstate Commerce Commission

19. Which of the following programs is the most expensive social welfare budget item in the federal budget?
    A. Social Security
    B. Medicare
    C. Medicaid
    D. Education
    E. Employment Assistance (welfare)

20. Who declared that "government is not the solution to our problem" in his inaugural address?
    A. Ronald Reagan
    B. Jimmy Carter
    C. Richard Nixon
    D. Dwight Eisenhower
    E. Bill Clinton

Practice essay questions
1. Americans have been arguing over the proper role, scope and powers of the federal government in the economy since the founding of the Republic. Analyze debates over the proper role of the federal government in the economy during TWO of the following four periods.
   - 1792-1808
   - 1828-1836
   - 1928-1940
   - 1976-1988

2. How closely did presidents Thomas Jefferson and Andrew Jackson stick to their principles of states' rights and limited federal government?

3. Alexander Hamilton and Thomas Jefferson articulated different visions of the federal government's economic and political powers. Whose vision triumphed? Limit your answer to the period 1788 – 1945.

Answers to Multiple Choice Questions
1. E
2. C
3. C
4. D
5. E
6. A
7. A
8. C
9. D
10. C
11. E
12. E
13. A
14. E
15. A
16. D
17. E
18. C
19. A
20. A

American History Tutoring Guide Paul Pinto

TOPIC 4: THE CONSTITUTION

Overview

The durable success of the US Constitution after two and a quarter centuries often veils the troubled birth of the document as a political compromise that failed to satisfy many of the Framers of the Constitution.[3] To obtain sufficient support for ratification, those in favor of the Constitution had to include provisions defending the rights of small as well as large states and slave as well as free states, and they also had to address the concerns of Anti-Federalists who feared the strong central powers proposed for the federal government. The result was an ambiguous document whose meaning soon came to be fiercely contested by the Framers of the Constitution themselves.

Improving on the Articles of Confederation

Befitting a people who had committed themselves to a long and difficult war to rid themselves of a powerful central authority, the successful revolutionaries of the United States designed a remarkably weak central government in the form of the Articles of Confederation. Congress did not have the power to impose taxes; it could only request funds from the states, who were free to refuse. This meant that Congress was always short of money for the most crucial administrative tasks, most glaringly the funding of armies needed to quell domestic rebellions or put foreign powers in their place. The Articles also lacked the presence of a single executive figure who could act with the speed and efficiency necessary to solve festering security and financial issues. Underlying these practical problems was the central question of sovereignty:[4] real power rested with the states, not the confederation; the fact that unanimity was required for making amendments to the Articles made each state a quasi-kingdom of its own. The one bright spot of the Articles was the **Northwest Ordinance (1785)**, which specified the process by which unorganized territories might equip themselves with representative forms of government, apply for statehood, and join the union on an equal basis with the existing states. The troubled period in the 1780s leading up to the creation and ratification of the Constitution is known as the **Critical Period** because of the fragility of the union and the very real possibility that it might splinter into separate parts.

Centralization and Compromise under the Constitution

The men who had spent years fighting the British Army in order to gain independence were not going to sit back and let the United States fall apart due to the weakness of the government under the Articles. Leaders like James Madison of Virginia, Alexander Hamilton of New York and James Wilson of Pennsylvania took the lead in drafting a new document that shifted much more power to the central (federal) government, while retaining significant powers for the states. Congress under the constitution was given the power to tax and to borrow money, key powers that allowed the federal government to come up with a credible plan to consolidate and pay back the massive loans incurred by most states during the Revolutionary War. The constitution also envisaged a single executive magistrate – the president – who was granted control over the entire "executive power" of the government and named the commander-in-chief of the armed services. The

---

[3] The term "framer" refers to individuals like Alexander Hamilton or James Madison who "framed" or put into place constitutional principles and text

[4] Sovereignty may be defined as "the right to rule". Something is sovereign if it has the authority and power to rule over some territory or group of people.

office of the president therefore possessed the power to act quickly and decisively to suppress rebellions such as the Whiskey Rebellion and also act as a credible representative of the United States in foreign policy matters. Finally, the president had the power to veto legislation, although his veto could be overcome by a two-thirds majority of both houses. The preferences of small states were recognized in the Constitution by the creation of a Senate composed of two senators from each state, regardless of population size (known as the **Great Compromise**). The South was also granted disproportional power by the **Three-Fifths Compromise**, which counted slaves towards overall congressional representation in the House of Representatives according to a ratio of five slaves for every three free persons.[5] The Three-Fifths Compromise magnified the representation of the southern states by about 50 percent. All these compromises provided a quite fitting preparation for the new government, because passing laws under the Constitution was designed to be an extremely difficult exercise: backers of a new law had to obtain majority support in both the House and the Senate (sometimes supermajority in the latter in order to defeat a filibuster); the support of the President (or support in two-thirds of both houses to override his veto); and the willingness of the Supreme Court to leave the law unchallenged on constitutional grounds. Therefore, only those laws that won the support of a supermajority of Americans could pass.

Bringing the Constitution to the People

If the process to create the document was an elite-driven one driven by impending domestic crises, the process of ratification was a laudably democratic exercise. Special state ratification conventions were called, and delegates to each convention were elected by the people at large, with very few election qualifications required of voters. Eleven of the thirteen colonies had ratified the Constitution by the summer of 1788 and the final two (North Carolina and Rhode Island) joined by 1790. The authority of the Constitution thus resided in both the approval of the states, and, through the democratic state conventions, the people. By using a strategy of "taking the Constitution to the people," the Federalists defused one of the strongest critiques of the Anti-Federalists, who up to that point had stoutly argued that the Constitution was anti-democratic and opposed to the spirit of the Revolution.

The text of the Constitution

The preamble or introductory statement to the Constitution begins with the ringing declaration "We the People of the United States, in Order to form a more perfect Union, establish Justice, insure domestic Tranquility, provide for the common defence, promote the general Welfare, and secure the Blessings of Liberty to ourselves and our Posterity, do ordain and establish this Constitution for the United States of America." The focus on "We the People" clearly connects and justifies the power of the new federal government to the needs and desires of the people.

The first three articles of the United States Constitution deal respectively with the legislative, executive, and judicial branches of government. Some main insights from these articles are presented in the table below:

---

[5] A slaveowner with one hundred slaves would be counted for purposes of representation as sixty-one people, or three-fifths multiplied by one hundred plus one.

Article I	Article II	Article III	Other Articles
• Legislative Power granted to US Congress • House of Representatives responsive to the people, reps elected to 2 year terms • Senate supposed to take a broader view, six year terms • Section 8 outlines the powers of Congress: tax, spend, borrow, declare and finance war, create courts below the Supreme Court, make all laws "necessary and proper" to execute the above powers	• Full Executive Power granted to a single office: the Presidency • Elected to a four year term by an Electoral College (only office to be voted on by the whole country) • Executive Branch responsible for administering the laws of Congress - Treasury State, Justice, War • President Commander-in-Chief of the armed services and chief diplomat • Veto power	• Judicial power granted to a Supreme Court • Justices selected by the President, with approval of Senate, for lifetime terms • Although the power of judicial review, or the ability to determine whether a law is constitutional or not, is not explicitly stated in the Constitution, the Court has claimed this power since *Marbury v. Madison* (1803)	• Article IV mutually recognizes the deeds and acts of individual states and extends the privileges and immunities of citizens of a given state to other states • Article V specifies the amendment process, which involves super-majorities of Congress and of the state legislatures

- The Framers of the Constitution realized that changing times and political needs would require additions and alterations to the Constitution. Three main political movements placed their stamp on constitutional amendments:
    — The **Bill of Rights (1st-10th)**, the work of Anti-Federalists concerned that the federal government created by the Constitution threatened personal liberties
    — The **Civil War Amendments (13th-15th)**, the work to the Republican Party which eliminated slavery (successfully) and sought to defend the rights of African-Americans and build a multiracial democracy (unsuccessfully)
    — The **Progressive Amendments (16th-19th)**, which sought to ameliorate the excesses of the Gilded Age with a federal income tax, direct election of Senators, Prohibition and women's suffrage.

Although the New Deal wrought a major shift in the power of the federal government to manage the economy, the Roosevelt administration did not aim to pass a set of constitutional amendments to enshrine these economic changes, preferring instead to rely on the precedent of Supreme Court opinions that recognized and thus legitimized the new powers of the government. Unfortunately for FDR, the Supreme Court at first rejected many key pieces of New Deal legislation, such as the Agricultural Adjustment Act, declaring that these acts authorized federal government intervention in the economy in a manner that was plainly unconstitutional. Roosevelt responded in 1937 with the infamous **Judicial Procedures Reform Bill of 1937,** better known as the **Court-Packing Plan** for its intent to increase the number of (pro-New Deal) justices under the guise of expanding and modernizing the federal court system. Although this plan failed, it had the desired effect in that the Supreme Court came to support and unofficially ratify the key claims of the New Deal. The table below summarizes key points of selected amendments:

#	Content
1	• Freedom of religion (no established state religion; no limit on practices of religious groups) • Freedom of speech • Freedom of the press • Right of the people to peaceably assemble • Right of the people to petition their government
2	• Right to bear Arms
4	• Government has no power to conduct unreasonable searches/seizures of property
5	• Prevents people from being compelled to testify against themselves in court (known as "pleading the Fifth") • Requires "due process of law" to be carried out before people can be deprived of their rights of "life, liberty, or property"
6	• Guarantees an impartial jury trial with a defense attorney supplied by the state if necessary
10	• Reserves all powers "not delegated to the United States by the Constitution, nor prohibited by it to the States" back "to the States respectively, or to the people"
13	• Bans slavery
14	• Guarantees citizenship to all people born or naturalized in America (federalizes citizenship) • Gives the federal government the power to prevent any individual state from denying the "privileges and immunities of citizens of the United States" and to prevent any state from taking the "life, liberty and property" of any citizen without due process of law (in other words, it "federalizes" the Fifth Amendment)
15	• Guarantees the right to vote to any (male) citizen regardless of race, color or previous condition of servitude.
16	• Federal income tax
17	• Direct election of US Senators
18	• Prohibition: banned the sale or manufacture of alcoholic beverages (later repealed)
19	• Women's right to vote

Comparing the Constitution to the Declaration of Independence

The Declaration of Independence was designed to set off a revolution and win people's hearts and minds, a task brilliantly accomplished by its talented author, Thomas Jefferson. The Declaration is based on the English philosopher John Locke's **contract theory of government**, which argues that because government is based on the consent of the governed, who have delegated their power to it in order to enjoy the blessings of peace and liberty, the people reserve the right to rise up against a government that denies them their 'natural rights' of life, liberty and property. This is essentially the case Jefferson leveled against the King and Parliament: he argued that taxation without representation violated the rights of the colonists and that the Revolution was a justified response by a people seeking to restore their rights.

Like the Declaration of Independence, the Constitution is rooted in the concept of popular sovereignty – the people hold the ultimate authority that underpins its form of republican government (note that the Preamble to the Constitution starts off with "We the People"). However, the Constitution is also a practical document whose role it was to define the basic ground rules of the society; it therefore had to deal with society as it was rather than how people might wish it. James Madison, the leading thinker behind the Constitution, argued that because governments, no matter how well formed, tend to attract ambitious people, the powers of the government had to be separated into different functions, each of which would check the power of the other. This **separation of powers** theory of government is an idea drawn from the Baron de Montesquieu, a French philosopher (in his book *The Spirit of the Laws*). The Constitution indeed divides the powers of the United States federal government into three parts: legislative (Congress), executive (presidency) and judicial (courts), and allows each branch to compete with and block the others. The Constitution was also forced to reckon with the institution of slavery. Whereas Jefferson (a slaveowner) was able to write in ringing tones that "all men are created equal," the Constitution had to settle for a Three-Fifths compromise that counted slaves as the equivalent of three-fifths of a person. Perhaps the way to think about the relationship between the two documents is to observe that generations of American reformers have made it their mission to align the Constitution with the values of the Declaration of Independence. This is what the Radical Republicans tried (and partially failed) to do during Reconstruction; what female reformers pushed for in the battle to win the vote in 1920; and what Martin Luther King, Jr. called on the South to concede during the Civil Rights Movement.

Concluding Thoughts and Supreme Court Cases
It is interesting to wonder what the Founding Fathers would have made of the enduring power of the Constitution. Jefferson, for one, believed that democratic societies should rewrite their constitutions every nineteen years, to ensure that constitutions kept pace with societal changes. Perhaps Jefferson might be placated by the amendments to the Constitution, which have certainly helped the document adapt fundamental changes in the society. On the other hand, he might also concede that the continuing relevance of (and reverence for) the Constitution reflects its core values of liberty and democracy, values that remain as important today as they were in 1788.

Although the Constitution has generally enjoyed the reverence of the American people, it has endured challenging periods. The **nullification crisis** of the 1820s and 1830s posed a challenge to the authority of the Constitution when leaders like John C. Calhoun of South Carolina argued that states could reject or 'nullify' federal laws that they found repugnant to the basic liberties of their people. The nullification crisis was precipitated by the Tariffs of 1828 and 1832, which were (generally) supported by northerners and opposed by southerners. South Carolina responded to what it considered a particularly unjust tariff rate by holding a state convention that issued an **Ordinance of Nullification** in 1832. The matter was resolved by Andrew Jackson, who obtained a **Force Bill** from Congress that authorized military force to bring South Carolina back into line; this threat, along with the renegotiation of the tariffs on terms more acceptable to South Carolina, settled the issue. Nourished by its tradition of nullification, it is no accident that South Carolina was the first state to secede from the Union in 1860.

It is important to note that specific sections of the Constitution or specific amendments have been interpreted by the Supreme Court in very different ways at different times. The

Fourteenth and Fifteenth Amendments, plainly written to defend the civil, constitutional and voting rights of former slaves, were deemed by the Supreme Court to no longer serve this purpose in 1883 (in the Civil Rights Cases, which ruled that Congress could pass no laws defending black civil rights unless states passed clearly discriminatory laws first). In a different context and time period, the 1960s, the Court famously "discovered" rights not explicitly written down in the Constitution such as the "right to privacy" that underpinned *Roe v. Wade*, the 1973 Supreme Court decision guaranteeing women the right to an abortion.

The central role of the Supreme Court in determining how the Constitution is interpreted requires a basic familiarity with some of the main constitutional cases:

Case	Date	Constitutional Principle	Details
Marbury v. Madison	1803	Judicial Review	• The Supreme Court has the power to review and strike down laws in conflict with the Constitution • Chief Justice John Marshall: "It is emphatically the province and duty of the judicial department to say what the law is"
McCulloch v. Maryland	1811	Federal legal supremacy	• Federal law is superior to state law; therefore states are not allowed to do things like tax federal institutions such as the Bank of the United States
Johnson v. M'Intosh	1823	Native lands inalienable (cannot be sold)	• Only the federal government has the authority to purchase or establish control Native American lands; private (white) individuals have no power to do so
Gibbons v. Ogden	1824	Interstate Commerce	• Supreme Court ruled that only Congress (not the states) can regulate interstate commerce
United States v. The Amistad	1841	Rights of slaves to contest illegal slave trade	• Slaves from Western Africa en route to Cuba revolted on board the Spanish Ship *L'Amistad*, capturing the ship and ending up in the United States. A federal court ruled that because the international slave trade had already been banned at this point (in 1831), the slaves had the right to contest their illegal capture in Africa up to and including the use of force; galvanized abolitionists.
Dred Scott v. Sanford	1857	Black citizenship; federal power over slavery	• Court rules that (1) African-Americans, because they are a different race, have no right to American citizenship (whether slave or free) and (2) Congress has no power to regulate slavery in the western territories
Texas v. White	1869	State secession	• The Court rules that states that had seceded during the Civil War did so illegally and remained legally part of the Union during the War; all acts of secession were thus retroactively declared "absolutely null"
Civil Rights	1883	Limitations on	• Court rules that Congress does not have the

Cases		Fourteenth Amendment	power under the Fourteenth Amendment to prevent racial discrimination by private individuals and corporations. Furthermore, the court ruled that the Civil Rights Act of 1875, which guaranteed equal racial access to all public institutions and organizations, was unconstitutional. This ruling definitely ended Reconstruction and laid the foundation for Jim Crow segregation laws in the South and, unofficially, in many places in the North
LDS Church v. United States	1890	Polygamy	• The Court rules that the charter of the Corporation of the Church of the Latter-Day Saints (Mormon Church) was revoked and its property could be seized by the federal government as a result of the church's unwillingness to give up the practice of polygamy (plural marriage). Faced with this threat, the Mormon Church officially discontinued polygamy
Plessy v. Ferguson	1896	Segregation of public facilities	• Court rules that public facilities segregated by race are legal provided that equal facilities are provided for African-Americans
Williams v. Mississippi	1898	Voter Discrimination	• Court finds that a Mississippi law that requiring literacy tests and the payment of voting (poll) taxes was constitutional as it applied to all voters (notwithstanding the fact that white officials applied the act predominantly against African-Americans).
Lochner v. New York	1905	Economic Regulation	• Court rules that states have no right to limit the number of hours individuals can work, calling this an "arbitrary interference with the right and liberty of an individual to contract" his labor with his employer. This ruling was part of a broader effort by the Court to prevent unions and states from regulating the market to prevent abuses like excessive hours and brutal working conditions
Muller v. Oregon	1908	Economic regulation	• The Court does allow state laws limiting hours worked for women, justifying this as a matter of women's health
West Coast Hotel Co. v. Parrish	1937	Economic regulation	• The Court rules that states actually do have the authority to pass laws regulating working hours and conditions. This law thus reversed *Locher v. New York*(1905) and recognized the political changes of the New Deal. Because one conservative judge shifted his vote, the decision is often seen as a concession to FDR's attempt to

			"pack the court." From this point, the Court no longer challenges the right of the government (federal or state) to regulate the economy
NLRB vs. Jones & Laughlin Steel Co.	1937	Economic regulation	• Declares that the National Labor Relations Board is constitutional, as is the act that authorized it (Wagner Act of 1935). This decision further concedes power to Congress to regulate the economy as it sees fit
Korematsu v. United States	1944	Japanese interment	• Court rules that Executive Order 9066, which authorized the internment of Japanese-Americans, is constitutional given the plausible risk of Japanese espionage
Sipuel v. Board of Regents of Univ. of Oklahoma	1948	African-American rights	• Court rules that African-Americans have the right to equal access to legal education from a state institution under the equal protection clause of the Fourteenth Amendment. The case was argued before the court by NAACP attorney Thurgood Marshall
Brown v. Board of Education	1954	Segregation of public facilities	• Court reverses *Plessy v. Ferguson* by stating that separate public schools are inherently unequal and violate the equal protection clause of the Fourteenth Amendment. Thurgood Marshall argues this case before the Court
Hernandez v. Texas	1954	Rights of other racial minorities	• Court rules that the equal protection clause of the Fourteenth Amendment protects Mexican-Americans and other racial groups
Gideon v. Wainwright	1963	Right to counsel	• Court rules that states are required to provide legal counsel to those unable to afford a lawyer under the due process clause of the Fourteenth Amendment (Federal Government already required to do so by the Sixth Amendment)
Griswold v. Connecticut	1965	Right to privacy	• The Constitution protects a right to individual privacy that means that the use of contraceptives (the specific issue in the case) are permissible. The concept of the right to privacy was later expanded to the right to abortion
Miranda v. Arizona	1966	Right to due process of law for those under arrest	• Right against self-incrimination and right to a lawyer. Note that the Supreme Court under Earl Warren (Chief Justice from 1953-69) made a concerted effort to protect individual liberties
Loving v. Virginia	1967	Miscegenation	• Declares that race-based limitations or bans on marriage are unconstitutional
Roe v. Wade	1973	Right to privacy, abortion	• A woman has the right to choose whether or not to have an abortion

American History Tutoring Guide   Paul Pinto

QUESTIONS

Multiple Choice

1. Which Supreme Court justice articulated a robust national viewpoint that included opinions defending the supremacy of federal over state law, the supremacy of Congress in regulating interstate trade, and the right of the Court to determine the constitutionality of both federal and state laws?
    A. John Jay
    B. John Marshall
    C. Roger B. Taney
    D. William Howard Taft
    E. Louis Brandeis

2. The doctrine of the separation of powers forms a key element of the Constitution. Which eighteenth-century philosopher outlined this theory in his work *The Spirit of the Laws*?
    A. Voltaire
    B. Diderot
    C. Pascal
    D. Rousseau
    E. Montesquieu

3. Which of the following arrangements correctly links articles of the Constitution to their appropriate content?

	Article I	Article II	Article III	Article IV	Article V
A.	Executive	Legislative	Amendment Process	Relations between States	Judicial
B.	Legislative	Executive	Judicial	Relations between States	Amendment Process
C.	Legislative	Judicial	Executive	Amendment Process	Relations between States
D.	Executive	Legislative	Judicial	Relations between States	Amendment Process
E.	Judicial	Legislative	Executive	Relations between States	Amendment Process

4. Guarantees protecting freedom of religion, speech, the right to peaceably assemble and to petition the government were all included in the Constitution at the behest of
   A. Anti-Federalists
   B. James Madison
   C. Alexander Hamilton
   D. John Jay
   E. Benjamin Franklin

5. Both the Declaration of Independence and the Constitution as originally ratified agree on which of the following principles?
   A. Republican government based on the ultimate authority of the people
   B. The inalienable rights of all men and women
   C. The right to revolution
   D. The right of the people to be represented by a unicameral legislature
   E. All of the above

6. According to *McCulloch v. Maryland* (1811), which of the following actions are not permissible?
   A. The creation of a National Bank
   B. State taxation of the Bank of the United States
   C. Federal acquisition of new territories to the West
   D. Congressional regulation of interstate commerce
   E. Federal control of international trade

7. *Roe v. Wade* (1973) declared that abortion is legal and gives decision-making power to a woman and her doctor based on which constitutional principle?
   A. The right to property
   B. The right to pursue happiness
   C. The right to privacy
   D. The right to American citizenship
   E. None of the above

8. Under the Constitution, the President has which of the following powers?
   A. The veto
   B. Control over the entire executive power of the United States
   C. Command of the armed forces
   D. Control of foreign affairs subject to the advice and consent of the Senate
   E. All of the above

9. Under the original terms of the Constitution, an area containing ten plantations each with an average slave population of 50 and an average free population of 10 would be apportioned as if it had how many American citizens?
   A. 10
   B. 100
   C. 310
   D. 400
   E. 620

10. Which of the following pairs of amendments eliminated the Three-Fifths Compromise?
    A. Tenth and Eleventh
    B. Twelfth and Thirteenth
    C. Thirteenth and Fourteenth
    D. Sixteenth and Seventeenth
    E. Eighteenth and Nineteenth

11. *Plessy vs. Ferguson* (1896) declared that
    A. Segregated public facilities were to be the law of the land throughout the nation
    B. Segregated public facilities were acceptable provided they were equal
    C. Segregated public facilities were inherently unequal
    D. Segregated public facilities could only apply to Native Americans, not African-Americans
    E. None of the above

12. All of the following are examples of checks and balances amongst the branches of the federal government EXCEPT
    A. A presidential veto
    B. The Supreme Court declaring a law unconstitutional
    C. Congress overriding a presidential veto with two-thirds support from both houses
    D. The direct election of Senators
    E. The House of Representatives filing impeachment charges against the president

13. Which Supreme Court decision enunciated the principle of judicial review?
    A. *Plessy v. Ferguson*
    B. *McCulloch v. Maryland*
    C. *Marbury v. Madison*
    D. *Brown v. Board of Education*
    E. *Roe v. Wade*

14. Which Chief Justice of the Supreme Court led a movement to protect and expand personal
    liberties in the 1960s?
    A. Roger B. Taney
    B. Harlan Stone
    C. Louis Brandeis
    D. William Rehnquist
    E. Earl Warren

15. All of the following decisions expanded personal liberties EXCEPT
    A. *Gideon v. Wainwright*
    B. *Miranda v. Arizona*
    C. *Plessy v. Ferguson*
    D. *Roe v. Wade*
    E. *Brown v. Board of Education*

16. Which of the following constitutional amendments was repealed by the Twenty-Second Amendment in 1933?
    A. Thirteenth
    B. Fourteenth
    C. Fifteenth
    D. Sixteenth
    E. Eighteenth

17. All of the following are rulings of the Warren Court (1953-1969) that expanded civil rights and liberties EXCEPT
    A. *Lochner v. New York*
    B. *Gideon v. Wainwright*
    C. *Brown v. Board of Education*
    D. *Griswold v. Connecticut*
    E. *Miranda v. Arizona*

18. *Korematsu v. United States* (1944) confirmed which action of the Roosevelt Administration?
    A. Dropping the atomic bomb on Japan
    B. The internment of Japanese-Americans
    C. The hanging of enemy spies without a trial
    D. The cession of the Philippines to Japan during World War II
    E. All of the above

19. All of the following Supreme Court decisions are correctly matched with the constitutional amendment or decision that overruled them EXCEPT
    A. *Lochner v. New York* (1905) – *West Coast Hotel Co. v. Parrish* (1937)
    B. *Plessy v. Ferguson* (1896) – *Brown v. Board of Education* (1954)
    C. *Dred Scott v. Sanford* (1857) – The Fourteenth Amendment (1868)
    D. *Civil Rights Cases* (1883) – *Brown v. Board of Education* (1954)
    E. *Marbury v. Madison* (1803) – The Thirteenth Amendment (1865)

20. To gain passage, a proposed constitutional amendment must gain the support of
    A. A majority of both houses of Congress plus a majority of state legislatures
    B. A majority of both houses of Congress plus three-fourths of state legislatures
    C. Two-thirds of both houses of Congress plus three-fourths of state legislatures
    D. Two-thirds of both houses of Congress plus two-thirds of the states legislatures
    E. Two-thirds of both house of Congress plus three-fourths of state legislatures plus the signature of the President of the United States

Essay Questions
1. Explain the changes in the legal and political rights of African-Americans from 1776 to 1965. Be sure to cite relevant laws, court decisions, and amendments.

2. How did the struggle for American Independence, including the Revolutionary War itself, influence the form and powers of the new national government under the Articles of Confederation?

3. Compare and contrast the powers of the national government under the Articles of Confederation and under the Constitution.

4. Should the Supreme Court have the exclusive right to determine what the Constitution says?

5. In what ways did Reconstruction serve as a second Constitutional Convention?

6. Do major constitutional changes require constitutional amendments? Discuss, using a comparison of the Progressive Era and the New Deal as examples.

Answers to Multiple Choice Questions
1. B
2. E
3. B
4. A
5. A
6. B
7. C
8. E
9. D
10. C
11. B
12. D
13. C
14. E
15. C
16. E
17. A
18. B
19. E
20. C

TOPIC 5: BUSINESS AND ECONOMY

The treatment of economics in US history textbooks is uneven and uncertain: uneven because the narrative history favored by many textbooks prioritizes vivid short-term events like depressions and panics over longer-term patterns of economic growth or decline; and uncertain because the narrative format of textbooks makes it difficult to squeeze coherent explanations of complex economic causes and consequences within the space of a few pages. One result is that many students are often vaguely familiar with certain economic events but find it difficult to answer multiple choice questions that require the application of some basic economic logic. Consider the following question selected from a leading test preparation guide (Bach and Fitzgerald 2005):

1. If the policies of the Greenback Party had been enacted it would have had the same effect on the money supply as when the Federal Reserve:
   A. raises the discount lending rate
   B. manipulates the price of gold
   C. tightens the money supply
   D. lowers the discount lending rate
   E. insures bank deposits

We will return to this question at the end of the section, once we have unpacked economic concepts like **supply and demand** (how many things are produced versus how much things are purchased), **market equilibrium** (how the market helps balance the amount of things produced with the amount of things purchased), **money and prices** (how the market, with a helping hand from the government, determines how different things are valued), and the **business cycle** (how economies get into and out of depressions and expansions). Do not fret if you dislike abstract economic discussions: the explanations below include practical examples as well as a main takeaway point or two that you can simply memorize while working towards developing increasing familiarity with economic logic.

This section begins with a review of business history, which serves as a warm-up to our overview of the principles of economics and their application to United States history. Remember that if an **economy** is a social institution that determines what is produced, how it is produced, and for whom it is produced, a **business firm** is an organization within the economy that attempts to earn a profit by selling things in the marketplace that people and other businesses want to buy. Businesses make profits (or losses) by selling quantities of goods or services for a specific price or set of prices (the product of which is called their sales or revenues) and deducting the costs of manufacturing, selling and marketing their products. Businesses whose sales are less than their costs will soon or later go out of business, and their position in the marketplace will be taken by more competitive businesses. **Adam Smith**, the great Scottish economist whose work *The Wealth of Nations* was published in 1776, makes the important point that competition between business firms is a great blessing for societies in that individual firms are constantly driven to improve their products, lower their prices and invent better products in order to compete in the marketplace, thereby making society far better off than if such competition was restrained by the government. In Smith's elegant language, it is as if an "Invisible Hand" is guiding the uncoordinated competitive actions of individual firms via the mechanism of competition to produce the most productive results for society as a whole. Smith's ideas formed the basis for an economic philosophy known as *laissez-faire* ("let it be," or "leave us alone!"), which was used by 19th century industrialists and businessmen to argue against government intervention in the economy. One problem with *laissez-faire* reasoning, of course, is that the benefits to society of an unfettered competitive market accrue when many small firms compete vigorously in a market no single firm controls. **Monopolies**, where one firm dominates an entire industry, and **oligopolies**, where a few firms dominate an industry, are situations in which the competition mechanism is impaired and firms have little incentive to improve their performance and lower their prices, making consumers and society worse off. In other words, monopolies violate the competition mechanism that makes the "Invisible Hand" work; in fact, they should be seen rather as a "Visible Hand" that controls what consumers pay and thus detracts from overall social welfare. The second half of the 19th century – the **Gilded Age** – was an age of dominant monopolies or **trusts** (a term used to describe a set of overlapping financial arrangements which concentrated the control of an industry in one or a few people's hands) which fought to restrain competition and used their market power to generate massive profits and buy control of the political system. Many of the leaders of Gilded Age monopolies loudly proclaimed their belief in laissez-faire capitalism while vigorous attempting to throttle competition in their industries in order to raise prices and make more money.

Business history as it is tested on the AP and SAT II exams consists of two main components: (1) the history of great inventions and technological advances, and (2) the history of major businessmen and companies. The table below lists some of the major inventions in American history, along with their inventors or early pioneers and their social and economic impact. Pay particular attention to the date of the invention; test questions frequently require you to place specific innovations in their proper time period.

Invention	Date	Inventor	Social and Economic Impact
Bifocals	1784	Benjamin Franklin	• Allowed their wearer to simultaneously correct both near and far-sightedness
Cotton Gin	1793	Eli Whitney	• A mechanical device that separated cotton seeds, the cotton gin vastly improved the productivity of plantations, helping "King Cotton" become the dominant cash crop of the South, supplying the raw material to drive the mechanized textile production of the Industrial Revolution, and further increasing the centrality of slavery
Interchangeable Machine Parts	1798	Eli Whitney, others	• Allowed inventors to mix & match different parts to produce new types of machines; lowered production costs
Steam Engine	1802	Oliver Evans (US)	• Used to supply power in factories, mines and, later for locomotives

Reaper	1831	Cyrus McCormick	• Mechanical harvester to chop grain
Revolver	1836	Samuel Colt	• Pistol that could fire six shots in quick succession
Ether	1842	Crawford Young	• Chemical used in surgery to anesthetize patients quickly and painlessly
Telegraph	1844	Samuel Morse	• Allowed for the transmission of messages by Morse code over telegraph lines; revolutionary change in long-distance communication
Sewing machine	1846	Elias Howe	• Sped up clothing production in both factories and homes
Rotary printing press	1847	Richard Hoe	• Rapidly increased the speed and lowered the cost of printing
Passenger elevator	1853	Elisha Otis	• Made rapid vertical transport in buildings possible (foreshadowing skyscrapers)
Oil Well	1859	Edwin Drake	• Helped launch one of America's largest industries – oil
Pullman Railroad Cars	1859	George Pullman	• Made long-distance train journeys practical and enjoyable for passengers
Typewriter Cash Register Adding Machine	1867 1879 1888	Various	• Made business transactions much faster and more accurate
Kodak cameras and film	1879, 1888	George Eastman	• Allowed non-professionals to take their own photographs
Meat packing	1870s	Gustavus Swift	• Transport of beef in refrigerated railroad cars makes beef accessible to the urban masses
Mail-order catalog stores	1872	Richard Sears; Montgomery Ward	• Created impersonal mass consumption of goods and services
Telephone	1876	Alexander Graham Bell	• Continued the revolution in communication
Phonograph	1877	Thomas Edison	• Recorded and played back sounds; created the record industry
Electric light bulb	1879	Thomas Edison, others	• Transformed life at night, as businesses, homes and places of entertainment were able to transform night into day; 2 million electric lights manufactured by 1900
Skyscrapers	1884	William Le Baron Jenney	• Buildings more than several stories made possible

Subway/Streetcar Systems	1887	Frank Sprague	• First streetcar system in Richmond, Virginia
Tractor	1892	John Froelich	• Further mechanization of farming → lower demand for farm laborers
Assembly lines	1900s	Various innovators, including Henry Ford	• A product is created by the sequential addition of different parts along a line; each part is controlled by a worker or group of workers, who specializes in that part and nothing else; allows for the efficient mass production of cars and other large industrial goods
Air conditioning	1902	Willis Carrier	• Allows for the cooling and control of temperature indoors for the first time; causes population mobility by enticing more people to move to the "Sunbelt" areas of the country
Airplane	1903	Wilbur and Orville Wright	• Made rapid long-distance transportation across oceans as well as land possible; a powerful new weapon of war
Model T Ford	1908	Henry Ford	• Four-cylinder automobiles that were small, relatively inexpensive, and designed for the mass market – created era of physical mobility for the middle class
Radio broadcasting	1920s	Various	• Created a mass public audience; standardized American culture
Hollywood	1920s	Various	• Audiences of tens of millions by the 1920s
Television	1950s	Various	• First developed in the 1920s, TVs became a household staple in the 1950s, quickly becoming a dominant mode of communication
Atomic Bomb	1940s	Robert Oppenheimer, others	• Top secret Manhattan Project spends $2B to develop an atomic weapon • Used to end the war in Japan
Space flight	1950s-60s	Werner von Braun, others	• Soviet send first satellite – Sputnik – into space in 1957, setting off the space race • Soviets send first man into space in 1962 • Neil Armstrong the first man on the moon in 1969
Computers	1940s	Various	• Revolutionized business computations, science, the military, communications, and much more

American History Tutoring Guide

Sources: (Deitch 2001; Divine et al. 2007: 526-7)

Business leaders rose to great social prominence during the Gilded Age, when the first large industrial monopolies created unparalleled levels of wealth for their owners. Wealth in the period before the industrial age was generated primarily from the land, with large estates established in colonies like New York (held by families like the Van Rensselaers and the Livingstons) and, of course, the tobacco, rice, sugar, and (later) cotton plantations of the South. In the years leading up to the Civil War, the largest plantations were found in the Deep South and Virginia. Another route to great wealth in the antebellum era came from trans-Atlantic shipping and was centered in port cities like Boston, New York, Philadelphia and Charleston. Finally, New York emerged as the financial capital of the United States and created a number of substantial fortunes in commercial banking, merchant (later called investment) banking, and investments.

The table below summarizes the careers of some of the most important business leaders in American history.

Name/Industry	Social and Economic Impact
Andrew Carnegie (Steel)	• A Scottish immigrant, Carnegie possessed a natural charm that partially leavened his ruthless business practices. His Carnegie Steel Company aggressively entered all aspects of the steel production process (**vertical integration**) and also tried to acquire competitors (**horizontal integration**). His charm did not prevent him from crushing a union strike with force (the **Homestead strike**, 1892). Carnegie built his company into the largest steel company in the world by 1900, and then sold it in 1901 to J.P. Morgan to become a philanthropist. His charitable endowments include concert halls, museums, libraries, and more.
Cornelius Vanderbilt (Railroads)	• Vanderbilt used his shipping fortune to acquire an initial stake in the New York Central Railroad, which he eventually parlayed into control of thousands of miles of railroad tracks.
George Pullman (Railroad cars)	• Pullman was both an inventor and a businessman. His major business innovation was the creation of luxurious passenger train cabins known as Pullman sleepers. He hired many African-Americans to serve as porters on his train lines, and suppressed these workers violently during a strike in 1894. He created a "Pullman company town" in Illinois which he ran as a benevolent dictatorship.
John D. Rockefeller (Oil)	• A highly disciplined and religiously devout man, Rockefeller was also a ruthless businessman. His business strategy focused on finding economies of scale, which enabled his Standard Oil refining company to undercut the competition with lower prices, which further increased his market share. He also resorted to shadier practices like buying off politicians and spying on competitors, and succeeded in building a near-monopoly in the oil-refining business by 1879. He earned a massive fortune of $1B (equivalent to hundreds of billions of dollars today), much of which he donated to philanthropic causes in education, African-American welfare, and health
J.P. Morgan (Banking)	• Adopted a strategy of using finance to "rationalize" industries like steel and railroads by merging firms to reduce "wasteful" competition and increase the size and stability of profits. Morgan commanded so much capital and influence that he was able to lead a group of private investors to provide the financing that eased the Panic of 1907; this experience pushed Congress to authorize the creation of a national bank system in 1913 (Federal Reserve)
William Hearst (Newspapers)	• Built up an empire of newspapers and magazines partially through his practice of printing sensationalist stories (**yellow journalism**)
Thomas Edison (Electricity, Research)	• Pioneered the creation of the modern research laboratory designed to professionalize the innovation process. Edison's lab produced the phonograph (record player) and the incandescent light bulb.
Thomas Watson (Computers)	• Created International Business Machines (IBM), a corporation that produced punch-card tabulation machines that helped businesses and the government track and organize vast amounts of data. After World War II, IBM moved into the nascent computer industry and grew into the dominant producer of very large "mainframe" computers used by large corporations

Understanding the Role of the Economy in US History

To understand the role of the economy in shaping United States history, it is necessary to gain a basic familiarity with a few fundamental economic concepts:
- Gross Domestic Product (GDP) – the statistics that measures the size of the economy
- Money and banking, including inflation
- The economic cycle of expansion and contraction

Gross Domestic Product and the National Economy

Businesses in a competitive marketplace like the United States seek to sell their products or labor at the highest possible prices and minimize their costs in order to maximize their profits. When a business generates a profit, we say that it has **added value** to the economy equivalent to the amount of profit generated (Profit = [Total Units Sold x Average Price Per Unit] – Total Costs). The Gross Domestic Product is simply the sum, across the whole economy, of the value added by all the businesses in the country. Economists compute GDP as follows:

GDP = Consumption + Investment + Govt. Spending + Net Exports (exports - imports), where

Consumption = the total value of all goods and services sold in a given year
Investment = business spending on new equipment, buildings, materials, etc.
Government Spending = total spending on goods and services by all levels of government
Net Exports = Value of goods sold to overseas customers (exports) minus value of goods purchased from overseas sellers (imports)

GDP was not reliably computed as a national figure until the 1930s, when the onset of the Great Depression compelled the federal government to start collecting reliable national economic information. The charts below show GDP in three phases from 1929-2011.

Gross Domestic Product, GDP, 1929-1950 (constant 2005 $B)

Source: Bureau of Economic Analysis (BEA), www.bea.gov

The toll of the Great Depression can be seen in the decline of GDP from about $1 trillion in 1929 to about $700 billion in 1933; the New Deal provided a partial rebound back to $1 trillion in 1937, at which point the government's effort to balance the budget pushed the economy back into recession. The advent of World War II restored demand (to put it mildly) to the economy, and GDP doubled by 1945.

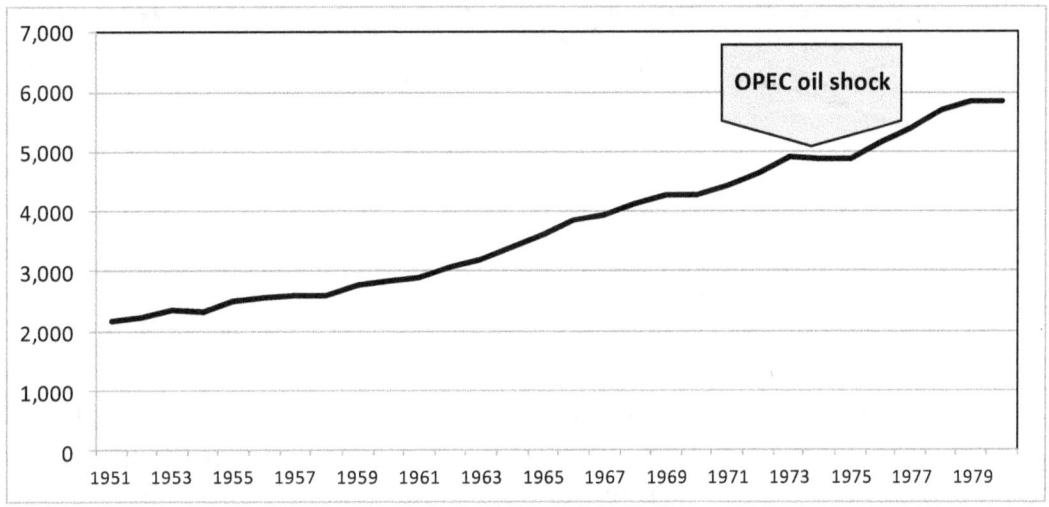

Gross Domestic Product, GDP, 1951-1980 (constant 2005 $B)

The United States enjoyed a long economic expansion from 1951-1973, the fruit of government investments in wartime technology and postwar infrastructure (national highways) and education combined with strong business and manufacturing performance. However, economic growth came to a virtual halt in the mid-1970s thanks largely to the OPEC oil price shock. OPEC (the Organization of Petroleum-Exporting Countries) was formed by the largest oil-producing nations (Saudi Arabia, Iran, Iraq, Venezuela, Russia, and others), who realized that they accounted for the majority of the world's oil production and could therefore act like a **cartel**, or a group of firms who coordinate their supply in order to raise prices. OPEC members coordinated a calculated reduction in production which drove up global oil prices fivefold in the early 1970s, producing rapid price inflation and stagnant growth in the world's industrial economies, including the United States. The world's industrial economies at the time depended on oil as a crucial source of energy in a vast range of manufacturing and transportation industries. Accustomed to cheap oil, these economies were unable to respond quickly to a price increase of this magnitude and a larger number of businesses found themselves in deep financial difficulties, which they responded to by laying off workers and cutting back on new investments. This unpleasant situation of high inflation, high unemployment, and low growth is called **stagflation**.

Gross Domestic Product, GDP, 1981-2011 (constant 2005 $B)

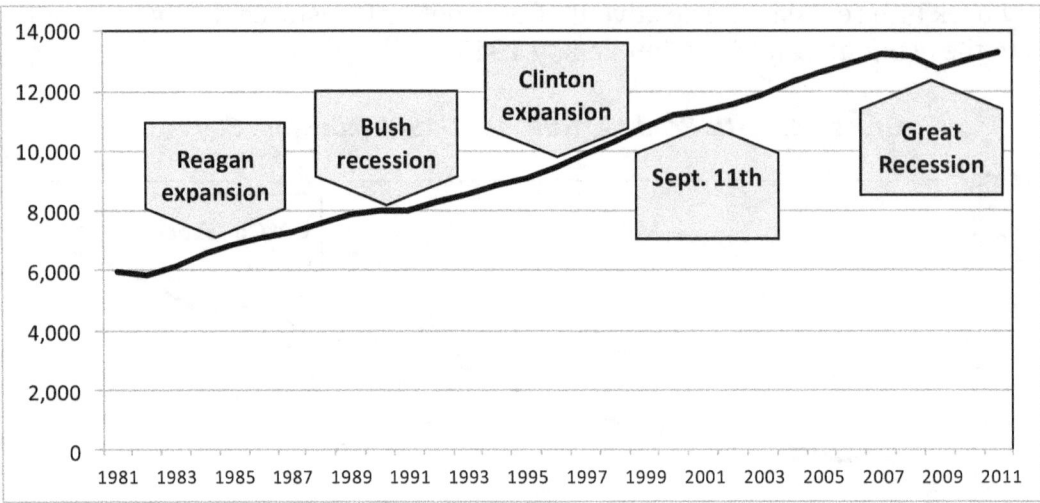

Ronald Reagan's economic agenda of the 1980s consisted of cutting taxes (a reduction in the top personal tax rate from 70% to 28%, along with additional reductions on taxes on investment and corporate income), reducing government spending, and rolling back government regulation of industry. Reagan's policies, although politically controversial and socially disastrous for the less affluent, succeeded in restoring growth to the United States economy, which, after a brief recession in the early 1990s, grew rapidly from the early 1980s all the way until 2000. However, Reagan's push towards deregulation in financial services resulted in the growth of what economists call the **shadow banking system**, a vast unregulated arena in which investment banks and other securities firms were able to make an interconnected series of extremely risky bets on various sectors of the economy. The broad rise in house prices from 1990 to 2008 was accompanied by a massive expansion in investment securities based on house prices, which eventually led to a massive financial panic in 2008 when the market turned. The government was forced to bail out many large Wall Street firms, and the resulting financial carnage led to a deep and lengthy recession.

The overall positive trend line in GDP during most periods of US history disguises broader changes in the economy that emerge when GDP is graphed by its four components (consumption, investment, government spending, and next exports). The chart below breaks out the four components from 1929-2011:

Gross Domestic Product by Components, 1929-2011 (constant 2005 $B)

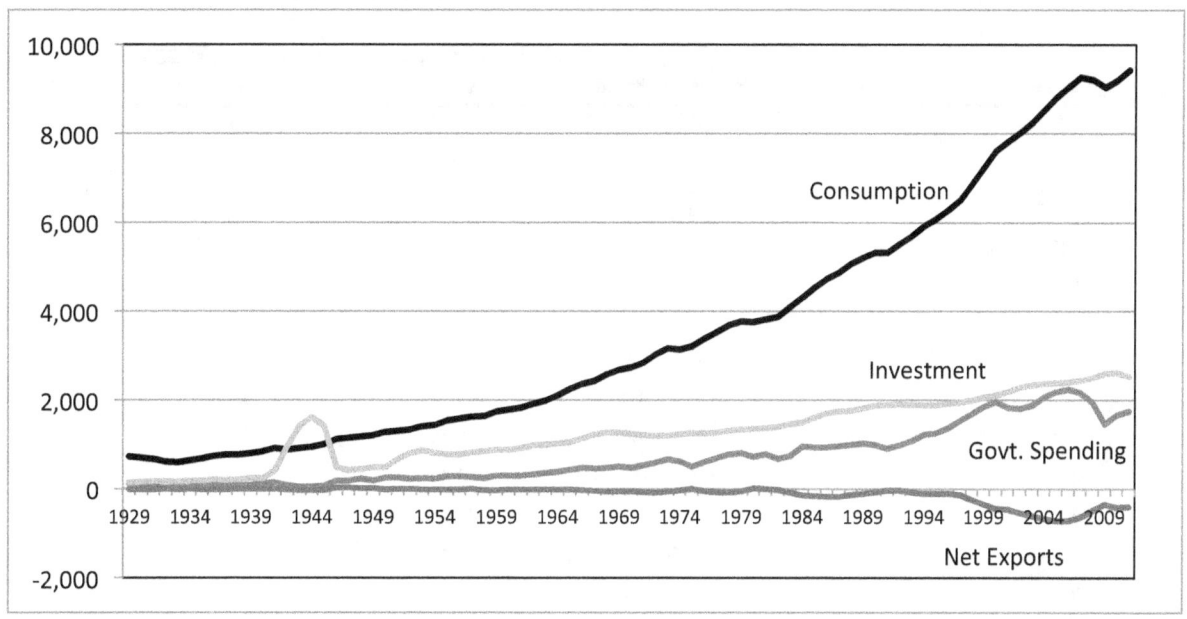

Growth in GDP was relatively balanced from 1945 to the 1960s, with growth led by consumption and business investment, government spending growing at a modest pace, and balanced imports and exports. However, from the 1970s onward, growth has been largely fueled by consumption, government spending has grown rapidly, and imports have outweighed exports by a large degree (which makes net exports negative, because net exports equal imports minus exports). The decline in the balance of trade is somewhat ironic given the central role of the United States in creating a system of global free trade from 1945 onwards and encouraging other nations to join this system. The table below summarizes two of the main trade agreements created by the United States.

Economic Treaties

Treaty	Achievement
GATT (WTO)	• The General Agreement on Tariffs and Trade (GATT) was a recurring series of trade talks and agreements to reduce trade barriers and tariffs from 1958-93 between a large number of governments including the USA. GATT was replaced in 1993 by the World Trade Organization (WTO), which holds rounds of global trade discussions every few years with the goal of reducing barriers to trade, negotiating labor and environmental standards and competition issues (if a country feels that another country is not living up to its trade promises for a certain industry, it can file suit with the WTO)
NAFTA	• The North American Free Trade Agreement reduced trade barriers between Canada, the United States and Mexico. It was signed into law by President Clinton in 1994

The political importance of GDP growth is perhaps best seen by comparing rates of growth for different presidential administrations. The chart below shows GDP growth from 1929-2011:

Real GDP Growth by Presidential Term, 1929-2011

President	Term	Years in Office	% of Popular Vote	Average Real GDP Growth (%)
Hoover	1	1929-1932	58.2%	-9.4%
FDR	1	1933-1936	57.4%	10.9%
FDR	2	1937-1940	60.8%	4.3%
FDR	3	1941-1944	54.7%	14.2%
FDR/Truman	4	1945-1948	53.4%	-2.7%
Truman	1	1949-1952	49.6%	6.7%
Eisenhower	1	1953-1956	55.2%	2.8%
Eisenhower	2	1957-1960	57.4%	2.9%
Kennedy/Johnson	1	1961-1964	49.7%	5.4%
Johnson	2	1965-1968	61.1%	4.6%
Nixon	1	1969-1972	43.4%	2.9%
Nixon	2	1973-1976	60.7%	1.5%
Carter	1	1977-1980	50.1%	2.8%
Reagan	1	1981-1984	50.8%	3.2%
Reagan	2	1985-1988	58.8%	3.6%
G.H.W. Bush	1	1989-1992	53.4%	1.7%
Clinton	1	1993-1996	43.0%	3.4%
Clinton	2	1997-2000	49.2%	4.4%
G.W. Bush	1	2001-2004	47.9%	2.6%
G.W. Bush	2	2005-2008	50.7%	1.4%
Obama	1	2009-2011	52.9%	2.1%

Sources: BEA, www.whitehouse.gov

The sustained decline in GDP during President Herbert Hoover's term of office helps explain how Hoover, who was elected with 58.2% of the popular vote in 1928, found himself losing badly in 1932 (Franklin Roosevelt won 57.4% of the vote). The strong recovery of the economy from 1933-36 helped Roosevelt win reelection in 1936 with a near-dominant margin (60.8%); however, the relatively muted growth of 1936-40 reduced FDR's winning margin by quite a bit in 1940. The natural decline in growth after the end of World War II caused most experts to predict a Truman defeat in 1948, although Truman managed to slip by Thomas Dewey in that election. The relatively robust growth during the Eisenhower years made it difficult for John F. Kennedy to defeat Richard Nixon (Eisenhower's Vice President) in the election of 1960, although Kennedy, by the slimmest of margins, squeaked by Nixon. The rapid growth of the early to mid-1960s made Lyndon Johnson an extremely popular president until Vietnam brought him down in 1968. Lackluster growth in the mid-1970s due to the OPEC oil crisis made Jimmy Carter a one-term president, while the restoration of growth under Ronald Reagan allowed Reagan to cruise to a dominant re-election victory in 1984 (58.8% of the vote). The continuing Republican era of growth earned George H.W. Bush a strong election victory in 1988, but the recession that set in shortly after the Gulf War of 1991 resulted in a Bush defeat to Bill Clinton in 1992. Clinton's enduring popularity is largely due to the rapid economic growth of the 1990s, while the poor economy in 2004 forced George W. Bush to scratch out a narrow reelection victory over John Kerry. The financial crisis of 2008 basically lost the election for the Republican party, with Barack Obama securing 52.9% of the popular vote.

Unemployment Rate
The unemployment rate, or the proportion of people seeking work who are unable to find a job, is a statistic of great economic and political importance.

Here is the unemployment rate from 1890-2010:

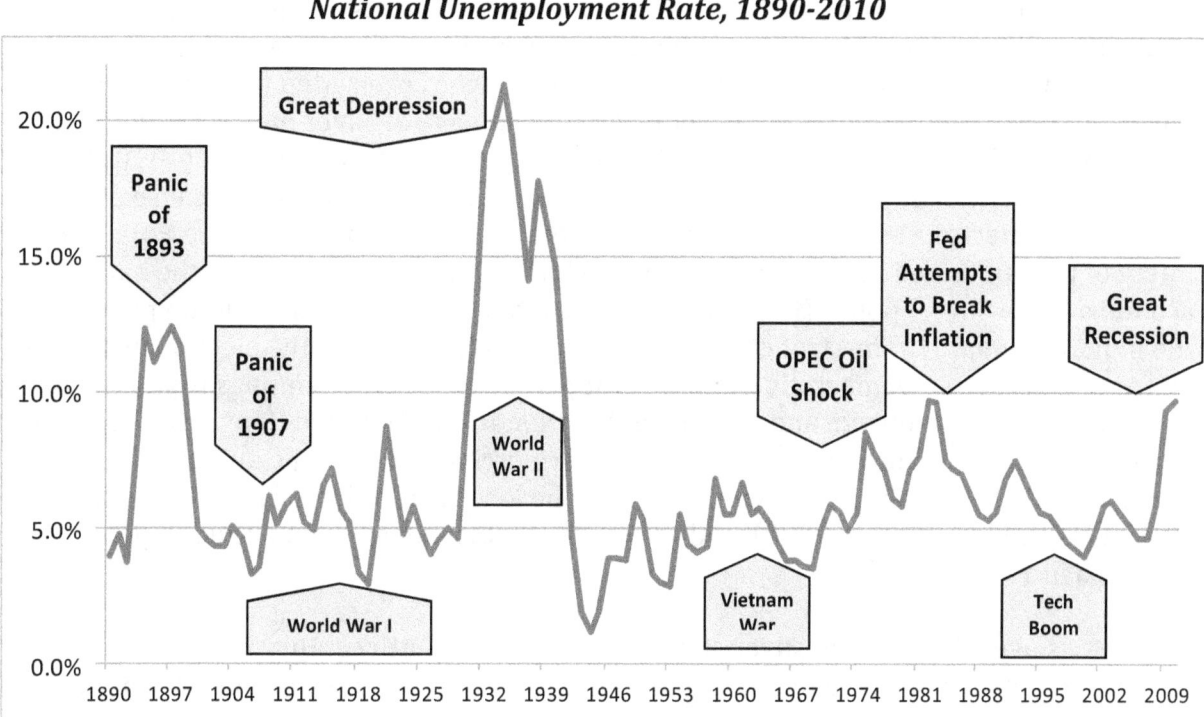

Sources: Bureau of Labor Statistics (bls.gov), Coen 1973; Romer 1986

As the chart demonstrates, unemployment tends to increase rapidly after financial crises, especially the Panic of 1893, the Great Depression, and the Great Recession of 2008. Unemployment fell rapidly during World War I and World War II thanks to the mass mobilization of society and the economy.

Money and Banking
The economic system of the United States relies on a system of money and banking that combines both private and public elements. All economies use money as a neutral means of exchange, because this saves people from having to trade goods directly (barter) which is both inefficient (it's hard to consistently match the value of one good to another) and time consuming. The tricky thing is that the value of money itself can change over time depending on a variety of economic factors. In order to anchor the value of money, especially paper money, governments have often chosen to tie the value of money to tangible sources of value such as gold or silver. Congress, which was granted the power to regulate coinage under the Constitution, passed the Mint and Coinage Act in 1792, which established a bi-metallic standard of money for the United States (i.e., a standard based on both gold and silver). In the early years, both the federal government under the First Bank

of the United States and state governments possessed the authority to issue paper currency that was supposed to be backed up by gold and silver. This changed during the Civil War, when the National Banking Act (1863) made the federal government the sole issuer and guarantor of currency accepted as legal tender in the United States. The economic pattern from 1860-1930 was one of eastern manufacturers and bankers prioritizing "tight" money based on very close adherence to a gold standard versus debt-burdened southern and western farmers who hoped for a "looser" monetary policy based on the supply of silver in addition to the supply of gold. The **Bland-Allison Act** (1878) responded to demands from farmers and (more influentially) owners of silver mines to increase the quantity of silver coinage relative to gold coinage. The discovery of large deposits of silver in the West in the 1880s led to louder demands from farmers and silver miners for more coinage of silver. This led to the formation of the **Greenback Party**, which represented farmers anxious to lower their debt burdens with easier money (more coinage of silver meant higher inflation, which made debts easier to pay back).[6] The **Sherman Silver Purchase Act** (1890) further increased government purchase and coinage of silver, but was repealed because of its inflationary effects in 1893. The Greenback Party was later surpassed by the **Populist Party** of the 1880s and 1890s, which attempted to organize farmers across the nation around a "Free Silver" policy (i.e., a policy that wanted to use silver in addition to gold as the money standard). The strength of the Populist Party peaked in the election of 1896, in which the darkhorse Democratic candidate for president William Jennings Bryan ran on an explicitly Populist campaign and pledged at the Democratic National Convention that "you shall not crucify mankind upon a cross of gold" (referring to the gold standard). Unfortunately for Bryan and the Populist cause, he lost the election of 1896 to William McKinley (and lost again in 1900), and the United States moved to an exclusive gold standard in 1900.

The battles over the gold and silver standard in the nineteenth century increased in importance as the number and size of banks in the country rose. **Commercial banks** are institutions that accept deposits from individuals and businesses and in return pay interest on these deposits. These banks make money by lending their depositors' funds to businesses that need money in order to, for example, build factories, hire new employees, or develop new products. These businesses pay the bank a higher rate of interest on their business loans than the bank pays its depositors. It is important to realize that the business success of commercial banks relies in large part upon confidence: at any given time, a typical bank will hold ten percent or less of the total value of its deposits in its vaults (the rest has been lent out to businesses). That means that virtually no bank is able to redeem its deposits if all of its depositors try to withdraw their money on the same day. Although customers rarely descend on banks en masse to demand their funds, this does happen during widespread economic panics. These panics can be self-fulfilling in that if enough depositors panic and try to withdraw their funds, even healthy and profitable banks can go bankrupt, worsening the cycle of panic and causing even more banks to collapse. Under

---

[6] To understand why inflation hurts savers and helps borrowers, consider the following example. Joe T. Farmer owes $100 in 1890 to Philip A. Banker. Inflation equals the percentage change in the value of money from one year to the next. If the inflation rate in a given year is 0%, Joe Farmer will owe Philip Banker $100 in 1891. If inflation is 5%, however, Joe Farmer will still have to pay Philip Banker $100 in 1891, but that $100 will only buy 95% of what it would have the year before. Joe Farmer's debt has thus been effectively reduced by 5%, and Philip Banker only receives 95% of his initial investment in real terms.

these conditions, only a lender of last resort is capable of calming the panic with a very large infusion of money that is lent out to banks so that they can redeem the requests of their depositors.

In contrast to commercial banks, which have been present in the United States since the colonial era, **investment banks** developed in the United States in the mid-nineteenth century when the government required financial institutions to sell enormous quantities of war bonds to finance the Civil War and emerging industrial firms required both equity (stock in the firm that provides the buyer with a portion of the firm's overall value) and debt (bank loans) to finance their activities. Like commercial banks, investment banks help channel money from investors toward businesses; unlike commercial banks, their financing schemes often involve the possibility of large or even total losses on a given investment. The risky nature of investment banking makes this type of banking very profitable during good years but also highly prone to collapse during periods of economic crisis. During the **Gilded Age** (1880-1930), investment bankers like J.P. Morgan and Cornelius Vanderbilt used their financial power to create enormous business corporations capable of influencing or even dominating entire industries (steel, oil, coal, railroads, sugar, copper, etc.). To help manage risky investment banks and maintain control over their financial affairs, many countries set up national banks that could tap the financial power of the nation to professionally manage the money supply and halt banking panics. The United States, of course, set up a First Bank of the United States in 1791 (charter expired in 1814) and a Second Bank of the United States in 1816. After the great **Bank War**, in which Andrew Jackson rallied farmers, workers and ordinary citizens against a Bank which in his view had become a corrupt tool of the wealthy and powerful, the charter of the Second Bank of the United States expired in 1836. The United States thus went through the Civil War and the Industrial Revolution without a central bank to manage the money supply or provide a financial backstop during financial panics. One result was that citizens such as JP Morgan were required to intervene with private funds to solve financial panics by using their vast financial resources. The Panic of 1907 and the Progressive movement towards more active government pushed Congress to create a new national bank in the form of the United States Federal Reserve in 1913. Rather than a single national institution, the Federal Reserve combines a Board of Governors that is headquartered in Washington, DC.; twelve regional banks such as the New York Fed and the San Francisco Fed; and a Federal Open Market Committee that sets basic **interest rates** such as the **federal funds rate**, or the rate that banks charge one another to borrow money, and the **discount rate**, or the rate that the Federal Reserve charges banks who want to borrow money directly from the Federal Reserve. The Federal Reserve can flood the market with money by lowering interest rates during times of panics; this makes it easier for banks to calm panics by giving them the extra money they need to redeem any requests from panicky depositors. By raising interest rates, the Federal Reserve can also prick so-called bubbles in the market that are caused whenever the private markets start to overspeculate due to irrational exuberance in markets like railroads, the Internet, or house prices.

The chart below outlines some of the key downturns and depressions in American economic history:

Economic Downturns: Depressions and Financial Panics

Depression	Causes and Consequences	Resolution
Post-Revolutionary War	• Deeply indebted states try to finance their deficits by printing more money; leads to high inflation and financial instability	• Hamilton creates national debt and national bank to buy up state debts; provides financial stability and unity • Passes tariff of 5% on imports to fund the federal government
Embargo of 1807	• Jefferson's administration cuts off trade with Britain and France to punish them for impressment of American ships • Deeply damages American economy: most American traders try to violate the embargo causing the federal government to imposed intrusive and punitive regulations	• Democratic-Republicans forced to repeal the embargo in 1809
Financial Panic of 1837	• Financial crisis caused by international factors; made worse by the fact that Jackson/Van Buren had destroyed the Bank of the United States	• Democratic administration not able to take active countermeasures; Whigs victorious in election of 1840
Panic of 1893	• Caused by railroad overinvestment bubble and by the decision of President Cleveland to abandon the dual money standard (gold + silver) in favor of gold alone	• Democrats suffer major defeat in election of 1894 • Free silver advocates, who preferred the dual standard, did not give up the fight
Panic of 1907	• Collapse of stocks due to speculators trying to corner the copper market • Government not able to solve the panic with an injection of cash into the system because there is no national bank • J.P. Morgan, the private banker, organizes other bankers to provide a private bailout	• Leads to the creation of the Federal Reserve system (central bank)
Great Depression	• Enormous levels of financial speculation and risk-taking left thousands of banks and brokerage firms insolvent when the stock market crashed in 1929; • Panicked bank customers pull their money, leading to collapse of banks and downward economic spiral in which corporations began laying off works • Unemployment rises from 4% to 25% of the workforce; major contraction of GDP under Hoover;	• The New Deal: federal government takes active role in the regulation of the national economy • Bank insurance, union bargaining rights, social security to provide old-age income, work relief programs • New Deal brings the American economy back from the dead but not to full health (WWII does)

The Business Cycle: Understanding Why Busts follow Booms, and Vice Versa

Economic growth occurs through a number of different mechanisms. First, if the quality of **economic inputs** – typically land, labor and capital (things like factories or machines) –

improves, then the economy grows. Second, economies grow by trading with one another because different countries can specialize in different sectors of the economy, concentrate on what they do best, and subsequently trade with each other so that the maximum total number of goods are produced and both sides get to enjoy a variety of different goods. Third, the economy grows if **technology** (basically the methods and knowledge that allow us to convert economic inputs into useful goods and services) improves. Finally, economic growth is most likely where there is a stable political system that protects the rule of law and encourages wealth creation.

The United States has successfully followed each of these four paths to growth. English legal and political institutions and culture of respect for property rights created a beneficial environment for economic growth (even as this system sometimes ignored the property and human rights of workers). Protestant evangelism centered at first in New England created a highly disciplined, well-educated, and dedicated workforce that spread the gospel of work along with the actual Gospel all across the United States with the First and Second Great Awakenings. The availability of enormous quantities of land to the west proved to be an engine of economic growth by attracting enterprising farmers and business owners from all over the United States and Europe. A focus on education and practical innovation led to the growth of science and technology, and the trade routes across the Atlantic and Pacific contributed to substantial economic growth in industries like shipping, agriculture (tobacco, cotton) and manufacturing. Finally, American law consistently defended the right of business owners to make free choices to maximize profits.

During normal economic periods, the free market typically does an excellent job of matching supply to demand through the price mechanism. In a competitive market, suppliers and buyers respond to changing tastes, preferences and income levels by changing the amount offered for sale and the average price charged per unit. If too few people want to buy a given product at a given price, suppliers must reduce their prices in order to sell the desired amount of the product. When they reduce their price, supply meets demand (because more people are willing to buy the product at the lower price), and the market 'clears', meaning that the quantity demanded matches the quantity supplied. The process works in reverse as well: increased demand for a product leads to a higher price for that product, and the price continues to rise until the number of people willing and able to buy the product drops to a level at which demand equals supply. So far, so good. Problems arise, however, during economic booms, which occur when people start to believe that the economy has changed in some fundamental way and that even ridiculously high prices for a given product are worthwhile because of that fundamental change. These 'new economy' manias are as old as capitalism: the Dutch tulip bulb boom of the 17th century resulted in a market in which a single tulip bulb was valued equal to the price of a house; needless to say, the tulip bulb market collapsed back to a more "normal" level shortly thereafter, and many people lost their entire net worth in this collapse. In United States history, speculative manias occurred in the 19th century with railroads and in the twentieth century with the stock market bubble that led to the crash on Wall Street in 1929 and the ensuing Great Depression. Let us take this stock market bubble as an illustrative example. For the first time in the 1920s, ordinary people began to 'play' the stock market, and new technologies like the telegraph spread stock price information far and wide. The market was largely unregulated, and many financial firms sought to use unorthodox and unscrupulous methods to 'game' the system and profit financially. Although the 'proper' purpose of a stock market is to use the principle of competition (this time over financial resources) to allocate money to worthy corporations, the market can also be used like a casino to make bets and profit solely on a financial rather than a fundamental basis. As more and more ordinary investors joined the stock market during the boom years of the 1920s, more and more people felt that the market was going to continue to rise indefinitely, which led to more and more buying (this consistent positive uptrend in the market is what is called a **Bull Market**). Stock prices rose to tremendous heights by the late 1920s, at which point more and more people slowly began to realize that the market was in a mania or bubble in which prices no longer reflected reality. This slow realization all of a sudden became national news on "Black Thursday," October 24, 1929, when the New York Stock Exchange suddenly fell 11% in a single day. Although Wall Street bankers tried to halt the slide by forming a fund and buying up major stocks, the decline continued on Black Monday, October 28, when the market fell another 13%, and Black Tuesday, a further 12% decline. The stock market did not return to its high of September 1929 until November of 1954.

Government Remedies for Economic Recessions and Depressions
Economies that enter depressions caused by financial panics or recessions caused by somewhat milder financial or economic shocks are characterized by a lack of **aggregate demand**, a situation in which businesses recognize that the economic boom is over and decide that in order to preserve profits they need to cut costs, cancel or reduce future spending plans, and sit tight until the depression is over. Although this kind of cost-cutting and budget-balancing may be rational for each individual business, the economy as a whole suffers if every business cuts back at the same time, because there will be little overall demand for products and services. This low demand will cause individual businesses to cut back even more, created a self-reinforcing spiral downwards. Under these circumstances, the private sector will find itself mired in a recession that lasts until some positive external factor induces businesses to start spending and investing again. This external factor could be a technological development such as the advent of electrical lights in the 1920s, or the rise of a rapidly growing economy such as China today. However, it is typically government spending that provides the **stimulus** to aggregate demand necessary to get individual businesses going again. The government has the ability to stimulate the economy through two main mechanisms: **fiscal policy**, in which the federal government cuts taxes or raises spending and **monetary policy**, in which the central bank reduces the interest rate it charges to member banks, which in turn lowers the cost of money to banks and (ideally) makes banks more willing to lend to businesses. Let us consider fiscal policy first. When the government cuts taxes, this leaves more money in the hands of individuals and businesses, which makes people and firms more likely, on the margin, to buy more things, which increases aggregate demand and gives businesses the confidence to increase spending and investment. The government can also increase its spending on goods and services, to achieve much the same effect. Monetary policy works slightly differently. When a borrower borrows from a lender, the lender expects his or her money back plus an extra sum of money. The percentage we get by dividing the extra sum of money by the total amount borrowed is the **interest rate**. The Federal Reserve, the central bank of the United States, has the power to manipulate this rate by raising or lowering the money supply (which it controls because it controls the amount of money in circulation in the

economy). When the Fed increases the rate, its member banks increase their rates, which makes it harder for businesses and consumers to obtain loans, thereby reducing both consumer spending and business investment. The Fed increases interest rates when it feels that the economy is overheating, and lowers rates when the economy is in a recession. When it lowers interest rates, banks lower their rates, which enables more individuals and businesses to obtain loans that they desire, which then causes an increase in business and consumer activity and gets the economy going again.

One final economic relationship worth noting is the relationship between inflation (the percentage change in prices in the economy from one year to the next) and unemployment. To make this relationship easy to understand, think of the economy as containing a certain amount of money. When economic activity heats up, the amount of money in circulation increases, causing prices to rise (more people have money to buy things, so prices get bid up); this increased economic activity typically causes unemployment to fall. So the usual relationship is: economic activity (growth) increases, inflation increases, and unemployment falls. During depressions, economic activity falls, inflation falls (sometimes becoming negative, which is called deflation), and unemployment rises. There is therefore an inverse relationship between inflation and unemployment: when one goes up, the other typically goes down. The main exception to this is if some external factor causes inflation (the best example of this is the OPEC oil price shock). If this happens during a domestic economic downturn, then **stagflation** occurs (low growth, high unemployment and high inflation). Government stimulus does not work very well in this situation, because pouring government money in only causes inflation to go higher,

We are now ready to answer the question presented at the beginning of this section:
1. If the policies of the Greenback Party had been enacted it would have had the same effect on the money supply as when the Federal Reserve:
   A. raises the discount lending rate
   B. manipulates the price of gold
   C. tightens the money supply
   D. lowers the discount lending rate
   E. insures bank deposits

We know that the Greenback Party, a predecessor of the Populist Party, supported Free Silver, or a money standard based not only on gold but also on silver. A bimetallic money standard would expand the money supply, creating more economic activity and making it easier for debtors (such as farmers) to pay back creditors (bankers and industrial machinery corporations). We also now know that the Federal Reserve expands the money supply when it lowers the discount lending rate, or the rate at which member banks can borrow from the Fed (the member banks then lower their rates, making it easier for consumers and businesses to get bank loans). The correct answer is therefore answer choice (D).

Concluding Thoughts
Calvin Coolidge famously said that "the chief business of the American people is business." Whether an overstatement or not, this claim underlines the central role played by business and economics in the construction of the country and its rise as a global power. Blessed

abundantly with natural resources, land and water, the United States also benefited from a number of other positive economic attributes, including a legal culture that stressed the importance of private property rights, political traditions emphasizing limited government and the rule of law; and social values of discipline, hard work, and education. All these factors combined together to produce what became, in a relatively short period of time, the largest economy in the world.

QUESTIONS
Multiple Choice

1. America benefited from which of the following factors of production to grow into an industrial power by the 1890s?
   A. A comparatively well-educated work force
   B. A ready supply of immigrant labor
   C. Large quantities of fertile land
   D. Pro-growth government policies
   E. All of the above

2. Wealthy capitalists operating trusts during the Gilded Age
   A. Were in favor of policies to guarantee unrestrained competition
   B. Preferred to manage competition by acquiring or coordinating with competitors
   C. Supported a federal income tax
   D. Supported the aspirations of the Populist Party
   E. None of the above

3. Which of the following industrial actions corresponds to horizontal integration?
   A. Migration into related markets to control the entire production process from raw materials to finished product for sale
   B. The acquisition or takeover of other firms in the same market
   C. The use of financial techniques to drive a competitor out of business
   D. Recognizing and negotiating with the local labor union
   E. All of the above

4. Which of the following business leaders managed to control 90% of the nations' oil refining capacity by 1890?
   A. Andrew Carnegie
   B. Thomas Edison
   C. John D. Rockefeller
   D. Cornelius Vanderbilt
   E. George Pullman

5. Adam Smith's *Wealth of Nations* (1776) discusses the concept of the Invisible Hand, which argues that
   A. Competition in markets compels individual firms to constantly improve their products and reduce prices and creates the greatest efficiencies for society
   B. Government should quietly act to make sure that corporations are meeting their obligations
   C. Private property rights are vital to economic growth
   D. Individual firms can provide greater efficiencies than the market by minimizing transactions costs
   E. Mercantilism is a viable system provided it be dominated by the English and the Dutch rather than the Spanish

6. Which of the following actions are most likely to halt a financial panic?
   A. Public hearings that reveal the true financial condition of leading banks
   B. A public announcement that the government or private investors are organizing a fund that will meet all outstanding obligations among troubled banks
   C. The sale of additional bonds or shares by troubled banks to raise surplus capital
   D. The passage of laws that prioritize the rights of individual borrowers to access their funds in troubled banks on the basis of a lottery
   E. All of the above

7. Which of the following caused the United States to move towards creating the Federal Reserve System?
   A. The bailout of the financial system organized by J.P. Morgan in the Panic of 1907
   B. Hyperinflation during the Civil War
   C. The repudiation of Confederate War debts
   D. The need to consolidate Revolutionary War debt
   E. The expenses of World War I

8. The Roosevelt Administration took which of the following actions during the New Deal to ensure the safety and stability of the financial system?
   A. The establishment of the Federal Deposit Insurance Corporation, which provided insurance for bank deposits up to a certain amount
   B. The creation of the Securities and Exchange Commission (SEC) to prevent abuses on Wall Street associated with insider dealing and the reporting false company information
   C. The passage of the Glass-Steagall Act, which separated commercial banking from investment banking
   D. Congressional hearings (the Pecora investigation) into the causes of the Great Depression
   E. All of the above

9. The main motivation behind the "Free Silver" campaigns of the Greenback and Populist parties was
   A. To help the owners and operators of silver mines in the West
   B. To expand the money supply and reduce the debt burden on farmers
   C. To construct a global central bank that could better manage the economic system
   D. To create a Federal Reserve System that could better manage the monetary system
   E. To reform campaign finance rules

10. Which of the following sets of inventions were all created between the end of the Civil War and the advent of World War I?
    A. The cotton gin, bifocals, and interchangeable machine parts
    B. The computer, the radio and the airplane
    C. The Pullman railway car, refrigerated meat packing, and the telephone
    D. The electric light bulb, the airplane, and the atomic bomb
    E. The sewing machine, oil well, and phonograph

11. All of the following people established and operated large business corporations EXCEPT:
    A. Upton Sinclair
    B. John D. Rockefeller
    C. Cornelius Vanderbilt
    D. J.P. Morgan
    E. Andrew Carnegie

12. During the Gilded Age, Congress protected the rights of large corporations over those of individuals and labor unions for which of the following reasons?
    A. Political donations and influence-peddling by large corporations
    B. A belief that the Constitution did not allow Congress to intervene in the private relationship between employer and laborer
    C. Suspicion that labor unions were affiliated with communism
    D. Support from the Supreme Court that pro-business legislation was both legal and proper
    E. All of the above

13. Market economies tend to go through boom and bust cycles for all the following reasons EXCEPT?
    A. New technologies or products create the belief that a new economy is emerging in which old expectations about prices are outdated
    B. Overinvestment in new industries eventually leads to financial losses and retrenchment
    C. Business insiders rig the system for their own profit, in the process causing markets to fail to operate properly
    D. Prices in the market system adjust smoothly to changes in supply and demand
    E. The discovery and exploitation of major natural resource deposits

14. The Gross Domestic Product (GDP) consists of which components?
    A. Consumption, Investment, and Net Exports
    B. Consumption, Investment, Government Spending, and Net Exports
    C. Consumption, Investment, Government Spending, and Exports
    D. Consumption and Investment
    E. Consumption and Government Spending

15. All of the following presidents enjoyed strong economic growth during their term(s) of office except for:
    A. Franklin Roosevelt
    B. Ronald Reagan
    C. Bill Clinton
    D. John F. Kennedy
    E. George H.W. Bush

16. Which of the following correctly defines the term stagflation?
    A. Low growth, high unemployment, and high inflation
    B. High growth, high inflation and high unemployment
    C. High unemployment and low inflation
    D. Low inflation and low unemployment
    E. High growth, low unemployment, and low inflation

17. All of the following contributed to the Great Depression EXCEPT for:
    A. Depressed economic conditions in Europe
    B. The great stock market crash of 1929
    C. The failure of the Hoover administration to address growing economic problems
    D. Depressed agricultural conditions
    E. Land speculation in the West

18. Which of the following would constitute a stimulus to the economy from the government?
    A. The Federal Reserve raises interest rates
    B. State governments raise taxes
    C. The federal government cuts taxes
    D. A banking syndicate offers a bridge loan to the government
    E. Detroit automakers cut prices on new cars

19. Which president's political prospects were complicated by high unemployment rates?
    A. Lyndon Johnson
    B. John F. Kennedy
    C. Ronald Reagan
    D. Bill Clinton
    E. Jimmy Carter

20. The Federal Deposit Insurance Corporation (FDIC) supports the stability of the financial system by
    A. Providing funds to individuals whose mortgages are underwater
    B. Insuring bank deposits up to $250,000
    C. Providing direct loans to consumers during financial panics
    D. Changing interest rates charged to member banks
    E. All of the above

Essay Questions
1. What factors explain why the North industrialized while the South failed to industrialize?

2. What economic, political, and social factors contributed to the rise of the Gilded Age economy?

3. Why did farmers in the late 19th century campaign with such vigor for Free Silver?

4. Select TWO of the following inventions and discuss how they transformed American society.
   A. The cotton gin
   B. Electric lighting
   C. The Model T Ford
   D. Railways

5. Compare and contrast how the following presidents dealt with the problem of high unemployment.
   A. Herbert Hoover
   B. Franklin Roosevelt
   C. Ronald Reagan

Answers to Multiple Choice Questions
1. E
2. B
3. B
4. C
5. A
6. B
7. A
8. E
9. B
10. C
11. A
12. E
13. D
14. B
15. E
16. A
17. E
18. C
19. E
20. B

American History Tutoring Guide Paul Pinto

TOPIC 6: THE PATH TO INDEPENDENCE

The path to American independence can be modeled as a conflict between those who believed that the American colonies should be independent, or at minimum self-governing, and those who thought that the English parliament as constituted in the 1750s was sufficient in meeting the political needs of the American colonies. In between these two poles stood the mass of colonists, who recognized valid arguments on both sides. After the French & Indian War, which was part of a lengthy global struggle between England and France, the British government found itself in need of additional revenue to pay for its troops in North America. This desire for additional revenue without allowing the colonies to participate in the taxing process through their legislative assemblies resulted in a number of crises that steadily pushed the colonies toward independence. The timeline below starts with the end of the French and Indian War (1763) and ends with the fighting at Lexington and Concord (1775).

Path to Independence Timeline

Towards Compromise	Event	Towards Conflict
• Shared military experience as colonial soldiers served as part of the British army • Thrill of victory over French and Indians	French & Indian War (1756-1763)	• British soldiers/statesmen viewed colonial militias as poorly organized and ill-funded • Cost of the war leads British government to abandon policy of salutary neglect • Proclamation of 1763 prohibited colonists from settling in the west
	Sugar Act (1764)	• Taxes on foreign sugar/other luxury goods
	Quartering Act (1765)	• Required colonists to provide room and board for British soldiers
• Repeal of the Act by Parliament, partially as a response to colonial protest, partly as a change of prime minister	Stamp Act (1765) Repeal (1766) Declaratory Act (1766)	• Required revenue stamps to be placed on most printed paper in the colonies (first direct tax) • Nine colonies meet in 'Stamp Act Congress' in NYC, resolve that only elected reps can pass taxes • Formation of Sons of Liberty to intimidate tax collectors • Declaratory Act restates Parliament's claim to tax the colonies as it pleased

Towards Compromise	Event	Towards Conflict
• Repeal of Townshend Acts with the accession of Lord North as prime minister; retained small, symbolic tax on tea	Townshend Acts (1767) ... Repeal (1768)	• New taxes on colonial imports of tea, glass, paper • Independent crown officials to collect tax; allowed to search private homes • Less protest than Stamp Act b/c of indirect nature • James Otis/Samuel Adams send Mass. Circular Letter to colonial legislatures urging colonists to petition Parliament for repeal
• John Adams, a colonial leader, defends the soldiers and earns their acquittal	Boston Massacre (1770)	• British soldiers fire on crowd protesting their presence and taxation, kill five Americans
	Boston Tea Party (1773)	• Response to the Tea Act of 1773, which attempted to push colonists in purchasing British East India company tea • Colonists dumped tea into Boston harbor
	Coercive (Intolerable) Acts (1774)	• Port of Boston closed • Power of Mass. legislature reduced • Royal officials in Mass. removed from colonial justice system • British troops to be quartered in
	First Continental Congress (1774)	• All colonies sent delegates except Georgia to determine how to respond to Coercive Acts • Claims of the Congress dismissed by the King, Mass. declared to be in rebellion
	Lexington and Concord (1775)	• British troops sent to seize colonial military supplies stored in Concord • Colonists warned by Paul Revere and William Dawes • Fighting breaks out in Lexington

Concluding Thoughts

The main lesson from the timeline is the almost complete lack of substantive compromise between the two sides. In particular, reformers in the British government never used the worsening colonial protests as an opportunity to rethink the constitutional links between the mother country and the colonies. British politicians remained firmly wedded to the idea of **virtual representation**, which argued that Parliament as the national representative body protected the rights and liberties of all the people, regardless of whether those people had their own representative or representatives in Parliament. These politicians noted that many people living in England did not have their own representative due to the vagaries of medieval procedures of seat selection, which, in a prominent example, provided a Parliamentary seat to an old village containing a few people, while completely ignoring the neighboring large and growing industrial town (villages of this sort were known as **rotten boroughs**). Perhaps not surprisingly, the rotten borough argument did not find much support amongst American colonists who had enjoyed over a century's experience with a far more democratic and responsive system of legislative assemblies. Rather than offer the colonists a deal in which colonial assemblies could vote to approve or reject Parliamentary taxation measures or take a truly bold leap of faith and offer the colonies actual representation in Parliament, British politicians clung to the tried and true practice of insisting that the colonies ought to be satisfied with virtual representation.

The American colonists, for their part, had used their century or more of experience with representative assemblies to work out a political theory of representation and liberties that combined the thinking of philosophers like John Locke with the Puritan idea of the covenant relationship. Locke argued that free men form governments by their mutual consent in order to more fully enjoy their natural rights of life, liberty, and property without fear of dispossession or loss of life. Because government is formed by consent, government can also be reformed if it infringes on the natural rights of the people. Locke's theory of government is thus a **contract** theory in which governments are formed by free choice. This theory dovetailed nicely with the Puritan view of the covenant relationship, in which God had freely offered man a covenant (contract) under which both man and God had specific rights and duties. By the 1770s, the American contractual theory of government had deep philosophical and religious roots that could not be easily reconciled with British Parliamentary traditions.

American History Tutoring Guide Paul Pinto
QUESTIONS

Multiple Choice
1. Jefferson's famous words in the Declaration of Independence that all men are "endowed by their Creator with certain unalienable Rights, that among these are Life, Liberty, and the pursuit of Happiness" draws from ideas from which of the following works of political philosophy?
   A. *The Spirit of the Laws*
   B. *The Social Contract*
   C. *Two Treatises of Government*
   D. *On Liberty*
   E. *Reflections on the Revolution in France*

2. All of the following actions during the period 1763-1776 worsened relations between Britain and her North American colonies EXCEPT:
   A. John Adams's defense of British soldiers after the Boston Massacre
   B. The Intolerable Acts
   C. The Boston Tea Party
   D. The Townshend Acts
   E. The Stamp Act

3. During the period of protest from 1763-1776, American colonists opposed all of the following EXCEPT:
   A. The Proclamation of 1763
   B. The Stamp Act
   C. The Tea Act
   D. The quartering of British soldiers in American homes
   E. Repeal of the Townshend duties

4. Parliament refused to consider direct representation for the colonists because
   I. It believed that the theory of virtual representation met the needs of the colonists
   II. It was unwilling to tolerate limits on its power as the dominant sovereign body in the British Empire
   III. It did not believe that the colonists deserved the rights of Englishmen

   A. I only
   B. II only
   C. III only
   D. I and II
   E. I, II and III

5. The Coercive or Intolerable Acts
   A. closed the port of Boston
   B. quartered British soldiers in Massachusetts homes
   C. removed royal officials and tax collectors from the legal jurisdiction of Massachusetts
   D. diminished the power and independence of the Massachusetts legislature
   E. all of the above

6. The British decided to tax the colonies more heavily in 1763 primarily because
   A. The king decided that the colonies had become too independent and wanted to bring them to heel
   B. The French & Indian War had cost a great deal of money and Parliament wanted the North American colonies to pay their share of the burden
   C. The Navigation Acts were no longer brining in any revenue to the Treasury
   D. Native American tribes were planning a massive invasion to retake Massachusetts that required increased British military spending to defend against
   E. All of the above

7. The thirteen colonies, despite their differing histories, political cultures, and views on the wisdom of challenging Parliament, were able to ally together to declare independence because
   A. They believed that the mistreatment of Massachusetts would eventually extend to mistreatment of other colonies
   B. They recognized that their best chance of defending their natural rights was by making common cause against the British
   C. They were shocked by British willingness to kill colonists in Massachusetts in 1775
   D. They realized that Britain was unwilling to offer them substantive political representation
   E. All of the above

8. The Stamp Act provoked particularly loud protests from the colonists because
   A. Stamps were rare commodities that cost a great deal of money
   B. The tax was a direct tax paid by individual colonists
   C. The tax threatened to bankrupt Massachusetts and Rhode Island
   D. The tax was an indirect tax paid primarily by merchants
   E. All of the above

9. Contract theories of government argue that
   A. The will of the people is sovereign
   B. Governments that violate the will of the people deserve to be replaced by the people
   C. Governments exist to protect the natural rights of the people
   D. The right to resistance is legitimate when natural rights are threatened
   E. All of the above

10. The Proclamation of 1763
    A. Banned British North America from trading with France
    B. Prevented settlement by American colonists west of the Appalachian Mountains
    C. Purchased Florida from Spain
    D. Created the political basis for a joint Anglo-French canal connecting the Hudson River Valley to the Great Lakes
    E. Commanded Native Americans living in Georgia to move to what is now North and South Dakota

Essay Questions
1. Why and how did the French and Indian War transform the relationship between Great Britain and the thirteen American colonies?

2. Define the British concept of virtual representation and explain why the American colonists refused to embrace it as a viable alternative to revolution.

3. What are the three most important reasons why the American colonies declared independence from Great Britain?

4. Discuss why and how each of the following incidents marked a turning point in the road to independence:
   A. The Stamp Act
   B. The Boston Tea Party
   C. Lexington and Concord

Answers to Multiple Choice Questions
1. C
2. A
3. E
4. D
5. E
6. B
7. E
8. B
9. E
10. B

American History Tutoring Guide Paul Pinto

TOPIC 7: POLITICAL PARTIES

Political parties are voluntary political organizations that compete to win office in order to put into place some kind of political program. Parties serve as coordination mechanisms – they unite smaller groups of individuals, each with their own set of political preferences and ideas – into a relatively disciplined body organized around a few main principles. The process of uniting smaller groups together into a party that can compete and win a majority of the vote is called **building a coalition**. Although different parties may be interested in different political priorities, whether it be abolishing slavery in the West or rolling back the welfare state, they share one central goal: to win elections for offices at the local, state and national level.

Although political parties are one of the most important elements in the American political system, they do not appear in the Constitution. The Framers of the Constitution distrusted what they called 'factions,' defined by James Madison in Federalist Paper no. 10 as: "a number of citizens, whether amounting to a majority or minority of the whole, who are united and actuated by some common impulse of passion, or of interest, adverse to the rights of other citizens or to the permanent and aggregate interests of the community." That is to say, Madison defines parties as groups that prioritize some interest or goal that is at odds with the general interests of the country. This is quite a harsh assessment, and a rather ironic one given that Madison ended up as one of the leaders of a very successful 'faction', the Democratic-Republican party! It ought to be pointed out that the Founding Fathers had ample experience with parties, albeit ones of a less organized nature: during the path to independence, they represented the party for independence (the **Patriots**), while **Loyalists** like Peter Oliver represented those in favor of sticking with Great Britain. Furthermore, the men who produced the Constitution – whom we call the **Federalists** - themselves constituted a party who had to politically defeat the **Anti-Federalist** party that was deeply skeptical of the centralizing powers of the Constitution. In any case, shortly after the passage of the Constitution, the Founding Fathers split into two antagonistic parties: the **Federalists,** led by Alexander Hamilton, who favored the growth and further development of the federal government, a substantial national debt with a national bank to manage it, an active role for the government in the economy, and an economic strategy based on mercantile trade with Britain; and the **Democratic-Republicans**, led by Thomas Jefferson, who favored the retirement of the national debt, a federal government limited to its explicit powers, and an economic strategy based on internal agricultural development. Spurred on by fundamental ideological disagreements and the competitive nature of elections for Congress and the presidency, the party system took shape in the 1790s and forced all major political figures to choose a side. This included even George Washington, whose administration eventually moved decisively towards the Federalists. After leaving Washington's cabinet, Thomas Jefferson faced a period of political persecution under the Adams administration but responded in a constructive way by continuing to build a coalition that could capture the presidency. The election of 1800 was characterized by a high degree of partisan intensity. Jefferson and the Democratic-Republicans won the day against the Federalists because the Democratic-Republicans took more interest in appealing to ordinary farmers, who constituted the vast majority of eligible voters. By the time the Federalists realized that their party needed at least a measure of popular support, Jefferson had already concluded the Louisiana Purchase, which vastly increased the arable land in the new nation, removed its economic focus from Atlantic trade with Britain to internal farming and trade along the Mississippi, and – the cherry on the top – expanded Jefferson's core constituency of farmers.

The dramatic victory of the Democratic-Republicans over the Federalists demonstrated that every vote counted and that voters could be mobilized according to their economic interests (there were many more ordinary farmers than merchant traders in the early Republic). Indeed, the victory of the Democratic-Republicans (who shortened their name to simply the Democrats in the 1820s) was so powerful that there was no major opposition party until the formation of the **Whig Party** in the 1830s. The Whigs took up the mantle of the old Federalist party by arguing that the American economy needed support from the federal government in the form of a protective tariff for young manufacturing industries and increased federal funding for internal improvements like roads, bridges and canals. Both the Whigs and the Democrats competed vigorously for votes, with the Whigs stronger in the Northeast and towns and cities, and the Democrats stronger in the South, the West and rural areas. Andrew Jackson, a Democrat, demonstrated the increasing electoral importance of ordinary citizens in politics by practicing the **politics of the common man**, which sought to appeal to farmers and workers. These ordinary citizens understood and supported Jackson's attack on the Bank of the United States, which they viewed as a corrupt institution that doled out financial and political favors to the rich and powerful.

The rise of slavery as a major political issue in the 1830s complicated the American political map and caused great difficulties for the national political parties. Abolitionists in the north at first tried to convince Southerners of the evils of slavery with rallies, pamphlet distribution and meetings across the south. Not only did they fail to win over any planters, but they found slavery so embedded in the culture and politics of the south that even friendly venues like churches proved unwilling to listen to their message. However, the abolitionist cause continued to grow rapidly in the north and began to strain the Democratic party in once-reliable strongholds in the mid-Atlantic states of New York and New Jersey (the Democrats could not favor any moves toward abolition because of its base in the south). Although abolitionism at first affected the Whig party to a lesser degree given the greater strength of the Whigs in the north and the sympathy many Whigs held for the anti-slavery cause, the failure of party leaders to respond creatively to the new situation proved to be an eventual disaster for the party, which found itself cast aside by the politics of sectionalism and war. In summary, the rise of emancipation as a political issue complicated American politics by providing two dimensions of political competition: an economic dimension, which tended to separate the middle class and the wealthy from the common man, and an abolitionist dimension, which tended to separate anti-slavery northerners from everyone else.

As the nation moved towards civil war, the politics of slavery split the Democratic Party into northern and southern wings, each of which supplied a presidential nominee in the election of 1860. The equivocating Whig Party was cast aside by the **Republican Party**, which provided a clear champion for free soil and free labor in the western territories. The Republican Party and the Democratic Party went on to compete politically from the 1850s until the present day as the two dominant American parties.

The Republican Party's platform of free soil, free labor and free people married to federal government promotion of business and commerce served as the dominant political force in American politics from the 1850s until the 1930s, when the party's laissez-faire attitude to the Great Depression resulted in an electoral shellacking at the hands of FDR's New Deal coalition. Representing nearly two-thirds of the American voting public, the New Deal coalition stood for active government involvement to help ameliorate the boom-and-bust economic cycle and the creation of a social welfare state to help people struggling in the marketplace. This broad and diverse coalition included white Southerners; urban political machines; ethnic, racial and religious minorities; intellectuals; labor unions; and blue-collar workers. The coalition splintered in the 1960s with the rise of the civil rights movement; Democratic President Lyndon Johnson's signing of the Civil Rights Act in 1964 led to a steep drop in Democratic support among Southern racists and a portion of northern working-class people. The unpopular Vietnam War, which divided Democratic party intellectuals from ordinary party members, completed the decline of the party. The Republican party began a process of transformation in the 1970s to attract Southern religious and racial conservatives in addition to its core of business conservatives and military cold warriors. The resulting Reagan Republican coalition of the 1980s swept the Democratic party out of power in the White House and the Senate, becoming the dominant political movement with priorities of limited government, tax cuts, a strong military, and social conservatism.

How political parties work

Parties have two basic functions – (1) to select candidates and (2) help these candidates win in a general election. In the early years of the Republic, candidates for the presidency were generally selected by a group of prominent leaders or congressmen – this is known as the **caucus nominating procedure**. In 1831, the selection of presidential candidates became democratized with the arrival of national **party conventions**, in which all the party members were allowed to vote in order to select a candidate. Finally, in the twentieth century the selection of candidates was further democratized to allow ordinary party members to vote on their preferred presidential and congressional candidates (known as the **direct primary**).

Political parties raise money in order to pay for the costs of conducting a political campaign. During the nineteenth century, it was common for parties to work on a patronage basis, in which donors to the party would expect to be given jobs and offices in return (the **spoils system**). For example, a party supporter might expect to be given a Post Office branch to run, allowing him or her to benefit financially and to dole out further patronage of his or her own.

Party organization at the national level

The separation of powers in the United States Constitution makes coordination and cooperation between the presidency and Congress necessary to pass laws. Parties serve as the mechanism of coordination. The party that holds the majority in the House of Representatives selects from its members the leader of the House, known as the Speaker of the House. The party that holds the majority in the Senate does the same for the position of Senate majority leader, not to be confused with the Senate President Pro Tempore, a position of mostly ceremonial leadership usually given to the most experienced senator.

Party leaders in both houses decide which members of Congress are assigned which positions on Senate or House Committees, the bodies that carry out most of the actual lawmaking. Committee chairmen and chairwomen have the power to control whether or not a bill comes up for a vote by the full House or Senate. The president provides his allies in Congress with a political agenda consisting of his favored policies. When one party controls the presidency and the other at least one house in Congress, a situation of **divided government** or **gridlock** exists, and the chances of major legislation passing during these periods is slim.

Political Parties in American History

Period	Party (Leaders)	Platform	Party (Leaders)	Platform	Other Parties
Early Republic (1788-1812)	Democratic-Republicans (Jefferson, Madison)	Limited government; states' rights; agrarian republic	Federalists (Hamilton, Adams)	Govt. role in the economy; national debt; national bank;	
Era of Good Feelings (1812-24)	Democratic-Republicans (Jefferson, Madison, Monroe)	Limited government; states' rights; agrarian republic			
Antebellum (1824-50)	Democrats (Jackson, Van Buren, Polk)	Limited government; states' rights; agrarian republic	Whigs (Clay, Harrison, Webster)	National economic development	Free-Soil (anti-slavery)
Prelude to War (1850-60)	Democrats (Pierce, Douglas)	Limited government; states' rights; pro-slavery	Republicans (Lincoln)	Free labor, soil and markets, nationalism	Know-Nothings (anti-immigrant)
Civil War (1860-65)	Republicans (Lincoln, Seward, Stevens)	Free labor, soil and markets, nationalism	Northern Democrats (Breckinridge)	Limited government; states' rights; compromise on slavery	Southern Democrats in rebellion
Reconstruction (1865-77)	Republicans (Stevens, Grant)	Free market economy and multiracial democracy	Democrats (various)	Limited government, white power	Union (President Johnson)
Gilded Age (1877-1900)	Republicans (Hayes, Garfield, McKinley)	Free market economy, national unity	Democrats (Cleveland)	Limited government, white power	
Progressive Era (1900-20)	Republicans (T. Roosevelt, Taft)	Torn between free markets and progressivism	Democrats (Wilson)	Torn between limited government and progressivism	Progressive (Roosevelt) Socialist (Debs)
Interwar (1920-32)	Republican (Coolidge,	Free markets	Democrats (Smith)	Moving towards	Progressive (La

	Hoover)			government activism	Follette)
New Deal (1932-65)	Democrats (FDR, Truman, Johnson)	New Deal activist state + Southern Dixiecrats	Republicans (Eisenhower)	Limited government	
Modern Era (1965-present)	Democrats (Carter, Clinton)	Activist government + Civil Rights	Republicans (Reagan, Bush)	Limited government, strong military + social/ religious conservatism	Dixiecrats (1968, Wallace)

American History Tutoring Guide Paul Pinto

QUESTIONS
Multiple Choice

1. Why did the Federalist Party lose ground to the Democratic-Republicans from 1796-1816?
   A. The Federalists no longer had a major party leader to rally around after the retirement of George Washington
   B. The Federalists were far less willing to appeal to the interests and desires of farmers, workers and other ordinary people who accounted for an increasing share of the electorate
   C. The Federalists believed in the politics of the common man
   D. The Democratic-Republicans managed to win the merchant vote from the Federalists with centralizing economic policies
   E. The National Bank failed miserably within a few years of its founding

2. Despite the stated preference of the Democratic-Republican Party for limited government and a strict construction of the Constitution, the party came out in full-throated support of the Louisiana Purchase, which doubled the size of the nation. Which of the following reasons best explains this apparent abandonment of party principle?
   A. By providing access to new lands in the West and the transportation waterway of the Mississippi, the Louisiana Purchase allowed the party to fulfill its dream of building an agrarian republic
   B. Fundamental party principles always change once the party enters political office
   C. The Democratic-Republicans decided that limiting the power of the federal government was no longer in the best interests of the nation
   D. Because the Louisiana Purchase was strongly supported by the Federalists, the Democratic-Republicans had to support it in order to prevent being outflanked on the issue
   E. Revenues from the Louisiana Purchase would allow the Democratic-Republicans to close the National Bank

3. Which of the following parties ran on a platform of free soil, free labor and free people?
   I. The Republicans
   II. The Free-Soil Party
   III. The Democratic-Republican Party

   A. I only
   B. II only
   C. I and II
   D. II and III
   E. I, II and III

4. Which of the following parties adopted many of the economic principles and programs of Alexander Hamilton?
   A. The Whigs
   B. The Know-Nothings
   C. The Greenback Party
   D. The Populist Party
   E. The Progressive Party

5. How did the political coalition governing the South change from 1865 to 1896?
   A. An alliance of African-Americans and Republicans gave way to Democratic dominance based on the idea of single party government in order to restore white racial control
   B. The Democratic Party came to adopt many of the principles and programs of Reconstruction
   C. The Republican Party conducted a disciplined drive to disenfranchise African-Americans
   D. The Democratic Party sought to appeal to poor African-Americans in order to build a cross-racial coalition of farmers
   E. All of the above

6. Which of the following positions did the Republican Party take on slavery in the late 1850s?
   A. Slavery ought to be abolished throughout the United States
   B. Slavery should be abolished in the Western territories
   C. Slave states should immediately start a program of gradual emancipation
   D. Northern states should fund a program of compensation for Southern states willing to give up slavery
   E. The Dred Scott decision was the best guide to solving the difficult problem of slavery

7. Which of the following presidents benefited from divisions in a major political party in order to win an election?
   I. Woodrow Wilson
   II. Abraham Lincoln
   III. Theodore Roosevelt

   A. I only
   B. II only
   C. I and II
   D. II and III
   E. I, II and III

8. The Progressive Party succeeded in passing elements of its program into state and federal legislation by relying on which of the following parties?
   I. The Republican Party
   II. The Democratic Party
   III. The Progressive Party

   A. I only
   B. II only
   C. III only
   D. II and III
   E. I, II and III

9. The Republican Party in the post-Civil Rights era has transformed itself into a party with dominant geographical strength in
   A. The rural South and West
   B. The Northeast
   C. California
   D. The Midwest
   E. New England

10. The New Deal coalition included
    A. Labor union
    B. Intellectuals
    C. Urban immigrants
    D. Farmers
    E. All of the above

Essay Questions
1. How did the Democratic-Republican party of Thomas Jefferson get the best of the Federalist Party of Alexander Hamilton and John Adams?

2. How did the Republican Party build a majority coalition in the North by 1860?

3. Discuss the factors that led the following groups to change political party affiliation:
   A. African-Americans from the 1920s to the 1940s
   B. Southern whites from 1948 to 1970

4. Why did the New Deal coalition formed by Franklin Delano Roosevelt in 1932 splinter in 1968?

American History Tutoring Guide

Answers to Multiple Choice Questions

1. B
2. A
3. C
4. A
5. A
6. B
7. C
8. E
9. A
10. E

TOPIC 8: FOUNDING COLONIES

The experiences of the founding colonies in British North America are worthy of close study because they established social and political precedents that have lasted for centuries. All thirteen colonies worked their way towards republican forms of government with legislative assemblies and broad-based manhood suffrage. Despite vast differences of geography and climate, all thirteen found sufficient common ground to hang together during the difficult years of the Revolutionary War. And yet an observer cannot help but be struck by profound differences in social structure and political culture across colonies like Massachusetts, Virginia and New York. A shorthand version of the differences in the founding traditions may be summarized as follows:

The Holy Experiment(s)

Massachusetts, along with Connecticut and Rhode Island, was founded on a bedrock of Puritanism, a strand of Protestant Christianity deeply concerned with religious piety and individual sincerity as the requirements for salvation. Puritans unhappy with religious tolerance in England migrated with their families to New England in order to create pure (hence the name Puritan) religious communities dedicated to God. In the process of working out their salvation, they developed democratic and voluntary communities that placed the church at the center of social, political and religious life. Their relentless dedication to both religion and ordinary work (they believed that God blessed both prayer and work) led to great economic productivity, and New England eventually became a world center of education, commerce and industry. Pennsylvania, under the proprietorship of wealthy English Quaker William Penn, developed an independent version of a Holy Experiment based on Quaker religion. Quakers shared many of the same religious and political principles as Puritans, differing in two important respects: Quakers were (1) significantly more tolerant of other types of Christianity; and (2) more likely to deal fairly (at least in the early years of settlement) with Native American tribes.

Plantations, Slavery and Democracy

Virginia was settled by planters not particularly curious about religion but far more interested in making profits. After a few difficult years, the colony discovered tobacco as a cash crop and began to grow rapidly. Large tobacco plantations required a significant labor force, and the colony moved towards importing African slaves when white indentured servants proved unwilling to remain on the plantations for more than a few years. As slaves became a larger proportion of the population, laws regulating them became stricter, making it virtually impossible for slaves to free themselves. Virginia also moved towards a republican form of government with an elected legislature based on white manhood suffrage, but many historians argue that it did so as a security measure to keep poor whites on the side of the planters and maintain control over the slave population. Like New England, Virginia blossomed commercially and culturally, growing into the largest of the thirteen colonies at the time of independence with a population of nearly three-quarters of a million people; however, nearly forty percent of these were slaves.

American History Tutoring Guide   Paul Pinto

An Uneasy Melting Pot

Captured from the Dutch in 1664, New York was defined by a large degree of diversity blending Dutch aristocracy, wealthy English merchants, African slaves, Native Americans and a range of other ethnicities and social classes. New York possessed neither the religious fervor and relative social uniformity of New England nor the plantation-style economy of Virginia. It was rather a *entrepot*, a meeting place of different cultures. Dutch settlers in New York were granted religious tolerance and free use of their language. Other ethnic groups were not accorded the same privileges, but managed to get along with one another in the broader interest of making money. The granting of a representative assembly in 1683, the result of concerted political action by colonists from New England, gave New York political freedom to underpin its economic vitality.

	New England	**Mid-Atlantic**	**Chesapeake**	**South**
Colonies	MA, NH, CT, RI	NY, NJ, PA	MD, DE	VA, NC, SC, GA
Founding motive(s)	Puritan religion (MA, CT, NH)	Colonial rivalry w/ Dutch (NY, NJ)	Catholic refuge (MD)	Plantations (VA, NC, SC)
	Religious freedom (RI)	Religious freedom for Quakers (PA)	Offshoot of Pennsylvania (DE)	Plantation/Penal Colony (GA)
Society & Family	Homogeneous English Puritan population; balanced gender ratio	NY and PA a mix of ethnicities and races	Large Catholic population in MD; high mortality, high male-female ratio	High male-female ratio (6:1 in early VA)
Average Education Level	High	Middle	Low	Low
Economy	Mostly farming, with shipping and fishing	Shipping, trade, finance, farming	Tobacco planting, farming	Tobacco, cotton, sugar and rice planting, farming
Prominent figures	William Bradford, Puritan gov. of MA	Peter Stuyvesant, Dutch governor or New York	Lord Baltimore, Catholic gov. of MD	John Rolfe, Jamestown merchant leader
	Anne Hutchinson, religious exile from MA	William Penn, Quaker and founder of PA		John Smith, Jamestown military leader
	Roger Williams, champion of religious liberty, RI			Nathaniel Bacon – leads rebellion of poorer whites against planters

	New England	Mid-Atlantic	Chesapeake	South
Colonies	MA, NH, CT, RI	NY, NJ, PA	MD, DE	VA, NC, SC, GA
Rise of democracy	Church membership conferred right to vote for political leaders	Quaker religion strongly supports democracy (PA), NY/NJ initially royal colonies but later obtain legislatures	Baltimore tries to set up a feudal govt; it fails and settlers demand representative government	Broad-based democracy among whites strengthens slave system
Total Population, 1790	MA = 378,787 CT = 237,946 NH = 141,885 RI = 68,825	PA = 434,373 NY = 340,120 NJ = 184,139	MD = 319,728 DE = 59,094	VA = 747,610 NC = 393,751 SC = 249,073 GA = 82,548
% of Population Slaves in 1790	MA = 0% NH = 1% CT, RI = 2%	PA = 1% NY, NJ = 6%	DE = 15% MD = 32%	SC = 43% VA = 39% GA = 35% NC = 26%

Relations with foreign powers

During the colonial period, the American colonies were bordered by the Spanish empire to the west and south; French territories to the west; and Native American tribes being pushed constantly west by colonial settlement. Relations between the British colonies and these other political groups covered a range of activities from trade to warfare.

The Spanish Empire

Spain's empire in North America ranged across the entire southern portion of the Continental United States, from Florida to San Francisco. Spanish settlers established farms and plantations, and Jesuit missionaries sought to convert Native American tribes such as the Pueblo Indians living it what is now the state of New Mexico. Settlers attempted, often successfully, to force Native Americans in their territories to work as indentured laborers. Because of its vast size and distance from Mexico City, North America remained something of a political backwater for Spain.

Louisiana and New France

The strong economic and population growth of the British colonies posed a rising threat to French territories. French officials in the 1750s aimed to capture the Ohio Valley before American colonists could move in. Troops from Virginia under the command of a young George Washington tried but failed to defeat an army of French and Indian soldiers.

Native American Tribes and Confederacies

Metacom, chief of the Wampanoags (known to the colonists as King Philip, 1638-1676) formed an armed confederation of New England tribes and attacked English settlers in 1675. King Philip's War resulted in thousands of deaths on both sides, with the destruction of a number of towns and villages. The colonial forces eventually won and thus ended Native American armed resistance in New England.

American History Tutoring Guide Paul Pinto

QUESTIONS
Multiple Choice

1. In which of the following colonies was church membership a necessary qualification for political voting?
   A. Massachusetts
   B. New York
   C. Virginia
   D. Georgia
   E. South Carolina

2. All of the following colonies had slave populations that accounted for more than 25% of their overall population in 1790 EXCEPT for
   A. South Carolina
   B. Georgia
   C. Virginia
   D. Maryland
   E. New York

3. Which Northern colony had the largest population in 1790?
   A. Pennsylvania
   B. New York
   C. Massachusetts
   D. Rhode Island
   E. Connecticut

4. New England colonies differed from colonies in the Chesapeake area in that
   A. Colonists in the Chesapeake were mostly from areas outside the British Isles
   B. The ratio of women to men was far more balanced in New England
   C. Colonists in the Chesapeake were mostly Catholic, while those in New England were mostly Protestant
   D. The Chesapeake colonies failed to develop representative institutions
   E. All the New England colonies developed established churches

5. Spain valued its colony of Spanish Florida primarily for its
   A. central role in the system of Catholic missions in the New World
   B. role as a strategic buffer against British settlement
   C. valuable fishing waters
   D. strategic control of the Gulf of Mexico
   E. natural resource wealth

6. Which of the following provides the best general description of the central purpose of British, French and Spanish colonies in the New World?
   A. Britain – settlement; France – commerce; Spain – conquest
   B. Britain – conquest; France – conquest; Spain – conquest
   C. Britain – commerce; France – commerce; Spain – commerce;
   D. Britain – conquest; France – conquest; Spain – commerce
   E. Britain – conquest; France – settlement; Spain – commerce

7. All of the following individuals believed in religious pluralism and tolerance for unorthodox ideas EXCEPT:
   A. Anne Hutchinson
   B. Roger Williams
   C. William Bradford
   D. William Penn
   E. Lord Baltimore

8. Which of the following colonies failed to establish representative government by 1700?
   A. Maryland
   B. Virginia
   C. Massachusetts
   D. New Jersey
   E. None of the above

9. Analysis of shipping rosters listing individuals migrating from England to New England in the 1630s would reveal the presence of a large number of
   A. Merchants
   B. Planters
   C. Intact families
   D. Unmarried males
   E. Slaves

10. Which of the following colonies had slave populations amounting to less than 5% of their total population by 1790?
    A. Massachusetts
    B. Rhode Island
    C. Pennsylvania
    D. Connecticut
    E. All of the above

Essay Questions
1. Discuss how TWO of the following factors shaped settlement patterns and governing traditions in the American colonies:
   A. Religion
   B. Soil quality
   C. Health conditions
   D. Transatlantic trade

2. How and why did New England and Virginia develop in very different ways during the seventeenth century?

Answers to Multiple Choice Questions
1. A
2. E
3. A
4. B
5. B
6. A
7. C
8. E
9. C
10. E

TOPIC 9: THE RIGHTS OF WOMEN

Overview

The efforts of generations of American reformers to win equal political, social and economic rights for women constitutes a fundamental change in American history. The patriarchy – or rule by the father, husband, or other dominant male figure – was fundamental not just to American culture but to almost all societies around the world, and remains so in many places. To win their liberation, American women had to find a way to convince men at both the personal and the political level that they deserved a role beyond domestic affairs. Although many contemporary female reformers would say that true gender equality has still not been attained, with many women still forced into either/or choices between child rearing and careers, there can be no mistaking the major victories for women's rights that have been won in terms of law, politics, and economics.

Both the SAT II and AP tests have included questions on the role, status, and reform efforts of women in increasing quantity over the past decade – this topic is clearly growing in importance. To properly answer these questions, it is necessary to develop a basic knowledge of the status of women in society at four different periods in history:
- The era of colonial settlement
- The mid-nineteenth century
- The suffragette period leading to the vote in 1920[7]
- The women's liberation movement of the 1960s-70s

During the **era of colonial settlement (1600s-1776)**, many middle-class women, particularly in New England, were educated church members who managed household financial affairs as well as social responsibilities. Indeed, women represented a majority of church members in New England. Despite their evident capabilities, women enjoyed only limited legal rights of property ownership and were granted neither the right to vote nor the right to hold public office. At the family level, a woman's legal and property rights were dominated first by her father, and then by her husband, which meant that widows and unmarried women often had more legal control over their property than their married counterparts!

By the **mid-nineteenth century**, women reformers centered in the Northeast (many of whom were evangelical Protestants) had created a political movement pushing for the public rights of women, including the right to vote. This movement held a convention at Seneca Falls, New York (1848), where its delegates issued a Declaration of Sentiments that broadened the claims of the Declaration of Independence to explicitly include women. Momentum towards female suffrage and equal legal rights faltered, however, with the sectional crisis leading to the Civil War. Women reformers who had assisted the abolitionist movement were deeply wounded by the fact that the Fourteenth and Fifteenth Amendments, which protected the citizenship and voting rights of African-American males, included no such protections for women. The nineteenth century rather became an age that glorified the **cult of domesticity** and the **separate spheres of public affairs and the home**, relegating women to duties of wifehood and motherhood.

---

[7] The word suffrage refers to the right to vote; for example, universal manhood suffrage means that all men are eligible to vote in elections. A suffragette refers to a woman claiming the right to vote.

Prominent female social reformers such as Jane Addams cleverly turned the concept of separate spheres on its head in order to draw attention to the public contribution women might make if they were only granted the right to vote. Addams and her fellow reformers argued that women's expertise in the home and family earned them the right (and duty) to serve as public leaders in ameliorating the dangerous, unhealthful and un-Christian conditions of modern urban life. Women proved their capacity for public participation by serving in a range of social movements including temperance (reduced consumption of alcoholic beverages), public health, improving labor conditions for women and children, financial support for widows, and women's suffrage. The movement achieved its biggest goal – the right of women to vote – with the passage of the **Nineteenth Amendment** in 1920.

Although women now possessed the most powerful right in a democracy – the ability to vote – the cult of domesticity remained powerful, and few women were able to win influential positions in public or commercial life. Exceptions included Frances Perkins, the first female cabinet secretary (of Labor, in the Roosevelt administration), Mabel Walker Willebrant, a US Assistant Attorney General who played a major role in the legal enforcement of Prohibition, and Amelia Earhart, a female aviator. During World War II, male labor shortages caused by mobilization into the armed forces gave women an unprecedented opportunity to work in factories and office buildings in jobs previously filled by men. Their obvious success in these roles was a powerful refutation of the stereotype of female unfitness for the public sphere. Yet the end of the war and the return of millions of soldiers meant the return of many of these women to their prior roles at home. Indeed, the rise of a broad-based prosperity in the 1950s allowed middle-class women to push domesticity to its limit, as more and more families could afford suburban houses, cars, plenty of food and consumer goods. The idealized family life of the 1950s, in which the man worked as the breadwinner and the woman managed the home, appeared to be extremely solid – until, quite quickly, it wasn't. Women like Betty Friedan began to ask why women could not have it all in terms of a public career and a successful family life. Friedan's book *The Feminine Mystique* (1963) posed the question of whether a woman could be fulfilled by domestic achievements alone. This led to the **Women's Liberation Movement** of the 1960s and 1970s. Women fought to pass an **Equal Rights Amendment (ERA)** to the Constitution, which stated that "equality of rights under the law shall not be denied or abridged by the United States or by any State on account of sex," and obtained its passage through Congress and approval from 35 states by 1972, just short of the 38 needed for ratification. However, changing political winds and the rise of conservatism by the late 1970s prevented the amendment from winning any more states. Although the federal ERA failed to pass, twenty-one states passed equal-rights amendments to their state constitutions. In addition, the women's movement as a whole, symbolized by organizations such as the National Organization of Women, won a number of legal and social victories that transformed the role of women in society. More women went to college and took up professional jobs, and advances in medical technology and contraception allowed women to (controversially) manage their family planning so as to better combine work and family responsibilities. In 1984, Geraldine Ferraro became the first female Vice-Presidential nominee (followed by Sarah Palin in 2008), and Hilary Clinton nearly won the Democratic nomination for President in 2008.

American History Tutoring Guide — Paul Pinto
Timeline of women's rights

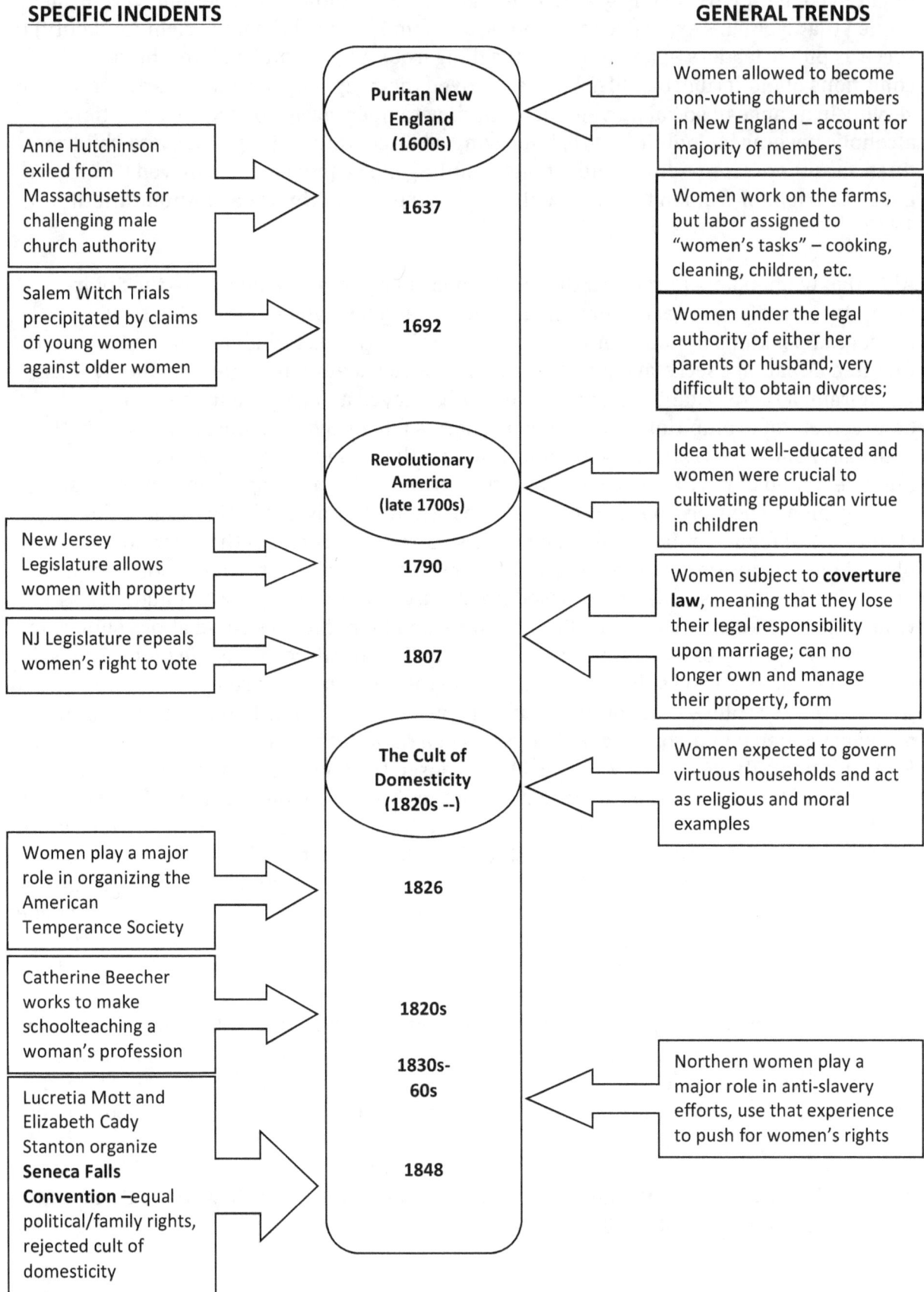

SPECIFIC INCIDENTS

- Anne Hutchinson exiled from Massachusetts for challenging male church authority → **1637**
- Salem Witch Trials precipitated by claims of young women against older women → **1692**
- New Jersey Legislature allows women with property → **1790**
- NJ Legislature repeals women's right to vote → **1807**
- Women play a major role in organizing the American Temperance Society → **1826**
- Catherine Beecher works to make schoolteaching a woman's profession → **1820s**
- Lucretia Mott and Elizabeth Cady Stanton organize **Seneca Falls Convention** — equal political/family rights, rejected cult of domesticity → **1848**

Timeline periods: Puritan New England (1600s); Revolutionary America (late 1700s); The Cult of Domesticity (1820s --); 1830s-60s

GENERAL TRENDS

- Women allowed to become non-voting church members in New England – account for majority of members
- Women work on the farms, but labor assigned to "women's tasks" – cooking, cleaning, children, etc.
- Women under the legal authority of either her parents or husband; very difficult to obtain divorces;
- Idea that well-educated and women were crucial to cultivating republican virtue in children
- Women subject to **coverture law**, meaning that they lose their legal responsibility upon marriage; can no longer own and manage their property, form
- Women expected to govern virtuous households and act as religious and moral examples
- Northern women play a major role in anti-slavery efforts, use that experience to push for women's rights

American History Tutoring Guide — Paul Pinto
Timeline of women's rights (continued)

SPECIFIC INCIDENTS — **GENERAL TRENDS**

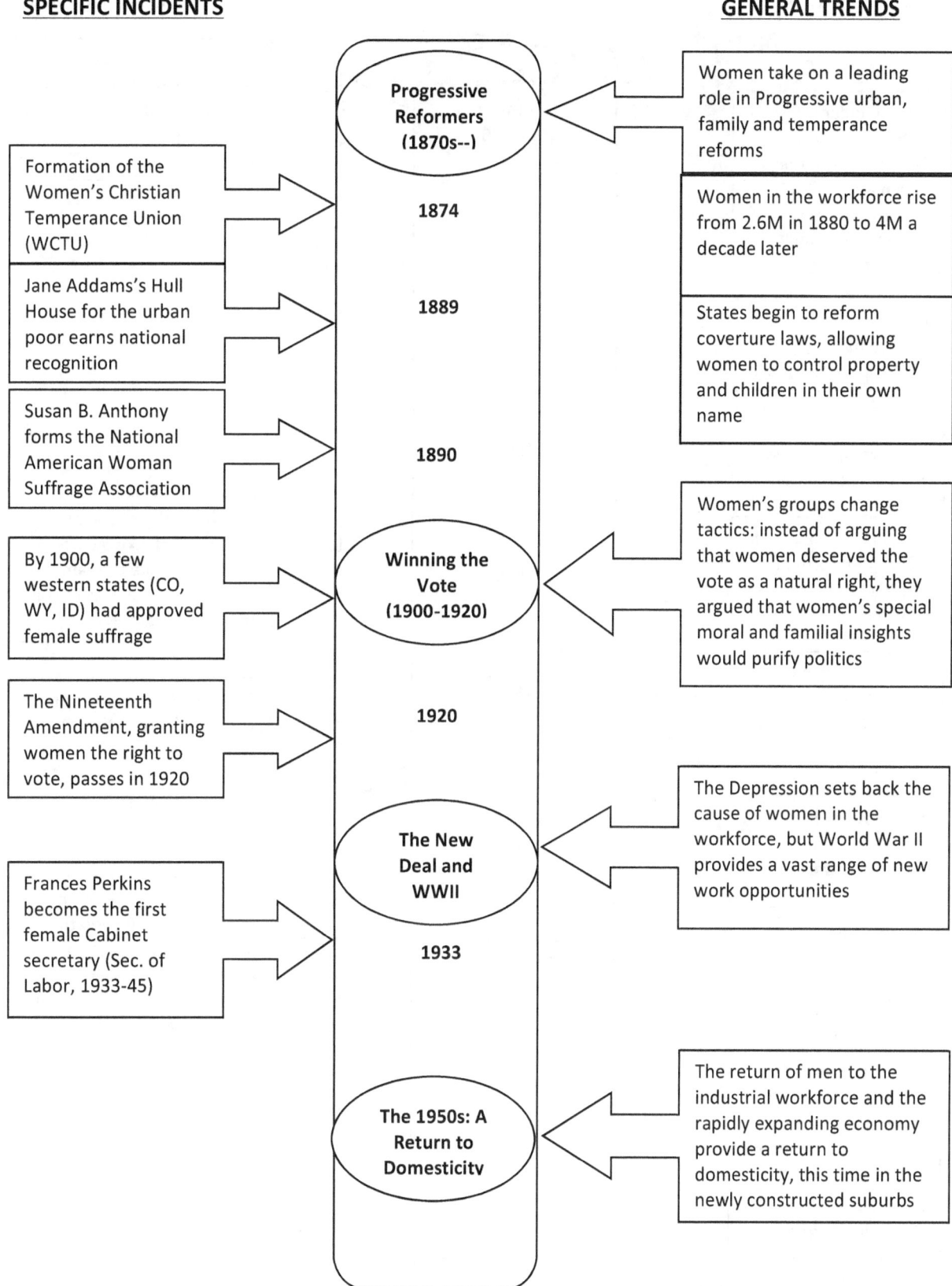

Progressive Reformers (1870s--)

- Women take on a leading role in Progressive urban, family and temperance reforms
- Women in the workforce rise from 2.6M in 1880 to 4M a decade later
- States begin to reform coverture laws, allowing women to control property and children in their own name

1874 — Formation of the Women's Christian Temperance Union (WCTU)

1889 — Jane Addams's Hull House for the urban poor earns national recognition

1890 — Susan B. Anthony forms the National American Woman Suffrage Association

Winning the Vote (1900-1920)

- By 1900, a few western states (CO, WY, ID) had approved female suffrage
- Women's groups change tactics: instead of arguing that women deserved the vote as a natural right, they argued that women's special moral and familial insights would purify politics

1920 — The Nineteenth Amendment, granting women the right to vote, passes in 1920

The New Deal and WWII

- The Depression sets back the cause of women in the workforce, but World War II provides a vast range of new work opportunities

1933 — Frances Perkins becomes the first female Cabinet secretary (Sec. of Labor, 1933-45)

The 1950s: A Return to Domesticity

- The return of men to the industrial workforce and the rapidly expanding economy provide a return to domesticity, this time in the newly constructed suburbs

American History Tutoring Guide Paul Pinto

Timeline of women's rights (continued)

SPECIFIC INCIDENTS | GENERAL TRENDS

Women's Liberation (1960s-70s) ← Women who had worked in the civil rights and student movements decided to start their own liberation movement

1963 ← Betty Friedan publishes *The Feminine Mystique*, which attacks the idea that women were totally fulfilled

1964 ← The 1964 Civil Rights Act makes it illegal to discriminate by gender as well as race

1965 ← *Griswold v. Connecticut* legalizes contraception (right

1966 ← National Organization of Women formed; quickly becomes radicalized | Overheated rhetoric of feminists attacking core institutions like the family and home cause loss of some female support

1972 ← The Equal Rights Amendment (ERA) passes Congress and is sent to the states | Millions more women enter the workforce in the 1970s, tend to take lower-paying jobs (women's wages less than two-thirds of men for the

1973 ← *Roe v. Wade* legalizes abortion (right to privacy)

Conservative Counterattack (1970s-80s) ← Phyllis Schlafly leads conservative campaign against ERA | Reagan coalition of limited government conservatives and evangelicals attempts to counter feminism in the name of social and religious conservatism

1982 ← Deadline for ratification of the Equal Rights Amendment arrives with the amendment still three states short

1984 ← Geraldine Ferraro becomes the first female vice-presidential nominee

American History Tutoring Guide Paul Pinto

QUESTIONS

Multiple Choice
1. Female reformers in the nineteenth century worked on all the following reform movements EXCEPT:
   A. Temperance
   B. Abolitionism
   C. Support for the mentally insane
   D. Religious evangelism
   E. Laissez-faire capitalism

2. *Roe v. Wade*, the 1973 decision that legalized abortion at the national level was based on the concept of
   A. The right to personal sovereignty
   B. The superiority of women
   C. The right to privacy
   D. The need to control population growth
   E. All of the above

3. Anne Hutchinson was expelled from Massachusetts Bay because
   A. she posed a threat to the religious and gender power structure in the Colony
   B. she advocated religious tolerance for Quakers
   C. she wanted to marry a Native American leader
   D. she campaigned for the right of women to run for office
   E. all of the above

4. All of the following increased the economic opportunities of women EXCEPT:
   A. Mobilization for World War II
   B. New jobs created in offices and cities as a result of the Industrial Revolution in the late nineteenth century
   C. Rising educational standards among women throughout the twentieth century
   D. The legalization of contraception following *Griswold v. Connecticut* (1963)
   E. The revivification of women's roles as wives and mothers in the 1950s

5. The feminist movement of the 1970s spurred a strong conservative backlash for which of the following reasons?
   A. The legalization of abortion
   B. Concern that two-earner households were damaging traditional family structures
   C. Anger at radical feminist critiques of male dominance in business and politics
   D. Evangelical religious convictions that stressed a subordinate position for women
   E. All of the above

6. Which of the following female leaders opposed the goals of the women's movement?
   A. Phyllis Schlafly
   B. Geraldine Ferraro
   C. Betty Friedan
   D. Hillary Clinton
   E. None of the above

7. Which of the following banned gender discrimination by public institutions?
   A. The Fourteenth Amendment
   B. The Fifteenth Amendment
   C. The Nineteenth Amendment
   D. The Equal Rights Amendment
   E. The Civil Rights Act of 1964

8. The *Feminist Mystique* (1963) argued that
   A. Women should aspire to manage their households more efficiently by adopting new principles of home economics
   B. Women were not completely satisfied with their opportunities limited to their roles as wives and mothers
   C. Women should work to change society by influencing their husbands
   D. Women should use their special talents and insights as wives and mothers to improve society
   E. All of the above

9. Coverture laws of the nineteenth century
   A. Limited the independent legal rights of women
   B. Placed women under the authority of their fathers or husbands
   C. Made it difficult for women to obtain divorces
   D. Limited the ability of women to obtain university educations
   E. All of the above

10. Delegates at the Seneca Falls Convention of 1848 declared that
    A. Women have the same natural rights as men
    B. Coverture law should be reformed
    C. Women should be able to own property in their own names
    D. Women should have the right to vote
    E. All of the above

American History Tutoring Guide Paul Pinto

Essay Questions
1. Explain the doctrine of "separate spheres" for men and women and discuss how this doctrine shaped opportunities for women from the birth of the Republic to the women's rights movement of the 1960s and 1970s.

2. Compare and contrast the women's rights movements of 1900-1920 and 1960-1980. What were women fighting for during each of these movements? What political or social claims did they make? What did each of these movements achieve, and what, if anything, was left incomplete by each movement?

3. Select THREE of the following leaders and discuss their contribution to American history and to the expansion of women's rights:
   A. Harriet Tubman
   B. Elizabeth Cady Stanton
   C. Jane Addams
   D. Betty Friedan
   E. Hillary Clinton

4. How did World War II (1941-45) and the Civil Rights Movement (1954-1965) create new opportunities for women?

Answers to Multiple Choice Questions
1. E
2. C
3. A
4. E
5. E
6. A
7. E
8. B
9. E
10. E

American History Tutoring Guide Paul Pinto

TOPIC 10: AMERICAN LITERATURE AND PHILOSOPHY

American literature and philosophy from the seventeenth to the early nineteenth century were deeply influenced by and derivative of broader trends in English and European culture. For example, both of the great intellectual currents in early American history – Puritanism and the Enlightenment – trace their descent from European antecedents. The Puritans were part of a fundamental European debate between Protestantism and Catholicism that dated back to the Reformation leaders Martin Luther (a German monk) and John Calvin (a French theologian and lawyer). Many of the core precepts of Puritanism came directly from Calvin's major work *The Institutes of the Christian Religion (*1549), which argued that man's inherent sinfulness could only be overcome by the grace of God, who selected some individuals for salvation (predestination) while consigning the rest to damnation. This idea of a group of the 'elect' who were granted salvation while the majority perished fortified the Puritans with sufficient religious confidence to separate themselves from the English church and society. The (very different) intellectual movement which we call the Enlightenment was also based on European thought. Major Enlightenment figures in American history such as Benjamin Franklin and Thomas Jefferson were deeply influenced by thinkers in Paris, Oxford and Cambridge. European philosophers and scientists such as Voltaire, Denis Diderot, John Locke and Isaac Newton sought to combine the best of classical philosophy and modern science to explain the world in rational and reasonable terms (the Enlightenment is also sometimes called the Age of Reason). Jefferson directly adapted the core ideas of the Declaration of Independence – that individuals are born with inalienable rights to life, liberty and property (the pursuit of happiness); that government is formed to protect these rights; and that individuals have the right to change their government if it fails to protect these rights – from the English philosopher John Locke's *Two Treatises of Government* (1689).

The Enlightenment generated powerful counterreactions in both Europe and America. In America, the response emerged in religious garb with the **Great Awakening**, a mass revival stressing the importance of inner religious experience, emotion in faith, and personal salvation. In Europe, individuals similarly frustrated by the cool reason of the Enlightenment created the **Romantic** movement in art, literature, and music. Romantic composers, artists and writers stressed values like emotion, passion, and drama, and set their art in fantastic or exotic landscapes to further enhance the depth of feeling. The Romantic movement crossed the Atlantic and influenced the first wave of major American novelists, including James Fenimore Cooper, Nathaniel Hawthorne, and Herman Melville.

Romanticism

Author	Works	Content
James Fenimore Cooper	• *The Leatherstocking Chronicles* (1820s), including *The Last of the Mohicans*	• Tales of life on the frontier • Main character Natty Bumppo, a white man raised by Native Americans who travels (not without difficulty) across racial and cultural lines
Nathaniel Hawthorne	• *The Scarlet Letter* (1850)	• Passion and love collide painfully with New England religious mores as a woman bears an illegitimate child
Herman Melville	• *Moby Dick* (1851)	• Story of a sailor (Captain Ahab) obsessed with pursuing a large white whale

By the 1840s, America had begun to develop its own intellectual and literary traditions. These traditions are rooted in the unique characteristics of the United States – its undeveloped, virginal 'natural' frontier characterized by interesting subcultures and a whiff of danger (regional literature from James Fenimore Cooper and Mark Twain); its vigorous work ethic that produced a powerful business civilization and equally powerful critiques of that civilization (F. Scott Fitzgerald's *Great Gatsby* and Upton Sinclair's *Babbitt*); and its African-American citizens whose plight and continuing battle for freedom and equality produced profound literature and poetry (the Harlem Renaissance of the 1920s).

Ralph Waldo Emerson, Henry David Thoreau, and other New England thinkers and writers articulated the first properly American philosophy, **Transcendentalism**. At the root of Transcendentalist philosophy are concepts of self-reliance, independent thinking, and the purity of man in the state of nature. Emerson pointed out that the pressures and temptations of society reduce the ability of individuals to think and act for themselves. He suggested that the spark of divinity and the genius of original thought could be found in the majesty of nature and the natural world if only individuals would find the courage to venture outwards in order to search inside themselves. In his famous essay titled *Self-Reliance* (1841), he argues that "a man should learn to detect and watch that gleam of light which flashes across his mind from within," because "none but he knows what that is which he can do, nor does he know until he has tried." Therefore, each person, no matter how humble, should "trust thyself: every heart vibrates to that iron string." Emerson's friend Henry David Thoreau put transcendentalist philosophy into practice by living independently in a cottage he built with his hands near Walden Pond, Massachusetts. Thoreau's famous book from this experience, *Walden; or, Life in the Woods* (1854) contains reflections on independent thinking, civil disobedience (the peaceful refusal of an individual to comply with unjust or evil laws), and the conformity that society forces upon its members.

Transcendentalism

Author	Works	Content
Ralph Waldo Emerson	• *Nature* (1836) • *Self-Reliance* (1841)	• Lays out transcendental philosophy, specifically the idea that nature contains elements of the divine • Challenges individuals to think and act independently, to resist the temptation to conform to society's expectations and demands
Henry David Thoreau	• *Walden, or, Life in the Woods* (1854)	• Account of life alone in a cabin in the woods, reflecting on the individual and his or her place in society • Thoreau's writings on civil disobedience and peaceful resistance influenced Gandhi and Martin Luther King, Jr.

Regionalist books in American literature fit less easily into well-defined literary categories. These books are grounded in local culture, dialects and rhythms: the sights, smells and sounds of the Mississippi River, for example, in the work of Mark Twain. The best of these works use the local scenery as a foundation on which to communicate something of fundamental importance about the human condition. Twain, for instance, uses an adventure story about a boy and a man on a boat, floating down the river, to explore larger issues of freedom, slavery, race, and friendship. Regionalist books tend to cluster around these areas with the most vivid and idiosyncratic cultures: New England, the deep South, the Mississippi, and the West.

Regionalism

Author	Works	Content
Mark Twain (Samuel Clemens)	• *The Adventures of Tom Sawyer* (1876) • *The Adventures of Huckleberry Finn* (1884)	• Stories about a boy famous for getting into adventures in Mississippi • Written in the vernacular (local dialect), *Huckleberry Finn* is a critique of the racism and hierarchy of the South. A youthful runaway with a hardscrabble life, Huck meets Jim, an escaped slave, on the Mississippi. His conversations with Jim teach him about the realities of life under slavery, helping him to mature and think for himself.

William Faulkner	• *The Sound and the Fury* (1929)
	  As I Lay Dying (1930)
	  Light in August (1932)
		• Novels set in fictional Yoknapatawpha County (in Mississippi), and deal with issues of race, inheritance, hierarchy and family
		• Faulkner combines Southern regionalism with the "stream-of-consciousness" style popularized by European writers like James Joyce

Protest or **Social Movement** books aim to inform and arouse the general public about social injustices. These books have a long tradition in American history, from abolitionist books and pamphlets published in the antebellum period to works detailing the injustice faced by African-Americans and Native Americans in the nineteenth and twentieth centuries to the battle for women's rights. These works, published in the context of an expanding literary market based on a better-educated readership and improved printing technology, made a significant contribution to public debate and often resulted in political or social change. A popular, if apocryphal (unverified) story states that Abraham Lincoln, upon meeting abolitionist author Harriet Beecher Stowe, remarked "So this is the little lady who started this great war."

Protest and Social Movement Books

Author	Works	Content
Harriet Beecher Stowe	• *Uncle Tom's Cabin* (1852)	• Details the injustices of slave life through the story of escaped slaves; in keeping with Stowe's evangelical faith, the role of Christianity is emphasized as a redemptive and unifying force. Despite its real contribution to emancipation, the book was later criticized for its one-dimensional portrayals of African-Americans
Helen Hunt Jackson	• *A Century of Dishonor* (1881)	• Based on the investigative work Jackson performed for the Department of the Interior, *A Century of Dishonor* criticized the 1871 Indian Appropriations Act, which made Native Americans the wards of the American state, and American policy towards Indians in general. She mailed copies of the book to Congressmen in the hopes that United States government would deal more honorably with the Native American tribes
Dee Brown	• *Bury My Heart at Wounded Knee* (1970)	• The book takes its name from Wounded Knee, a village in South Dakota that was the site of the last major armed conflict between the US Army and Native Americans. It details the long history of military conflict, land expropriation, and humiliation

W.E.B. Du Bois	• *The Souls of Black Folk* (1903)	• A Harvard-trained sociologist, Du Bois used data and interviews to demonstrate the unfairness and injustice of segregation and racial prejudice in the South and the North. This collection of essays is unified by a central thesis – that the American political and social system needed reform in order to guarantee African-Americans equal rights in voting, legal justice and education. Du Bois opposed Booker T. Washington's focus on industrial education and political quietism for blacks, arguing that African-Americans needed to uplift themselves and protest against the system itself
Rachel Carson	• *Silent Spring* (1962)	• Described the ways in which pollution and pesticides had damaged plant and animal life. The book is credited as one of the founding tomes of the environmental movement
Betty Friedan	• *The Feminine Mystique* (1963)	• Seized on the sense of grievance and discrimination that developed among white middle-class women in the 1960s. She attacked the prevailing view that women were completely contented with their housekeeping and child-rearing tasks, claiming that housewives had no self-esteem and no sense of identity.

Naturalism is a term for a literary movement characterized by a realistic portrayal of life that rejected transcendentalist beliefs in self-reliance and the ability of individuals to make independence choices. Influenced by Charles Darwin's theory of evolution, naturalist authors demonstrated rather how underlying factors of inheritance and environment acted to limit the free agency of people. Leading authors in this tradition include Ernest Hemingway (*The Sun Also Rises*) and Sinclair Lewis (*Main Street* and *Babbitt*).

Naturalism

Author	Works	Content
Ernest Hemingway	• *The Sun Also Rises*	• Novel about American and British expatriates in Paris who travel to Spain. Featured Hemingway's spare writing style and his restrained use of description to convey characterizations and action.
Sinclair Lewis	• *Main Street* • *Babbitt*	• Satirized the values of small-town America as dull, complacent and narrow-minded; poked fun at the commercialism of the 1920s.

The **Harlem Renaissance** (1920-40s), a literary and cultural movement among African-Americans in Northern cities beginning in the 1920s, drew artistic inspiration from the injustices of life in segregated America. As Langston Hughes put it in his famous poem "I, Too, Sing America":

> I, too, sing America.
> I am the darker brother.
> They send me to eat in the kitchen
> When company comes,
> But I laugh,
> And eat well,
> And grow strong.

Some of the other leading literary lights in the movement were Zora Neale Hurston (*Their Eyes Were Watching God*, 1937); Countee Cullen (*The Black Christ and Other Poems*, 1929); and James Weldon Johnson (*American Negro Spirituals*, 1925, 1926).

Harlem Renaissance

Author	Works	Content
Langston Hughes	• *The Weary Blues* (1926)	• Book of poems in which Hughes expressed his pride in African-American and his desire to articulate an independent black identity that could hold its head up on an equal basis with the broader culture
Zora Neale Hurston	• *Their Eyes Were Watching God* (1937)	• Exploring both gender and race, this book examined the efforts of a young African-American woman in Florida to articulate her independence
Countee Cullen	• *The Black Christ and Other Poems* (1929)	• Controversial poem which compares the lynching of an African-American to the crucifixion of Christ
James Weldon Johnson	• *The Book of American Negro Poetry* (1922) • *American Negro Spirituals* (1925)	• Weldon collected over one hundred poems (some written by himself) whose topics range from love and family to race and politics • Weldon collected and edited a range of African-American spirituals, many of which dated back to the antebellum period

Critiques of Modernity and Capitalism (1920s-present). A number of authors have taken up the problems of modernity and capitalism – an obsession with money; the soul-deadening character of industrial work; the decline of faith and family; loneliness amidst urban crowds; social conformity – as the topic of their social critiques. Some of these works are clear criticisms of industrial excess and urban corruption, such as Upton Sinclair's *The Jungle* (1906) or Lincoln Steffens *The City* (1904). Other works seek to transcend capitalism altogether with utopian fantasies of the future, as in Edward Bellamy's *Looking Backward: 2000 to 1887* (1887). Still others take a less direct but perhaps more profound line of criticism. F. Scott Fitzgerald's *The Great Gatsby* (1925) provides a searing criticism of the emptiness, lack of human concern, and snobbery below the glittering surface of the lives of New York's wealthy and powerful (whom Fitzgerald describes as "the beautiful and damned"). Fitzgerald's work, published during the height of the Roaring Twenties, may be usefully paired with Depression-era life as depicted by John Steinbeck in *The Grapes of Wrath* (1939), an account of the rural poverty and social desperation of migrant farmers in Oklahoma. Steinbeck's novel is suffused with a sense of profound outrage at the injustice of poor farmers facing ruin as a result of a Depression caused by Wall Street. The return of prosperity in the 1950s did not dull the critical pen of social observers; indeed, the very conformity and peace of the era may have compelled writers like William Whyte to condemn the death of individual man at the hands of faceless corporations (*The Organization Man*, 1956). Authors like J.D. Salinger extended these critiques of capitalism to modern society at large. His novel *The Catcher in the Rye* (1951) is an analysis of the alienation and loss of identity and freedom suffered by an individual in modern society.

Critiques of Capitalism and Modernity

Author	Works	Content
Upton Sinclair	• *The Jungle* (1906)	• Sinclair found health violations and labor abuses in a meatpacking market trying to produce meat as cheaply as possible. Led to the passage of the Meat Inspection Act
Ida Tarbell	• *The History of the Standard Oil Co.* (1902)	• Scathing review of how Standard Oil had abused competitive and labor practices to become a dominant monopolist.
Lincoln Steffens	• *The Shame of the Cities* (1904)	• Exposed the shabby state of life in the cities, and called for major urban reforms.
Edward Bellamy	• *Looking Backward: 2000 – 1887* (1887)	• The novel's protagonist, Julian West, falls asleep in 1887 and awakes in the year 2000. Wide-eyed, he finds himself in a socialist utopia. The government owns the means of production, and citizens share the material rewards. Cooperation, rather than competition, is the watchword.
F. Scott Fitzgerald	• *The Great Gatsby* (1925)	• Life among "the beautiful and the damned" on Long Island's North Shore is revealed to be based on emptiness and lack of human concern, reflecting the broader void at the heart of modern capitalistic society
John Steinbeck	• *The Grapes of Wrath* (1939)	• Description of the Depression-era plight and search for dignity of poor farmers subject to market forces
John Keats	• *The Crack in the Picture Window* (1956)	• A critique of the flaws of suburbia, this work describes the endless rows of tract houses "vomited up" by developers as "identical boxes spreading like gangrene." Their occupants –dubbed the Drones, the Amiables, and the Fecunds – lost any sense of individuality in their obsession with material goods.
William Whyte	• *The Organization Man* (1956)	• Whyte perceived a change from the old Protestant ethic, with its emphasis on hard work and personal responsibility, to a new social ethic centered on "the team" with the ultimate goal of "belongingness." The result was a stifling conformity and the loss of personal identity.
J.D. Salinger	• *The Catcher in the Rye* (1951)	• A tale of a young man's alienation from a conformist world and his desire for freedom and authenticity
Jack Kerouac	• *On the Road* (1957)	• Describes the anti-conformity "beatniks" who flouted the respectability of suburbia in favor of social, sexual and medicinal experimentation

Concluding Thoughts

American literature is unsurprisingly rooted in the central institutions, features and dilemmas of American life, from the Puritan doubt expressed in the *Scarlet Letter* to the stirring frontier life of *The Leatherstocking Chronicles* to the concern with the excesses of industrial capitalism. Note that some of the most striking social critiques emerge during periods of relative social peace and prosperity (for example, strong critiques of capitalism emerged in both the 1920s and 1950s). Finally, remember that literature is often a way for writers to protest or articulate the plight of discriminated-against or damaged groups of people.

QUESTIONS
Multiple Choice

1. Which literary tradition stresses self-reliance and independent thinking?
   A. Methodism
   B. Transcendentalism
   C. Naturalism
   D. Regionalism
   E. Romanticism

2. All of the following books are critiques of capitalism EXCEPT
   A. *History of the Standard Oil Company*
   B. *The Jungle*
   C. *The Grapes of Wrath*
   D. *The Organization Man*
   E. *A Century of Dishonor*

3. Which of the following Transcendentalist authors developed the theme of nonviolent civil disobedience?
   A. Ralph Waldo Emerson
   B. Harriet Beecher Stowe
   C. Zora Neale Hurston
   D. Henry David Thoreau
   E. Josiah Strong

4. Ordinary Americans responded to Enlightenment rationalism and science in the late eighteenth century by
   A. Converting to deism
   B. Applying the scientific method to the Bible
   C. Persecuting scientists
   D. Engaging in the religious revival known as the Great Awakening
   E. Building a coalition for a social revolution in the style of the French Revolution

5. Which of the following sold the most copies of any book apart from the Bible in the 1850s?
   A. *Pride and Prejudice*
   B. *A Century of Dishonor*
   C. *Uncle Tom's Cabin*
   D. *Their Eyes Were Watching God*
   E. *The Adventures of Tom Sawyer*

6. Authors criticizing capitalism and modern society in the twentieth century attacked which of the following?
   A. Social conformity
   B. Robber barons
   C. Corruption in urban politics
   D. The neglect of the poor by the rich
   E. All of the above

7. Penetrating critiques of capitalism are most likely to be found in which of the following decades of the twentieth century?
   A. The 1990s
   B. The 1920s
   C. The 1940s
   D. The 1910s
   E. The 1960s

8. The cultural creativity embodied by the Harlem Renaissance was made possible in part by
   A. Increased educational opportunities for African Americans
   B. De facto residential segregation in New York City
   C. The desire of African-American poets and writes to craft something true to their experiences and of equal quality to 'white' literature
   D. The skilful use of religious themes and imagery to levy social critiques
   E. All of the above

9. Authors writing in the Naturalist (or Realist) tradition repudiated Transcendentalism and instead stressed the
   A. embeddedness of characters in class, family and wealth structures
   B. free will of characters
   C. overriding power of love
   D. importance of nature
   E. all of the above

10. What did F. Scott Fitzgerald mean when he wrote that "the rich are different from you and me"?
    A. Rich people are inherently better
    B. Rich people are destined to rule society
    C. The wealthy care little for poor people
    D. Those born to wealthy backgrounds have an ingrained confidence and ease of manner
    E. The rich are rich because they work harder than the poor

Essay Questions
1. What concepts and subjects did American authors and thinkers draw on to create distinctively American forms of literature and philosophy?

2. What did Ralph Waldo Emerson and Henry David Thoreau mean by *self-reliance*? How is self-reliance related to nature? How does self-reliance help underpin a successful republic?

3. Compare the critiques of capitalism and materialism made by leading authors in the 1920s and the 1950s. Why did these critiques emerge during these periods of overall economic success?

4. Discuss the perspective of leading writers and thinkers of the Harlem Renaissance, specifically the tension between their mastery of arts and culture and their status as African-Americans in a segregated nation.

Answers to Multiple Choice Questions
1. B
2. E
3. D
4. D
5. C
6. E
7. B
8. E
9. A
10. D

TOPIC 11: THE PRESIDENCY

Overview

Article II of the Constitution lays out the powers of presidency with admirable economy. The "executive Power shall be vested in a President of the United States of America" who holds the office for a period of four years. The president is voted into office by a College of Electors, and thus does not depend on Congress for his political authority;[8] through the Electoral College he draws his power from the people, and he is the only nationally elected official under the Constitution. The Constitution binds the office of the president directly to it, stating at the end of Article II, Section 1 that the President must pledge an oath to "preserve, protect and defend the Constitution of the United States." Section 2 names the president commander-in-chief of the armed services of the federal government and of the state militias, and he is also granted the power, with the advice and consent of the Senate, to make foreign treaties, which makes him diplomat-in-chief. Section II also grants the president the power to appoint (and dismiss) individuals to a range of offices: military, judicial, diplomatic, bureaucratic, etc. Finally, going back to Article I of the Constitution, the president is given the power to veto legislation that he finds objectionable, meaning that he can take a bill signed by majorities in both houses and return it to Congress, whereupon the bill dies, unless Congress can muster a supermajority of two-thirds of both houses to pass it into law.

To sum up, the President is granted the following constitutionally-defined powers:
- He holds the **executive power** of the nation, meaning that he is responsible for making sure that laws passed by Congress are put into effect;
- To fulfill his executive duties, he is granted major **administrative powers**, namely the direction of the entire executive branch. He names all the leading officers, who serve at his pleasure;
- He runs the **foreign affairs** of the nation (with help from the Senate);
- He is the commander-in-chief of the **military**;
- He has extraordinary **legislative power** through the veto. Think it about it this way: if you were a congressman or congresswoman trying to pass a law, you would certainly want to make sure that the President approved, because while obtaining a majority is difficult, winning a two-thirds majority is significantly more challenging.

To this broad array of constitutionally-defined powers we may add an informal but significant power: the President, by virtue of his office, is the leader of his **political party**. He is thus the **politician-in-chief**, and that means that either his political party holds the majority and is passing his agenda into law or the president serves as the major veto point checking or limiting the agenda of the opposing majority party.

With all these powers, it is perhaps not surprising that the presidency has been described by contemporaries and scholars as an elective monarchy. As King William V of Holland said to John Adams, "Sir, you have given yourselves a king under the title of president."[9]

---

[8] The masculine gender is used here for convenience
[9] http://www.historytoday.com/frank-prochaska/american-monarchy

The Paradox of Presidential Power

The paradox of presidential power is that few presidents in American history have governed with the power and authority of (democratically elected) monarchs despite the panoply of written and unwritten presidential powers provided by the Constitution. Indeed, presidents who have exercised great authority are relatively easy to remember: Jackson, Lincoln, and Franklin Roosevelt, among others. It's much harder to recall the vast majority of presidents who did not govern with great authority and power (quick: name a president between Jackson and Polk, or between Lincoln and McKinley). There are two main schools of thought that explain why some presidents have exercised great powers and others have not. The first school of thought separates the presidency into premodern and modern eras, the latter starting with the rise of the administrative, regulatory and national security state during the New Deal and World War II. This 'periodization' approach argues that the new and major responsibilities of the presidency in the modern era required strong executive leadership in order to deliver the political changes necessary to keep pace with modern times (Neustadt 1960). There are two obvious problems with this argument. First, it can only explain powerful but premodern presidencies such as the Lincoln's as aberrations caused by emergencies. Second, it does not explain relatively weak presidencies in the modern era such as the Carter administration. A second school of thought, created by presidential scholar Stephen Skowronek, performs better. It argues that presidents are able to exercise great executive power only during those times where the country is ready for a new political movement and the president is the leader of that movement (Skowronek 1993). Consider the New Deal as an instructive example: the faith of Americans in the previously dominant Republican Party's trust in the unfettered free market plummeted as the unemployment rate rose to disastrous levels. Roosevelt and the Democrats came into office with an entirely new program of activist government and proceeded to build a welfare and regulatory state in which the federal government took a major new role in guiding and governing the economy. We can use Skowronek's framework and terminology to organize the presidents in terms of their relationship to new political movements. I assign a number of prominent presidents to one of the four groups: see if you can assign the others as an exercise.

Group 1: The Reconstructors
These presidents enter office at the head of a new political movement that offers convincing answers for the nation's problems. They are therefore granted a fair degree of political space to legitimately use the full powers of the presidency to effect major political changes

President	Dominant Political Movement	Relationship to Movement	Strategy and Achievements
Thomas Jefferson (1800-1808)	States' rights, limited government, agrarian republic	Leader	• Rejects Hamilton's national debt policy, designed to bind the nation to mercantile trade and Britain, by reducing the size of the national debt • Reduces size of the federal govt. • Refocuses the nation on westward development rather than Atlantic trade
Andrew Jackson	Politics of the common man	Leader	• Reduces the power of political elites • Destroys the Bank of the United States

				• Uses veto power to restrain federal govt. role in the economy
Abraham Lincoln (1860-65)	Republican vision of free soil, free labor, free market nationalism	Leader	• Defeats the South in the Civil War and restores the union • Emancipates the slaves • Provides for the industrial and educational development of the West and Midwest (railroads, land-grant colleges)
Franklin Roosevelt (1932-45)	New Deal welfare/ regulatory state	Leader	• Creates a range of federal agencies to regulate the economy • Creates federal agencies to provide welfare services to citizens to protect them from worst of the market • Creates a national security state to win World War II
Ronald Reagan (1980-88)	Conservative rollback of New Deal in favor of limited government	Leader	• Tax cuts to reduce the revenues of the federal government • Deregulates many industries to reduce federal economic control • Fights activist government intervention in the economy and in society

Group 2: The Articulators

These presidents carry on the legacies of the Reconstructors; the political movement they represent remains strong, but not quite as strong as during the time of the Reconstructors

President	Dominant Political Movement	Relationship to Movement	Strategy and Achievements
James Monroe (1800-1808)	States' rights, limited government, agrarian republic	Articulator (main disciple of Jefferson)	• Tries to maintain national unity built by Jefferson/Madison ("era of good feelings") • Walks a tightrope between limited government principles and national development needs
Theodore Roosevelt (1901-1908)	Free soil, free labor, free market nationalism	Articulator (saw himself as the heir of Lincoln)	• Pushes Republican party to adapt to challenges of industrial development and global politics • Tries to make Republican Party progressive, but struggled with conservative old guard • Explodes the system by trying to create a wholly new Progressive Politics, which split the Republican Party
Lyndon Johnson (1963-1968)	New Deal welfare/ regulatory state	Articulator (completing FDR's work)	• Extends New Deal with new programs (Medicare/Medicaid for health and welfare) and new groups of people eligible to receive benefits (African-Americans via civil rights) • Splits New Deal coalition by losing southern Democrats due to civil rights

Group 3: The Preemptors

These presidents are from the political party in opposition to a dominant political movement. Their role is to limit, co-opt, or restrict the achievements of that movement

President	Dominant Political Movement	Relationship to Movement	Strategy and Achievements
Andrew Johnson (1865-1868)	Free soil, free labor, free market nationalism	Opposed (supports efforts of southern states to maintain white control)	• Attempts to recreate the political coalition of the Democratic Party on a post-Civil War basis (accepts emancipation but seeks to subordinate freedmen and women) • Lenient towards the South • Fights the dominant Republican Party to create his own program; loses the political battle and is nearly removed from office
Richard Nixon (1968-73)	New Deal welfare/regulatory state	Opposed (wants to cut back New Deal)	• Approves Environmental Protection Agency (pro-regulatory state) • Imposes wage and price controls (pro-intervention in economy) • Resigns after facing impeachment charges for obstruction of justice due to Watergate
Bill Clinton (1992-2000	Conservative rollback of New Deal	Opposed (tries to co-opt or limit Republican welfare reforms)	• Tries and fails to pass New Deal-style health care reform • Settles for co-opting Republican welfare reform initiatives (declares that "the Age of Big Government is over") • Impeached by Republicans in 1997

Group 4: The Last Defenders

These presidents belong to a dominant political movement that is long past its prime; as defenders of this weakened ideology they must deal with constant political dissatisfaction

President	Dominant Political Movement	Relationship to Movement	Strategy and Achievements
Herbert Hoover (1924-28)	Free labor, free market nationalism	Last Defender	• Could not rally his party to deal with the Depression given commitments to free market • Tried a number of initiatives but could not achieve the scale/scope to rally society
Jimmy Carter (1976-80)	New Deal welfare/regulatory state	Last Defender	• Tries to defend and fix the problems of the fading New Deal program despite bad economy • Warned his constituents that "government has its limits and cannot solve all our problems" • Could not manage all the splintering elements of the New Deal coalition • Brought down by economic troubles (stagflation) and Iran hostage crisis

We can summarize this presidential framework in general terms as follows:

		Position of President Relative to Dominant Political Movement	
		Opposes Movement	*Leads Movement*
Strength of Dominant Political Movement	*Strong and Vibrant*	③ Preemptors	② Articulators
	Weak and Ready for a New Movement	① Reconstructors	④ Last Defenders

The best position from which to exert presidential leadership and power is the bottom left cell, position #1. In this position, the dominant political movement no longer has good answers or strategies to address the challenges of the day, and a president leading a new movement to reform or change politics finds himself with a great deal of political space in which to reconstruct politics. He is therefore relatively free to use the great powers of the presidency to their full potential. FDR is a great example of a Reconstructor president – he put in place the New Deal welfare state on the ashes of the failed Republican laissez-faire economic approach. Presidents following Reconstructor presidents serve as political heirs whose job it is to further develop or articulate the political programs first presented by the Reconstructor. Lyndon Johnson is a good examples of an Articulator president (top right cell, position #2); his Great Society set of social programs extended or completed many New Deal initiatives. Presidents from the minority party who manage to get elected while a dominant political movement is in full swing find themselves constantly battling and resisting the majority party in Congress. These Preemptor presidents (top left cell, position #3) are often forced to accept many of the basic facts and assumptions of the opposing political movement. A good example of a Preemptor president is Richard Nixon, who signed the Environmental Protection Act into law and imposed wage and price controls. Finally, a president occasionally has the bad luck to enter office when the political movement led by his party is showing major signs of fatigue. These Last Defender (bottom right, position #4) presidents are handcuffed by their principles of their declining political movement and are thus restrained from responding creatively to new challenges. Jimmy Carter is a good example of a Last Defender: his failure to solve the economic difficulties of the 1970s by reworking the welfare state has more to do with the political constraints he faced from his own party than any personal failures of leadership.

American History Tutoring Guide Paul Pinto

QUESTIONS
Multiple Choice

1. Which of the following presidents did NOT come to power at the head of a major new political movement?
   A. Franklin D. Roosevelt
   B. Ronald Reagan
   C. Dwight D. Eisenhower
   D. Thomas Jefferson
   E. Abraham Lincoln

2. Which of the following presidents was faced with an extremely difficult strategic situation in which the political and economic commitments of his party limited his options to address the needs of the nation?
   A. Franklin D. Roosevelt
   B. Ronald Reagan
   C. Bill Clinton
   D. John F. Kennedy
   E. Herbert Hoover

3. All of the following presidents changed the relationship between the federal government and the economy in a fundamental way EXCEPT
   A. Andrew Jackson
   B. Franklin D. Roosevelt
   C. Ronald Reagan
   D. Lyndon Johnson
   E. Bill Clinton

4. The Constitution grants all of the following powers to the office of the President EXCEPT
   A. Control over the executive power of the nation
   B. Command of the armed forces
   C. Power to negotiate foreign treaties (subject to the advice and consent of the Senate)
   D. Power to veto legislation
   E. Power to levy new taxes

5. Which of the following presidents was not the de facto leader of the political party that brought him to power?
   A. Abraham Lincoln
   B. John F. Kennedy
   C. Theodore Roosevelt
   D. Woodrow Wilson
   E. Andrew Johnson

6. Which of the following presidents sought to limit the power of financial and political elites in favor of ordinary Americans?
   A. Andrew Jackson
   B. James K. Polk

C. John F. Kennedy
D. Dwight D. Eisenhower
E. Richard M. Nixon

7. Stagflation, an economic situation in which high inflation coexists with low growth and high unemployment, proved to be devastating politically as well as economically for Jimmy Carter for all of the following reasons EXCEPT
   A. Stimulus policies based on Keynesian economics failed to improve the situation, casting doubt on the capability the federal government to manage the economy
   B. High unemployment is almost always damaging to the political fortunes of a presidential administration
   C. Gas shortages due to OPEC supply reductions resulted in Americans having to queue for hours to get gasoline
   D. High inflation caused interest rates to rise, making it harder for Americans to obtain bank loans and mortgages
   E. Union workers failed to obtain wage increases to match higher inflation

8. Which of the following presidents made the veto a political weapon, vetoing more bills during his administration than all his predecessors combined?
   A. Andrew Johnson
   B. Andrew Jackson
   C. Theodore Roosevelt
   D. James K. Polk
   E. James Monroe

9. Which of the following presidents advocated a "Third Way" approach to politics that aimed to combine both the efficiency of markets with a robust role of the federal government in the economy?
   A. Ronald Reagan
   B. George H.W. Bush
   C. George W. Bush
   D. Bill Clinton
   E. Jimmy Carter

10. Presidential power has typically expanded most rapidly during
    A. Economic booms
    B. Divided government caused by one party controlling Congress and the other the White House
    C. National security crises
    D. Periods of assertiveness by the Supreme Court
    E. All of the above

Essay Question
1. Compare and contrast the way that Franklin Roosevelt and Herbert Hoover dealt with the Great Depression. Why were some of FDR's solutions off limits to Hoover?

Answers to Multiple Choice Questions
1. C
2. E
3. E
4. E
5. E
6. A
7. E
8. B
9. D
10. C

American History Tutoring Guide Paul Pinto

TOPIC 12: NATIVE AMERICANS

The history of the Native American peoples since the arrival of European settlers has been a challenging one, with moments of triumph and cooperation scattered amidst a larger history of military defeat, forced migration, and cultural imperialism. Even the most creative and strategically sophisticated efforts of Native American leaders to adapt and benefit from the arrival of Europeans failed to prevent the eventual defeat, expropriation or expulsion of almost all Native American tribes by American settlers hungry for land.

The history of the Native American peoples may be summarized by four main periods:
- (1) Balance and competition (1600s-1763)
- (2) Migration west (1763-1840)
- (3) Final conquest (1865-1890)
- (4) Finding a place in the American state (1890-present)

Balance and competition (1600s-1673)

Although the English colonists arriving in New England and Virginia in the early seventeenth century were the beneficiaries of a culture with superior economic productivity and military technology, Native Americans were able to use their greater numbers, knowledge of the land, military prowess, and alliances with French traders to maintain a rough balance of power. It is important to remember that geographic dispersal across a vast area often resulted in significant social differences between Native American tribes, including differences of language, economic methods, and forms of political organization. These differences made it possible for Europeans to strategically form alliances with rival tribes in order to divide and rule. The figure below is a vastly simplified map showing the location of many prominent Native American tribes in the 17th century. It contains only those tribes that tend to be mentioned frequently on American history tests. Familiarize yourself with the location of these tribes in order to master specific facts such as that Virginians were in contact and conflict with the Powhatan and New Englanders with the Wampanoag.

Map of Selected Native American Tribes in North America (17th Century)

John Eliot, a Puritan minister at Harvard College, attempted to convert a number of local Indian tribes in the 1640s. He learned their languages and organized a group of Christianized Indians into what contemporaries called "praying villages," places where Indians could organize their own church congregations and enjoy a measure of self-government. He also attempted to start a college for Indians at Harvard. The praying villages lasted for about thirty years, but were greatly weakened by King Philip's War and the spread of disease.

Native Americans tribes along the coast, such as the Wampanoags and Narragansett, benefited at first from the presence of New Englanders through trade. However, the continual growth of the coastal towns and the desire of settlers to expand onto territory owned by the neighboring Indian tribes led to military conflict. **King Philip's War (1675-78)** was a bloody conflict between English colonists and a confederation of tribes lead by Metacom, chief of the Wampanoag tribe. Hundreds of people from both sides died in the conflict, and many villages were burned. The conflict was severe enough to raise doubt over the viability of New England, but in the end the settlers captured Metacom and won the war. The main significance of the war lies in the definitive establishment of military superiority by the colonists over the Native Americans. The Indians were forced retreat west, and the dynamic of continual westward settlement by Europeans was put into place.

War between the two sides was underpinned by a fundamental conflict over economic and social organization. New England towns were based on the notion of private property: each settler was given a plot of land over which he exercised full control. As settlers sought to expand their properties, and new settlers pushed westwards in search of farmland and cattle pastures, Native American tribes were pushed further and further west. By the early 1700s, Native American tribes had mostly retreated across the Appalachian Mountains, ceding the territory to the east to English settlers. Tribes on the move attempted to integrate with other Native American groups, forming confederations for mutual economic and military support. Native Americans continued to depend on trade with Europeans in order to maintain their supply of finished goods, including weapons.

By playing the French off against the English, Native American tribes were able to survive and thrive in the "middle ground" between the Mississippi River and the Appalachians. However, the defeat of their French allies in the Seven Years' War (1756-63) left the Indians without allies and American settlers all the more eager to take their land.

Migration west (1763-1850)

The founding of the American Republic initiated a period of great difficulties for Native American tribes east of the Mississippi. The army of the United States was sufficiently large and powerful that no confederation of Native American tribes could challenge it in open warfare. Native tribes were therefore left to the faint hope that the American government would protect their rights to the land from American settlers. Making matters more difficult was the tendency of individual Indian tribes to break their alliances with fellow tribes and sell their land to settlers for scandalously low prices. The efforts of leaders like Tecumseh, a Shawnee ruler in the Indiana territory, to push for unity in a desperate attempt to maintain Indian political and cultural independence failed at the hands of armed white settlers. Although President Washington and Jefferson each made efforts to carve out large territories for the Native Americans, these plans came to naught given the intense desire for land amongst white settlers. The **Louisiana Purchase** (1803), which doubled the size of the United States and extended its territories to the Rocky Mountains, offered a solution of sorts by providing additional land to settle displaced Indians. The **Lewis and Clark** exploration mission that mapped the territory (1803) benefitted from the aid of a Shoshoni Indian woman named **Sacagawea**.

Tribal leaders like Tecumseh realized that the central conflict between Native Americans and white Americans was rooted in the different relationship each group held with regard to the land. Tecumseh responded to General William Henry Harrison's entreaty to sell or concede land in the Indiana Territory in 1810 by interjecting: "Sell a country! Why not sell the air, the clouds, and the great sea, as well as the earth? Did not the Great Spirit make them all for the use of his children?" While the pastoral and agricultural system of the Native American tribes allowed for shared use of the land among multiple populations, the system of private property and constant improvement and exploitation of land by European Americans could tolerate only a single owner of a given property. Recognizing this fundamental difference between Native American and European cultures, and alarmed by the constant increase of European settlers, Tecumseh attempted to ally his Shawnee people with other tribes in order to build a confederation of sufficient strength to repel European settlers. In a speech before a council of Choctaws and Chickasaws in 1811, he pleaded for unity: "Sleep not longer, O Choctaws and Chickawsaws, in false security and delusive hopes. Our broad domains are fast escaping from our grasp. Every year our white intruders become more greedy, exacting, oppressive, and overbearing." Tecumseh used the opportunity afforded by the War of 1812 to ally with the British in the hopes of driving out American settlers. However, he was killed in 1813 in a battle against American forces in Canada. His lament for the defeat of his fellow tribes is poignant and foreshadows the treatment of tribes further to the west:

> Where today are the Pequot? Where are the Narragansett, the Mohican, the Pokanoket, and many other once powerful tribes of our people? They have vanished before the avarice and oppression of the white man, as snow before the summer sun (Brown 1970)

Other Indian tribes, recognizing the futility of armed conflict against the United States, sought to acculturate themselves to Western civilization, hoping that by doing so they would benefit economically and obtain greater political recognition. Five great tribes of the Southeast – Cherokee, Chickasaw, Choctaw, Creek, and Seminole – were called the "Five Civilized Tribes" due to their mastery of white institutions, including settled agriculture, republican government, and slavery. Unfortunately, racism and the desire for land trumped the efforts of the Indians to acclimatize to white society. The federal government, eager to help whites obtain land, used a combination of threats and trickery to take the land of the Five Civilized Tribes. The accession to the presidency of Andrew Jackson, who championed an aggressive anti-Indian policy, set the stage for the removal of the Indian tribes.

Jackson viewed the Indians as inferior peoples whose land could and should be taken. His Indian Removal policy was based on the idea that the states had power over the Indians, despite the recognition of the rights of Indian tribes as foreign nations under the federal Constitution. In 1830, Jackson's Indian Renewal bill overcame northern opposition and the Five Civilized Tribes were forced west to the Oklahoma territory. Jackson supported Georgia's decision to defy the Supreme Court's ruling **(Worcester v. Georgia, 1832)** that reiterated the Constitution's view that the states had no foreign policy power over the Indian tribes. The difficult and bitter migration of the Cherokee to Oklahoma is known as the **Trail of Tears**, as thousands of Indians died on the path.

Final Conquest (1865-1890)

The end of the Civil War freed American settlers to concentrate on the task of conquering the remaining areas of Indian settlement. The United States Army was often dragged into conflicts between the settlers and the Indians, and its power ensured that the Indians got the worse of these conflicts. Native American tribes in the west such as the Pueblos and Apaches were dispossessed of their land and reassigned to federal Indian reservations by the 1870s.

The miserable fate of the Indians in the West after the Civil War occurred despite efforts by American policymakers in the 1830s to avoid this outcome. The federal government provided Indians with treaties protecting their land rights in the west, and passed the **Indian Intercourse Act (1834)**, which banned white settlers from entering Indian territories without special permission. However, white settlement headed for California and Oregon broke the status quo, and as increasing numbers of white settlers poured into Indian Country, the once-firm rights of the Indians became steadily weaker.

In 1865, the Sioux tribe of Montana revolted, and scored some successes against the US Army. Peace was arranged in 1867, and Peace Commissioners empowered by Congress set up a system of small reservations which would be protected under federal authority. Native Americans in these reservations would have to learn how to farm and would be

Christianized and civilized by American missionaries and teachers. Any Native Americans refusing to be confined by the reservations would be treated as enemy soldiers.

The **Dawes Severalty Act**, passed by Congress in 1887, attempted to Americanize Indian tribes with a series of measures:
- *Land reform to encourage private ownership:* Native reservations were divided and individual plots assigned to families; the remainder of the land was held by the federal government and later sold to fund schools for Native Americans
- *Labor Instruction and Education*: The federal government sent instructors and teachers to demonstrate Western farming methods and teach Western subjects
- *Citizenship*: American Indians who complied with the Dawes Act were made American citizens

The Dawes Act was a miserable failure: white settlers were able to trick or cheat the Indians out of much of their land, and when the policy was finally reversed, and Indian land ownership was reconverted to communal status, Indian territories had shrunk from 138 million acres to just 48 million acres.

The population of Native Americans in the United States declined from 600,000 in 1800 to 250,000 in 1900.

Finding a place in the American state (1890-present)
Life for Native Americans began to improve, somewhat, in the twentieth century. The **Indian Reorganization Act (1934)** continued the reversal of the Dawes Act by trying to shore up Indian institutions of self-government and cultural unity. Nevertheless, most Indians remained and remain trapped in lives of poverty, crime and alcoholism.

Since the 1970s, Native Americans have attempted to improve their economic situation by utilizing their special legal status as tribes to specialize in activities restricted by the general laws of many states, most prominently gambling. The **American Indian Movement**, founded in the 1960s in Minnesota, attempted to use the methods and tools of the Civil Rights Movement to fight for redress of Native American grievances. Native Americans have also acted to protect the dignity of their cultural identity by challenging the use of Native tribes as mascots for sports teams.

American History Tutoring Guide Paul Pinto

QUESTIONS
Multiple choice

1. All of the following Native American individuals or tribes aided or allied with American colonists EXCEPT for
   A. Sacagawea
   B. Tasaquantum (Squanto)
   C. The Cherokee until the 1830s
   D. The Creek until the 1830s
   E. Metacom

2. Provisions of the Dawes Severalty Act (1887) included
   A. The division of tribal land into individual and family plots converted into private property
   B. The provision of American citizenship to those Native Americans willing to participate
   C. The provision of American education
   D. The teaching of American agricultural methods
   E. All of the above

3. The Dawes Severalty Act (1887)
   A. was a major success in converting Native Americans to a (white) American way of life
   B. created broad-based prosperity among Native American tribes
   C. preserved most of Native American land it sought to reorganize
   D. resulted in settlers paying Native Americans above-market prices for their land
   E. none of the above

4. What did the "Five Civilized Tribes" hope to gain by adopting white institutions such as farming, slave-owning, literacy and political democracy in the early nineteenth century?
   A. The economic strength to declare independence and ally with the British
   B. Legal and political recognition and incorporation in the American state on a relatively equal basis
   C. Positions in the United States Army
   D. Time to build up their strength to expel white Americans from Georgia and Florida
   E. All of the above

5. What policy did Andrew Jackson favor with regard to Indian tribes in Georgia in the 1830s?
   A. Alliance with the Indians against the French and Spanish
   B. Removal of the Indians to what is now Oklahoma
   C. Paying the Indians above-market prices to encourage them to sell their land
   D. Using the Supreme Court to deny the Indians legal title to the land
   E. Recruiting the Indians to serve in the United States Army

6. The Proclamation of 1763
   A. was designed by the British government to reduce conflict between American settlers and Native American tribes
   B. was designed to sell the Northwest Territory back to the French
   C. encouraged American settlers to move into Ohio River Valley and establish homesteads
   D. provided a place for Native American tribes in Canada
   E. all of the above

7. In the second half of the nineteenth century, the policies of the federal government with regard to Native American tribes included
   A. policies to Christianize and westernize Native Americans
   B. policies to push Native American tribes into specially reserved areas
   C. policies to use the United States Army to help white settlers obtain Native American land
   D. policies to teach Native Americans literacy and modern agricultural methods
   E. All of the above

8. What was the result of King Philip's War (1675-78)?
   A. Native American tribes were forced west by New England settlers
   B. Thousands of Native Americans were killed
   C. Hundreds of American colonists were killed
   D. The development of New England was set back by many years
   E. All of the above

9. Which of the following tribes came into conflict with settlers in Virginia in the 17th century?
   A. Wampanoag
   B. Pequot
   C. Miami
   D. Powhatan
   E. Creek

10. Why did Tecumseh seek to ally a confederation of tribes against American settlers?
    A. He believed that American settlers would eventually drive his people and other Native Americans out of their lands
    B. He realized that the thirst for land among settlers would outweigh possibilities for cooperation or compromise
    C. He did not believe that acculturation to European norms would spare the tribes
    D. He thought that Native American tribes could drive a harder bargain if they were unified and willing to fight
    E. All of the above

Essay Questions

1. How did the concept of private property shape relations between Native American tribes and settlers from 1620-1870?

2. Assimilation and acculturation are terms that can be used to describe efforts to spread Western culture and ways of life to the Native American peoples. Both voluntary assimilation as epitomized by the Five Civilized Tribes in the 1820s and forced assimilation through the Dawes Act in 1887 failed. Explain why assimilation failed in each case and what the overall failure means for relations between the United States and its Native American citizens.

Answers to Multiple Choice Questions
1. E
2. E
3. E
4. B
5. B
6. A
7. E
8. E
9. D
10. E

TOPIC 13: THE LABOR MOVEMENT

To labor simply means to work; in US history, it typically refers to those who make a living working for someone else. The history of labor follows the experiences of those working in plantations or factories owned by other individuals. From the founding to the Civil War, some laborers were paid for their wages, while others were forced to work permanently (slaves) or temporarily (indentured servants) for no compensation other than the food and shelter necessary to keep them alive.

Throughout American history, farm and factory owners have endeavored to obtain labor forces that were cheap, disciplined and flexible (meaning they could be easily hired or fired). The main issue for landowners in early colonial New England, Maryland and Virginia was a lack of people to work the abundant fields. The few Indians that could be coerced into labor often died from disease or fled west, leaving the labor gap unresolved. Puritans in New England, blessed with balanced family structures and a more healthful climate that enabled the stable growth of their population independent of immigration, solved the labor problem by (1) working themselves to the bone and (2) making their children work extremely hard on the farms from a young age (the famed **Puritan work ethic**). The profit-minded landowners of Maryland and Virginia, blessed and cursed with a climate highly conducive to the large-scale planting of tobacco, cotton and rice, but also less healthful (high mortality rates for laborers), selected a labor solution that relied on economics rather than religion. They initially tested **indentured servitude** as a way of building a suitable workforce. Indentured servants were (primarily) Europeans, mostly young men but also some young women (6 to 1 male to female ratio), who agreed to work for a fixed period (typically four to seven years) for no wages except for free passage across the Atlantic and food and shelter; upon completion of their terms, they could become free wage laborers. Studies estimate that around eighty percent of whites who traveled to Maryland and Virginia in the seventeenth century were classified as indentured servants(Divine et al. 2007: 72). Indentured servitude did not solve the labor problem in the South: white servants were too interested in obtaining their own land, and too apt to complain about the meager conditions of their servitude. **Bacon's Rebellion (1676)** was an uprising of indentured servants (mostly white but including some Africans) resentful of the policies of the planters and their political representative, Virginia governor William Berkeley. The uncertainty and political difficulty posed by indentured servitude thus pushed planters towards a labor force made up of African slaves.

The rise of the American industrial economy in the second half of the nineteenth century created a new category of workers – industrial laborers. These people, drawn from rural America and European countries like Ireland, Italy, Poland and Germany, came to the cities to work in the factories and attempt to build a better life for themselves and their families. They were often confronted by jobs that required long hours of labor in appalling conditions for low wages. One common response among people in this situation was to group together to collectively bargain for a better deal. However, the prevailing free-market ideology of the time viewed unions as a stepping-stone towards the communist overthrow of the capitalist system and factory owners suppressed unions violently, often with help from the government. Although in Europe the labor movement often led to socialism or communism, socialist parties in the United States struggled to gain more than a few percent of the vote, a result indicative of the consistent desire of the labor movement to remain within the mainstream of American democratic politics. The labor movement is the story of how industrial workers found a way to band together and win the sympathy of the American people and the support of at least one of the major political parties. By doing so, they won the right to form unions, collectively bargain, and earned for themselves a better quality of life. The main watershed for the labor movement was the New Deal; the passage of the National Labor Relations Act (commonly known as the Wagner Act) in 1935 legalized unions across many industries and provided a government body (the National Labor Relations Board) to help work out disagreements between labor and management. The dominance of American industry in the 1950s and 1960s led to a halcyon period for the labor movement, which enjoyed great negotiating power and provided major salary increases and benefit perks to its union members. The rise of strong industrial competitors in Germany and Japan and the stagnation of the American economy in the 1970s led to reforms that reduced the power of unions. Today, labor unions remain an important constituency of the Democratic party (including newer unions like the Service Employees International Union – SEIU), but they are far smaller and weaker than a half-century ago.

Labor Terminology
• **Closed shop**: a labor agreement where management agrees to hire union employees only, and all employees must be members of the union.
• **Open shop**: labor agreement where employees are not required to be members of nor financially support a union
• **Arbitration**: the process of settling labor disputes through a third party or a joint committee
• **Collective bargaining**: the process where employees band together to negotiate in order to obtain a better deal with management
• **Injunction**: court order preventing either labor or management from taking an action the court deems dangerous to public safety, welfare or property rights

Major Unions and their Constituencies

Union	Date Formed	Size	Leaders	Workers Represented	Political Views
Knights of Labor	1869	1882: 42,000 1885: 110,000 1886: 730,000 1890: 100,000	Uriah S. Stephens; Terence Powderly	All who "toiled", including women and blacks	Willing to work with owners that were not monopolists; reluctant to strike; desired eight-hour day/abolition of child labor
American Federation of Labor (AFL)	1886	1904: 1.7M 1940: 5.0M	Samuel Gompers	Craft Unions (skilled white male workers)	Conservative, focused on working within the system, excluded women, minorities
Industrial Workers of the World (IWW)	1905	1910: 100,000	Eugene V. Debs, Big Bill Haywood	All workers	Socialist, believed in the unity of the working class, workplace democracy, and abolition of wage system
Women's Trade	1903	1910: 50,000	Margaret	Female	Sought legislation to

Union League (WTUL)			Dreier Robins, Jane Addams	Workers	protect female workers
Brotherhood of Sleeping Car Porters	1925	15,000 in 1940	A. Philip Randolph	Railways	First union led by African-Americans to obtain recognition from the AFL
Congress of Industrial Organizations (CIO)	1935	5.0M by 1940	John L. Lewis	Steel, Mining, Autos	Used collective bargaining authority under the Wagner Act to organize steel and autos

Major Events in the Labor Movement

- **1869**: **Knights of Labor** forms the first broad-based labor organization, stressing the values of family, free labor, and a decent quality of life for workers. Advocated cooperation between management and labor.
- **1886**: **American Federation of Labor** founded to represent skilled workers (the 'aristocracy of laborers'); generally excluded women and African-Americans
- **1886**: Haymarket Riot in Chicago deals the Knights of Labor a serious blow after unaffiliated anarchists set off a bomb at a peaceful labor rally.
- **1892**: Homestead strike by the Amalgamated Association of Iron and Steel Workers (AA) against the Carnegie Steel Company. The AA was seeking to build on its relatively successful strike in 1889, but this time Carnegie used both private police agencies (the Pinkertons) and the state militia to break the strike. The result was a disaster for the AA union and a general setback for labor relations.
- **1894**: Pullman strike by the American Railway Union, led by Eugene V. Debs. The strike was broken up by federal troops who killed 13 strikers; Debs was sent to jail for his role in the strike
- **1902**: Teddy Roosevelt brokers a deal for striking Pennsylvania coal miners but does not recognize the legitimacy of their union, the United Mine Workers
- **1914**: The **Clayton Antitrust Act** exempts unions from being counted as unlawful combinations restraining trade
- **1917-18**: AFL cooperates with the War Labor Board to keep war production strong
- **1919**: United Mine Workers under John L. Lewis go on strike for increased wages. Attorney General A. Mitchell Palmer tries to break the strike on national security grounds, and by linking unions to communism he succeeds in getting Lewis to call off the strike
- **1935: Wagner Act** (aka National Labor Relations Act) provided federal support for union collective bargaining. Outlawed union-breaking tactics and articulated a democratic principle giving negotiating power to the union as long as it could get 50% of the workers to sign up
- **1938: Fair Labor Standards Act** established a national minimum wage and maximum work hours (exempts industries like farmworkers)
- **1947: Taft-Hartley Act** bans the closed shop for unions, drastically weakening union bargaining power. Also allowed individual states to pass "right-to-work" laws that forbade unions to require that all workers join or financially support the union
- **1952**: United Steelworkers of America go on strike against US Steel and other major steel producers. The Truman administration, in desperate need of steel due to the Korean War, nationalizes the industry to maintain production, a decision which is subsequently reversed by the Supreme Court
- **1963: Equal Pay Act**. Mandates equal pay for equal work performed.

American History Tutoring Guide Paul Pinto

QUESTIONS
Multiple Choice

1. "Labor is prior to, and independent of, capital. Capital is only the fruit of labor, and could never have existed if labor had not first existed. Labor is the superior of capital, and deserves much the higher consideration."
    -- Abraham Lincoln, Annual Message to Congress, 3 Dec. 1861

    Which of the following individuals would agree with Lincoln's sentiment?
    A. George Pullman
    B. Andrew Mellon
    C. John L. Lewis
    D. John D. Rockefeller
    E. Andrew Carnegie

2. All of the following union leaders would have been satisfied with union recognition, fewer working hours, better pay, and improved working conditions EXCEPT for
    A. A. Philip Randolph
    B. Samuel Gompers
    C. Uriah S. Stephens
    D. Eugene V. Debs
    E. Terence Powderly

3. The National Labor Relations Act, commonly known as the Wagner Act, authorizes or provides which of the following?
    A. Federal protection for the right of employees to bargain collectively through unions
    B. The creation of a federal National Labor Relations Board to arbitrate disputes between labor and management
    C. A ban against violent strike-breaking
    D. Support for a democratic principle of union organization in which only the body that attracts majority support of employees has the legal right to bargain with employers
    E. All of the above

4. All of the following laws advanced the cause of unions EXCEPT
    A. Wagner Act
    B. Clayton Antitrust Act
    C. Fair Labor Standards Act
    D. Taft-Hartley Act
    E. Equal Pay Act

5. Which of the following events or factors resulted in rising industrial wages?
    A. The Panic of 1893
    B. Immigration from Southern and Eastern Europe
    C. Industrial competition from Europe
    D. The Great Depression
    E. World War II

6. Early applications of the Sherman Antitrust Act tended to levy cases against
   A. Urban machines like Tammany Hall
   B. The Standard Oil Company
   C. Electrical utilities
   D. Railways
   E. Labor unions

7. Congress, the Supreme Court and various presidential administrations applied which of the following arguments to limit union mobilization from 1865-1932?
   A. Union bargaining violated the property relation between owner and worker
   B. Unions were associated with communism
   C. Unions were a threat to competition
   D. Unions were associated with socialism
   E. All of the above

8. The Gospel of Wealth preached
   A. Support for unions to bargain collectively
   B. The obligation of capitalists to provide philanthropy and support for society
   C. Profit-sharing with workers
   D. The creation of labor union councils to work with corporate boards of directors
   E. Support for a wealth tax

9. The passage of right to work laws permitted by the Taft-Hartley Act in 1947
   A. eliminated the closed shop under which all workers were required to sign up with a single union
   B. created an injunction to ban collective bargaining in a range of industries
   C. lowered the barriers to union organizing
   D. enabled employers to easily send manufacturing jobs overseas
   E. all of the above

10. Since the 1970s
    A. Labor unions have continued to grow as a percentage of the economy
    B. Private sector labor unions have drastically shrunk as a percentage of the economy
    C. Labor unions have gained increasing political power within the Democratic Party
    D. Labor unions have become increasingly intransigent towards management
    E. All of the above

Essay Questions
1. What strategies did business owners and their political allies use to delegitimize unions from the 1880s to the 1930s? How did unions respond to these attacks?

2. How did each of the following presidents advance the cause of labor rights?
   A. Theodore Roosevelt
   B. Woodrow Wilson
   C. Franklin Roosevelt

Answers to Multiple Choice Questions
1. C
2. D
3. E
4. D
5. E
6. E
7. E
8. B
9. A
10. B

American History Tutoring Guide   Paul Pinto

TOPIC 14: IMMIGRATION

The history of immigration to the United States is in many ways the history of the United States itself. From Plymouth Rock to Ellis Island, immigration has transformed, enriched, and complicated American society and politics. The country has experienced waves of immigration from virtually every country on earth, as English, Irish, Scottish and Dutch settlers were joined by people of African, German, Italian, Polish, Chinese, Japanese, and Latin American heritage, to name only some of the largest immigrant groups.

Immigration has always been closely connected to issues of culture. In the United States, the generally dominant culture of Anglo-Saxon Protestantism, or English-speaking people who adhere to the Protestant faith, often persecuted or sought to marginalize groups who did not share its language, religion or customs. Northern European Protestants such as the Dutch in New York or Germans in Pennsylvania and Wisconsin were generally able to integrate successfully into American social and political life. Irish immigrants generally faced quite a lot of prejudice, as did their fellow Catholic Italian and Polish brethren, but all three of these groups were allowed despite significant discrimination to establish positions of social and political strength in the form of urban ethnic enclaves, and in time were permitted to integrate fully into American life. The "**Know-Nothing" or American Party** of the 1840-50s, which ran on a primary plank of lengthening the period of naturalization of Catholic immigrants, so as to prevent them from voting in the short term, capitalized on the decline of the Whig party to win a number of major elections, and reached a membership of around one million by 1854. The party then collapsed in 1856, and most of its votes were swept up by the new Republican Party, which took a more liberal view of immigration.

Immigration to the United States in the nineteenth century was fueled by improvements in transportation, the availability of cheap or even free land, a strong economy that generated millions of new jobs, and the opportunity of making a better life for one's children. The promise of becoming an American citizen and participating in its democracy was also a significant benefit for many if not most immigrants. Finally, political turmoil and agricultural disasters such as the Irish potato famine often pushed immigrants to the United States.

In 1850, the US Census for the first time included a question about place of birth, which allowed census officials to track the growth of the foreign-born population. The chart below presents the foreign-born population from 1850-2010, along with prominent immigrant groups and legislation affecting immigration:

Foreign-Born Population in the United States, 1850-2010 (millions)

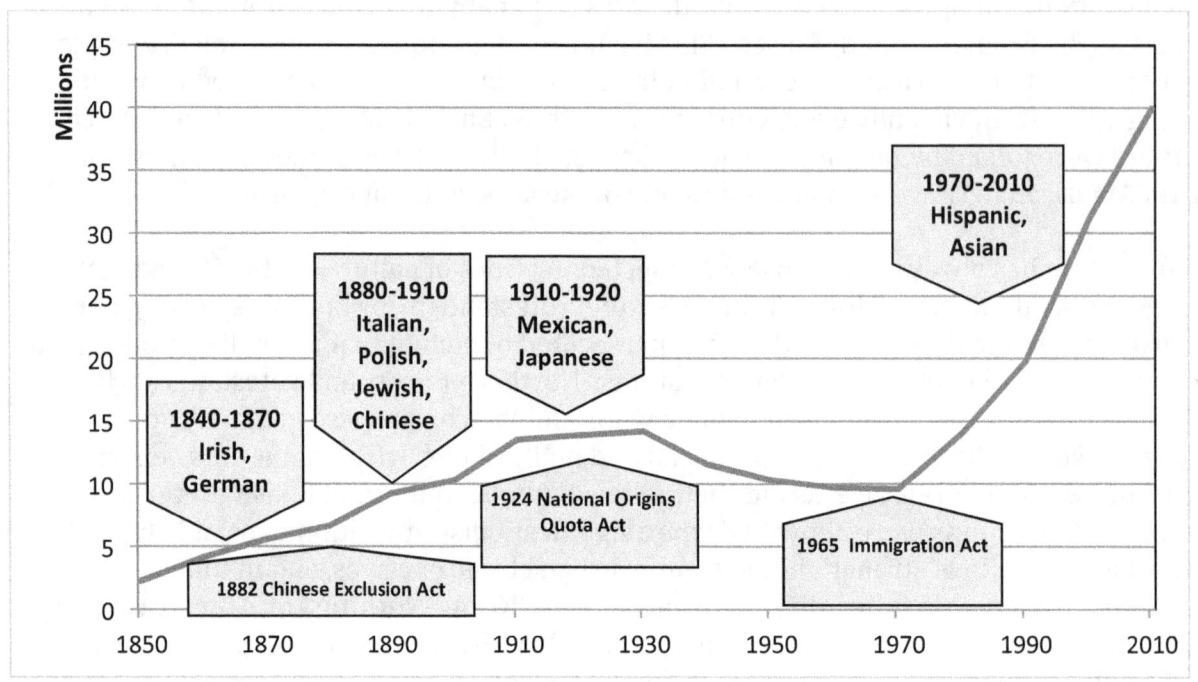

Source: US Census Bureau

Immigrants as a % of Total Population:

10%   14%   15%   15%   12%   7%   5%   8%   13%

Heavy immigration from Europe from 1850-1910 produced a rise in the foreign-born population from 2.2 to 13.5 million, or from 10 to 15% of the total population. Immigrants during this period were drawn mostly from Europe, with German and Irish immigrants joined by the end of the century by Italians, Poles, and Jews. The rise of non-European immigration in the form of Chinese, Japanese, and Mexican immigrants set of a nativist backlash that exceeded that of the 1850s. The arrival of hundreds of thousands of Chinese laborers for work on the railroads in the 1880s precipitated the **Chinese Exclusion Act (1882)**, a law that prohibited Chinese workers for a decade; this Act was subsequently renewed until the **1924 National Origins Quota Act,** which capped European immigration to 150,000 people per year and banned all immigration from Asia. The act was motivated by more than just anti-Asian animus: it reserved most of the European immigration places to British, Irish, German and Scandinavian immigrants, thereby screening out southern and eastern Europeans. As the chart shows, the foreign-born population declined precipitously after the Quota Act's passage, both in absolute (from 14.2 million people in 1930 to 9.7 million in 1960) and proportional (from 12% in 1930 to just 5% of the nation's total population) terms. It is worth noting that the Quota Act passed with large majorities in both houses of Congress and was enthusiastically signed by President Coolidge.

In the 1930s, working-class European immigrants in large cities (Poles, Yugoslavs, Italians, Jews, and more) began voting for the Democratic party in large numbers, and became a key element in the New Deal coalition, a 'big tent coalition' that also included African-Americans, urban progressive intellectuals, labor unions, city machines, farmers, and white Southerners.

In 1965, the Johnson administration revolutionized the immigration system without fully intending to. The administration kept the quota system that limited immigration by region, but opened it up to Asia, Africa, and Latin America. The result was a major transformation in the ethnic and racial composition of the American population, as a table of the foreign-born population of the United States in 2010 demonstrates:

Foreign-Born Population in the United States by Region of Birth, 2010 (millions)

Region	Foreign-Born Population	%
Latin America	21.2	53%
Asia	11.3	28%
Europe	4.8	12%
Africa	1.6	4%
Other	1.0	3%
Total	40.0	100%

The rapid growth of the foreign-born population through immigration has resulted in a steady transformation of the ethnic and racial composition of the United States; today, non-white members of the population represent about one hundred million people, or one-third of the overall population.

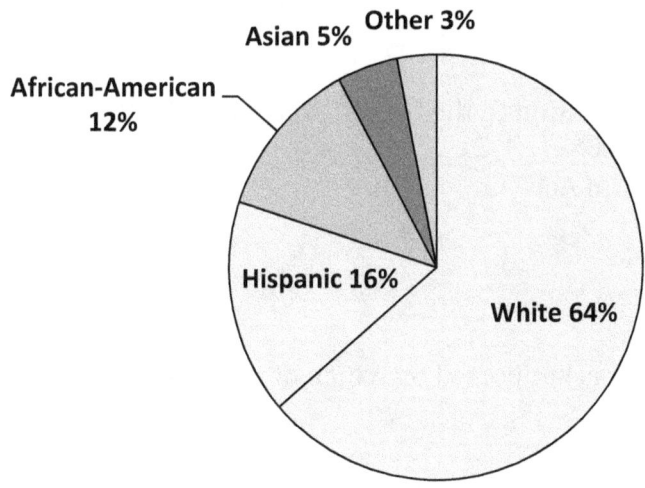

Population of the United States by Race/Ethnicity, 2010
(Total Population = 314 million people)

QUESTIONS
Multiple Choice

1. The region which has supplied the most immigrants to the United States since 1965 is
   A. Africa
   B. Asia
   C. Latin America
   D. Europe
   E. The Pacific Islands

2. Which ethnic or racial group was the first to be explicitly banned from immigration to the United States by law?
   A. Japanese
   B. Chinese
   C. Italian
   D. Russian
   E. Filipino

3. Immigration from Southern and Eastern Europe peaked during which period?
   A. 1820-1850
   B. 1850-1880
   C. 1880-1910
   D. 1930-1950
   E. 1950-1965

4. All of the following limited immigration to the United States EXCEPT?
   A. The 1924 National Origins Act
   B. The 1965 Immigration Reform Act
   C. The Chinese Exclusion Act
   D. World War II
   E. The Great Depression

5. The 1924 National Origins Act was supported by which of the following groups?
   A. The Ku Klux Klan
   B. A majority of Americans
   C. Those favoring the new "science" of eugenics
   D. Anti-Semites
   E. All of the above

6. The proportion of the foreign-born as a percentage of the overall US population peaked during which of the following periods?
   A. 1830-1850
   B. 1850-1870
   C. 1870-1890
   D. 1890-1910
   E. 1910-1930

7. The Know-Nothing Party achieved short-lived but massive levels of support in the 1850s by running on a platform of
   A. Temperance
   B. Evangelicalism
   C. Anti-immigration
   D. Progressive Reform
   E. Abolitionism

8. All of the following factors encouraged immigration to the United States except?
   A. Poor economic conditions in Europe
   B. Rapid economic growth in the United States
   C. The comparative availability of land in the United States
   D. The reputation of the United States as an opportunity society
   E. The passage of laws based on nativist principles

9. Immigrants to the United States in the nineteenth century typically migrated to
   A. Economic centers
   B. Large metropolitan areas
   C. Boomtowns in the West
   D. Places where they had friends or family
   E. Rural areas in search of land

10. Which of the following immigrant groups was subsequently persecuted by the government during World War II?
    A. Latin Americans
    B. German Americans
    C. Italian Americans
    D. Japanese Americans
    E. Chinese Americans

Essay Questions
1. Compare and contrast social, economic and political experiences of THREE of the following immigrant groups in the United States:
   A. Irish
   B. Italian
   C. Jewish
   D. Chinese
   E. Japanese

2. Immigrants from Europe were joined in American cities by African-Americans from the South. Compare and contrast the treatment of these two groups from 1880 to 1960.

Answers to Multiple Choice Questions
1. C
2. B
3. C
4. B
5. E
6. D
7. C
8. E
9. D
10. D

American History Tutoring Guide   Paul Pinto

TOPIC 15: THE PROGRESSIVE MOVEMENT

The Progressive Movement was a political movement from 1880-1920 that sought to improve the lives and opportunities of the working poor whose labor fueled the Industrial Revolution. Drawing upon their own northern middle-class social and religious values, Progressive Reformers sought to use education, bureaucratic organization and the power of modern government to remake American democracy and society for the Industrial Age. The movement achieved a great deal, including:

- A **federal income tax (Sixteenth Amendment, 1913)** that offered a new source of revenue (and thus power) to the federal government and inaugurated the principle of progressive taxation (charging higher tax rates for higher incomes);
- The **direct election of senators (Seventeenth Amendment, 1913)**, which offered the promise of greater democratic (and less corporate) control over Congress;
- **Prohibition (Eighteenth Amendment, 1919)**; the ill-fated "Noble Experiment" that banned the production and sale of alcohol for non-medicinal purposes and provided the federal government with powerful enforcement powers through the Volstead Act.
- Women's **right to vote (Nineteenth Amendment, 1920)**
- Federal regulatory agencies to police large corporations and monopolies
- Regulations to protect the health and safety of consumers
- A conservation movement to create and protect national forests and parks

Like many political movements, the Progressive movement contained notable flaws, among them a disregard approaching disdain for the values of the working-class people Progressives aimed to uplift; an unwillingness to challenge racial policies limiting the opportunities of African-Americans; and a belief bordering on certainty in the power of technocratic government to solve any and all social problems. An example of the overreach of the Progressive Movement is **Prohibition**, which confused the noble aim of fighting alcohol abuse in working or middle class families with the impractical solution of a blanket federal ban on the sale or manufacture of alcohol. The result was mass noncompliance, leading to the growth of organized crime, an upsurge in violence and repeal in 1933.

Progressive reformers recognized that the industrial economy had thrown American democracy out of kilter by concentrating a great deal of wealth among capitalists, who happily proceeded to buy off the political classes of the nation in order to stave off laws to regulate industrial competition, factory conditions, female and child labor, and union organization. In addition, industrial development and immigration had rapidly outstripped the ability of governments to cope in urban areas. Workers, especially recent migrants, were crammed by the thousands into tenement housing blocks; lack of proper sewage and bathroom facilities in these blocks led to unsanitary conditions, and industrial pollution blighted the city environment. Political bosses in cities ran voting machines that traded jobs and aid to immigrants and the poor in return for votes. To address the excesses of industrialism and urbanization, Progressive reformers aimed to transform both government and society. Transforming government required laws to democratize the vote, regulate business, protect workers, mothers, children and consumers and conserve the environment. Transforming society included settlement houses for the poor, better schools to educate immigrants, family planning for women, the temperance (anti-alcohol) movement, and the growth of churches in the cities.

American History Tutoring Guide Paul Pinto

Social, Political and Economic Problems:

| Urban overcrowding | Political corruption | Unregulated Business | Social Ills | Environmental Degradation |

Progressive Solutions:

Settlement Houses	Experts & Democratizing the Vote	Business Regulation	Moral Reformation	Conservation
• Reformers create settlement houses that provided better living conditions, education and culture to the urban poor • Hundreds of such houses founded by 1910 • Well-known houses include Jane Addams's **Hull House** in Chicago (1889) and Lillian Wald's Henry Street Settlement in New York (1903)	• City reformers create boards of noncorrupt experts to improve taxes, voting, water and sewage • Urban reform leagues to maintain progressive momentum • Progressives champion secret ballot to break power of machines; • Direct primary elections, to let the people choose candidates • **17th Amendment** provides for direct election of Senators (1913) • **19th** provides women right to vote (1920) • Use of referendums and recall elections	• Muckraking journalists call for action to monitor and regulate business • Upton Sinclair's *The Jungle* calls attention to filth in meat-packing plants (1906) • Creation of the Food & Drug Administration (FDA) to monitor safety and efficacy (1906) • Renewed emphasis on regulating trusts and big businesses: Clayton Antitrust Act (1914) • 16th Amendment imposes federal income tax on wealthy	• Alcohol abuse, particularly in urban areas, results in high levels of spousal and child abuse • Cities also plagued by problems such as prostitution, crime and lack of public health systems • Women's Christian Temperance Union (1874) led by Annie Wittenmyer and Frances Willard worked against alcohol and other social problems • 18th Amendment bans sale and consumption of alcohol • WCTU sets up Ellis Island office for immigrants	• Industrial development and commercial farming result in the destruction of forests on the East Coast and in the Midwest • Rise of ecology as a science results in the creation of Forestry Schools and a national Forest Service • Roosevelt and Forest Service chief Gifford Pinchot create the first national conservation policy • Increase acres under conservation from 45M to 195M

Concluding Thoughts

The Progressive Movement was very much a reformist rather than a transformative or revolutionary movement. It set out to improve and further develop American democracy and society without changing its fundamental principles, culture, or underlying economic system. An illustration of the nonrevolutionary tendency of the Progressive Movement is the campaign for female suffrage. Women like Jane Addams or Frances Willard were very much independent political actors and leaders, using their education and leadership abilities to improve society in much the same way as male reformers. Yet Addams and Willard did not defend their social activism as rooted in their skills or intellect but rather as an extension of their particular female expertise in the home and family. They justified their social activism as an extension of the female sphere, thereby preserving the political and economic realm for men. In the same way, female suffragettes from 1910-1920 no longer argued that they deserved the vote as a matter of natural right or basic equality. They rather argued that their particular moral sensibilities as wives and mothers commended them as good candidates for the vote; female suffrage, so the argument went, would add a much-needed moral and familial dimension to American politics. This helps to explain why the Nineteenth Amendment did not by itself lead to revolutionary changes in the way women worked, ran the household, raised children, or participated in politics.

The Progressive Movement provided a political legacy and framework for other social and political movements to follow and fulfill. For example, Franklin Roosevelt's desire to save rather than abolish capitalism was a faithful extension of the Progressive vision. Overall, the Progressive Movement demonstrated that the American system could respond to major socioeconomic changes in innovative and useful ways and taught that modernization was something the American government, led by wise federal officials, should embrace.

American History Tutoring Guide Paul Pinto

QUESTIONS
Multiple Choice

1. All of the following correctly match a Progressive-era problem to a Progressive solution EXCEPT
   A. Gilded Age income inequality: Sixteenth Amendment
   B. Lack of women's voices in public affairs: Nineteenth Amendment
   C. Corruption in election of US Senators by state legislatures: Seventeenth Amendment
   D. Chronic alcoholism and alcohol abuse: Eighteenth Amendment
   E. Suppression of labor unions: Wagner Act

2. Women played an important role in Progressive politics in all of the following areas EXCEPT:
   A. Settlement houses in cities
   B. Women's suffrage
   C. Temperance
   D. Muckraking journalism
   E. Banking reform

3. Each of these muckraking journalistic books is correctly aligned with its author EXCEPT
   A. *History of the Standard Oil Company* – Ida Tarbell
   B. *The Shame of the Cities* – Lincoln Steffens
   C. *The Jungle* – Sinclair Lewis
   D. *How the Other Half Lives* – Jacob Riis
   E. All of the above are correct

4. The most successful argument offered by Progressive women reformers seeking to win the vote was that
   A. Women deserved the vote as a matter of natural law
   B. Women possessed equal capacities with men in all respects
   C. Women possessed special insights into improving public affairs through their roles as wives, mothers and nurturers
   D. The Industrial Revolution had enabled women to work in the same managerial and professional roles as men
   E. All of the above

5. The Progressive movement's effect in American politics was
   A. Primarily restricted to the Republican party
   B. Primarily restricted to the Democratic party
   C. Primarily restricted to the Progressive party
   D. Primarily restricted to the Socialist party
   E. Robust across a number of parties and presidents

6. Theodore Roosevelt made which of the following contributions to Progressive politics?
    A. The conservation of millions of acres of land as national parks and forests
    B. The passage of the Pure Food and Drug Act
    C. Enforcing the Sherman Anti-trust act
    D. Helping to negotiate a settlement between mine owners and the United Mine Workers
    E. All of the above

7. Jane Addams's Hull House in Chicago was designed to do which of the following?
    A. Provide low-cost housing and moral instruction to members of the urban poor
    B. Create a new political machine in Chicago for women voters
    C. Provide a finishing school for young women seeking to enter the University of Chicago
    D. Provide training and jobs in the professional sector for women
    E. All of the above

8. The Progressives aimed to improve American life in all of the following sectors EXCEPT
    A. Consumer safety
    B. Conservation
    C. Urban life
    D. Civil rights
    E. Women's rights

9. All of the following are Progressive measures EXCEPT
    A. The Volstead Act
    B. The Agricultural Adjustment Act
    C. The Clayton Act
    D. The Pure Food and Drug Act
    E. The Seventeenth Amendment

10. The Progressive Movement was inspired by all of the following ideologies EXCEPT
    A. Women's rights
    B. The Social Gospel
    C. Middle-class propriety
    D. Communism
    E. The application of science to social problems

Essay Questions
1. In what ways did the Progressive movement transform the role and responsibilities of the federal government? Discuss, using at least TWO of the following categories:
   A. Social issues such as temperance
   B. Industrial regulation
   C. Corruption and political patronage in the cities
   D. Economic inequality

2. What role did muckraking journalists play in generating political awareness of and support for Progressive initiatives?

3. How did the Progressive movement generate opportunities for women to hold positions of public leadership?

Answers to Multiple Choice Questions
1. E
2. E
3. C
4. C
5. E
6. E
7. A
8. D
9. B
10. D

American History Tutoring Guide Paul Pinto

TOPIC 16: RELIGION IN AMERICAN HISTORY

Overview

Religion, specifically the Protestant religion, has fundamentally shaped the culture, work ethic, social institutions and political traditions of the United States. Puritanism provided America with a multifaceted founding culture in New England that blended faith and individualism with voluntarism and democracy. During the eighteenth century, led by preachers such as the great Jonathan Edwards, Puritan thinkers transcended their narrow concern with those that had already been saved (the elect) and turned their faith outward in a great evangelical effort to bring the message of salvation to all Americans. This Great Awakening was only the first of a number of broad religious campaigns led by Puritans (aka Congregationalists), Methodists, Baptists and many other Protestant denominations. The transformations wrought by these religious campaigns frequently led to major social and political changes. Yet Protestantism's status as the dominant religion in America certainly did not mean that it calmly presided over the development of American history. Protestant denominations competed vigorously against one another for converts; the religion was forced to accommodate the presence of a broad range of other faiths, including Catholicism, Native American religions, Judaism and more; and the claims of the faith were challenged first by Enlightenment philosophy and later by the rise of modern science.

Religion in American history has played a particularly prominent role in a number of historical events or processes, including:
- Puritan New England
- Evangelical Protestantism, the Great Awakenings and the social reform movements
- Conflict over religious pluralism in the 19th century
- The battle between religion and science
- The Civil Rights Movement
- The rise of the Religious Right in the 1970s

A way to connect all these movements together is to root them in what scholars have called a Protestant *theory of agency*.[10] An *agent* is a representative of a client whom we call the *principal*. Agents are dedicated to fulfilling the commands laid upon them by their principal. Protestants, in this view, consider themselves to be agents of God (the ultimate principal!), and as such feel responsible for reconstructing human institutions so as to be in accordance with God's will. Many American Protestants believed that God had charged them with a mandate to change the world in order to meet the requirements of their faith. This leads us to expect that periods of religious fervor will be associated with Protestant activism in politics and society, a pattern that has persisted with impressive regularity throughout American history.

Puritan New England

To understand Puritan society, it is necessary to outline the basic religious principles of the faith:

---

[10] Richard Block, *A Nation of Agents*.

Puritan Beliefs and Social Practices

Religious Principle	Explanation	Social Implications
• *Individual Salvation through faith alone*	• Only God has the power to provide salvation → no human priest has the power to intercede on behalf of sinners → everyone therefore has to be his or her own priest, responsible for his or her own soul	• Great importance placed on individual responsibility and conscience; complete rejection of the Catholic church and its hierarchy of priests and bishops
• *Voluntary communities of faith*	• The only way that individuals sincerely striving for salvation can succeed is to be surrounded by those equally sincere about their faith	• 'Pure' churches must be made up solely of those voluntarily committed to the faith → separation from Church of England → establishment of New England
• *The Bible as the main authority*	• Since the universal church and its priests can no longer be trusted (it must contain sinners, because the world contains sinners), Scripture becomes the sole authority to guide the path to salvation	• Every true Puritan must learn how to read and think about the Bible for himself or herself in order to work out their own salvation → universal literacy
• *Predestination: only some are chosen by God*	• The most difficult belief in Puritanism: the idea that only a small minority of people are designated for salvation by God (the elect). Puritans conceded that only God knows who will be saved, but they also believed that success in this life was a marker of elect status	• Puritans had to work hard and pray hard; slackness of effort and lack of worldly success was a dreaded sign that they were not one of the elect

The religious beliefs of the Puritan faith, taken together, help to explain why so many Puritans risked death, disgrace and dispossession to start a new life in what they considered the wilderness of New England. The very act of sailing three thousand miles away from civilized society symbolized the value they placed on the opportunity to create an unspoiled religious community of the faithful. Puritans strongly believed in a voluntary church of the religiously committed, and required each individual believer to bear testament to his or her personal experience of salvation as a condition of gaining church membership. Because all church members shared the exalted status of being part of God's elect (i.e., those saved by God), Puritan churches governed themselves democratically, with all church members having a say in key decisions such as the election of their minister, the election of church governing board members, and whether or not to admit candidates to church membership. Puritanism's democratic principles extended through the church into the town and the colony at large. Arrivals to Plymouth plantation famously pledged themselves to the **Mayflower Compact (1620)**, promising to govern themselves democratically. Puritan town communities were based on an egalitarian distribution of the land, and citizenship and the right to vote in the General Court (legislature) of the colony were based on church membership. Democracy in Puritan communities worked well because these communities boasted an average level of education superior to that found anywhere in the world. The mandate to read and understand the Bible pushed even the poorest of Puritans to master literacy, and eventually resulted in near universal literacy among adult members of the community, an extraordinary social achievement. In terms of economic life, the Puritan conscience, in which God was always watching, drove New Englanders to work as hard as possible. Success in worldly life, although it risked the danger of corruption by money or power, was deemed a sign of membership of the elect. By the mid-eighteenth century, Puritans in New England had created a successful farming, shipping and fishing economy, which eventually grew into a global center of education, finance and trade. This work ethic became known as the Puritan work ethic, later broadened to the Protestant work ethic and finally the American work ethic.

Challenges to the Puritan way of life emerged almost immediately. Although the Puritans sought to recruit only true believers, some of the travelers joining in the Great Migration of the seventeenth century from England to New England were not particularly interested in the great matters of faith that enthralled the Puritan mind. These settlers were more interested in the availability of arable land, and many of them left coastal Puritan communities to go further inland and find land to cultivate. In addition, the profound rigor of Puritanism created internal difficulties, none more challenging than what to do about the salvation potential of the second and third generation of Puritan children. The problem, of course, was that only God determined who could be saved, and only those who had undergone a personal saving experience from God were deemed worthy of becoming church members. Merely being the child of a church member could not, on its own, guarantee that one would be saved. Faced with the agony of deciding between their faith and their children, Puritan churchmen developed a compromise known as the **Halfway Covenant (1662)**, which allowed children of church members to join the church without the privileges of full membership. Yet another challenge to the stability of Puritan communities was the battle over the social status of women. The religious logic of Puritanism suggested that both men and women should be equally deserving of God's grace. Indeed, Protestant communities that pushed the logic of Puritanism even further than the Puritans, such as the Quakers, came to practice gender equality. The Puritans of New England, however, although genuinely torn about the issue, retained the patriarchal or male-dominated worldview of their fathers. The issue was put to the test by **Anne Hutchinson**, a well-educated Puritan woman in Massachusetts who was skilled in Biblical interpretation to the point that she would conduct her own classes in religious instruction. These classes attracted many of the women of the colony, who looked to Hutchinson rather than the (male) minister for spiritual and social guidance. This threatened the local religious and political power structure, and the Governor of the colony, William Bradford, had Hutchinson placed on trial. During the trial, Hutchinson claimed that she had received a direct religious revelation from God, which allowed the judges and Bradford to exile her to Rhode Island. Hutchinson's belief that she had received a personal revelation is an extreme form of **antinomianism**, or the belief that all individuals, male or female, are equally capable of receiving God's grace, even in the form of a new religious revelation or prophecy. The last challenge to the Puritan way of life was the one that eventually overturned Puritanism as a way of life: the challenge of **religious toleration**. Puritan leaders in New England faced a paradox that they did not face in England: they strongly proclaimed the importance of a church of voluntary believers, since voluntarism was the only route to sincerity in matters of faith. Yet they also exercised political control in colonies like Massachusetts, and used that control to suppress other faiths, going as far as to hang Quakers who dared to openly practice their religion. Roger Williams, despite being an extremely staunch Puritan, was exiled from Massachusetts for his opinion that other religions had the right to profess their faith openly. Williams founded Providence colony in what became Rhode Island as a haven for those with unorthodox religious beliefs (1636). Williams was an exceptional man who managed to combine extremely robust religious faith with understanding and compassion for those who did not share his faith. He advocated fair dealing with the local Native American tribes in Providence, paying them full value for their land; he worked to ban slavery in the colony; and he remained committed to his belief in religious tolerance to the end of this long life. Williams demonstrated that it was possible to successfully run a colony with no established church.

Evangelical Protestantism, the Great Awakenings and the reform movements
The Protestant idea of **predestination**, or the marking out by God of the elect (those granted access to heaven) from everyone else (damned to hell), greatly inhibited Protestant missionary work, for it seemed to Protestants the will of God that only a few were blessed with their faith. However, the survival and success of Protestantism in northern Europe and north America led to a rethinking of predestination. Many Protestant preachers began to spread the alternative idea that God really wanted everyone to be saved. These preachers, who included the Englishmen George Whitefield and John Wesley, and the American Congregationalist Jonathan Edwards, traveled through the American colonies spreading the Gospel in revival meetings. They crossed denominational boundaries, preaching to Congregationalists (Puritans), Methodists, Presbyterians, Baptists and more. This mid-18th century revival is known as the **Great Awakening (1740s-1770s)**. The Great Awakening provided a template for religious revival led by preachers seeking to provide salvation, a template that was to be used over and over in American history. As preachers spread Protestantism, they also spread its social practices: voluntary church organization, democratic church government, including the election of the minister, the organization of the church around a covenant or contract, the cultivation of literacy amongst church members, and more. The Great Awakening thus further democratized American society. Many of those who supported the American Revolution did so because of their faith in democracy and self-government from their experiences in church. Historians also generally consider the Great Awakening as a nation-building event, because it easily crossed colonial boundaries with a common message and culture.

The evangelical spirit, in addition to favoring democracy, strongly opposed the institution of slavery. The Quakers, who practiced perhaps the most undiluted form of Protestantism, took the lead in opposing slavery. It is no surprise that those states in which evangelical Protestantism was at its strongest – New England and Pennsylvania – took the lead in abolishing slavery in their state constitutions. It should be noted, however, that even evangelicals generally failed to establish equitable relationships with freed African-Americans, who were often only offered subordinate positions in white churches. Some African-Americans, like Richard Allen in Philadelphia, responded by forming their own democratically governed churches (Allen founded the African Methodist Episcopal Church in 1814).

If the First Great Awakening contributed to the success of the American Revolution, the **Second Great Awakening** (1800-1840s) led to reform movements focused on moral revival, abolition, temperance (anti-drinking), increased religious piety and missionary work. These reform movements were characterized by their voluntary nature: ordinary people came together in self-governing associations whose work they funded themselves. Here are some of the societies that emerged from the Second Great Awakening (most founded from 1800-1840s).

Society	Leader	Purpose
American Bible Society	• Revered Samuel John Mills	• Printed and distributed hundreds of thousands of Bibles, primarily for the unchurched West
American Tract Society	• Various ministers	• Printed religious pamphlets and books for unchurched groups like sailors and native Americans
American Temperance Society	• Rev. Lyman Beecher and other ministers	• Believed that alcohol was a great evil in that it lead to lust and lack of self-discipline; worked to cut down drinking amongst members of the poor; 5,000 local branches by 1834
American Board of Commissioners for Foreign Missions	• Rufus Anderson; Congregationalist ministers	• Recruited and sent out missionaries overseas, to India, Africa and Asia
American Home Mission	• Baptist ministers	• Preaching and church-building on the American frontier

Evangelicals also played a major, if not always dominant, role in the following societies:

Society	Leader	Purpose
American Anti-Slavery Society	• William Lloyd Garrison	• Abolition of slavery
Women's Rights Movement	• Lucretia Mott (Quaker) • Elizabeth Cady Stanton	• Rights of women to vote and retain their property and legal rights when married

Conflict over religious pluralism in the 19th century
The fervent beliefs of Protestant evangelicals often resulted in the persecution of other religions. The Church of Jesus Christ of Latter-day Saints, better known as the Mormon Church, was founded by Joseph Smith in upstate New York in 1830. Smith believed that he

had received a revelation from an angel of God, who provided him with a new Biblical text (the Book of Mormon). He intended to use this text to create a new faith that combined Christianity with new elements. Although Mormons practiced the same kind of voluntary self-reliance and communal spirit as other Protestant denominations, their new beliefs and especially their practice of polygamy (men taking multiple wives) resulted in major tension with neighboring Christians. Smith was murdered in Illinois in 1844, which convinced other Mormons that they needed land of their own for security and religious freedom. Smith's successor Brigham Young led the people to what is now Utah, where Mormons built up what was virtually an independent nation. Indeed, in 1857 the United States Army was sent to Utah to discipline the Mormons and force them to renounce polygamy; fortunately for both sides, bad weather prevented the army from reaching its destination in time, and the dispute was settled without violence. In 1892, Utah joined the union as a state, on condition that the Mormon Church abandon the practice of polygamy (the Church accepted).

The arrival of significant numbers of German and Irish Catholics in the 1840s created a backlash amongst many Protestant evangelicals, who worried that the immigrants would expand the influence of the Catholic Church in America. These fears grew in the latter part of the 19th century, as Irish immigration was accompanied by Italian and Polish immigration, further increasing the number of Catholics in the United States. Protestant fears of Catholics contributed directly to the **1924 National Origins Quota Act**, which attempted to reduce immigration from Catholic southern Europe in favor of immigration from Protestant northern Europe. The fears of Protestants proved generally unfounded, as American Catholics nourished their Catholic roots with healthy doses of American democracy and voluntarism. Many Catholic parishes gave quite a lot of influence to church boards made up of lay Catholics, in a manner somewhat analogous to self-governing Protestant churches. Catholics also quickly mastered the culture of democratic politics, and many American Catholics were deeply disappointed (and quietly rejected) Pope Pius IX's condemnation of liberal democracy (among other things) in 1864. The American Catholic Church continued to grow in size (it is now the largest single Christian denomination, with nearly 80 million members) and social acceptance throughout the twentieth century, and Catholicism has become a core element of America's religious fabric.

The battle between religion and science

The leading position of Protestantism in American faith and culture has been challenged in American history, first by Enlightenment philosophy and more recently by the rise of modern science.

Many of the leaders of the founding generation were influenced by Enlightenment philosophy and therefore tended to take a rather dim view of organized religion. Founders like Thomas Jefferson and Benjamin Franklin were prominent adherents of a deist view of religion that accepted the existence of God but denied that God took an active role in the management of human affairs. Jefferson pioneered the concept of separation of church and state in Virginia, with the basic idea being that churches should be protected from control by the state, to preserve freedom of religious opinion, and that the state should be protected from an established church, which would inevitably use the power of the state to coerce or harass believers of other faiths. Jefferson's concept found its way into the First

Amendment of the Constitution, which states that "Congress shall make no law respecting an establishment of religion, or prohibiting the free exercise thereof." The first part prevents the creation of a state church, and the second means that the government has no power to regulate religious activity, so churches are free to do whatever they feel is necessary to practice their faith without breaking the general laws of the country.

During the 19th century, Protestant ministers and believers prided themselves in their joint faith in religion and science. The discovery of the principle of natural selection as the governing force behind evolution by Charles Darwin greatly complicated this happy alliance. Darwin's theory provided a highly compelling and scientifically defensible alternative explanation for the origin of mankind, thus forcing a wedge between religion and science. Although many Protestants came to accept evolution by reading the Bible less literally, the bedrock importance of Scripture pushed many others to reject evolution. Matters came to a head during the so-called **Scopes Monkey Trial (1925)**, in which a high school biology teacher in Tennessee, John Scopes, was accused of breaking a Tennessee law that prevented the teaching of evolution in public schools. Clarence Darrow, a well-known and highly skilled trial lawyer, defended Scopes, while the prosecution hired three-time presidential candidate William Jennings Bryan as lead counsel. The trial received national attention for the issues being debated in it, particularly over literal interpretations of the Bible. Darrow took a risk by calling Bryan as a witness, and cross-examined Bryan over his knowledge of the Bible and evolution, making Bryan look like something of a fool. Scopes was found guilty of teaching evolution and required to pay a small fine.

The Civil Rights Movement
The Civil Rights Movement was an African-American led political and social movement designed to overturn segregation in the South. The ability of white Southerners to overturn Reconstruction, which granted African-Americans political and civil rights, was codified by the Supreme Court in the case of **Plessy v. Ferguson (1892)**, which held that states were allowed to separate the races so long as the separated facilities were considered generally equal. The result was a **Jim Crow** system of racial separation (segregation), in which whites controlled virtually all political and economic power in the South. The only institution which was left to African-Americans was the church, which is why most of the leaders of the Civil Rights Movement were pastors and students. The Civil Rights Movement began to take shape with the Supreme Court's decision in **Brown v. Board of Education (1954)**, which rejected Plessy v. Ferguson, arguing that separate facilities were inherently unequal. The Civil Rights Movement was led by Dr. Martin Luther King, Jr., a Baptist minister from Atlanta who attended desegregated seminaries in Pennsylvania and Boston. King's insight was to combine Christian love with Thoreau's concept of nonviolent civil disobedience (practiced successfully in India by Gandhi) in order to win over Northern whites, whose votes could convince Congress to pass national legislation protecting black civil rights. King drew on a national network of black churches for support, and also received support from many white Protestants and Jews. Although the Civil Rights Movement was a long and difficult struggle, its success through nonviolence reinvigorated the Christian tradition of fighting for social justice and made King one of the most admired figures in American history.

The Rise of the Religious Right

The rapid social changes of the 1960s and 70s, especially the Sexual Revolution and the legalization of abortion in *Roe v. Wade* (1973) galvanized conservative Christians in the south and west of the country to organize politically. Conservative Christian leaders such as Jerry Falwell, Pat Robertson, James Dobson, and Billy Graham became major political players, with Robertson even running for the Republican presidential nomination in 1988. Believing that the overall cultural and education system of the United States had become hostile to Christian beliefs, Christian conservatives worked to create new universities, encouraged home schooling, and opposed the teaching of evolution in public schools. Despite the political success of the movement, which did much to reinvigorate the Republican Party, Christian conservatives have not been successful in overturning *Roe v. Wade*, and appear to be currently losing in their effort to permanently ban gay marriage.

American History Tutoring Guide   Paul Pinto

QUESTIONS
Multiple Choice

1. Protestant evangelicalism has contributed significantly to all of the following social or political movements EXCEPT
   A. Abolitionism
   B. Temperance
   C. The resurgence of the Republican Right in the 1980s
   D. The Civil Rights Movement
   E. The Free Silver movement

2. Why were so many of the leaders of the Civil Rights Movement of the 1950s and 1960s African-American preachers?
   A. Churches were one of the few truly independent African-American institutions in the south
   B. African-American churches served as a powerful social network coordinating individuals and resources throughout the country
   C. African-American preachers were well trained in the philosophy and theology of nonviolent resistance and social liberation
   D. African-American preachers had the religious connections and background necessary to effectively coordinate with white ministers and social reformers in the North
   E. All of the above

3. Which of the following groups have been persecuted in America due to their differences with mainstream Protestant culture?
   A. Chinese Americans
   B. Japanese Americans
   C. African-Americans
   D. Members of the Church of Jesus Christ of Latter Day Saints (Mormon Church)
   E. Members of the Presbyterian Church

4. The Scopes monkey trial of the 1920s
   A. Proved that evolution was false
   B. Resulted in the acquittal of John Scopes
   C. Resulted in the conviction of William Jennings Bryan
   D. Demonstrated to a national audience that Biblical literalism was inconsistent with the evidence presented by Darwin's theory of evolution
   E. All of the above

5. Why did Northern evangelicals oppose slavery so adamantly in the first half of the nineteenth century?
   A. Slave plantations competed with Northern production of cotton
   B. The Second Great Awakening taught them that all people possessed human dignity
   C. A decline in church rolls in the Northeast caused many ministers to eye slaves as potential new converts and church members
   D. They wanted to beat the British in the race to emancipate the slaves
   E. All of the above

6. Which of the following individuals defended the cause of religious liberty in the seventeenth century?
   A. Joseph Smith
   B. Roger Williams
   C. William Bradford
   D. Arthur Dimmesdale
   E. John Winthrop

7. Quakers supported which of the following ideas?
   A. Abolition of slavery
   B. Relative equality for men and women
   C. The organization of church congregations according to the democratic principle
   D. Opposition to war
   E. All of the above

8. All of the following are well-known present day conservative evangelicals EXCEPT?
   A. Jerry Falwell
   B. Pat Robertson
   C. Billy Graham
   D. James Dobson
   E. Rachel Carson

9. Protestants in the 19th and early 20th centuries denigrated Catholic immigrants by arguing which of the following?
   A. Catholic immigrants were not capable of understanding or practicing democracy
   B. The Catholic Church was a corrupt autocracy
   C. Catholics were mandated to answer to Rome rather than the Constitution
   D. Catholicism was against modernity and progress
   E. All of the above

10. The Calvinist doctrine of predestination argues that
    A. God provides salvation to all
    B. God provides salvation to all Christians
    C. God provides salvation to all repentant Christians
    D. God provides salvation to all Puritan Christians
    E. God provides salvation to those he elects for salvation

Essay Questions
1. How and why did the Second Great Awakening contribute to nineteenth-century social reform movements?

2. How did Puritanism shape the social, economic and political formation of the New England colonies?

3. Why did Protestants in the United States frequently discriminate against Catholics in the nineteenth and early twentieth centuries?

4. Why did so many leaders of the Civil Rights Movements have religious backgrounds?

5. What contributions to American history were made by TWO of the following religious figures forced into exile for their beliefs?
   A. Anne Hutchinson
   B. Roger Williams
   C. Joseph Smith

Answers to Multiple Choice Questions
1. E
2. E
3. D
4. D
5. B
6. B
7. E
8. E
9. E
10. E

TOPIC 17: SOCIAL AND DEMOGRAPHIC TRENDS

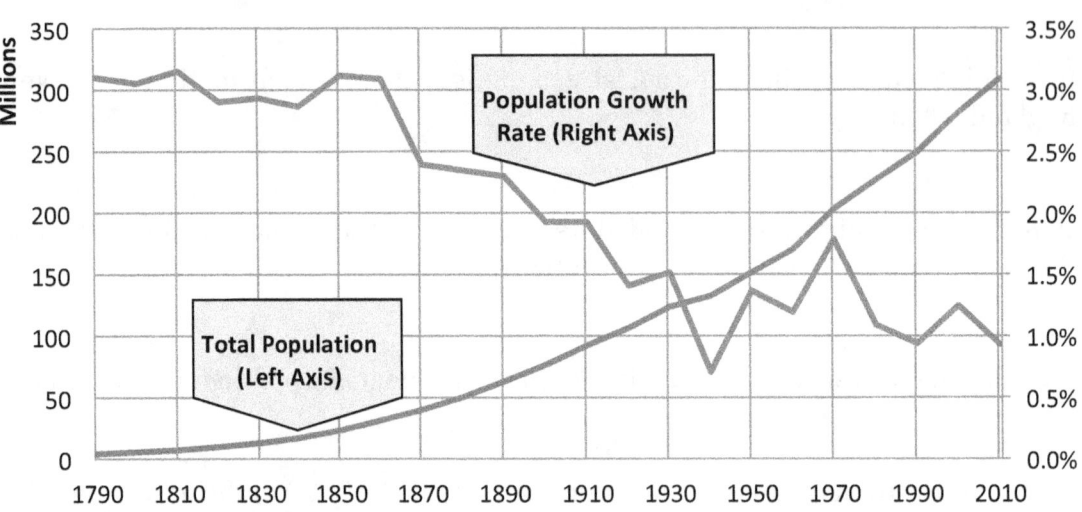

Total Population of the United States, 1790-2010 (millions)

The population of the United States of America has increased from 3.9 million people in 1790 to 308 million today. The population grew at a robust rate of 3% until the 1860s, and ranged between 2-3% until the 1920s, when immigration quotas, depression and war sent the growth rate plunging below 1%. The baby boom and the reopening of the immigration system in the 1960s sent the growth rate back up near 2%, but it has declined back to 1% in the last twenty years.

Population Migrations in American History

Migration	Description
Great Migration (1620s-1640s)	• Movement of between 20,000-30,000 Puritans leaving England for New England to avoid the rule of pro-Catholic King Charles I • The English Civil War, in which a Puritan-led army defeated, tried and executed King Charles, slowed down subsequent migration • The Great Migration ensured the viability of New England
The Middle Passage (1500s-1888)	• Refers to the part of the triangular Atlantic trade in which slaves were shipped from Africa to the Americas • Brutal manner of cramming slaves onto ships →high mortality rates
European immigration	• (1840s-1920s); See Topic on Immigration for more details
Native-American migration	• (1820s-90s); See Topic on Native Americans for more details
African-American Great Migration (1910-1970)	• Movement from South to the cities of the North and West • Millions of blacks left the south to find work in Northern factories • Government creation of the **Fair Employment Protection Committee** (FEPC, 1941), designed to ban racial discrimination in wartime industries, draws 700,000 blacks to Northern cities
World War II and postwar migration to the Sunbelt (1940-80)	• Army installations in the Sunbelt (southern portion of the United States from southern California to southeastern Georgia) draw millions of people • Invention of air conditioning further increases migration south • Sunbelt the fastest-growing region during the 1970s

Mass Culture

Cultural Form	Period of Growth	Social, Cultural and Legal Impact
Movies	1910-1920	<ul><li>Hugely popular: 10,000 movie theaters by 1910, with an audience of 10 million people (Divine et al. 2007: 647)</li><li>D.W. Griffith's film *Birth of a Nation* (1915), a movie glorifying the exploits of the KKK in restoring white supremacy in the South, opens to huge audiences in both the north and south</li><li>Movies with sound begin in 1929 with weekly attendance of nearly 100 million people</li></ul>
Radio	1920s	<ul><li>800 local radio networks, NBC forms the first national network in 1929</li></ul>
TV	1950s	<ul><li>Three dominant networks (NBC, CBS, ABC), audience of 40 million people</li><li>Strong revenue growth fueled by advertising</li><li>Development of standard TV program formats like the evening news, sitcoms (situation comedies), westerns, and variety shows</li></ul>
Music	1890-1910 1910-1930	<ul><li>Phonograph records also popular, hundreds of millions of records sold</li><li>Ragtime music, popularized by Scott Joplin and Irving Berlin</li><li>Dance: fox-trot, tango</li><li>Jazz music, a black art form from New Orleans that used wind instruments and stressed creativity and improvisation, becomes popular (Louis Armstrong, Duke Ellington, etc.)</li></ul>
Vaudeville	1920s	<ul><li>Song-and-dance shows</li></ul>
Sports	1870-1900 and 1950-70	<ul><li>First World Series in 1903</li><li>Baseball becomes national pastime by 1910</li><li>Golf becomes an extremely popular sport in the 1920s</li><li>Boxing rises to new heights with champs like Jack Dempsey</li><li>NFL becomes most important national sport by 1980s</li><li>US national hockey team defeats Russia in 1980 Winter Olympics</li></ul>
Youth Culture	1960	<ul><li>Broad-based challenge to traditional values of work, marriage, sex, clothing, music, and more</li><li>Rise of "hippie" culture based on free love and drug use (centered in places like the Haight-Ashbury district in San Francisco)</li><li>Psychedelic rock n' roll, led by the Beatles, Jimi Hendrix, Janis Joplin</li></ul>

High Culture

Cultural Form	Period of Growth	Social, Cultural and Legal Impact
Art	1910s	• **Ashcan School** paints realistic scenes of urban life
Philosophy	1890-1920	• **Pragmatism:** a school of philosophy that stressed the importance of experience and measurement rather than pure theory (William James, John Dewey)
Poetry	1910-1920	• Robert Frost, *North of Boston* (1914) • Carl Sandburg, *Chicago Poems* (1916) • T.S. Eliot, *The Waste Land* (1922); *The Hollow Men* (1925)
Literature	1920s 1950s	• "**Lost generation**" lamenting the Great War: • Hemingway, *Farewell to Arms* (romance set in WWI) • F. Scott Fitzgerald, *The Great Gatsby* (critique of American materialism) • Sinclair Lewis, *Main Street* (1920) and *Babbitt* (1922) (critiques of American small town provincialism and commercialism) • **Critics of American materialism** emerge again in the 1950s: • John Keats' *The Crack in the Picture Window* rails against the blandness of suburbia • William Whyte's *The Organization Man* (1956) criticized the conformity of the corporate life in the suburbs • C. Wright Mills *Power Elite* (1956) argued that corporations drained the individuality and life out of their workers • The **Beats**, led by Jack Kerouac (*On the Road*, 1957) and Allan Ginsberg, rejected consumer society entirely for a life of traveling freedom
Harlem Renaissance	1920s	• Blend of scholarship, art, music, and literature dealing with the black experience • NAACP magazine *The Crisis: A Record of the Darker Races* publishes a lot of influential black scholarship and literature • Claude McKay, *White Shadows* (1922), attacking racial injustice • Langston Hughes, a "jazz poet," wrote "The Negro Speaks of Rivers," a poem about African-American life in America and the challenges of blending the legacy of African slavery with the optimism of America
Music	1890-1920	• Phonograph records also popular, hundreds of millions of records sold • Ragtime music, popularized by Scott Joplin and Irving Berlin • Dance: fox-trot, tango • Jazz music, a black art form from New Orleans that used wind instruments and stressed creativity and improvisation, becomes popular (Louis Armstrong, Duke Ellington, etc.)

American History Tutoring Guide Paul Pinto

QUESTIONS
Multiple Choice

1. Which of the following films that glorified the effort to "Redeem the South" attracted large audiences throughout the country in 1915?
   A. *The Birth of a Nation*
   B. *Gone with the Wind*
   C. *The Catcher in the Rye*
   D. *The Wizard of Oz*
   E. *Citizen Kane*

2. Each of the following describes some aspect of African-American migration from 1619-1965 EXCEPT
   A. The Middle Passage
   B. The Great Migration of 1620-1640
   C. The Underground Railroad
   D. Migration to the North from the South from 1910 to 1970
   E. All of the above

3. The "Baby Boom" of the 1950s was driven by all of the following factors EXCEPT
   A. The end of the Second World War
   B. The restoration of prosperity to the American economy
   C. The growth of the suburbs
   D. The Army GI Bill
   E. A decline in the marriage rate

4. All of the following contributed to the formation of a shared national culture EXCEPT
   A. Film
   B. Broadcast television
   C. Sports like boxing, golf and horse racing
   D. Service in the world wars
   E. The Harlem Renaissance

5. The counterculture rebellion of the 1960s and 1970s was caused or fueled by which of the following factors?
   A. The Baby Boom
   B. The Vietnam War
   C. New developments in music and art
   D. The Civil Rights Movement
   E. All of the above

6. Which of the following factors led to a pronounced postwar trend of migration from the North and Midwest to the South and West?
   A. The construction of Army bases and installations during World War II
   B. The widespread use of air conditioning
   C. The development of the post-Civil Rights "New South"
   D. The growth of Florida, California and the Southwest as retirement destinations
   E. All of the above

7. All of the following represent a rebellion against or critique of mainstream culture EXCEPT
   A. *On the Road*
   B. *The Catcher in the Rye*
   C. *Sgt. Pepper's Lonely Hearts Club Band*
   D. *The Power Elite*
   E. *North of Boston*

8. The population of the United States is correctly associated with the time period in all of the following EXCEPT
   A. 1860: 31 million
   B. 1890: 63 million
   C. 1920: 106 million
   D. 1950: 250 million
   E. 2000: 280 million

9. Which of the following books criticized the conformity of corporate life in the 1950s?
   A. *The Great Gatsby*
   B. *Babbitt*
   C. *The Organization Man*
   D. *The Crack in the Picture Window*
   E. *On the Road*

10. The rate of total population growth in the United States was highest during which of the following periods?
    A. 1990 – 2010
    B. 1970 – 1990
    C. 1950 – 1970
    D. 1930 – 1950
    E. 1870 – 1890

Essay Questions

1. Explain how and why the baby boom starting in the late 1940s contributed to major social change in the 1960s.

2. How did World War II set the stage for the revitalization and reinvention of the South and Southwest regions of the United States?

3. Outline the social consequences of TWO of the following population migrations
    A. The Great Migration of the Puritans (1620-1640)
    B. Immigration from Southern and Eastern Europe (1880-1920)
    C. The migration of African-Americans from the South to Northern cities (starting in 1910)

American History Tutoring Guide

Answers to Multiple Choice Questions
1. A
2. B
3. E
4. E
5. E
6. E
7. E
8. D
9. C
10. E

American History Tutoring Guide Paul Pinto

TOPIC 18: THE CIVIL WAR

Introduction

The Civil War is probably the central event and pivotal turning point in American history. During the course of the four year conflict, slavery was destroyed, the rebellious southern states suffered defeat in a total war that cost the lives of hundreds of thousands of Americans,[11] and the United States was forged into a unified nation by the fires of war. The Civil War began as a constitutional crisis precipitated by the southern states, who preferred the risks of secession and war to a future in which the federal government might regulate or prohibit slavery first in the western territories and ultimately in the South. The vast human, material and moral cost of the war transformed public opinion and emotions in the North and made the abolition of slavery throughout the United States a real possibility. The Emancipation Proclamation (1863), which freed all the slaves in those states still in rebellion, made the war a social revolution as well as a constitutional battle over the rights of states. The war tested both sides to their breaking point, with the North finally achieving victory thanks to the strong performance of the Republican Party and the president of the United States, Abraham Lincoln.

The Advantages and Disadvantages of the North and South

Both sides in the Civil War could rely on relative strengths and strategic advantages, the combination of which made for a long and difficult conflict. The South was fighting for its independence and the retention of its characteristic way of life, and its military strategy was correspondingly clear: win enough battles to draw Great Britain into the conflict and force the Union to accept secession,. Many of the best military officers in America came from Southern families, including the Virginian Robert E. Lee, who was offered command of both the Union and Confederate armies (he chose the latter). The North was faced with the daunting challenge of comprehensively subduing the South, a task that required millions of soldiers spread across thousands of miles of enemy terrain. To meet this challenge, the North had a number of advantages: its soldiers were also fighting for a powerful cause – the preservation of the Union, and, for some, the battle against the evil 'slave power' – and it could claim an enormous population (22 million against a free Southern population of 5.5 million), economic (85% of factories and manufacturing), and military-industrial advantage over the South. The internal politics of the North and South also provided the North with a powerful advantage – a vibrant party system and active federal government to coordinate the struggle. The South, although governed by a relatively unified planter class, struggled to coordinate its efforts in an efficient manner because individual southern states were reluctant to give power to the Confederacy's central government. Indeed, the very unity of the planter class proved to be a drawback when the Confederacy failed to develop a competitive internal two-party system. Without a disciplined and well-connected party apparatus behind him, President Davis was frequently left with no recourse when southern governors refused his requests for money, men or material. On the other hand, an apparent weakness of the North – the continued existence of the Democratic party as a political force – helped ensure the continued discipline and dedication of the Republican Party, which played a huge role in helping President Lincoln to coordinate the war effort

---

[11] Recent research suggests that about 620,000 Americans died during the Civil War, constituting about 2% of the American population of 31 million people. Historians calculate that a war of similar intensity today would cost the lives of over six million Americans. For more information see Faust, Drew Gilpin. 2008. *This Republic of Suffering: Death and the American Civil War*. New York: Alfred A. Knopf.

and maintain public support during the numerous military setbacks suffered by the North. Lincoln also had the advantage of using the ample powers of the presidency and the federal government to their limit: he was able to impose high levels of taxation, conscript soldiers into the army, and even hold enemy combatants without the right of habeas corpus.

A Focused Timeline of Civil War Events

Both the AP and SAT II US history tests avoid questions that exclusively test the military history of the Civil War (e.g., who won the battle of Spotsylvania?); rather, military events are tested insofar as they relate to broader political and strategic issues. The North, after initial hopes for a quick victory were dashed, devised a long-term strategy that consisted of (1) a naval blockade of Southern ports (known as the **Anaconda Plan**, the idea was to disrupt and eventually destroy Southern trade and resupply from Europe); (2) winning control of the Mississippi to divide the Confederacy; and (3) building an army strong enough to conquer Richmond, its capital.

The timeline below lists the main military-political events of the war:

Date	Event	Description and Significance
Nov – Dec 1860	• Lincoln elected to presidency; South Carolina secedes	• Lincoln receives no substantial political support in the South, and Southern states view his election as a threat to their liberties • South Carolina secedes in December 1860 • Lincoln forms a "Team of Rivals" cabinet made up of powerful political figures in the Republican party, including William Henry Seward at State and Salmon P. Chase, a prominent Radical, at Treasury. Both men believed they should have been president, but they help Lincoln unite and rally the Republican party in support of the war (Goodwin 2005)
June 1861	• Secession	• Ten other states secede (MS, FL, AL, GA, LA, TX, AK, NC, VA, TN), signifying a broad-based rebellion
July 1861	• Battle of Bull Run (northern Virginia)	• The first major battle of the Civil War, the First Battle of Bull Run, results in a Confederate victory over inexperienced Union troops. The battle shatters illusions in the North that the conflict will be short-lived
November 1861	• Trent Affair	• US navy seizes a British ship containing two Confederate diplomats headed for Britain. The British threaten war unless the diplomats are allowed to complete their mission. Lincoln agrees, but the diplomatic mission is a failure as Britain will not commit to supporting the Confederacy
March 1862	• Peninsula Campaign (Virginia)	• Union troops under George M. McClellan are defeated by Robert E. Lee, further demonstrating the superiority of the South's military leadership
September	• Antietam	• Lee hoped that a strategic victory against the North

1862	(Maryland)	would result in British support for the Confederacy; however, the Union army holds off the Confederate charge at great cost (22,000 men die on both sides). McClellan fails to pursue the weakened Confederate army, earning Lincoln's scorn.
1 January 1863	• Emancipation Proclamation	• Lincoln issues an executive order freeing the slaves in all states still in rebellion against the Union
May 1863	• Siege of Vicksburg (Mississippi)	• General U.S. Grant manages to conquer the well-defended port city by ranging into enemy territory and attacking from the east. Control of the Mississippi allows the Union to split the Confederacy
May 1863	• Battle of Gettysburg (Pennsylvania)	• The Union Army achieves a major victory when it turns back Lee's attacking force; however, the Union Army fails to pursues Lee's retreating forces, missing a chance to quickly end the war
March 1864	• U.S. Grant promoted to general in chief	• Grant's willingness to take risks and win battles earned him the promotion; however, this same boldness cost the lives of tens of thousands of Union soldiers in 1864 without victory
November 1864	• Lincoln wins reelection	• Running against the general he fired (George McClellan) Lincoln emerged with a strong victory after a number of military successes including General William T. Sherman's campaign in Georgia. Sherman's **March to the Sea** in the winter of 1864 illustrates the rigors of total war, as his army destroyed both military and economic targets • Democratic northerners in favor of peace even at the price of secession were known as **Copperheads**
April 1865	• Lee surrenders at Appomattox Courthouse (Virginia)	• The war is ended when Lee decides not to conduct a policy of guerrilla warfare and surrenders his army to General Grant
April 14, 1865	• Lincoln is assassinated	• John Wilkes Booth and a small group of accomplices succeed in killing Lincoln and nearly killing Secretary of State Seward

Coming to terms with the sacrifices of the Civil War

Both the Union and the Confederacy sought to develop a moral vocabulary to deal with the immense destruction wrought by the Civil War and the sacrifices felt by so many of its citizens. The historian Harry Stout argues that "only as casualties rose to unimaginable levels did it dawn on some people that something mystically religious was taking place, a sort of massive sacrifice on the national altar. The Civil War taught Americans that they really were a Union..." Christian ministers on both sides sought to justify and frame the war in religious and sacrificial terms; many preachers argued that their cause was hallowed by God, and still more fused traditional religion with what can be called an emerging civil religion or national spirit. During the war, the Confederacy held many public days of fasting to bond the southern people together. These fast days explicitly framed the Confederacy as a holy nation bonded together by the principles of Christianity and willing to suffer collectively in order to achieve its independence from a tyrannical North. President Lincoln sought to take something of a more balanced stance, especially before and in the early years of the war. During the Lincoln-Douglas debates, Lincoln stated that "I have no prejudice against the Southern people. They are just what we would be in their situation…"(Ibid: 53) However, Lincoln would brook no compromise on the issue of extending slavery to the territory, and he began appealing to the Declaration of Independence to justify his arguments. This culminated in the Gettysburg Address, the text of which is worth quoting in full:

> Four score and seven years ago our fathers brought forth, on this continent, a new nation, conceived in Liberty, and dedicated to the proposition that all men are created equal.
>
> Now we are engaged in a great civil war, testing whether that nation, or any nation so conceived and so dedicated, can long endure. We are met on a great battle-field of that war. We have come to dedicate a portion of that field, as a final resting place for those who here gave their lives that that nation might live. It is altogether fitting and proper that we should do this.
>
> But, in a larger sense, we can not dedicate—we can not consecrate—we can not hallow—this ground. The brave men, living and dead, who struggled here, have consecrated it, far above our poor power to add or detract. The world will little note, nor long remember what we say here, but it can never forget what they did here. It is for us the living, rather, to be dedicated here to the unfinished work which they who fought here have thus far so nobly advanced. It is rather for us to be here dedicated to the great task remaining before us—that from these honored dead we take increased devotion to that cause for which they here gave the last full measure of devotion—that we here highly resolve that these dead shall not have died in vain—that this nation, under God, shall have a new birth of freedom—and that government of the people, by the people, for the people, shall not perish from the earth.

In the Gettysburg Address, Lincoln weaves together the theme of profound sacrifice with the idea of the preservation and redemption of the deepest ideals of the Declaration of Independence: the willingness of thousands soldiers to die for their country – the depth of their sacrifice – is what will allow for the rebirth of freedom and democracy in a reconstituted and blessed American republic. It is worth noting that 200,000 African-American soldiers served in the Union Army, and many of these men paid the ultimate sacrifice. For example, the 54th Massachusetts Colored regiment, led by the white abolitionist Robert Gould Shaw, lost half of its men storming Fort Wagner in July 1863. Two years later, Lincoln's Second Inaugural Address (March 4, 1865) sums up the Civil War and its moral costs and equivalencies with remarkable cogency. He begins by noting, gently, that the Southern states were responsible for initiating the war:

> ...Both parties deprecated war; but one of them would make war rather than let the nation survive; and the other would accept war rather than let it perish. And the war came.

He continues by underling the centrality of slavery to the conflict:
> One-eighth of the whole population were colored slaves, not distributed generally over the Union, but localized in the Southern part of it. These slaves constituted a peculiar and powerful interest. All knew that this interest was, somehow, the cause of the war...

He then points out that both sides felt that God was with them:
> Both read the same Bible, and pray to the same God; and each invokes his aid against the other. It may seem strange that any men should dare to ask a just God's assistance in wringing their bread from the sweat of other men's faces; but let us judge not, that we be not judged. The prayers of both could not be answered—that of neither has been answered fully.

And then defines the great sacrifices of the war as terrible payment for two and a half centuries of slavery:
> Yet, if God wills that it continue until all the wealth piled by the bondman's two hundred and fifty years of unrequited toil shall be sunk, and until every drop of blood drawn with the lash shall be paid by another drawn with the sword, as was said three thousand years ago, so still it must be said, "The judgments of the Lord are true and righteous altogether."

Lincoln's words take on an even deeper resonance in the context of his assassination five weeks later, one last terrible sacrifice to the Civil War.

Social and Political Changes Wrought by the Civil War

By directing the full attention of American society towards the funding, equipping and conduct of total war for four years, the Civil War led towards a number of profound social, economic and political changes. Some of these changes were temporary in the sense that they ceased after the emergency had passed. Others provided for lasting changes in American society.

Temporary changes:
- *The rise of a social welfare state.* The huge number of Union dead led to public demand by Americans that the government provide for the widows and orphans of soldiers who had sacrificed their lives for the Union. For the next twenty years or so, the American government thus created the largest and most generous welfare state in the world. However, when the generation of Civil War beneficiaries passed on, the government did not try to extend these benefits to other cities, and would not establish a broad-based welfare state until the New Deal.

- *The creation of multiracial democracy.* Reconstruction was a bold and noble attempt to create multiracial democracy in the South. However, the reluctance of white Southerners to commit to its promise led to resubjugation of African-Americans in the South and de facto segregation in the North. White Northerners and Southerners joined hands to

Permanent changes:
- *The destruction of slavery.* Although freedmen would not get to enjoy full political and social equality in the South, slavery, the central economic institution of the South, was destroyed by the war.

- *The rise of an industrial state.* The secession of the South and the emergence of the war cleared the way in Congress for the Republican-led government to put into place an American System of the type dreamed of by Alexander Hamilton and Henry Clay. The government provided free or cheap lead to (white) settlers in the West (the Homestead Act), and donated more land for the establishment of universities of agriculture and science (Morrill Act land grant colleges). Even more importantly, the war trained a great many professionals in the army in the art of logistics and technology. These men (and some women) helped to build complex industrial corporations in industries like railways, oil, and manufacturing. Women in particular gained expertise in running philanthropic associations dedicated to "women's tasks" such as nursing and teaching.

- *A revised relationship between the states and the federal government.* The Civil War made it clear that the secession of individual states or groups of states was something that the federal government would not tolerate. The federal government thus demonstrated by force of arms and the votes of the majority of Americans in the North and West that the federal government was supreme over the states. In addition, the Civil War itself stirred the fires of nationalism, as national institutions such as the Union Army brought individuals from all over the North together in a common cause.

QUESTIONS

Multiple Choice

1. Which of the following strategic advantages did the North NOT enjoy over the South in 1860?
   A. Naval dominance
   B. Industrial superiority
   C. A larger population
   D. A strong cadre of top military leadership
   E. A robust two-party system

2. Who declined an offer to command the Union Army in order to serve his home state of Virginia in the Civil War?
   A. Stonewall Jackson
   B. Joseph E. Johnston
   C. George B. Crittenden
   D. John C. Breckinridge
   E. Robert E. Lee

3. Which former general of the Union Army challenged Abraham Lincoln in the presidential election of 1864?
   A. George B. McClellan
   B. Andrew Johnson
   C. Edwin Stanton
   D. William Seward
   E. Salmon P. Chase

4. President Lincoln issued the Emancipation Proclamation in 1863 using his authority as
   A. Commander-in-chief of the armed forces
   B. Chief legislator
   C. Chief diplomat
   D. Republican party leader
   E. None of the above

5. The Emancipation Proclamation of 1863
   A. Freed all the slaves in the United States
   B. Freed the slaves in the border states
   C. Arranged for the transportation of freed slaves back to Africa
   D. Freed the slaves in states still in a state of rebellion against the United States
   E. Freed all the slaves in the North

6. Which of the following displays the proper order of Civil War events or battles?
    A. Secession of the South, Battle of Bull Run, Antietam, Gettysburg, Sherman's March to the Sea
    B. Battle of Bull Run, Secession of the South, Gettysburg, Antietam, Sherman's March to the Sea
    C. Secession of the South, Battle of Bull Run, Sherman's March to the Sea, Gettysburg, Antietam
    D. Secession of the South, Antietam, Battle of Bull Run, Gettysburg, Sherman's March to the Sea
    E. Secession of the South, Gettysburg, Battle of Bull Run, Antietam, Sherman's March to the Sea

7. Jefferson Davis struggled to organize the Confederate war effort due to which of the following reasons?
    I. The Confederacy failed to develop a vibrant two-party system
    II. The dominant ideology of the South was states' rights, which complicated efforts to demand cooperation between the Southern states
    III. The Confederacy had very few railway lines, which made movement of troops by rail extremely difficult

    A. I only
    B. II only
    C. I and II
    D. II and III
    E. I, II, and III

8. Which of the following pieces of legislation passed during the Civil War helped fulfill one of the goals of Henry Clay's American System?
    A. The Morrill Land Grant Act of 1862
    B. *Ex Parte Milligan* (1866)
    C. The Thirteenth Amendment
    D. The 1867 Alaska Purchase
    E. The Emancipation Proclamation

9. Which of the following correctly defines the Reconstruction Amendments?
   I. Thirteenth: Abolition of slavery;
      Fourteenth: Right to equal protection of the laws, right to due process, and national citizenship for all Americans;
      Fifteenth: Voting rights guaranteed for African-Americans

   II. Thirteenth: Abolition of Slavery
       Fourteenth: Right to Vote
       Fifteenth: Right to own property for Freedmen

   III. Thirteenth: Abolition of Slavery
        Fourteenth: Right to equal protection of the laws, right to due process, and national citizenship for all Americans
        Fifteenth: Right to vote for women

   A. I only
   B. II only
   C. I and II
   D. II and III
   E. I, II and III

10. Which prominent Radical Republican politician served as Secretary of the Treasury in Lincoln's Cabinet?
    A. Salmon P. Chase
    B. William H. Seward
    C. Stephen Douglas
    D. Ralph Waldo Emerson
    E. None of the above

11. "It was further strongly recommended by me to the President that all men of property to whom he was offering pardon should be conditioned to provide a small homestead or something equivalent to each head of family of his former slaves; but President Johnson was amused and gave no heed to this recommendation. My heart ached for our beneficiaries, but I became comparatively helpless to offer them any permanent possession."

    The speaker above was the head of which federal agency?
    A. The Homestead Commission
    B. The Freedmen's Bureau
    C. The Bureau of Revenue
    D. The Union Army
    E. The Department of Indian Affairs

12. How did ordinary people not serving as soldiers demonstrate their support for the war?
    A. Paying taxes
    B. Participating in public days of fasting and prayer
    C. Reading newspapers and popular literature that supported their side
    D. Serving as nurses, band members, and military chaplains
    E. All of the above

13. Which of the following summarizes the core message of the Gettysburg Address?
    A. The South should be condemned for killing so many noble Union soldiers
    B. The South should liberate its slaves immediately
    C. The sacrifice of Union soldiers has provided America with a renewed opportunity to live up to her deepest ideals of liberty and democracy for all
    D. Both sides will be condemned by God for their sins
    E. The soldiers of both sides should be honored for their sacrifices

14. Women during the Civil War won themselves the right to
    A. vote
    B. participate in the war in women's occupations like nursing and sanitation
    C. serve as auxiliary soldiers
    D. serve in political office
    E. none of the above

15. In order to mobilize a sufficient number of men for the conflict, both the North and South resorted to
    A. large payment bonuses for enlistment
    B. the recruitment of Chinese immigrants to serve in the armed forces
    C. the recruitment of Scottish immigrants to serve in the armed forces
    D. conscription laws
    E. None of the above

16. Copperheads is a term used to describe
    A. Southern spies in the North
    B. Northern spies in the South
    C. Escaped African-American slaves who returned to the South
    D. Northern Democrats who preferred peace with the South
    E. Stonewall Jackson's elite troops

17. The 200,000 African-American soldiers serving in the Union Army
    A. served in segregated units
    B. served under white officers
    C. were typically paid less than their white counterparts
    D. generally served with honor and distinction
    E. All of the above

Federal Government Revenues and Expenditures, 1860-65

Year	Receipts	Outlays	Balance
1860	$56.1M	$63.1M	-$7.1M
1861	41.5	66.5	-25.0
1862	52.0	474.8	-422.8
1863	112.7	714.7	-602.0
1864	264.6	865.3	-600.7
1865	333.7	1,297.6	-963.8

Source: US Census Bureau, *Historical Statistics of the United States 1789-1945*

Use the chart above to help answer question 18.

18. How did the North primarily finance its prosecution of the Civil War?
    A. By raising taxes
    B. By printing large quantities of dollars that could not be redeemed in gold and silver
    C. By borrowing from Great Britain
    D. By making the soldiers pay for their own equipment and training
    E. None of the above

19. Why did the South struggle with mass hunger during the Civil War despite its agricultural productivity?
    A. Its transportation and production system were geared towards export crops like cotton and tobacco
    B. Southern states completely refused to share with one another
    C. The North was immediately successful in taking control of the Mississippi
    D. Leading planters were eager to convert their plantations into the production of food for the people rather than goods for export
    E. All of the above

20. Lincoln's assassination by John Wilkes Booth
    A. Reversed the emancipation of the slaves
    B. Reduced the influence of the Radical Republicans in Congress
    C. Caused General Robert E. Lee to rethink his surrender
    D. Allowed Andrew Johnson to ascend to the presidency
    E. None of the above

Essay Questions
1. How and why did the Civil War evolve from a war to preserve the Union to a war to emancipate the slaves?

2. In what ways did the Civil War change the relationship between the federal government and the states, and between the states and the people?

3. How did President Lincoln weave together the issue of slavery and the issue of preserving the union in the Gettysburg Address?

Answers to Multiple Choice Questions
1. D
2. E
3. A
4. A
5. D
6. A
7. C
8. A
9. A
10. A
11. B
12. E
13. C
14. B
15. D
16. D
17. E
18. B
19. A
20. D

American History Tutoring Guide   Paul Pinto

PART TWO: HOW TO STUDY

LESSON ONE: HOW TO READ THE TEXTBOOK

When you read your history textbook, it should always be with a specific purpose in mind. Before you begin reading, think about the following issues:
- What does my teacher want me to get out of this chapter or section? What topics, events or historical figures has my teacher really focused on in his or her lectures?
- How will reading this chapter or section help me prepare for an upcoming test?
- What method or methods of highlighting or taking notes will help me most when I return to this chapter at the end of the month/semester/year?

There are two major ways of capturing useful information from the textbook – highlighting and note-taking. You can choose to mostly highlight, or mostly note-take, but it's usually best to combine the two (highlighting is probably out of the question if you don't own the book). Both techniques have the same purpose – to help you isolate, from the vast sea of information, the specific pieces of information that are likeliest to show up on the test.

If you are note-taking, take ten or twenty minutes at the end of your reading and write down the answers, in as few words as possible, to the following questions:
- What is (are) the main historical process(es) described in this section/chapter?
- What is the tension/conflict at the center of each process?
- Who are the main historical actors on either side of this tension/conflict?
- What events define the unfolding of the process (beginning, middle, end)?
- How is the process resolved (is it resolved at all)? What happens to the individuals on either side of the conflict?

For example, if you are reading a chapter on the presidencies of George Washington and John Adams, the answers to the questions above would look something like the following:
- *Main historical process*: The rise of party politics (Federalists vs. Democratic-Republicans), and the competition between the two parties over the meaning of the constitution
- *Tension/conflict*: Federalists believed in a developmental path that would make America more like Britain – a commercial republic, focused on Atlantic trade, with a strong federal government deeply involved in the economy; Democratic-Republicans believed in a limited federal government and an economy primarily concerned with small and medium-sized farmers (an agrarian republic)
- *Leaders*: Hamilton was the strong leader of the Federalists, with Washington and Adams more moderate members of the same party; Jefferson led the Democratic-Republicans, helped by James Madison and James Monroe
- *Main events:* the main events in the beginning are the efforts of Hamilton, as Secretary of the Treasury, to create a national debt, a national bank, and an agreeable policy of trade with Britain; the middle involves the disenchantment of Jefferson, and the end involves the departure of Jefferson from Washington's administration to set up his own party apparatus and campaign for the presidency
- *Resolution:* the process is resolved by the victory of Jefferson in 1800 (the Revolution of 1800). The Federalists are basically defeated as a party, while the Democratic-Republicans enjoy the next generation of party dominance

In my experience, the ten minutes it takes to summarize your thoughts at the end of reading a section is just as valuable as the hour or more spent reading the textbook, given that you will normally only be able to retain a fraction of the total information read by the time you are tested on the material.

Taking book notes on the computer is an excellent way to build up a repository of information that will prove invaluable during test time. An electronic document makes it easier to find and look up key terms, copy information rapidly, and reorganize information depending on new understanding or needs.

LESSON TWO: ESSAY WRITING

Writing exam essays under time pressure is a specialized skill that requires a lot of practice. To produce a successful AP US History free-response essay, it is important to get into the habit of checking off the following key boxes each and every time you write an essay.

1. *Understand the question.* Reading the essay prompt carefully is a simple but extremely important step. The prompt almost always contains valuable clues and hints and sometimes even the seeds of an argument to answer the question.

    Consider the following prompt:
    "Evaluate the extent to which the Articles of Confederation were effective in solving the problems that confronted the new nation."

    Notice that the prompt states clearly that the new nation faced problems, with the implication being that the Articles of Confederation were not quite up to par as a governmental system. The prompt also tells us exactly what to do: evaluate and assess how well the Articles performed against a range of problems, whether economic, political, or of some other sort.

    Taken together, the hints suggest an argument or, at least, the skeleton of an argument, something like this:

    "Although not without its successes, the Articles of Confederation generally failed to deliver main governmental functions and solve the problems of the nation."

    A basic structure for the essay may also be deduced: two or three body paragraphs devoted to explaining how the Articles performed on vital economic, political and military challenges, accompanied by a short body paragraph acknowledging its successes.

    With practice, you should be able to extract key insights from the prompt in less than a minute or two.

2. *Organize the essay before writing.* Organization of the essay can be divided into two processes: (1) *brainstorming*, where you write down as many key terms and general insights dealing with this topic as you can recall; and (2) *outlining*, where you place the terms and concepts generated by brainstorming into a five-paragraph essay form (introduction with thesis, body paragraphs, conclusion). For the question above, an ideal brainstorming list might look like the following:

    <u>Characteristics of the Articles of Confederation</u>
    — States sovereign, weak central government
    — Single legislative body
    — Each state given single vote
    — No independent executive
    — No veto over legislative decisions

— No powers of taxation, only voluntary contributions from states
— Unanimity required for amendments

<u>Problems faced by the new nation</u>
— Financial crisis caused by wartime debts
— Could not enforce peace treaty with Britain; British troops remain in NW Territory
— Spain closes lower Mississippi
— Individual states running up irresponsible debts and refusing to pay
— Shay's Rebellion; poor farmers in western Mass. rising up against taxes and creditors; Congress did not have the money to support an army to put down the rebellion

The purpose of brainstorming ideas is to generate raw material amongst which connections can be drawn. For example, perhaps the single biggest problem with the Articles was the inability of Congress to impose taxes; this diminished all Congress's other powers, because it often did not have the money to, say, pay for an army to put down a rebellion or push the British out of the Northwest Territory.

The raw material and its various connections can then be organized into an outline, the most crucial step of the entire process. A good outline provides the basic structure on which the argument and its defense hang. The structure of a generic outline is as follows:

A. Introduction
   1. Introductory sentence(s): present the essay and draw the reader in (quickly)
   2. Thesis statement: presents an argument and describes how the argument will be defended
B. First body paragraph
   1. Topic sentence: presents the first main point of the argument
   2. Presentation of evidence in favor (2-5 sentences)
   3. Acknowledgement and rebuttal of contradictory evidence (1 sentence if applicable)
C. Second body paragraph
   1. Topic sentence: presents the second main point of the argument
   2. Presentation of evidence in favor (2-5 sentences)
   3. Acknowledgement and rebuttal of contradictory evidence (1 sentence if applicable)
D. Third body paragraph
   1. Topic sentence: presents the third main point of the argument; if there are only two points in favor, this paragraph can be rewritten to acknowledge and then dispatch a contradictory argument
E. Conclusion
   1. Restates the main argument
   2. Adds any further implications of the argument (e.g., fundamental importance to American history, foreshadowing of future developments, etc.)

An example outline for the Articles of Confederation prompt might look as follows. Note that the only sentence worth writing out in full is the thesis statement.

A. Introduction
   1. *Introductory sentence:* Articles, formed in war by committed republicans rebelling against British govt. → weak central govt.; authority → states
   2. *Thesis:* The weakness of the central government under the Articles, specifically its lack of a taxing power, produced a government incapable of maintaining a stable national economic, political and diplomatic order. Despite rare successes such as the Northwest Ordinance, the Articles proved unequal to the problems of the new nation.
B. Body paragraph #1:
   1. *Topic sentence*: Articles create weak central govt., no power of taxation; no independent national executive
   2. Makes sense given tradition of American Revolution
   3. Implication 1: Central govt. could not pay for national army; states' voluntary contributions no good b/c states have little money
   4. Implication 2: Central govt. could not regulate national economy
   5. Implication 3: Central govt. could not defend national interest overseas
C. Body paragraph #2: Inability to address problems
   1. *Topic sentence:* Lack of tax revenue major implications for economic, political, diplomatic order
   2. Economic: no tax power = no ability to take central financial measures to control ruinous wartime inflation; each state debasing its own currency, no stable financial system; states putting up tariffs against each other; states engaged in boundary disputes
   3. Political: no ability to raise funds to suppress rebellions (Shay's rebellion, western Mass.); no central executive looking to defend the national interest; unanimity required for amendment (v. difficult)
   4. Diplomatic: no ability to stick to the terms of the Treaty of Paris; no funds for army to push British out of NW Territory
D. Body paragraph #3: Successes (mini-paragraph)
   1. AC able to provide a legal framework for the addition of new states
   2. However, this is perhaps the sole success of the Articles, and does not compensate for the other very real troubles faced by the nation
E. Conclusion
   1. Despite few successes, AC too weak to provide effective national leadership; had it continued, likely would have resulted in the division of the US into northern and southern republics, possibly further splintering
   2. Primary issue was inability of the central government to create common economic framework
   3. No balance between local republicanism and national interest – creation of Constitution would address this with nationally elected president and independent judiciary

3. *Craft the essay*. A good outline simplifies the writing process in a number of ways. First, the outline logically divides the argument and the pieces of evidence into manageable

parts, which helps to order and streamline the number of words necessary to present and defend the main ideas. Second, the process of writing the outline gets the mind thinking about a rough cut of what the words will look like, which then eases the process of composition when it actually begins. Third, the outline format lends itself to a well sign-posted essay that is easy for the reader to follow.

4. *Proofread.* The essay format does not allow for much in the way of revision and changes given the time constraints, but always try to set aside a minute or two to quickly review your work and correct obvious spelling mistakes.

5. *Grade the essay.* Grading your own essays is a useful way to get a better sense for what makes a good essay. Go through your essay, and evaluate yourself on each of the following points:
    — a clear thesis that uses the right kinds of evidence in an elegant and concise manner;
    — a well-written and organized essay;
    — the ability to deal with contradictory pieces of evidence;
    — the ability to conclude by drawing out one or more of the deeper implications raised by the essay.

6. *Additional considerations.* The College Board provides a number of sample essay questions (see the Key Resources section below) with multiple sample responses (http://apcentral.collegeboard.com/apc/members/exam/exam_information/2089.html). The website also contains summary statistics for all students, which allows you to see the answers to questions you may have like "What percent of students get a 5 on the AP Test?"

American History Tutoring Guide Paul Pinto

LESSON THREE: THE DBQ

The Document Based Question offers a different challenge from the free-response essays by asking you to integrate background knowledge of a topic with primary documents. The question challenges you to make an argument and deal with the range of opinions (for and against) presented in the primary material. The process to write a successful DBQ essay is similar to that of the free-response essays: you need to come up with a clear argument or position, defend that argument with reference to the primary documents and your background knowledge, and deal intelligently with contradictory pieces of evidence. Here's an example:

1. Outline the main political, economic, and social factors that explain why Reconstruction succeeded in the short term but failed in the long term to deliver equal rights for African-Americans.

Document A

Source: Alexander Stephens, March 21, 1861

Our new government is founded upon exactly the opposite idea; its foundations are laid, its cornerstone rests, upon the great truth that the negro is not equal to the white man; that slavery and subordination to the superior race is his natural and normal condition. This, our new government, is the first, in the history of the world, based upon this great physical, philosophical, and moral truth ... Those at the North, who still cling to these errors, with a zeal above knowledge, we justly denominate fanatics ... They assume that the negro is equal, and hence conclude that he is entitled to equal privileges and rights with the white man. If their premises were correct, their conclusions would be logical and just but their premise being wrong, their whole argument fails.

Document B

Source: Abraham Lincoln, Gettysburg Address, November 19, 1863

But, in a larger sense, we cannot dedicate – we cannot consecrate – we cannot hallow – this ground. The brave men, living and dead, who struggled here, have consecrated it far above our poor power to add or detract. The world will little note, nor long remember what we say here, but it can never forget what they did here. It is for us the living rather to be dedicated here to the unfinished work which they who fought here have thus far so nobly advanced. It is rather for us to be here dedicated to the great task remaining before us – that from these honored dead we take increased devotion to that cause for which they gave the last full measure of devotion – that we here highly resolve that these dead shall not have died in vain – that this nation, under God, shall have a new birth of freedom – and that government of the people, by the people, for the people, shall not perish from the earth.

Document C

Source: Gen. Oliver Otis Howard, 1866

It was further strongly recommended by me to the President that all men of property to whom he was offering pardon should be conditioned to provide a small homestead or something equivalent to each head of family of his former slaves; but President Johnson was amused and gave no heed to this recommendation. My heart ached for our beneficiaries, but I became comparatively helpless to offer them any permanent possession.

Document D

Source: Fourteenth Amendment to the United States Constitution, Section 1

All persons born or naturalized in the United States, and subject to the jurisdiction thereof, are citizens of the United States and of the State wherein they reside. No State shall make or enforce any law which shall abridge the privileges or immunities of citizens of the United States; nor shall any State deprive any person of life, liberty, or property, without due process of law; nor deny to any person within its jurisdiction the equal protection of the laws.

Document E

Source: *Harper's Weekly*, December 1, 1866

Several of them have already acted. The Legislatures of Texas and Georgia have rejected the proposed Amendment. The Governors of Mississippi, South Carolina, and Alabama have recommended the rejection. The old political leaders who dragged their section into the war advise repudiation of the conditions. And the newspapers, the tone and manner of which are simply inconceivable to one who does not see them, disdain the Amendment with passionate contempt. That there are persons in the unrepresented States who deprecate this folly of Governors, Legislatures, leaders, and editors is very possible; but the practical drift of public opinion can be ascertained only through such channels. So long as those who, for whatever reason, approve the Amendment can not elect the Governors or a majority of the Legislatures, nor even organize to do so, we must regard what we see as the indication of the real state of feeling.

Document F

Source: House of Representatives Election Results, 1868-69

State	Total House Seats	Republican	Democratic
Alabama	6	4	2
Arkansas	3	2	1
Florida	1	1	0
Georgia	7	3	4
Louisiana	5	5	0
Mississippi	5	5	0
North Carolina	7	6	1
South Carolina	4	4	0
Tennessee	8	8	0
Texas	4	3	1
Virginia	8	3	5
Total	**58**	**44**	**14**

American History Tutoring Guide Paul Pinto

Document G

Source: Thomas Nast, *Harper's Weekly*, April 9, 1870

"TIME WORKS WONDERS."

IAGO (JEFF DAVIS): "FOR THAT I DO SUSPECT THE LUSTY MOOR HATH LEAP'D INTO MY SEAT: THE THOUGHT WHEREOF DOTH LIKE A POISONOUS MINERAL GNAW MY INWARDS." — OTHELLO

Document H

Source: Thaddeus Stevens, July 7, 1868

If you and your compeers can fling away ambition and realize that every human being, however lowly-born or degraded by fortune is your equal, that every inalienable right which belongs to you belongs also to him, truth and righteousness will spread over the land, and you will look down from the top of the Rocky mountains upon an empire of one hundred millions of happy people

Document I

Source: Frederick Douglass, August 15, 1888

I recognize the Republican party as the sheet anchor of the colored man's political hopes and the ark of his safety.

Document J

Source: James Henry Yarborough (judge from South Carolina), recollection of youth from interview in the 1930s.

When that cruel war was over, it would have been wiser had the whites and ex-slaves been left to their own resources and inventions, to work out their future welfare. There was no lack of affection or loyalty on the part of the Negro, nor was there a lack of love and an enlightened appreciation of self-interest upon the part of the whites. Things might have been different if suffrage had been granted gradually. But with immediate equal suffrage, or the right to vote, came the carpetbagger with his preachments of social equality and the tantalizing bag of tricks to get for every Negro 40 acres of land and a mule. The Negroes were credulous and believed all the absurdities the knaves told them. The result was an inevitable curse for the Negro and lots of trouble for the white people. It ended only when Hampton was elected in 1876. Hampton is still my hero and a man of greatest worth in the annals of South Carolina.

1. *Understand the question (1 minute).* The natural temptation with the DBQ is to read the question quickly and dive right into the primary sources. Resist this temptation and take one or two minutes to read and re-read the question, underlining and/or circling key terms:

   What are the political, economic, and social factors that help explain why Reconstruction succeeded in the short term but failed in the long term to deliver equal rights for African-Americans?

   The question, remember, sets the terms of the answer. It tells you exactly what needs to be explained, in this case equal rights for African-Americans. Note also that the phrasing of the question pushes us in the direction of two body paragraphs: one discussing the factors that explain the initial success of Reconstruction and the second discussing how those factors faded or were replaced by competing factors that led to the ultimate failure of Reconstruction. We underline as follows:

What are the political, economic, and social factors that help explain why Reconstruction succeeded in the short term but failed in the long term to deliver equal rights for African-Americans?

2. *Initial Brainstorm to Generate Outside Knowledge (2 minutes).* Before going to the documents, spend two minutes brainstorming. Write down the first few things you can remember about Reconstruction and its successes and failures. The purpose of doing this <u>before</u> you get to the questions is to help you generate and organize your outside knowledge independent of the documents. Remember that demonstration of outside knowledge is required for a top score on the DBQ. Here are some examples of what you might write down during this mini-brainstorming:
    — Abolitionists and African-Americans looking for full citizenship and equality
    — Many other Northerners sure about destroying slavery but less certain about equal rights for African-Americans
    — Southern whites strongly opposed, including President Andrew Johnson
    — Union Army occupying the South and forcing Southerners to comply (but this can't last forever)
    — Reconstruction Amendments

3. *Review the documents (8 minutes).* Carefully read the documents, underlining key terms and making connections in your head and/or on paper between your brainstorming and the key terms. Always take the time to look at the source of the document to see if you can identify the person in question and what political view he/she represents. Carefully note the date of the document in order to place it in its proper sequence of events. Timing is especially important for a question like this one that deals directly with the initial success and subsequent failure of an event or process. Finally, think about how different documents connect to one another, and show in your essay that you understand the nature of these connections.

Document A

Source: Alexander Stephens, March 21, 1861

Our new government is founded upon exactly the opposite idea; its foundations are laid, its cornerstone rests, upon the great truth that the negro is not equal to the white man; that slavery [and] subordination to the superior race is his natural and normal condition. This, our new government, is the first, in the history of the world, based upon this great physical, philosophical, and moral truth ... Those at the North, who still cling to these errors, with a zeal above knowledge, we justly denominate fanatics ... They assume that the negro is equal, and hence conclude that he is entitled to equal privileges and rights with the white man. If their premises were correct, their conclusions would be logical and just but their premise being wrong, their whole argument fails.

Key points:
— **Person:** Alexander Stephens was the Vice-President of the Confederate States of America
— **Date:** Writing at the beginning of the Civil War, he makes point that the whole basis of the Confederacy rests on denying that all men are created equal

— **Main point** is that white Southerners in 1861 were fundamentally opposed to equal rights; one additional point is that Stephens calls Northerners "fanatics" for supporting equal rights, demonstrating the depth of his feeling against equality

Document B

Source: Abraham Lincoln, Gettysburg Address, November 19, 1863

But, in a larger sense, we cannot dedicate – we cannot consecrate – we cannot hallow – this ground. The brave men, living and dead, who struggled here, have consecrated it far above our poor power to add or detract. The world will little note, nor long remember what we say here, but it can never forget what they did here. It is for us the living, rather to be dedicated here to the unfinished work which they who fought here have thus far so nobly advanced. It is rather for us to be here dedicated to the great task remaining before us – that from these honored dead we take increased devotion to that cause for which they gave the last full measure of devotion – that we here highly resolve that these dead shall not have died in vain – that this nation, under God, shall have a new birth of freedom – and that government of the people, by the people, for the people, shall not perish from the earth.

Key points:
- **Person**: President Lincoln
- **Date**: late 1863, a trying time for the North
- **Main point**: That the sacrifice paid in blood by Union soldiers is only worthwhile if it is paid back by reconstituting the United States on a basis of full freedom and equality for all
- **Logical Deductions/Outside Knowledge:** Since all white men already possessed equal rights prior to the war, we can deduce that Lincoln is moving toward a position of equal rights for African-Americans. Since he is the leader of the Republican party, it follows that the party as a whole is also moving towards this position. One important note of caution at this point, however: it is true that many Northerners at the time were willing to punish the South for killing Union Army soldiers by eliminating slavery, but it is also true that these Northerners were much more ambivalent about equal rights for African-Americans.

Document C

Source: Gen. Oliver Otis Howard, 1866

It was further strongly recommended by me to the President that all men of property to whom he was offering pardon should be conditioned to provide a small homestead or something equivalent to each head of family of his former slaves; but President Johnson was amused and gave no heed to this recommendation. My heart ached for our beneficiaries, but I became comparatively helpless to offer them any permanent possession.

Key points:
- **Person**: Oliver Otis Howard was a Union Army General who was given command of the Freedmen's Bureau, the federal agency set up to help recently freed slaves
- **Date**: 1866
- **Main point**: Howard recommends to President Johnson (who succeeded the assassinated Abraham Lincoln in summer 1865) that Confederate landowners who

had actively participated in the Civil War be required to give small portions of their land to their former slaves. Johnson literally laughs at Howard's suggestion.
— **Logical Deductions/Outside Knowledge**: Johnson's response is not surprising given his staunch opposition to equal rights for African-Americans (he is, after all, a conservative Southerner from Tennessee). Giving freedmen property in the form of land would have been one of the strongest guarantees of their prosperity and thus equal rights.

Document D

Source: Fourteenth Amendment to the United States Constitution, Section 1

All persons born or naturalized in the United States, and subject to the jurisdiction thereof, are citizens of the United States and of the State wherein they reside. No State shall make or enforce any law which shall abridge the privileges or immunities of citizens of the United States; nor shall any State deprive any person of life, liberty, or property, without due process of law; nor deny to any person within its jurisdiction the equal protection of the laws.

Key points:
— **Date**: Proposed in 1866, ratified in 1868
— **Main point**: Citizenship is no longer up to the individual states; the federal government is now bound to defend the core liberties – life, liberty and property – of all citizens, black and white, and further bound to prevent individual states from infringing upon these liberties. Every American citizen is now guaranteed the ability to challenge unfair treatment through the courts and all citizens are to be considered equal under the law.
— **Logical Deductions/Outside Knowledge**: On the surface, the Fourteenth Amendment, with its ringing declaration of equality, seems to permanently end the conflict over equal rights in favor of African-Americans. However, we must remember that the Amendment was passed over the massive resistance of Southern whites (Congress threatens to prevent Southern congressmen from participating in Congress at all if they refuse to accept the Amendment). As Southern whites regained their political and social power, they used every tool at their disposal – legal, illegal and violent – to hollow out the Amendment.

Document E

Source: *Harper's Weekly*, December 1, 1866

Several of them have already acted. The Legislatures of Texas and Georgia have rejected the proposed Amendment. The Governors of Mississippi, South Carolina, and Alabama have recommended the rejection. The old political leaders who dragged their section into the war advise repudiation of the conditions. And the newspapers, the tone and manner of which are simply inconceivable to one who does not see them, disdain the Amendment with passionate contempt. That there are persons in the unrepresented States who deprecate this folly of Governors, Legislatures, leaders, and editors is very possible; but the practical drift of public opinion can be ascertained only through such channels. So long as those who, for whatever reason, approve the Amendment can not elect the Governors or a majority of the Legislatures, nor even organize to do so, we must regard what we see as the indication of the real state of feeling.

Key points:
- **Person**: N/A
- **Date**: 1866
- **Main point**: The South, led by former Confederate leaders, is completely opposed to the (Fourteenth) Amendment.
- **Logical Deductions/Outside Knowledge**: The depth of opposition to the Amendment and the fact that former Confederate leaders have retained or regained political power in the South suggest that resistance will continue even if the Amendment is approved. *Harper's Weekly* was a prominent New York political magazine that served as a mouthpiece of Republican sentiment.

Document F

Source: House of Representatives Election Results, 1868-69

State	Total House Seats	Republican	Democratic
Alabama	6	4	2
Arkansas	3	2	1
Florida	1	1	0
Georgia	7	3	4
Louisiana	5	5	0
Mississippi	5	5	0
North Carolina	7	6	1
South Carolina	4	4	0
Tennessee	8	8	0
Texas	4	3	1
Virginia	8	3	5
Total	**58**	**44**	**14**

Key points:
- **Person**: N/A
- **Date**: 1868-9
- **Main point**: The Republican Party, the great enemy of the Confederacy, now has the vast majority of House seats in the former Confederate states.
- **Logical Deductions/Outside Knowledge**: This kind of vote distribution must be due to African-American votes for Republican candidates. In other words, Reconstruction is mutually supported by African-American voters in the South and the Republican party. As African-Americans start to be disenfranchised by tactics like poll taxes and literacy tests, Republican seats in the South should (and do) decline dramatically

American History Tutoring Guide Paul Pinto

Document G

Source: Thomas Nast, *Harper's Weekly*, April 9, 1870

Key points:
- **Person**: Thomas Nast, a well-known political cartoonist, depicts Jefferson Davis, the former President of the Confederacy and Senator from Mississippi, looking resentful at the election of his African-American replacement, Senator Hiram Revels
- **Date**: 1870
- **Main point**: Reconstruction, protected by the Republican Party, the Union Army, and the Fourteenth Amendment, was temporarily successful in granting African-Americans the right to vote and hold office. This caused deep resentment among the white Southern population, whose leaders plotted revenge and aimed for the white "Redemption" of the South. Jefferson Davis is portrayed as Iago, a devious character from Shakespeare's play *Othello*, who betrayed his master, the dark-skinned Othello.
- **Logical Deductions/Outside Knowledge**: Senator Hiram Revels was an African-American pastor and chaplain in the United States Army during the Civil War. He is shown in the company of leading Radical Republicans such as Salmon Chase.

Document H

Source: Thaddeus Stevens, July 7, 1868

If you and your compeers can fling away ambition and realize that every human being, however lowly-born or degraded by fortune is your equal, that every inalienable right which belongs to you belongs also to him, truth and righteousness will spread over the land, and you will look down from the top of the Rocky mountains upon an empire of one hundred millions of happy people

Key points:
- **Person**: Thaddeus Stevens, the Pennsylvania Republican congressman, leader of the Radical Republicans, and the most unabashed supporter of equal rights for African-Americans
- **Date**: 1868
- **Main point**: The United States, including the South, will be a much happier, more peaceful and freer nation if it can only accept the principle of equal rights for all
- **Logical Deductions/Outside Knowledge**: Stevens was viewed as a hero by African-Americans and many Northerners but as a tyrant by Southerners

Document I

Source: Frederick Douglass, August 15, 1888

I recognize the Republican party as the sheet anchor of the colored man's political hopes and the ark of his safety.

Key points:
- **Person**: Frederick Douglass, former slave and African-American leader
- **Date**: 1888
- **Main point**: African-Americans required the help of the Republican Party because the Democratic Party was completely opposed to racial equality
- **Logical Deductions/Outside Knowledge**: Reconstruction was only as strong as the political fortunes of the Republican Party. The election of 1876, in which the Republicans nearly lost the presidency, symbolized the declining fortunes of the party and paved the way for a deal with Democrats that ended Reconstruction in the South

Document J

Source: James Henry Yarborough (judge from South Carolina), recollection of youth during the Civil War from interview conducted in the 1930s.

When that cruel war was over, it would have been wiser had the whites and ex-slaves been left to their own resources and inventions, to work out their future welfare. There was no lack of affection or loyalty on the part of the Negro, nor was there a lack of love and an enlightened appreciation of self-interest upon the part of the whites. Things might have been different if suffrage had been granted gradually. But with immediate equal suffrage, or the right to vote, came the carpetbagger with his preachments of social equality and the tantalizing bag of tricks to get for every Negro 40 acres of land and a mule. The Negroes were credulous and believed all the absurdities the knaves told them. The result was an inevitable curse for the Negro and lots of trouble for the white people. It ended only when Hampton was elected in 1876. Hampton is still my hero and a man of greatest worth in the annals of South Carolina.

Key points/connections to make:

— **Person**: James Yarborough is not a famous historical figure but his quote remains useful as it explains the opinion of a white Southerner in his own words
— **Date**: 1930s (thinking back to the 1870s)
— **Main point**: The South should have been allowed to organize Reconstruction on its own. Equal rights and voting rights should not have been given to all African-Americans and should rather have been distributed slowly.
— **Logical Deductions/Outside Knowledge**: Yarborough illustrates the depth of anti-equality feeling among white Southerners. He regards a "Redeemer" politician like [Wade] Hampton as a hero for ending Reconstruction.

4. *Develop an Outline (5 minutes)*
   A. **Introduction**
      1. *Explain what Reconstruction was and what it set out to do*: Reconstruction described the political process designed to reintegrate the South back into the Union and to provide for the millions of freed African-Americans.
      2. **Thesis:**
         Structure the thesis to match the phrasing of the question:
         Reconstruction succeeded in the short term because of the strong coalition formed by Radical Republicans, African-Americans, and Northerners wanting to punish the South. It failed because this coalition could not obtain the consent of white Southerners who consistently opposed

   B. **Paragraph 1 – Why Reconstruction Succeeded in the Short Term**
      1. *Topic Sentence*: Reconstruction succeeded in the short term because of strong political support among the people of the North, the electoral power of the Republican Party, and the strength of the occupying Union Army
      2. Abolitionists in the North supported abolitionism from the start, which frightened staunch supporters of slavery like Alexander Stephens (Doc A).

Inspired by the Second Great Awakening's push to help all individuals find salvation from God, abolitionists by the 1860s were demanding the end of an institution that violated God's mercy and compassion.
3. Abolitionists were joined by many white Northerners and by African-Americans in the North and South to build a coalition that abolished slavery (13th Amendment) and offered the prospect of full equality for African-Americans (14th Amendment, Doc D).
4. White Northerners were more and more likely to join the coalition for equal rights because of the massive sacrifices suffered by the Union Army during the war (Doc B). These losses caused many Northern whites to want to punish the South, which led to support for the 13th Amendment and the end of slavery, but many of these whites were more ambivalent about the 14th Amendment, which guaranteed equal rights.
5. This coalition was temporarily so strong that it overcame the resistance of President Johnson by impeaching and nearly removing him from office and succeeded in pushing through the Fourteenth Amendment despite strong resistance from the South (Doc E)
6. African-Americans win equal rights, including the right to vote and hold office, which causes stunning scenes like the election of Senator Hiram Revels from Mississippi, who held Jefferson Davis's old seat in the Senate (Doc G)
7. The Republican Party dominated Congress from 1866 to 1872, but part of this dominance was due to success in the South thanks to African-American suffrage
8. Finally, the Union Army's presence in the South forced Southern whites to initially go along with the reforms of the 13th and 14th Amendments and the Civil Rights bills

C. **Paragraph 2 – Why Reconstruction Failed in the Long Term**
1. Reconstruction failed in the long term because of massive and sustained resistance from Southern whites, the waning of the Republican coalition, and the withdrawal of the Union Army
2. Alexander Stephens's declaration that the Confederacy was based in large part on the principle that the races were not equal is powerful evidence of the fundamental nature of Southern white opposition to equal rights for African-Americans (Doc A)
3. The Republican coalition for equal rights pushed through the Fourteenth Amendment and the Civil Rights Acts of 1866 and 1875 but did not generate enough support for reparations to slaves in the form of land given to them either by their former masters or by the federal government. President Johnson rightfully gets the blame for this (Doc C), but it is also notable that the Republicans do not push harder for this due to the longstanding American tradition against social welfare payments by the government. Widespread land ownership among African-Americans might very well have helped African-Americans maintain their equal rights even when abandoned after 1877.
4. The Union Army eventually had to leave the South, which made enforcement of equal rights very difficult; this process is sped up by the reintegration of

Southern whites into national politics and the corresponding decline in the fortunes of the Republican Party
5. As the Republican Party declines nationally, African-Americans are left without a strong political sponsor (Doc I)
6. Southern whites oppose Reconstruction almost unanimously: old Confederates are brought back to office, Redeemer politics are lionized for "restoring" politics by booting out Northern carpetbaggers and their African-American allies from office, the Ku Klux Klan uses force to threaten and intimidate African-American voters (Doc J)

D. Conclusion
1. *Sum up the essay*
2. *Draw out a deeper implication*: The United States has always been based on the concept of the consent of the governed. Reconstruction provided a very difficult test for this principle because Southern whites would not consent to the idea of equal rights for African-Americans. This massive resistance was overcome by the North, but the will of the North to suppress white Southerners began to fade after a few years and ultimately the North acquiesced and allowed Southerners to "Redeem" the South and restore white supremacy. Although Reconstruction ultimately failed, it provided equal rights to African-Americans for a brief window of time, which certainly made a difference to the people involved.

5. *Write the essay (40-45 minutes)*
Try to cultivate a writing style that emphasizes clarity and economy. Avoid using fancy vocabulary words unless you are able to do so with precision and a sense of proportion. Make sure that the essay is clearly signposted, meaning that each paragraph is linked via the topic sentence to the overall thesis. Make sure that your conclusion sums up the case made by the thesis and evidence and see if you can find a way to draw out a deeper implication at the very end.

American History Tutoring Guide   Paul Pinto

LESSON FOUR: MULTIPLE CHOICE

Success on multiple choice tests in American history is based on the mastery of three factors: (1) content knowledge; (2) logic governing the selection of correct answers and/or the dismissal of incorrect answers; (3) tactics such as where and when to guess. The relationship between the three may be visualized as a pyramid:

```
        Tactics
         Logic
    Content Knowledge
```

1. *Content knowledge.* The most important of the three factors, content knowledge supplies the foundation on which the others depend. Remember: content knowledge <u>does not mean</u> reading and understanding all the information contained in the 900+ pages of your textbook! Focus rather on mastering the logic and specific facts of each of the sixteen themes. To help retain the information in a theme, pratice exercises like making historical timelines of your own. In these timelines, lay out the major events, as well as how the events affected people on different sides of the historical conflict or process.

   Make sure that you read each multiple choice question carefully, underlining key terms as necessary, in order to maximize your ability to match your knowledge with what the question is actually asking.

   Some multiple choice questions will provide content clues twice, the first clue from naming an individual, and the second from naming the political, social or economic movement the individual represents. For example, a question like "Which of the following best characterizes the stance of the writers associated with the literary flowering of the 1920s, such as Sinclair Lewis and F. Scott Fitzgerald?" provides us with three reference points to get to the correct answer – Lewis, Fitzgerald, and the more general "literary flowering of the 1920s."

2. *The logic of correct & incorrect answers.* Although the logic of answering multiple choice questions produces the best results when married to a strong knowledge of content, logic on its own can still be useful for dismissing false answer choices.
   - *Anachronisms.* A common fallacy is a reasonable-sounding answer choice that is factually true but from a different historical period. For example, a question that deals with why Prohibition struggled to maintain compliance among the citizenry may have an answer choice that references the New Deal, and although this choice may be a narrowly true statement about the New Deal, it must be incorrect because

Prohibition was ended prior to the start of the New Deal. Although detecting anachronisms assumes a certain level of content knowledge, a simple alertness to the potential for anachronisms is enough to make a difference.

- *Nonrelated answer choices.* Nonrelated answer choices are similar to anachronisms in that they are technically true but not concerned with the specific intent of the question. Whether nonrelated answer choices are from a different time period, geographic region, or branch of government, their internal or narrow truth does not compensate for the fact that they do not address the question itself.
- *Opposite answer choices.* Opposite answer choices directly address the question but in exactly the wrong way. For example, if the correct answer deals with the fact that only a minority of whites in the South owned slaves, a false opposite answer choice might read something like the following: "majorities of whites in the South owned slaves."

Consider the following sample question:

D.W. Griffith's epic film *The Birth of a Nation* (1915) became controversial because of its
(A): Portrayal of the Sons of Liberty as a radical mob
(B): celebration of American freedoms at a time of protest against radical groups
(C): celebration of America's cultural diversity
(D): depiction of Ku Klux Klan's activities as heroic and commendable
(E): sympathetic treatment of Germany in the years before World War I

We can dismiss the incorrect answer choices as follows:

D.W. Griffith's epic film *The Birth of a Nation* (1915) became controversial because of its
(A): Portrayal of the Sons of Liberty as a radical mob ← *anachronistic, Sons of Liberty are from the colonial era*
(B): celebration of American freedoms at a time of protest against radical groups ← *nonrelated, the film is not concerned with protest against radical groups*
(C): celebration of America's cultural diversity ← *opposite, KKK repressed rather than celebrated diverse populations*
(D): depiction of Ku Klux Klan's activities as heroic and commendable ← *correct*
(E): sympathetic treatment of Germany in the years before World War I ← *nonrelated, KKK focused on America rather than Europe*

3. *Tactics.* Tactics in this context refers to making the right decisions given that content knowledge and logical analysis have reached the limits of their usefulness. The main tactical decision that you will need to make for the multiple choice test is where and when to guess.

The good news for AP US History test takers is that the College Board has removed the AP guessing penalty. Students should therefore never leave an answer choice blank: it is always preferable to guess, even if you are guessing blindly.

The SAT II US History test does have a guessing penalty of one-quarter point for each incorrect answer. Here are the expected-value calculations that demonstrate that <u>you are better off guessing as long as you can eliminate two of the five answer choices</u>. The logic is as follows: if the test has five answer choices, and you are randomly guessing, then you have a one-fifth probability of getting the question right, which means you get +1 point, and a four-fifths probability of getting it wrong, which means you incur the quarter point guessing penalty:

$$\text{Expected value for blind guessing} = (1/5)*1 + (4/5)*-0.25 = -0.05$$

This value is negative, which means that blind guessing is not an optimal tactic. If you can eliminate one of the answer choices, the equation shifts to:

$$\text{Expected value} = (1/4)*1 + (3/4)*-0.25 = 0$$

The results are neutral: there is no harm in guessing if you can eliminate just one answer choice; there is also no net benefit. If, however, you can eliminate two answer choices, the expected value becomes positive:

$$\text{Expected value} = (1/3)*1 + (2/3)*-0.25 = +0.08$$

The expected value, of course, gets higher the more answer choices you are able to eliminate. You should always guess when you can eliminate at least two of the five answer choices.

LESSON FIVE: HOW TO INTERPRET POLITICAL CARTOONS

Political cartoons are an effective and succinct way of communicating moral lessons, political principles and/or social critiques, and their ability to condense an important issue into a single image makes them ideal test question material. The multiple choice section of an average AP or SAT II US history test will contain at least a few cartoons that require both interpretation and analysis in order to identify the correct answer.

To answer questions dealing with political cartoons, follow these steps:
1. Look carefully at the picture to generate some initial hypotheses about the meaning of the cartoon. Try to situate the cartoon with reference to a specific time, place, or event
2. Read the question carefully, underlining key terms
3. Read and interpret the written message at the bottom of the cartoon and the other text in the cartoon; link the meaning of the text to the picture
4. Put everything together by linking the question to the picture, message, supporting text and background information
5. Consult the answer choices

Our first example is one of the most famous political cartoons in American history[12]:

QUESTION: Which of the following individuals would be MOST likely to agree with the message of the cartoon above?
A. Thomas Hutchinson
B. John Adams
C. Lord North
D. Citizen Genêt
E. Jefferson Davis

---
[12] Benjamin Franklin, *Pennsylvania Gazette*, 9 May 1754

Let's go through the steps:
1. *Look carefully at the picture to generate some initial hypotheses*
   The image of the snake in pieces clearly indicates that separation is worse than unity
2. *Read the question carefully, underlining key terms*
   "Which of the following individuals would be MOST likely to agree with the message of the cartoon above?"
3. *Read the text of the cartoon and link it to the picture*
   "JOIN, OR DIE" is the overall message; the remaining text serves to label the various parts of the snake with the various colonies or regions represented by the thirteen colonies. Note that New England represents the head of the snake.
4. *Put everything together*
   The overall message of this cartoon is relatively clear in this instance: without unity, the thirteen colonies have no power and might as well be dead
5. *Consult the answer choices*
   The most familiar names among the answer choices are (B) John Adams, the second President of the United States and a leader of the Revolutionary cause from Massachusetts and (E) Jefferson Davis, the president of the Confederacy. (E) is obviously incorrect as it is anachronistic. You may also be familiar with (C) Lord North, the British prime minister during the time of the American Revolution. The British were generally in favor of the political separation of the colonies, as it made each individual colony easier to control, so (C) is incorrect. Answer choice (A) Thomas Hutchinson refers to the Loyalist governor of Massachusetts, who opposed the Revolution, so (A) is incorrect, as is (D) Citizen Gênet, a French diplomat who does not come onto the scene until after the Revolution. The correct answer is therefore (B).

Let's try another cartoon, this one from the Gilded Age:

American History Tutoring Guide Paul Pinto

QUESTION: The artist who produced the cartoon above would probably express support for which of the following measures?
A. A federal income tax
B. More aggressive enforcement of the Sherman Antitrust Act
C. Recognition of the right of labor unions to organize and collectively bargain
D. The direct election of US Senators
E. All of the above

1. *Look carefully at the picture to generate some initial hypotheses*
   The image above shows three or four large and wealthy men clutching sacks of money and sitting atop a pier, which is kept aloft by a large number of beaten-down and tired looking individuals. The image that comes to mind is one of the idle rich being carried by the toil of the working poor.

2. *Read the question carefully, underlining key terms*
   The key terms here are "support" and "measures." To find the correct answer, we have to figure out which of the measures fit with the overall message of the cartoon.

3. *Read the text of the cartoon and link it to the picture*
   The text in the cartoon states the low wages per week earned by workers in various industries, as well as the names of famous captains of industry (robber barons) such as Jay Gould and Cornelius Vanderbilt.

4. *Put everything together*
   The message of the cartoon is clearly one of injustice: it is unfair for a few to live so well while so many of the hardworking poor are scraping by. This is supported by the image of the wealthy capitalists living high off the hog, while the mass of people scrape by on a few dollars per week.

5. *Consult the answer choices*
   We may reasonably infer that creator of the cartoon would favor policies that promise to level the playing field in the name of American democracy. The cartoonist would probably favor (A) the federal income tax, which at the time applied only to the very top of the income scale; (B) aggressive enforcement of the Sherman Antitrust Act to prevent capitalists from stamping out competition and collecting monopoly super-profits; (C) recognition of the right of labor unions to bargain in order to help increase wages and (D) the direct election of Senators, which was intended to remove the Senatorial selection process from easily corruptible state legislatures.

Exercise:
Follow the five steps to answer the following question about the cartoon on the next page:
QUESTION: Which of the following groups would agree with Lady Columbia?
A. Radical Republicans
B. Copperheads
C. Redeemers
D. Southern Democrats
E. Border state politicians

Source: Thomas Nast, *Harper's Weekly,* August 5, 1865

American History Tutoring Guide Paul Pinto

LESSON SIX: HOW TO READ AND INTERPRET CHARTS, GRAPHS AND TABLES

From the beginning of the Republic, the United States has made it a priority to gather statistics on the growth and development of the nation. Article I, Section 2 of the Constitution commands a census or "enumeration" of the population every ten years in order to apportion representatives to Congress. The Bureau of the Census has been tracking population and a number of other demographic, economic and social indicators since the first Census of 1790. These data are summarized in an extremely useful set of publications created called the *Historical Statistics of the United States* (http://www.census.gov/compendia/statab/past_years.html). Because many of the data table/graph questions on the tests are drawn from this data source, it is certainly worth your time to go to the link above and flip through the pdf files to familiarize yourself with the format, layout and content of the *Historical Statistics*.

We begin the lesson by drawing an excerpt from a historical population table.[13]

Population, Decennial Summary - Race: 1790-1860

Year	Total	Total White	%	Total Black	%	Free Black	%	Slaves	%
1860	31,443,321	26,922,587	85.6%	4,441,830	14.1%	488,070	1.6%	3,953,760	12.6%
1850	23,191,876	19,553,068	84.3%	3,638,808	15.7%	434,495	1.9%	3,204,313	13.8%
1840	17,069,458	14,195,805	83.2%	2,873,648	16.8%	386,293	2.3%	2,487,355	14.6%
1830	12,866,020	10,537,378	81.9%	2,328,642	18.1%	319,599	2.5%	2,009,043	15.6%
1820	9,638,453	7,866,797	81.6%	1,771,656	18.4%	233,634	2.4%	1,538,022	16.0%
1810	7,239,881	5,862,073	81.0%	1,377,808	19.0%	186,446	2.6%	1,191,362	16.5%
1800	5,308,483	4,306,446	81.1%	1,002,037	18.9%	108,435	2.0%	893,602	16.8%
1790	3,929,214	3,172,006	80.7%	757,208	19.3%	59,527	1.5%	697,681	17.8%

1. Which of the following is consistent with the information in the table above?
   A. The number of free African-Americans as a percentage of the overall population declined consistently from 1790-1860
   B. The number of slaves as a percentage of the overall population increased steadily from 1790-1860
   C. The number of free African-Americans as a percentage of the overall population declined from 1830-1860
   D. The white population more than doubled from 1790-1810
   E. The total population of the United States peaked in 1850

Solving data-intensive questions requires you to develop a simple but effective method of separating and emphasizing key pieces of information. The simplest general way to do this is to use your pencil to highlight important information, draw connections, or cross out less important information. Using your pencil in this way helps simplify a mass of information down to only those relationships that you need to answer the question. Follow the checklist below to successfully answer data questions.

Process to analyze data tables/graphs

---

[13] US Census Bureau. *Historical Statistics of the United States 1790-1945*. Series B 13-23. – Population, Decennial Summary – Sex, Urban-Rural Residence, and Race: 1790 to 1940

American History Tutoring Guide Paul Pinto

1. Read the table or graph title and headings to figure out what kind of data is being presented and what the main point of the data table or graph is
2. Read the question carefully, underlining key terms where necessary
3. Look at the data table or graph briefly to see if any major pattern or trend pops out
4. Combine your insights from steps 1-3 and quickly glance at each of the answer choices to see if you have a match
5. If you have a match, double check the choice with the data. If not, systematically go through each answer choice

Let's apply the steps to the problem above:
1. *Figure out what kind of data is being presented*
   The data table title makes it clear that race is the topic of the table, which means that we should be alert to the fact that the right answer is likely to involve some sort of comparison between the white population and the African-American population. The data table itself consists of columns of numbers and columns in percentage terms. Total population is shown on the left, followed by the total white population in terms of absolute numbers and as a percentage of the total population. The same data is presented for the total African-American population, which is then separated into free and slave components. Note that one can sum up to 100% by either adding the white population to the black population **or** adding the white population to the free black population and the enslaved black population. Finally, note that the Census Bureau convention at the time was to present the data in terms of descending rather than ascending dates.

2. *Read the question carefully, underlining key terms*
   In this case, the question does not provide us with any specific terms to underline. In many other cases, however, the question stem will include specific details that can be used to narrow down the answer choices.

3. *Look at the data table to see if any major pattern or trend pops out*
   In this case, we can see that the total population increases rapidly from 1790-1860; that the total black population also increases rapidly but not quite as rapidly as the total population; which means that the share of African-Americans among the total population is lower in 1860 than it was in 1790.

4. *Combine insights from steps 1-3 and see if an answer choice matches*
   Answer choices (A), (C), and (D) all fit with steps 1-3, which allows us to eliminate answer choices (B) and (E). (B) is contradictory in that it claims that the share of African-American slaves as a proportion of the total population is consistently rising when it is consistently falling. (E) is contradictory in that population in this chart hits its high in 1860, not 1850.

5. *Systematically check through the remaining answer choices.*
   Answer choice (A) is incorrect because free African-Americans as a share of total population increases then decreases; and answer choice (D) is incorrect because the white population does not quite double. Answer choice (C) is the correct answer.

American History Tutoring Guide Paul Pinto

Exercise

Answer the following question using the 5-step approach:

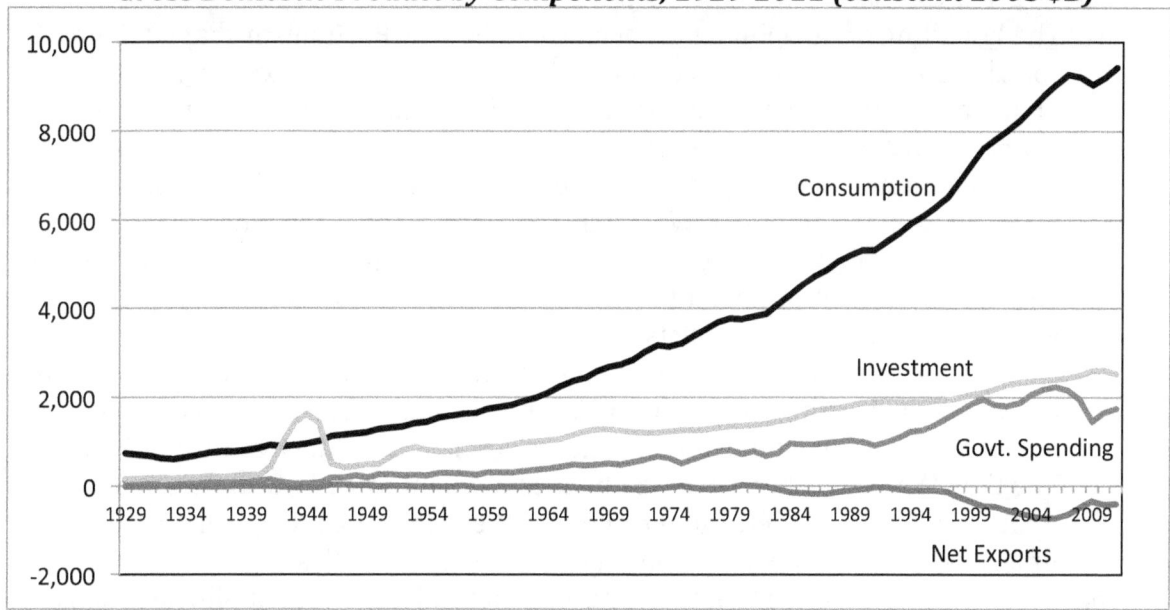

Note: GDP = Consumption + Investment + Government Spending + Net Exports (Exports - Imports)
Source: Bureau of Economic Analysis, www.bea.gov

1. According to the graph above, which of the following statements is NOT true?
   A. World War II produced an intense burst of investment spending
   F. Economic growth in the past twenty years has been largely fueled by increases in consumption and government spending
   G. The United States has run a negative balance of trade since the 1990s
   H. Consumption is the largest component of GDP
   I. Government spending accounts for the majority of GDP

LESSON SEVEN: FREQUENTLY TESTED ESSAY TOPICS

1. *Free-response essays.* Here are the findings from an analysis of 80 free response essay prompts given on AP tests over the past decade:
    - *Must-review topics*:
        1. The Founding of New England, specifically the way Puritanism shaped political, social and economic life, and a comparison of the founding experience in New England with those of the Chesapeake, Virginia, and, to a lesser degree, the Spanish Southwest and New France.
        2. The Road to Independence: tracing the evolution in the colonial relationship from the French and Indian War to the Declaration of Independence
        3. The Articles of Confederation and the Constitution, including the way that each addressed political, social and economic problems and the arguments of the Federalists and Anti-Federalists.
        4. Slavery, the origins of the institution in Virginia, its expansion in the South and decline in the North, its effect on social relations and economic development, the rise of the abolitionist movement, and its crucial importance to the Civil War
        5. The Civil War's effect on society: Changes wrought by the war in terms of the relationship of the federal government to the states; the fate of African-Americans; and the development of the South and the West.
        6. Social movements, or the efforts of groups excluded from the political arena to find their place in American democracy. The two main social movements relate to African-Americans and women.
            - The African-American Experience: life under slavery, freedmen in the North, emancipation, comparison of different African-American leaders and liberation movements, the politics of Reconstruction, life in segregated America, the Civil Right movement, comparisons over time (e.g., goals and achievements of black leaders in from 1890-1920 versus 1945-1968).
            - The Female Experience: life in the early colonies (especially New England), the nineteenth-century "cult of domesticity", the female contribution to the reform movements of the early 19th century, the women's liberation movement of the 1840s-1860s, female Progressive leaders, the suffrage movement, women in World War II, and the women's liberation movement of the 1960s; comparison of women's movements from one historical period to another.
        7. The Progressive Movement: its purpose, goals, achievements; its response to the challenges of urbanization and industrialism; its connection to religion; comparison to the New Deal
        8. Foreign Policy in the 20th century: early imperialism; involvement in WWI; Versailles/League of Nations; isolationism; World War II, the Cold War, and American global leadership; comparison of post-WWI response to post-WWII response
        9. Immigration: Attitudes towards and political movements for/against immigration; waves of immigration (Northern Europe 1780-1860; Southern Europe 1880-1920; rest of the world 1965-2000); challenges faced by immigrant groups

- *Important topics*
    10. <u>Economic Change and Sectionalism</u>: the development of the market system in the early 19th centuries and the way that the North, South and West came to occupy different economic identities with the rise of industrialism. An associated topic that is also important is <u>Economic Change and Social Development</u>, which deals with the way economic changes such as industrialism, transportation and trade led to different social and political patterns.
    11. <u>The Rise of the Modern Presidency</u>: analyzing the increase in the power, duties and image of the modern president, including changes in mass communication/the media, foreign policy/the military, and social welfare/the modern administrative state.
    12. <u>Opposition to central government</u>: colonial-era rebellions; states' rights movements; resistance to civil-rights and labor laws
    13. <u>Religion, society and politics</u>: Puritan era; 19th century social reformers (temperance, abolitionism)

Note that most of the key essay topics are the same or very similar to the key review topics from the multiple choice tests.

2. *The DBQ*
   An analysis of twenty past DBQ prompts reveals the most common topics:
   - Foreign policy (5);
   - Slavery (3);
   - Social movements (3);
   - American Revolution (2);

   Foreign policy is a favorite topic for the DBQ because the US made its largest foreign policy impact in the twentieth century and the documentary sources from the twentieth century (particularly political cartoons) tend to be far more readily available.

American History Tutoring Guide Paul Pinto

LESSON EIGHT: LINKING GENERAL THEMES TO SPECIFIC QUESTIONS

Learning how to work downwards from large themes to specific facts and how to organize specific facts within larger themes are both important historical skills. To illustrate this process, I use one of the central themes of American history: the efforts by African-Americans to establish an equitable place in American society.

1. *Describe, define and bound the theme*
   The vast scale of the slave trade – over three-quarters of the total number of individuals transported to the New World from 1500-1820 were African slaves – resulted in slaves representing 35% of the total population of the South in 1790. 'Representing' is perhaps an unfortunate word choice in that slaves had no basic political or social rights: neither the right to control their labor, nor their family, nor their community. This lack of rights was made all the more glaring by the democratization going on in the broader society, both in the North and the South. The African-American experience in the United States is thus the long and painful story of a community trying to regain control of itself – first over its very freedom and later over its struggle for political, civil and economic rights. This struggle illustrates not just the African-American community but rather the broader nature of American democracy and liberty.

2. *Outline the main tension, conflict, or logical process in need of being worked out*
   The main conflict is the ongoing effort of African-Americans to obtain an equal position in American history. To make this very large theme a bit more tractable, we can focus on three major processes: Emancipation, or the battle to free the slaves; Reconstruction, or the first effort to create a multiracial democracy; and the Civil Rights Movement, which succeeded in this effort a century later.

   The experience of slavery amplified pre-existing racial views to the point that the vast majority of the white community in the early nineteenth century agreed that, at best, whites and blacks were inherently different and that blacks should not be able to participate in American democracy on an equal footing. In other words, despite the general nature of the Declaration of Independence ('all men are created equal') and the refusal of the Constitution to link slavery to race, politics in the United States was run on racial lines. In the South, slavery plus the fact that blacks nearly accounted for majorities in South Carolina and Georgia meant that there was fierce resistance to black emancipation, let alone equality. Change begins around the 1820s with the rise of the anti-slavery movement, which succeeds in getting slavery banned in the British Empire in 1833. The anti-slavery movement was centered in Protestant New England and fueled by evangelical (Northern) Protestantism's desire to evangelize and liberate. The abolitionist movement remained a minority, however, and was generally outmatched by solid South support for slavery. There is further change, however, as southern intransigence on slavery and the rising popularity of a free-labor movement started to produce anti-slavery majorities in the North. Politics from the late 1840s until the Civil War is then consumed with the slavery issue, as the fearful South attempts to reach for more and more. A watershed is reached with the Supreme Court's *Dred Scott* (1857) decision, which rules that those Americans of African descent cannot be considered

American citizens. This ruling rejected the main idea of the Declaration of Independence and created a racial test for political participation.

The Civil War destroyed slavery but left unresolved the issue of whether blacks should be allowed to participate in a true multiracial democracy, a problem made even more difficult by the fact that large black populations were located in the very places in which racism was at its most virulent. Reconstruction was thus a competition between a coalition of African Americans and white liberals (Radical Republicans) versus Southern whites, with less-committed Northern whites as a "swing vote." Although Reconstruction resulted in some real achievements, culminating in the Fourteenth and Fifteenth Amendments, which guaranteed the citizenship and voting rights of African Americans (and any minorities that might be discriminated against), the ability of the Southern whites to resist implementation of the amendments eventually resulted in the reassertion of white domination in the South.

The Second World War, the Cold War, and the movement of many African-Americans from the South to the cities of the North eventually resulted in favorable conditions for a movement for civil rights. The purpose of this movement was not to win over white Southerners, who proved almost uniformly reluctant to grant blacks civil rights, but rather to prod the federal government to push the South into treating blacks equally. The civil rights movement combined a range of strengths – nonviolent protest, links to northern Congressmen of both parties, adroit use of the media, international support – to give African Americans the rights and liberties they had long sought, rights enjoyed by most other Americans.

In addition to giving African-Americans their rightful place in American society, the Civil Rights Movement helped to broaden opportunities for a range of other minority groups. Although some African-Americans today struggle with issues of poverty and crime, the community as a whole enjoys a real and profound political equality.

3. *Assign the main historical actors places on either side (or in the middle) of the conflict*
   I will break the conflict into three phases: (A) the battle over slavery; (B) Reconstruction; and (C) Jim Crow and the Civil Rights Movement.

   A. <u>Emancipation</u>

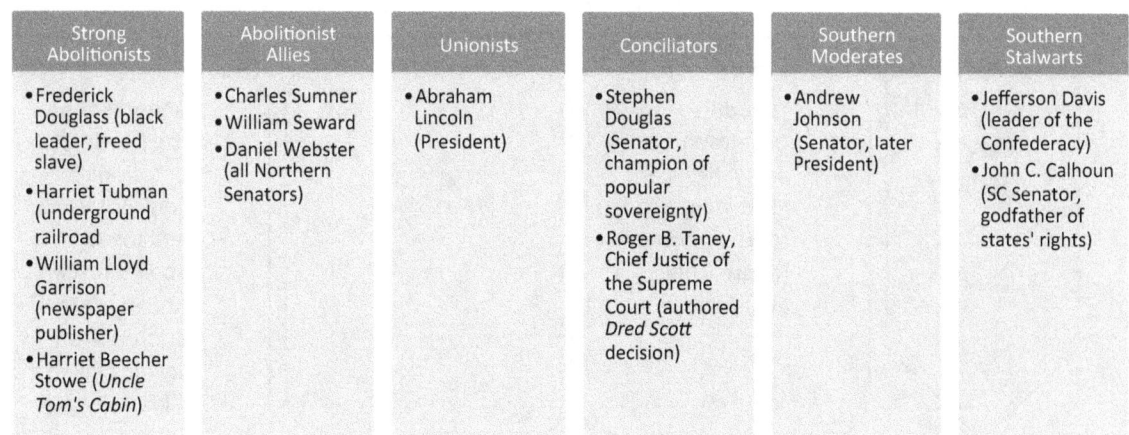

Strong Abolitionists	Abolitionist Allies	Unionists	Conciliators	Southern Moderates	Southern Stalwarts
• Frederick Douglass (black leader, freed slave) • Harriet Tubman (underground railroad) • William Lloyd Garrison (newspaper publisher) • Harriet Beecher Stowe (*Uncle Tom's Cabin*)	• Charles Sumner • William Seward • Daniel Webster (all Northern Senators)	• Abraham Lincoln (President)	• Stephen Douglas (Senator, champion of popular sovereignty) • Roger B. Taney, Chief Justice of the Supreme Court (authored *Dred Scott* decision)	• Andrew Johnson (Senator, later President)	• Jefferson Davis (leader of the Confederacy) • John C. Calhoun (SC Senator, godfather of states' rights)

B. Reconstruction

African American Leaders	Radical Republicans	Moderate Republicans	Unionists	Southern Stalwarts
• Frederick Douglass (black leader, freed slave) • Blanche K. Bruce (Senator from Mississippi)	• Charles Sumner (Senator) • Thaddeus Stevens (Congressman) • Gen. Otis Howard (head of Freedmen's Bureau)	• William Seward • Ulysses S. Grant	• Andrew Johnson	• Nathan Forrest (leader of the KKK) • Alexander Stephens (former VP of Confederacy)

C. Civil Rights Movement

African American Leaders	Democratic Party Leaders	Dixiecrats
• Martin Luther King, Jr. (preacher, movement leader) • John L. Lewis (student, movement leader) • Thurgood Marshall (lawyer for NAACP, later Supreme Court Justice) • Malcolm X (minister, Nation of Islam)	• John F. Kennedy (President) • Lyndon Johnson (President) • William Fulbright (Senator from Arkansas)	• Orval Faubus (Governor of Arkansas) • George Wallace (Governor of Alabama) • Police Commissioner Eugene "Bull" Connor (Birmingham, AL)

4. *Provide an event timeline that traces the progress of the conflict*
   For the sake of brevity, I focus on Emancipation and leave Reconstruction and the Civil Rights Movement as practice exercises.

Event	Abolitionists	Compromisers	Pro-Slavery
Founding of the *Liberator* (1831)	• Journal founded by Daniel Lloyd Garrison: called openly for immediate abolition		
Abolitionist Revivals (1835-7)	• Theodore Dwight Weld, an evangelical Protestant, tours Ohio and NY preaching abolitionism		• Angry mobs (in the North) occasionally confront Weld and fellow abolitionists • Abolitionist printer Elijah Lovejoy killed in Illinois

Event	Abolitionists	Compromisers	Pro-Slavery
Founding of the *North Star* (1847)	• Journal founded by Frederick Douglas to give black abolitionists a voice		
Compromise of 1850	• Abolition of slave auctions and depots in Washington, DC	• Henry Clay/Stephen Douglas arrange for NM and UT to decide slavery via popular sovereignty	• Strengthening of the Fugitive Slave Law; suspended right of jury trial for suspected fugitives
Kansas-Nebraska Act (1854)	• Many Northerners pushed into the abolitionist camp by repeal of the Missouri Compromise • Resulting political realignment leads to formation of Republican Party	• Bill organized by Douglas would allow Kansas and Nebraska to decide slavery via popular sovereignty, repealed Missouri Compromise	• Violence in Kansas caused by fighting for control of the territorial government
Dred Scott v. Sanford (1857)	• Decision provided increased support for the Republican Party, which takes a position of no slavery in the territories	• Made the popular sovereignty position of Stephen Douglas much more difficult	• Supreme Court ruled that no African-American could be a citizen • Congress had no power to prohibit slavery in any territory

Event	Abolitionists	Compromisers	Pro-Slavery
Lecompton Constitution (1858)	Convinced the Republican Party that the Democratic Party was completely subservient to the slave power	President Buchanan bows to southern pressure and pushes for Kansas to enter as a slave state despite majority opposition	Rigged election results in a pro-slavery legislature and constitution
Raid on Harper's Ferry (1858)	John Brown, a radical abolitionist, led men to seize the federal arsenal in VA and use the weapons to start a war to eradicate slavery	Common ground between Northerners and Southerners shrinking, as evidenced by widespread support for Brown's ends if	After Brown was caught and executed for treason, Southerners interpreted Northern sympathy for him as majority support for abolition
Election of 1860	Lincoln wins a majority in the electoral college but zero electoral votes in the South	Lincoln's moderation is not enough to placate the South • Democratic party splits between Douglas and Breckenridge	South moves irrevocably towards secession

5. *Practice sample multiple choice questions*:
   1. The Republican Party's position on slavery in 1860 was
      A. the immediate abolition of slavery
      B. to leave the question of slavery up to each state or territory
      C. to oppose the expansion of slavery into new territories
      D. to ignore the issue
      E. that slavery was a positive good

Emancipation required a coalition that included both committed white abolitionists and the more numerous free-soilers, who were not (until later) committed to abolition.

Lincoln represented both groups, and therefore would not have taken a position like (A). Choices (D) and (E) are both false given that the Republican Party defined itself by its view that slavery should not be extended into the territories. Finally, (B) may be ruled out as it was the position of Northern Democratic compromisers like Stephen Douglas. This leaves the correct answer, (C).

2. During a debate between Illinois senate candidates Democrat Stephen Douglas and Republican Abraham Lincoln in Freeport, Illinois, how did Douglas respond to Lincoln's assertion that the Dred Scott decision rendered the concept of popular sovereignty null and void?
   A. Douglas said he would push for a constitutional amendment that would recognize the legitimacy of the concept of popular sovereignty and supersede the Dred Scott decision.
   B. Douglas refused to discuss the issue of slavery, asserting that such discussions undermined national unity.
   C. Douglas argued that the Dred Scott decision did not impose slavery on free states and territories. The decision allowed only for slaves to be brought into these areas, not for slavery to be practiced there.
   D. Douglas acknowledged that the Dred Scott decision made it impossible for Congress to legislate against slavery but it did not prevent the president from ending slavery by executive order.
   E. Douglas argued that popular sovereignty was alive and well. Although slavery could not be outlawed by a territory, he insisted that slavery could not actually be practiced unless territorial legislatures passed legislation protecting it.

This is a difficult question that requires that the student think very carefully to isolate Douglas's position. (A) can be ruled out given that there would be no chance a constitutional amendment would be approved given that the South represented more than a quarter of the states. (B) can also be ruled out given that Douglas, to his credit, attempted to directly tackle the issue of slavery with his chosen instrument – popular sovereignty. (C) is internally contradictory, and (D) violates the Constitution. That leaves (E), which is the correct answer.

American History Tutoring Guide   Paul Pinto

LESSON NINE: HISTORICAL TIMELINES

Developing timelines to master a complicated series of events such as the process leading to American independence is an old but extremely useful technique. A good timeline goes beyond the mere memorization of a list of events by showing how different events and people are connected to the main process, and how that process is propelled forward by a conflict between two different sides.

For the purposes of this lesson, I focus on the path to American independence. Other topics in which the timeline can make a useful contribution are the path to the Constitution, the path leading to the Civil War, the Civil War itself, Reconstruction, the Progressive reforms, the New Deal, and the Civil Rights movement.

The path to American independence can be modeled as a conflict between those who thought the American colonies should be independent, or at minimum self-governing, and those who thought that the English parliament as constituted in the 1750s was sufficient in meeting the political needs of the American colonies. In between these two poles stood the mass of colonists, who recognized valid arguments on both sides. After the French & Indian War, which was part of a global struggle between England and France, the British government found itself in need of additional revenue to pay for its troops in North America. This desire for additional revenue without allowing the colonies to participate in the taxing process through their legislative assemblies resulted in a number of crises that steadily pushed the colonies toward independence. The timeline below starts with the end of the French and Indian War (1763) and ends with the fighting at Lexington and Concord (1775).

Path to Independence Timeline

Towards Compromise	**Event**	**Towards Conflict**
• Shared military experience as colonial soldiers served as part of the British army • Thrill of victory over French and Indians	French & Indian War (1756-1763)	• British soldiers/statesmen viewed colonial militias as poorly organized/ill-funded • Cost of the war leads British government to abandon policy of salutary neglect • Proclamation of 1763 prohibited colonists from settling to the west
	Sugar Act (1764)	• Taxes on foreign sugar/other luxury goods
	Quartering Act (1765)	• Required colonists to provide room and board for British soldiers

Towards Compromise	Event	Towards Conflict
Repeal of the Act by Parliament, partially as a response to colonial protest, partly as a change of prime minister	Stamp Act (1765) Repeal (1766) Declaratory Act (1766)	• Required revenue stamps to be placed on most printed paper in the colonies • First direct tax of colonists • 9 colonies meet in 'Stamp Act Congress' in NYC, resolve that only their elected reps can pass taxes • Formation of Sons of Liberty to intimidate tax collectors • Declaratory Act restates Parliament's claim to tax the colonies as it pleased
• Repeal of Townshend Acts with the accession of Lord North as prime minister; retained small, symbolic tax on tea	Townshend Acts (1767) … Repeal (1768)	• New taxes on colonial imports of tea, glass, paper • Independent crown officials to collect tax; allowed to search private homes • Less protest than Stamp Act b/c of indirect nature • James Otis/Samuel Adams of MA send Mass. Circular Letter to every colonial legislature urging colonists to petition Parliament for repeal
• John Adams, a colonial leader, defends the soldiers and earns their acquittal	Boston Massacre (1770)	• British guards fire on crowd critical of their presence, killing five
	Boston Tea Party (1773)	• Response to the Tea Act of 1773, which attempted to push colonists in purchasing British East India company tea • Colonists dumped tea into Boston harbor

Towards Compromise	Event	Towards Conflict
	Coercive (Intolerable) Acts (1774)	• Port of Boston closed • Power of Mass. legislature reduced • Royal officials in Mass. removed from colonial justice system • British troops to be quartered in
	First Continental Congress (1774)	• All colonies sent delegates except Georgia to determine how to respond to Coercive Acts • Claims of the Congress dismissed by the King, Mass. declared to be in rebellion
	Lexington and Concord (1775)	• British troops sent to seize colonial military supplies stored in Concord • Colonists warned by Paul Revere and William Dawes • Fighting breaks out on village green of Lexington

The timeline above is organized with the events in the center, efforts to compromise on the left, and efforts leading to increased conflict on the right. The relative paucity of events on the left provide a graphic illustration of the failure of moderate voices on either side to resolve the political tensions imposed by Parliament's taxation policies. Another way of organizing the timeline is to retain the events in the center, but place British policies on the left and colonial responses on the right.

After you have created a timeline, spend an hour memorizing as much information on the timeline as possible – some degree of memorization is necessary in order for you to successfully draw on this information when writing an essay.

American History Tutoring Guide Paul Pinto

PART THREE: REFERENCE MATERIALS

KEY RESOURCES

Your textbook, class lectures, and notes will supply you with most of the information you need for the test (along with this guide!). You may also consult the College Board and a number of useful online sources for additional information.

College Board Information
The College Board publishes helpful AP US History test information and preparation online (http://www.collegeboard.com/student/testing/ap/sub_ushist.html). Of particular interest is the AP US History Course Description document: (http://apcentral.collegeboard.com/apc/public/repository/ap-us-history-course-description.pdf), which provides lots of useful information, including:
- A listing of the main Themes and Topics of the course
- 40 sample multiple-choice questions
- Sample DBQ and free-response essay prompts

Online Sources
1. The US Census. The single best source of demographic, economic and political information (www.census.gov). The Census publications of greatest use may be found in the *Historical Statistics of the United States* (http://www.census.gov/compendia/statab/past_years.html), which contain an amazing

2. The Avalon Project. An excellent source for primary historical, legal and diplomatic documents such as the Constitution or the Monroe Doctrine (http://avalon.law.yale.edu/)

3. Digital History online. A website put together by Professor Steven Mintz at the University of Houston, which contains textbook materials, primary sources, analytical essays, and timelines. (http://www.digitalhistory.uh.edu/)

American History Tutoring Guide   Paul Pinto

SAMPLE FREE-RESPONSE ESSAY PROMPTS

1. Analyze the main factors that contributed to the formation of the American National Security State after World War II.

2. Compare and contrast the ways in which violations of the neutrality of the Atlantic contributed to America's involvement in the following wars:
   A. The War of 1812
   B. World War I
   C. World War II

3. How did World War II transform America at home? In your answer, focus on two or three of the many major social, economic, and demographic changes caused by the war.

4. How did American expansion westwards from 1819-1890 serve as a model for American imperial expansion in the late 19th century?

5. Select TWO of the following events and discuss how it marked a turning point in American foreign policy.
   A. The Spanish-American War
   B. World War II
   C. The Vietnam War

6. Use the example of America's evolving relationship with China from the 1880s to 1976 to illustrate the changing position of the United States in the world.

7. How did the Franco-American alliance help the United States win independence?

8. How did foreign policy shape domestic politics during TWO of the following time periods:
   1788 – 1808
   1880 – 1905
   1914 – 1920

9. Compare and contrast the role of the United States in shaping the League of Nations and the United Nations.

10. How did the foreign policy successes or failures of Franklin Roosevelt (1932-1945) and Lyndon Johnson (1963-68) affect prospects for the American welfare state at home?

11. Why did the Civil Rights Movement succeed where Reconstruction failed? In your answer, discuss at least TWO of the following factors:
    A. The size and scope of the federal government
    B. The Cold War
    C. The size, wealth and geographical distribution of the African-American population
    D. Racial attitudes among the American people

12. Compare and contrast the goals, strategies and approaches adopted by Martin Luther King and by Malcolm X.

13. How well did the political system of the United States deal with the challenge of extending slavery into the West from 1820-1860?

14. Assess the ways in which the practice of popular sovereignty exacerbated the sectional crisis from 1850-1860.

15. Why did the vast majority of Union Army troops consider John Brown to be a hero? Do you think Brown was a hero?

16. What factors are most responsible for the formalization and growth of the slave system of the American South from 1650-1850?

17. Compare and contrast the leadership strategies of W.E.B. Du Bois and Booker T. Washington. Which leader was more successful?

18. Slaves in the South lived lives dominated by the economic and social dictates of their masters. What social and cultural institutions and practices did slaves draw on to assert a small but significant degree of autonomy?

19. Americans have been arguing over the proper role, scope and powers of the federal government in the economy since the founding of the Republic. Analyze debates over the proper role of the federal government in the economy during TWO of the following four periods.
    1792-1808
    1828-1836
    1928-1940
    1976-1988

20. How closely did presidents Thomas Jefferson and Andrew Jackson stick to their principles of states' rights and limited federal government?

21. Alexander Hamilton and Thomas Jefferson articulated different visions of the federal government's economic and political powers. Whose vision triumphed? Limit your answer to the period 1788 – 1945.

22. Explain the changes in the legal and political rights of African-Americans from 1776 to 1965. Be sure to cite relevant laws, court decisions, and amendments.

23. How did the struggle for American Independence, including the Revolutionary War itself, influence the form and powers of the new national government under the Articles of Confederation?

24. Compare and contrast the powers of the national government under the Articles of Confederation and under the Constitution.

25. Should the Supreme Court have the exclusive right to determine what the Constitution says?

26. In what ways did Reconstruction serve as a second Constitutional Convention?

27. Do major constitutional changes require constitutional amendments? Discuss, using a comparison of the Progressive Era and the New Deal as examples.

28. What factors explain why the North industrialized while the South failed to industrialize?

29. What economic, political, and social factors contributed to the rise of the Gilded Age economy?

30. Why did farmers in the late 19th century campaign with such vigor for Free Silver?

31. Select TWO of the following inventions and discuss how they transformed American society.
    A. The cotton gin
    B. Electric lighting
    C. The Model T Ford
    D. Railways

32. Compare and contrast how the following presidents dealt with the problem of high unemployment.
    A. Herbert Hoover
    B. Franklin Roosevelt
    C. Ronald Reagan

33. Why and how did the French and Indian War transform the relationship between Great Britain and the thirteen American colonies?

34. Define the British concept of virtual representation and explain why the American colonists refused to embrace it as a viable alternative to revolution.

35. What are the three most important reasons why the American colonies declared independence from Great Britain?

36. Discuss why and how each of the following incidents marked a turning point in the road to independence:
    A. The Stamp Act
    B. The Boston Tea Party
    C. Lexington and Concord

37. How did the Democratic-Republican party of Thomas Jefferson get the best of the Federalist Party of Alexander Hamilton and John Adams?

38. How did the Republican Party build a majority coalition in the North by 1860?

39. Discuss the factors that led the following groups to change political party affiliation:
    A. African-Americans from the 1920s to the 1940s
    B. Southern whites from 1948 to 1970

40. Why did the New Deal coalition formed by Franklin Delano Roosevelt in 1932 splinter in 1968?

41. Discuss how TWO of the following factors shaped settlement patterns and governing traditions in the American colonies:
    A. Religion
    B. Soil quality
    C. Health conditions
    D. Transatlantic trade

42. How and why did New England and Virginia develop in very different ways during the seventeenth century?

43. Explain the doctrine of "separate spheres" for men and women and discuss how this doctrine shaped opportunities for women from the birth of the Republic to the women's rights movement of the 1960s and 1970s.

44. Compare and contrast the women's rights movements of 1900-1920 and 1960-1980. What were women fighting for during each of these movements? What political or social claims did they make? What did each of these movements achieve, and what, if anything, was left incomplete by each movement?

45. Select THREE of the following leaders and discuss their contribution to American history and to the expansion of women's rights:
    A. Harriet Tubman
    B. Elizabeth Cady Stanton
    C. Jane Addams
    D. Betty Friedan
    E. Hillary Clinton

46. How did World War II (1941-45) and the Civil Rights Movement (1954-1965) create new opportunities for women?

47. What concepts and subjects did American authors and thinkers draw on to create distinctively American forms of literature and philosophy?

48. What did Ralph Waldo Emerson and Henry David Thoreau mean by *self-reliance*? How is self-reliance related to nature? How does self-reliance help underpin a successful republic?

49. Compare the critiques of capitalism and materialism made by leading authors in the 1920s and the 1950s. Why did these critiques emerge during these periods of overall economic success?

50. Discuss the perspective of leading writers and thinkers of the Harlem Renaissance, specifically the tension between their mastery of arts and culture and their status as African-Americans in a segregated nation.

51. Compare and contrast the way that Franklin Roosevelt and Herbert Hoover dealt with the Great Depression. Why were some of FDR's solutions off limits to Hoover?

52. How did the concept of private property shape relations between Native American tribes and settlers from 1620-1870?

53. Assimilation and acculturation are terms that can be used to describe efforts to spread Western culture and ways of life to the Native American peoples. Both voluntary assimilation as epitomized by the Five Civilized Tribes in the 1820s and forced assimilation through the Dawes Act in 1887 failed. Explain why assimilation failed in each case and what the overall failure means for relations between the United States and its Native American citizens.

54. What strategies did business owners and their political allies use to delegitimize unions from the 1880s to the 1930s? How did unions respond to these attacks?

55. How did each of the following presidents advance the cause of labor rights?
    A. Theodore Roosevelt
    B. Woodrow Wilson
    C. Franklin Roosevelt

56. Compare and contrast social, economic and political experiences of THREE of the following immigrant groups in the United States:
    A. Irish
    B. Italian
    C. Jewish
    D. Chinese
    E. Japanese

57. Immigrants from Europe were joined in American cities by African-Americans from the South. Compare and contrast the treatment of these two groups from 1880 to 1960.

58. In what ways did the Progressive movement transform the role and responsibilities of the federal government? Discuss, using at least TWO of the following categories:
    A. Social issues such as temperance
    C. Industrial regulation
    D. Corruption and political patronage in the cities
    E. Economic inequality

59. What role did muckraking journalists play in generating political awareness of and support for Progressive initiatives?

60. How did the Progressive movement generate opportunities for women to hold positions of public leadership?

61. How and why did the Second Great Awakening contribute to nineteenth-century social reform movements?

62. How did Puritanism shape the social, economic and political formation of the New England colonies?

63. Why did Protestants in the United States frequently discriminate against Catholics in the nineteenth and early twentieth centuries?

64. Why did so many leaders of the Civil Rights Movements have religious backgrounds?

65. What contributions to American history were made by TWO of the following religious figures forced into exile for their beliefs?
    A. Anne Hutchinson
    B. Roger Williams
    C. Joseph Smith

66. Explain how and why the baby boom starting in the late 1940s contributed to major social change in the 1960s.

67. How did World War II set the stage for the revitalization and reinvention of the South and Southwest regions of the United States?

68. Outline the social consequences of TWO of the following population migrations
    A. The Great Migration of the Puritans (1620-1640)
    B. Immigration from Southern and Eastern Europe (1880-1920)
    C. The migration of African-Americans from the South to Northern cities (starting in 1910)

69. How and why did the Civil War evolve from a war to preserve the Union to a war to emancipate the slaves?

70. In what ways did the Civil War change the relationship between the federal government and the states, and between the states and the people?

WORKS OF AMERICAN FICTION AND NONFICTION

1. Bartolomé de las Casas, *Historia de las Indias* (1530s)
   Argued that Indians in Latin America possessed human rights and questioned the legitimacy of European conquest in Spain.

2. John Foxe, *Acts and Monuments* (1563) [commonly known as the *Book of Martyrs*]
   Written to commemorate Protestants burned at the stake by Queen Mary in the 1550s.

3. John Calvin, *Institutes of the Christian Religion* (1536)
   Powerful statement of the Protestant faith that spawned religious movements in most northern European countries, and which greatly influenced the Puritans

4. Benjamin Harris, *The New England Primer* (1690)
   Taught children both the alphabet and Puritan religion

5. Jonathan Edwards, *Sinners in the Hands of an Angry God* (1741)
   A fiery sermon that sought to return the people to the faith of their Puritan fathers but with an even greater evangelical fervor to spread the religion far and wide

6. John Locke, *Two Treatises of Government* (1690)
   Political theory that underpinned the Declaration of Independence: basically, a contract theory of government in which people choose to participate in society for mutual benefits and in return the government of that society must protect their God-given rights to life, liberty and property. The corollary of this theory, of course, is that rebellion is justified when these rights are abrogated by the government.

7. John Locke, *Some Thoughts Concerning Education* (1693)
   Argued that the mind was not formed at birth, and was there therefore a blank slate (*tabula rasa*). The child learned from experience, and if the infant witnessed violent, arbitrary behavior, then the baby would become an abusive adult.

8. James Madison, Alexander Hamilton & John Jay, *The Federalist Papers* (1787-88)
   Argued jointly in favor of the new Constitution. Federalist No. 10 (Madison) is one of the most famous; it argued that a large republic was desirable in that the clash of the many small factions within it would neutralize one another.

9. Thomas Jefferson, *Notes on the State of Virginia* (1785)
   Using Virginia as an example, Jefferson expresses his views about the nature of a good commonwealth. He argues in favor of separation of church and state, constitutional government, checks and balances, and individual liberty.

10. James Fenimore Cooper, *The Leatherstocking Tales* (series of novels from 1824-1841), includes *The Last of the Mohicans* (1826)
    The Leatherstocking Tales are a series of novels that chronicle the challenges, perils, paradoxes and glory of life on the frontier, with varying English, French, Indian and American protagonists. *The Last of the Mohicans*, considered to be Cooper's masterpiece, takes place during the French and Indian War, and describes the

difficulties faced by Indian tribes as they attempt to ally with and against the British and the French in order to survive.

11. Alexis de Tocqueville, *Democracy in America* (1835)
    De Tocqueville's book is framed around the notion that equality is the main social condition in America, and that it shapes all the other institutions – religious, political, etc.

12. Ralph Waldo Emerson, *Self-Reliance* (1841)
    Argues that society is often too overly conformist and that people should cultivate their capacity to reason and think independently and not too always seek "a false consistency" above all other virtues.

13. Nathaniel Hawthorne, *The Scarlet Letter* (1850)
    Penetrating critique of Puritan life pitting love and lust versus sin and societal expectations. A young woman is branded for committing adultery and the novel examines her life with her illegitimate daughter and the effect this has on the minister who is the real father.

14. Herman Melville, *Moby Dick* (1851)
    Story of a wandering sailor, Ishmael, and his captain, Ahab, who are in search of a legendary white whale. In a previous encounter, the whale attacked the ship and bit off Ahab's leg, and now Ahab is out for revenge. The book portrays obsession and monomania. The whaling captain Ahab, who brings destruction to himself and his ship by his relentless pursuit symbolized – among other things – the dangers facing a nation that was overreaching itself by indulging its pride and exalted sense of destiny with too little concern for the moral and practical consequences.

15. Walt Whitman, *Leaves of Grass* (1855)
    Collection of poetry that celebrates life in all its magnificence; often critiqued for its immoral celebration of free love. Exalts the body and the material world (influenced by both Emerson's Transcendentalism and Romanticism). Praises nature and the individual human's role in it.

16. David Walker, *Appeal to the Colored Citizens of the World* (1829)
    Walker, an African-American abolitionist, called for blacks to take up arms against slavery.

17. Hinton R. Helper, *The Impending Crisis of the South* (1857)
    Appeal to nonslaveholders to resist the planter regime. Called on lower-class whites to resist planter dominance and abolish slavery in their own interest. This book was suppressed with particular vigor; those found with copies were beaten up or even lynched.

18. *McGuffey's Eclectic Readers* (first appeared 1836)
    Taught the three R's (reading, writing, arithmetic) and the "Protestant Ethic" – industry, punctuality, sobriety, and frugality.

19. Daniel Lloyd Garrison, *The Liberator* (first published in 1831)
    Newspaper which took an uncompromising view on slavery – supported immediate emancipation without forced emigration of blacks.

20. Elizabeth Cady Stanton, Lucretia Mott, et al., *The Declaration of Sentiments* (1848)
    Document of a campaign for women's rights. Charged that "the history of mankind is a history of repeated injuries and usurpations on the part of man toward woman, having in direct object the establishment of an absolute tyranny over her." Demanded all women be given the right to vote and that married women be freed from unjust laws giving husbands control of their property, persons, and children.

21. Harriet Beecher Stowe, *Uncle Tom's Cabin* (1852)
    An enormously successful novel that fixed in the northern mind the image of the slaveholder as a brutal and cruel master. When the saintly Uncle Tom was sold away from his adoring wife and children, Northerners shuddered with horror and some Southerners felt a painful twinge of conscience.

22. Henry David Thoreau, *Walden; or, Life in the Woods* (1854)
    Thoreau put his philosophical beliefs in self-reliance and transcendentalism into practice by building a small cottage next to Walden Pond in Massachusetts where he spent better part of two years living on his own. Thoreau was not looking to become a hermit; in fact, he built his cottage on the outskirts of the nearby town that he quite frequently visited. He was interested, rather, in fully living life, and thought that relying almost entirely on himself for food, shelter, and the other necessities would help him to think more deeply about the human condition. He critiques society in the book, writing that "the mass of men lead lives of quiet desperation. What is called resignation is confirmed desperation" (Chapter 1: Economy).

23. Helen Hunt Jackson, *A Century of Dishonor* (1881)
    A description of the injustices suffered by Native Americans at the hands of settlers, the Army and the American government. Generated sympathy for the plight of the Native Americans, especially among Eastern reformers, whose preferred solution was the assimilation of the Native Americans through a program of Christianization, education and Anglicization.

24. Stephen Crane, *The Red Badge of Courage* (1895)
    Story about a young private during the Civil War who flees from the field of battle. Overcome with shame, he longs for a wound "a red badge of courage" to counteract his cowardice. When his regiment once again faces the enemy, he acts as standard-bearer. Novel is known for its realistic style and repeated use of color imagery and ironic tone.

25. D.W. Griffith, *The Birth of a Nation* (1915)
    Movie that depicts the Ku Klux Klan as saving white civilization from "bestial" blacks and preserving democracy for southern whites.

26. W.E.B. Du Bois, *Black Reconstruction in America* (1935)

Argued that Reconstruction was not a corrupt failure but instead was a noble effort to achieve a color-blind democracy, which failed because of the strength of white racism and conservative economic interests.

27. Frederick Jackson Turner, *The Significance of the Frontier in American History*
Argued that the existence of "free land" to the west explains American development by giving rise to values of independence, self-confidence, and individualism. The "escape valve" to the west also helped to keep social tensions relatively low by allowing those that were unhappy to simply move west.

28. Jacob Riis, *How the Other Half Lives* (1890)
Described life among the urban poor, who lived in crowded city tenements that were unsanitary and bad for health.

29. W.E.B. Du Bois, *The Souls of Black Folk* (1903)
Attacked Booker T. Washington and the philosophy of the Atlanta Compromise, which pledged no social agitation from blacks, acknowledged white domination, and called for slow progress through self-improvement in the manual crafts and trades. Du Bois, on the other hand, urged African Americans to aspire to professional careers, to fight for the restoration of their civil rights, and wherever possible, to attend college. Du Bois urged blacks to educate their "talented tenth," a highly trained intellectual elite, to lead them.

30. William Graham Sumner, *What Social Classes Owe to Each Other* (1883)
Argued that government action on behalf of the poor or weak interfered with evolution and sapped the species. Reform tampered with the laws of nature.

31. Henry George, *Progress and Poverty* (1879)
Saw modern society – rich, complex, with material goods hitherto unknown – as sadly flawed. Argued in favor of progressive taxation on land to provide benefits for the poor, to give them a fair chance in life.

32. Richard T. Ely, *History of Labour in the United States* (1885)
Economist who criticized free-market dogma then dominant in the discipline and urged government intervention in economic affairs.

33. Thorstein Veblen, *The Theory of the Leisure Class* (1899)
Viewed free-market economic laws as a mask for human greed. Analyzed the "predatory wealth" and "conspicuous consumption" of the business class.

34. Edward Bellamy, *Looking Backward, 2000-1887* (1887)
The novel's protagonist, Julian West, falls asleep in 1887 and awakes in the year 2000. Wide-eyed, he finds himself in a socialist utopia. The government owns the means of production, and citizens share the material rewards. Cooperation, rather than competition, is the watchword.

35. Washington Gladden, *Applied Christianity* (1886)

Preached the Social Gospel, which called for church members to fulfill their social obligations by helping the poor and finding ways to help employers and employees cooperate better for the improvement of all.

36. Walter Wyckoff, *The Workers* (1897)
Trying to understand the working man, he worked as an unskilled laborer in jobs from Connecticut to California, and summarized his findings in a book hailed as a major contribution to sociology.

37. Bessie and Marie Van Vorst, *The Woman Who Toils: Being the Experiences of Two Gentlewomen as Factory Girls* (1903)
Applied Wyckoff's approach in a work by women about women workers.

38. Israel Zangwill, *The Melting Pot* (1908)
A play that was a tribute to America's traditions of blending together races and nations in the common project of work. Critics scorned the play as "romantic claptrap," and indeed it was. But the metaphor of the melting pot clearly depicted a new national image.

39. Louisa May Alcott, *Little Women* (1868-69)
Depicted the lives of four girls in a New England family who were seeking to advance in society.

40. Horatio Alger, *Sink or Swim, Work and Win, Struggling Upward* (1860s-1870s)
Tales of poor youngsters who made their way to the top through hard work, thrift, honesty, and luck.

41. Mark Twain, *Life on the Mississippi* (1883); *Adventures of Tom Sawyer* (1876); *Adventures of Huckleberry Finn* (1884)
Used dialect and common speech instead of literary language, describing ordinary life in the South and West with a vivid eye and an open heart.

42. Jack London, *The Call of the Wild* (1903)
Classic tale of a sled dog that preferred the difficult life of the wilderness to the world of human beings. Written in the naturalist tradition that stressed the power of nature over civilized society.

43. Josiah Strong, *Our Country: Its Possible Future and Its Present Crisis* (1885)
Called on Western missionaries to civilize the world under the Anglo-Saxon races. Key part of this involved expanding trade as the necessary basis of civilization and [Western] culture.

44. Alfred Mahan, *The Interest of America in Sea Power* (1897)
Argued that America must use naval power to open up new markets for the surplus produced by its massive industrial production. Argued in favor of naval bases, a powerful oceangoing navy, a canal across the isthmus to link the East Coast with the Pacific, and Hawaii as a way station on the route to Asia.

45. Ida Tarbell, *History of the Standard Oil Company* (1902)
   Scathing review of how Standard Oil had abused competitive and labor practices to become a dominant monopolist.

46. Upton Sinclair, *The Jungle* (1906)
   Description of the meatpacking industry. Sinclair found health violations, labor abuses, etc. – really the market run wild in the effort to produce meat as cheaply as possible. Led to the passage of the Pure Food and Drug Act and the Meat Inspection Act.

47. Lincoln Steffens, *The Shame of the Cities* (1904)
   Exposed the shabby state of life in the cities, and called for major urban reforms.

48. Frederick Winslow Taylor, *The Principles of Scientific Management* (1911)
   Recommended standardization of methods, enforced adoption of the best implements and working conditions, and enforced cooperation between management and labor so as to produce goods and services efficiently.

49. William James, *Pragmatism* (1907)
   A new doctrine which was impatient with theories that regarded truth as abstract. Truth, he believed, should work for the individual, and it worked best not in abstraction, but in action. Praised "tough-minded" individuals who could live effectively in a world with no easy answers. In other words, truth is what works in the real world.

50. John Dewey, *School and Society* (1899) and *Democracy and Education* (1916)
   Opposed memorization, rote learning and dogmatic, authoritarian teaching methods; emphasized personal growth, free inquiry, and creativity.

51. T.S. Eliot, *The Waste Land* (1922) and *The Hollow Men* (1925)
   Evoked images of fragmentation, sterility and emptiness of modern life.

52. F.Scott Fitzgerald, *The Great Gatsby* (1925)
   Wrote about life among "the beautiful and the damned." Amid the glitter of life among the wealthy on Long Island's North Shore came the haunting realization of emptiness and lack of human concern.

53. Ernest Hemingway, *The Sun Also Rises* (1926)
   Novel about American and British expatriates in Paris who travel to Spain. An early and enduring Modernist novel which featured Hemingway's spare writing style and his restrained use of description to convey characterizations and action.

54. Sinclair Lewis, *Main Street* (1920) and *Babbitt* (1922)
   Satirized the values of small-town America as dull, complacent and narrow-minded; poked fun at the commercialism of the 1920s.

55. James Weldon Johnson, *Fifty Years and Other Poems* (1917)

An African-American professor of literature, this collection comments on the half century of suffering that had followed the Emancipation Proclamation, and called for the promise of that period to be redeemed.

56. Claude McKay, *White Shadows* (1922)
Expressed both the resentment of the author against racial injustice and his pride in blackness.

57. John Keats, *The Crack in the Picture Window* (1956)
Critique of the flaws of the new suburbia. Described the endless rows of tract houses "vomited up" by developers as "identical boxes spreading like gangrene." Their occupants – whom he dubbed the Drones, the Amiables, and the Fecunds – lost any sense of individuality in their obsession with material goods.

58. William Whyte, *The Organization Man* (1956)
Whyte perceived a change from the old Protestant ethic, with its emphasis on hard work and personal responsibility, to a new social ethic centered on "the team" with the ultimate goal of "belongingness." The result was a stifling conformity and the loss of personal identity.

59. David Riesman, *The Lonely Crowd* (1950)
Riesman described the shift from the "inner-directed" Americans of the past who had relied on such traditional values as self-denial and frugality to the "other-directed" Americans of the consumer society who constantly adapted their behavior to conform to social pressures. The consequences –a decline in individualism and a tendency for people to become acutely sensitive to the expectations of others – produced a bland and tolerant society of consumers lacking creativity and a sense of adventure.

60. C. Wright Mills, *White Collar* (1951) and *The Power Elite* (1956)
The corporation was the villain for Mills, depriving office workers of their own identities and imposing an impersonal discipline through manipulation and propaganda. The industrial assembly line had given way to an even more dehumanizing workplace, the modern office.

61. Jack Kerouac, *On the Road* (1957)
The name came from the quest for beatitude, a state of inner grace sought in Zen Buddhism. Flouting the respectability of suburbia, the "beatniks" were easily identified by their long hair and bizarre clothing; they also had a penchant for sexual promiscuity and drug experimentation. They were conscious dropouts from a society they found senseless.

62. Michael Harrington, *The Other America* (1962)
Exposé of the 40 million Americans living in poverty; changed the national conversation to the point that President Johnson declared "an unconditional war on poverty" in 1964.

63. Rachel Carson, *Silent Spring* (1962)

Described the ways in which pollution and pesticides had damaged plant and animal life. The book is credited as one of the founding tomes of the environmental movement

64. Betty Friedan, *The Feminine Mystique* (1963)
Seized on the sense of grievance and discrimination that developed among white middle-class women in the 1960s. She attacked the prevailing view that women were completely contented with their housekeeping and child-rearing tasks, claiming that housewives had no self-esteem and no sense of identity.

American History Tutoring Guide Paul Pinto

BIOGRAPHICAL SKETCHES OF MAJOR FIGURES IN AMERICAN HISTORY

1. Christopher Columbus (1451-1506)
   Italian explorer who discovered the New World on behalf of the Spanish monarchs Isabella and Ferdinand. Columbus was granted authority to rule a number of Caribbean territories as viceroy to the Spanish monarchs. Most of the colonies failed due to high mortality rates among the local population. Although he failed to discover a westwards path to the trading wealth of China and India, Columbus set the stage for permanent relations between Europe and the 'New World'.

2. John Smith (1581-1631) & John Rolfe (1585-1622)
   Military captain and chief planter, respectively, of the Jamestown plantation (founded 1607) in Virginia. These men held the fledgling plantation together until tobacco planting provided a basis for prosperity through its sale as a cash crop in Europe. The first African slaves were imported for work on tobacco plantations in 1619.

3. William Bradford (1590-1657)
   Governor of Plymouth colony. A mainstream Puritan, he sought to maintain religious discipline, orthodoxy and stability in building a holy, self-governing community. The Puritans of Plymouth colony signed the famous Mayflower Compact committing themselves to constitutionalism and self-government. In the secular realm, Bradford encouraged industries like fishing, farming, fur trapping and trading, and lumber.

4. John Winthrop (1587-1649)
   Leader of the group of Puritans who founded Massachusetts Bay Colony in the 1630s. Delivered the famous "City on the Hill" sermon aboard the *Arbella* en route to Massachusetts. Massachusetts was governed democratically but the franchise was limited to adult male members of the Puritan Church.

5. Nathaniel Bacon (1647-1676)
   Failed farmer who led a rebellion of farmers in western Virginia in 1676 against the royal governor and the chartered company. After initial successes, Bacon died of dysentery and the his rebel army collapsed. Bacon's rebellion was characterized by political tensions between small farmers and large planters, and also between colonists and royal authority.

6. Roger Williams (1603-1683)
   A committed Puritan who nonetheless championed the idea of complete religious freedom, religious toleration and the disestablishment of religion from government. For these ideas, he was expelled from Massachusetts Bay in 1636 and went on to found Providence, which became Rhode Island. This colony was famous for its toleration of all varieties of Protestants as well as Catholics and Jews. Williams also recognized the rights of Native Americans and compensated them for acquiring their land.

7. Anne Hutchinson (1591-1643)
Another committed Puritan who fell foul of the authorities in Massachusetts, Hutchinson's crime was her willingness to challenge the authority of the church based on her belief in *antinomianism* – the idea that salvation comes through faith alone and that anyone deserved to wield religious authority given sufficient faith. Her gender and challenge to the religious and political power structure resulted in her being placed on trial for heresy. Her testimony that she had received direct prophetic inspiration from God resulted in her being banished in 1638 to found the colony of Portsmouth, which later became part of Rhode Island.

8. Metacom, King of the Wampanoags (known to the colonists as King Philip) (1638-1676)
Formed an armed confederation of New England tribes and attacked the English settlers in 1675. King Philip's War resulted in thousands of deaths on both sides, with the destruction of a number of towns and villages. The colonial forces eventually won and thus ended Native American armed resistance in New England.

9. William Penn (1644-1718)
An English Quaker gentleman who turned a royal debt to his family into the colony of Pennsylvania. The Quakers, or the Religious Society of Friends, were a Protestant group that propounded Gospel teachings of equality, nonviolence and democracy of religion. Penn's colony served as a haven for persecuted English Quakers, and Penn himself was the source of a liberal state constitution that guaranteed free exercise of religion, civil liberties, and self-government.

10. Jonathan Edwards (1703-1758)
A Congregationalist (Puritan successor church) minister in New England who is credited with initiating the Great Awakening through a series of powerful revival sermons. His "Sinners in the Hands of an Angry God" sermon (1741), convinced thousands of people that only total repentance and recommital to Christianity would spare them from everlasting damnation.

11. George Whitefield (1714-1770)
A English preacher who took evangelical Protestantism out of the churches and directly to the people in farms and open fields. Whitefield, blessed with remarkable preaching gifts, started mass revivals on both sides of the Atlantic. He arrived in America in 1739 and preached up and down the Atlantic seaboard, attracting thousands of people to his sermons. He stressed the ability of ordinary people to understand and control their faith without having to rely on ministers to lead them

12. Benjamin Franklin (1706-1790)
An American polymath who became Philadelphia's leading citizen, Franklin was a printer, writer, inventor and scientist who became famous through his witty aphorisms and homespun wisdom in *Poor Richard's Almanack*. Responsible for inventing bifocal glasses and the Franklin stove, and a scientific pioneer who conducted experiments with electricity, Franklin became a political figure during the American Revolution and played a leading role in the Continental Congress. He edited the Declaration of

Independence, served as minister to France during the Revolutionary War, and supported the cause one final time with the passage of the Constitution.

13. Charles Townshend (1725-1767)
Named Chancellor of the Exchequer (chief finance minister) in 1767, Townshend's task was to produce increased revenues from the American colonies in order to pay off debts accrued during the French and Indian War. He set about imposing a range of taxes and duties on the American colonists, including the Townshend Acts (taxed tea, glass, and paper), which caused a strong colonial reaction and boycott and resulted in repeal in 1770.

14. John Dickinson (1732-1808)
Farmer in Pennsylvania who rose to political fame during the boycott against the Townsend Acts. In *Letters From a Farmer in Pennsylvania*, Dickinson argued that while Parliament had the power to regulate trade, it could not impose taxes without the consent of colonial assemblies. That is to say, he articulated in writing the principle of no taxation without representation.

15. Samuel Adams (1722-1803)
New England brewer and merchant who, with James Otis, wrote the Massachusetts Circular Letter that urged the colonies to petition Parliament to repeal the Townshend Act. In response, British officials ordered the retraction of the Letter and threatened to dissolve the Massachusetts legislature. A radical Patriot, Adams organized Committees of Correspondence in 1772 to monitor British violations of American liberties.

16. Lord Frederick North (1732-1792)
British prime minister who favored a middle ground policy with regard to the colonies. He advocated the repeal of the Townsend Act, but maintained that Parliament retained the power to tax the colonies as she saw fit.

17. John Adams (1735-1826)
Farmer and lawyer from Massachusetts who, despite his belief in the principle of no taxation without representation, defended the British troops who fired on a Massachusetts Crowd during the Boston Massacre of 1770 (he earned the acquittal of the troops). Adams went on to become a leader of the American independence movement, serving on a number of Continental Congress committees, playing a role in the drafting of the Declaration of Independence, and representing his country overseas as a minister to France, Holland and Britain. He served as the first Vice President of the United States, and later as the second President of the United States (1796-1800). A moderate Federalist, Adams found himself caught between the central government nationalism espoused by Alexander Hamilton and the states' rights republicanism of Thomas Jefferson. He struggled to craft a central course through these partisan battles, which were exacerbated by international tensions with France and Britain. Jefferson's victory in 1800 denied Adams a second term, and he retired to his farm in Massachusetts.

18. John Locke (1632-1704)
One of the preeminent Western philosophers, Locke articulated a contractual theory of government in which sovereignty (the right to rule) is embedded in the people, who agree to give up their power to a lawfully constituted government in return for its protection of their liberties (life, liberty, property). If the government violated the liberties of the people, the people were entitled to rise up and replace the government. Locke's work was hugely influential on the American colonists as they sought a way to redress the taxation imposed by Parliament after the Seven Years' War.

19. Thomas Paine (1737-1809)
An English pamphleteer whose radical and unabashed writings in favor of liberty, democracy republicanism, and independence helped rally uncertain Americans to the cause of the Revolution. Paine's *Common Sense* (1776) argued that it defied logic for a small island to rule over a continent, particularly when the government of the island had become autocratic and corrupt, and castigated those who shrank from sacrifice in the cause of liberty (he called these people "summer soldiers and sunshine patriots"). Paine later played a major role in the French Revolution, contributing heavily to the *Declaration of the Rights of Man*.

20. Patrick Henry (1736-1799)
A staunch republican lawyer from Virginia who made his name in that colony's House of Burgesses by protesting the Stamp Act in 1765. His ringing declaration in favor of freedom, "Give me liberty, or give me death!" became one of the rallying cries of the Revolution.

21. Thomas Jefferson (1743-1826)
A man whose contributions to the American republic are hard to overstate. A wealthy slave-owning planter from Virginia, Jefferson was a man of science, philosophy, arts and letters, and, not least, politics. A reluctant public speaker, he rose to prominence by writing the Declaration of Independence. He helped craft the constitution of Virginia, and founded its great public university. After serving as ambassador to Paris, Jefferson served as the first Secretary of State under Washington. He soon found himself embroiled in conflict with Alexander Hamilton, who favored a program of economic centralization in the interest of increasing the financial and political power of the young nation. Jefferson found himself deeply ambivalent about the power of the federal government, and soon came to lead a faction – the Democratic Republicans – who opposed the centralizing policies of Hamilton. Victorious in the elections of 1800 and 1804, Jefferson ironically exercised great central power in doubling the size of the nation with the Louisiana Purchase. The triumphs of his first term were somewhat lessened by the economic troubles of the second, most notably caused by a trade embargo that attempted to punish the British but only served to impoverish the United States.

22. George Washington (1732-1799)
    The Father of the Nation and the first President of the United States (1788-1796), Washington symbolized and preserved the fine line between democratic republicanism and unified, successful national government. His restraint in the office of the presidency set a number of valuable precedents, none more valuable than his refusal to serve more than two terms. His prestige and popularity forced the emerging Federalist and Democratic-Republican parties to refrain from all-out conflict until the young nation had a chance to stand on its own feet. Washington also served as the commanding general of the Revolutionary War army, and his defeat of the British Army made him a figure of global renown. In his Farewell Address, he counseled restraint in foreign affairs and the avoidance of entangling alliances with European powers.

23. Alexander Hamilton (1755-1804)
    The illegitimate son of a Caribbean planter, Hamilton was a man of great talent who rose to prominence in New York and distinguished himself as a lawyer. He served as Washington's *aide de camp* (chief deputy) during the Revolutionary War and established himself further as a talented administrator. Together with Madison and John Jay, Hamilton authored a number of the Federalist Papers which made the case for the Constitution. In Washington's first term, he served as Secretary of the Treasury and was really something of a de facto prime minister for Washington. He made a number of aggressive moves towards economic centralization, among them the creation of the Bank of the United States and its assumption of the wartime debts of the states. These moves were criticized by the Democratic Republicans, but the Bank did serve to stabilize the debts and currency of the young nation, setting the stage for a strong economic expansion.

24. James Madison (1751-1836)
    The Father of the Constitution, Madison was perhaps the preeminent political theorist of the Founding generation. An ally of Jefferson's, Madison served as the primary drafter and moving spirit of the Constitution, which he ably defended in the Federalist Papers. His skill at political rhetoric and reasoning managed to overturn many doubts about the feasibility of a large continental republic. For instance, he argued in Federalist No. 51 that a large nation was actually better for republicanism, because a large country would have more competing factions that would balance one another out and therefore serve the national interest. Jefferson served two terms as the fourth President of the United States (1808-1816), which were generally successful but marred by conflicts at sea with the British, which escalated into the stalemated War of 1812.

25. John Marshall (1755-1835)
    A lawyer from Virginia, Marshall served over thirty years as Chief Justice of the United States. In the case of *Marbury v. Madison* (1803), Marshall ruled in favor of Jefferson's administration in the matter of judges appointed at the last moment by the outgoing Adams administration, but at the same time laid down the principle of judicial review, which gave the Supreme Court the power to act as the final arbiter of the Constitution and thereby determine the constitutionality of any local, state or federal law ("it is emphatically the province and duty of the judicial department to say what the law is.")

If the Court found that a law passed by Congress violated the Constitution, it could strike down that law (and thus defeat the work of the other two, elected, branches). Note that the power of judicial review does not appear in Article III of the Constitution, which establishes the Supreme Court, but, thanks to Marshall, judicial review has become a bedrock constitutional principle. In *McCulloch v. Maryland*, the Supreme Court under Marshall argued that Congress had the implied power to create a National Bank even if that power was not explicitly stated in the Constitution. He further denied the ability of states to tax the Bank. This ruling therefore provided the foundation of federal power in vastly expanding Congress' power through the notion of implied rather than enumerated powers, and placed the laws of the federal government clearly above those of the states.

26. Aaron Burr (1756-1836)
Something of a black sheep amongst the Founding Fathers, Aaron Burr served as Vice President under Thomas Jefferson. Flaws in the electoral system in which each elector concurrently cast votes for President and Vice President almost resulted in Burr becoming President in 1800. An ambitious man, Burr wanted to displace Jefferson as the leader of the Democratic Republicans. Failing in this effort, he engaged in a number of schemes, including an effort to win the governorship of New York and lead that state with New England to secede from the union, as well as a far-fetched plot to take Mexico from Spain. He also shot Alexander Hamilton dead in a duel in 1804. The Mexican plot led to charges of treason, in which Burr was acquitted narrowly.

27. Meriwether Lewis (1774-1809) and William Clark (1770-1838)
Commissioned by Jefferson and Congress to conduct a scientific expedition of discovery to the West, Lewis and Clark went on an epic three-year journey starting in 1804. The traveled across the Rockies to the Pacific Coast in Oregon, and returned in 1806. The expedition mapped routes for fur traders, established or improved relations with Native American groups, and provided the first systematic scientific knowledge of the land in the West.

28. James Monroe (1758-1831)
The fifth President of the United States (1816-1824). A veteran of the Revolutionary War, Monroe's presidency has been termed the "Era of Good Feelings" because of the peaceful dominance of the Democratic-Republican party. Monroe supported a national program that emphasized expansion (the acquisition of Florida), sectional compromise (Missouri Compromise) and rising power (the Monroe Doctrine, which declared that Latin America was off-limits to European powers).

29. John Quincy Adams (1767-1848)
The sixth President of the United States (1824-1828), John Quincy Adams was the son of President John Adams, Secretary of State under President Monroe, and a distinguished diplomat in Europe and Russia. His election in 1824 was marred by allegations of a 'corrupt bargain' from Andrew Jackson, the winner of the popular vote who failed to win a majority in the electoral college thanks to the fact that there were four candidates, and lost when one of those candidates, Henry Clay, gave his support to Adams rather than Jackson. Adding fuel to Jackson's fire was the fact that Adams

named Clay his Secretary of State. A moderate nationalist, Adams favored a program of internal improvements and federal government investment in education (a proposed national university), science (national observatory) and aid to new industries like textile manufacturing.

30. Andrew Jackson (1767-1845)
    The seventh President of the United States (1828-1836), Jackson favored the 'Politics of the Common Man', a political program that encouraged political participation and education for virtually all white males. A slaveholder, Jackson considered himself a strict constructionist and aimed to restrict what he viewed as the overreaching of the federal government. He was the first president to use the veto as a systematic constitutional weapon, casting more vetoes (12) than all his predecessors combined, mostly against federal actions like the proposed funding of the Maysville Road, a highway running through Kentucky. Jackson's spectacular battle against the Bank of the United States, which he viewed as a corrupt institution that engaged in both financial and political influence-dealing, shaped the election of 1832, which Jackson won in a landslide over Henry Clay. Jackson also favored the forced removal and resettlement of Native Americans from Georgia, which he pushed through despite resistance from the US Supreme Court.

31. Eli Whitney (1765-1825)
    Inventor of the cotton gin (1793) and interchangeable rifle parts (1812). The cotton gin made it vastly simpler to separate cotton fiber from seeds and therefore more profitable to grow cotton rather than tobacco or indigo. This directly spurred the formation of large slave cotton plantations in the South, which shipped most of its production to British textile factories.

32. Henry Clay (1777-1852)
    A longstanding Congressman from Kentucky, Clay served as Secretary of State under John Quincy Adams and ran losing campaigns for President in 1824 and 1832. He favored a Hamiltonian program of American development through active government, which included the development of internal improvements such as roads and canals, support for the development of banking, manufacturing, and trade, and the encouragement of public education and science. Clay and his fellow believers in the Hamiltonian system formed the Whig party, which opposed Jackson and his Democratic supporters.

33. Nat Turner (1800-1831)
    A Virginia slave who led a revolt in 1831 that resulted in the deaths of 55 whites. Turner's revolt signified the suicidal difficulty of armed slave revolts (hundreds of blacks were killed by whites in retaliation). Fear of similar revolts suppressed antislavery sentiment in the south, creating a fortress mentality that made compromise on the slavery issue steadily more difficult.

34. Martin Van Buren (1782-1862)
The eighth President of the United States (1836-1840), Van Buren was a New York politician who served as adviser and then Vice President to Andrew Jackson. Famous as a master of the workings of party politics, Van Buren was not much of charismatic national leader and failed to win reelection in 1840.

35. Alexis de Tocqueville (1805-1859)
A French aristocratic and scholar, de Tocqueville visited the United States in the 1830s, which informed his epochal *Democracy in America*. Tocqueville argued that the founding condition of America was equality, from which all else followed. Because Americans were not divided into classes by their ownership of land (aristocrat vs. peasant), conditions for democracy, self-government, and local self-reliance were much more auspicious than in Europe. De Tocqueville drew a broad distinction between two founding traditions of America – the New England religious mentality and the Southern planter mentality, arguing that the slavery associated with the latter was a cancer that would not be resolved easily. He was generally pessimistic about the ability of blacks (free or slave) and Native Americans to integrate with broader American culture, arguing that democracy with its shared power among all was especially threatened by the presence of minority populations. Tocqueville was a great admirer of American constitutional traditions, particular the easy creation and operation of self-governing townships. He highlighted the contributions of religion to these self-governing traditions, noting that church congregations served as valuable social fora for public interaction, coordination, and civilization.

36. Joseph Smith (1805-1844)
Smith founded the Church of the Latter-Day Saints, or Mormons, in 1830 in upstate New York. He claimed that he had received a revelation from an angel of God, who provided him with a book of Scripture – the Book of Mormon. Smith believed that the Native American tribes were actually lost offshoots of the tribes of Israel, and argued further that he was destined to form a church of true believers and build a new Zion. His religious beliefs aroused hostility in his neighbors, and he was murdered by a mob in Illinois while trying to set up his religious community. His follower Brigham Young led the Mormons west until they reached the Great Salt Lake in Utah. The close link between Mormon theology and social cooperation resulted in a high degree of agricultural productivity as the Mormons "made the desert bloom." However, the separatism of Mormonism and its practice of polygamy resulted in a number of skirmishes with the government of the United States, which only allowed Utah into the union upon condition that the Mormon church abandon polygamy.

37. Ralph Waldo Emerson (1803-1882)
A New England scholar and lecturer, Emerson advocated the development of a new and original American culture that drew on American virtues such as self-reliance, independent thinking, and the primacy of spiritual over material matters ('transcendentalism'). Emerson became a strong critic of slavery in the 1840s and supported the Union in the Civil War.

38. Henry David Thoreau (1817-1862)
A friend of Emerson's, Thoreau placed some of their shared transcendental theories into practice. He spent two years living mostly on his own in the woods near Walden Pond, Massachusetts. His book, *Walden* (1854) is a reflection on his time spent there, and uses his isolation to think more deeply about social relations. Thoreau observed that many people in society feel trapped in their economic and social roles ('the mass of men live lives of quiet desperation') and advises the reader not to be afraid to rely on themselves to make their lives more independent and self-reliant. His essay "On Civil Disobedience" advocated non-violent resistance to unjust policies, and served as a model for both Gandhi and Martin Luther King, Jr.

39. Dorothea Dix (1802-1887)
A schoolteacher in Massachusetts, Dix fought to improve the cruel and punitive treatment of the mentally ill, who were locked up in jails with convicted criminals. Her research and testimony about the awful conditions pushed state legislatures to improve facilities and to build mental hospitals.

40. Horace Mann (1796-1859)
The leader of the common (public) schools movement that started in Massachusetts and spread across all of the United States outside of the South. The idea was to provide public education to all in order to make people better citizens and more moral people. Mann's program of taxpayer-funded education, compulsory attendance for all children, and better-trained teachers spread to other states beginning in the 1840s. In addition to standard subjects, the schools also taught values of hard work, punctuality, sobriety and self-discipline. The common schools movement tended to be strongly Protestant, which pushed the Catholic Church in North America to create schools of its own.

41. Lucretia Mott (1793-1880)
An activist who worked to abolish slavery and advance women's rights. Informed by her Quaker faith, which stressed the presence of the Divine within every individual, Mott became a Quaker minister in 1821 and preached against slavery. In 1833, her husband helped found the American Anti-Slavery Society, and she herself took part in founding the Philadelphia Female Anti-Slavery Society, which was integrated from its founding. She continued to work for abolitionism until the Civil War, and then for equal rights for women and blacks until her death. She was one of the founders of Swarthmore College.

42. Elizabeth Cady Stanton (1815-1902)
A convener of the Seneca Falls Convention of 1848, Stanton helped produce the Declaration of Sentiments, which declared that "all men and women are created equal." A committed women's rights activist, she fought for women to be placed on an equal legal footing with men with regard to property, custody, employment, and divorce rights. She strongly supported the cause of abolitionism, although, along with Susan B. Anthony, she refused to support the Fourteenth and Fifteenth Amendments on the grounds that they excluded the rights of women.

43. Susan B. Anthony (1820-1906)

A leading campaigner for women's rights, Anthony worked to support the temperance movement and the women's suffrage movement. She tried to unify the cause of women's suffrage and abolitionism, saying in an 1859 speech "Where, under our Declaration of Independence, does the Saxon man get his power to deprive all women and Negroes of their inalienable rights?" Like Elizabeth Cady Stanton, Anthony opposed the Fourteenth and Fifteenth Amendments, which split the black-female reform coalition of the 1850s.

44. William Lloyd Garrison (1805-1879)

A newspaper publisher and abolitionist leader, Garrison's *The Liberator* took an uncompromising line on slavery beginning with its publication in 1831. He advocated immediate and universal abolition of slavery throughout the country (state or territory), with no compensation for slaveowners. He founded the American Antislavery Society with other abolitionists in 1833, and, among other vivid gestures, burned the Constitution as a proslavery document. His uncompromising tone split the abolitionist movement, with many arguing for compensation for slaveowners and a more conciliatory tone towards the South.

45. Frederick Douglass (1818-1895)

A former slave and black leader who bore eloquent witness to the brutality and injustice of slavery. Douglass advocated for both political and direct action to end slavery and racial prejudice. A firm believer in the equality of all people, black and white, male and female, he fought to the end of his long life to help America deliver on the promise of the Declaration of Independence. He wrote the *Narrative of the Life of Frederick Douglass, an American Slave*, which became a bestseller and challenged the stereotype of blacks as incapable of producing top-quality literature. He became an advisor to both Presidents Lincoln and Johnson and served as the president of the Freedman's Savings Bank.

46. Harriet Tubman (1820-1913)

A former slave who risked her life working through the Underground Railroad, a network of safe houses run by antislavery activists to shepherd runaway and escaped slaves to the North. Tubman served during the Civil War as a cook, nurse, scout and spy, at one point leading an armed expedition that freed more than 700 slaves in South Carolina. After the war, she became active in the women's suffrage movement.

47. Sojourner Truth (1797-1883)

An escaped slave who fought first for her own freedom, then her son's (freed as a result of a lawsuit filed by Truth), and then for her people through her work as an abolition, racial equality, and women's rights activist. Delivered a speech "Ain't I a Woman?" in 1851 at the Ohio Women's Rights Convention in Akron. Helped to recruit black troops for the Union Army, and tried but failed to secure land grants from the federal government for former slaves.

48. General Antonio López de Santa Anna (1794-1876)

A Mexican political and soldier, Santa Anna played a huge role in the shaping of the early Mexican government (mostly for the worse). His role in American history is as the losing general in both the secession of Texas from Mexico and in the Mexican-American War.

49. Sam Houston (1793-1863)
Born in Virginia, Houston spent time in Tennessee, during which he was accepted into the Cherokee nation. After serving as Governor of Tennessee, he settled in Texas and became the leader of the Texas Revolution that led to secession from Mexico. He supported annexation by the United States, and became the first governor of Texas. He resigned his post in 1861 and refused to swear loyalty to the Confederacy.

50. John C. Calhoun
A senator, statesman, and Vice President of the United States from South Carolina, Calhoun started off his career as a nationalist congressman who favored internal improvements funded by the federal government and a strong foreign policy. After running on Andrew Jackson's ticket in 1828, Calhoun evolved into one of the foremost advocates of states' rights. He advanced the theory of nullification, which argued that each state could decide whether or not to obey a federal law (note that this conflicted with the Supreme Court's decision in McCulloch v. Maryland [1819], which declared federal law to supersede state law). In 1832, South Carolina held a special convention to nullify a federal tariff, which pushed Jackson, no full-blooded nationalist himself, to pass a Force Bill giving the president the power to take military action to compel South Carolina to comply with federal law. Calhoun was a staunch defender of the cause of the slaveholding South.

51. James Polk (1795-1849)
A protégé of Andrew Jackson, Polk emerged as the proverbial 'dark-horse' candidate in the election of 1844 when the Democratic party could not agree on a nominee. He was an experienced politician at the time of the nomination, having served as both Speaker of the House of Representatives and Governor of Tennessee. Polk's main platform was expansionism – he was in favor of annexing Texas and claiming all of the Oregon territory for the United States. And this came to fruition: during his presidency, Mexico ceded New Mexico and California to the United States; Britain worked out a deal to split the Oregon territory at the 49th parallel; and Texas became a state. Polk promised to serve only one term and stuck to that promise; he died shortly after he left office in 1849.

52. David Wilmot (1814-1868)
A congressman from Pennsylvania, Wilmot entered politics as a Jacksonian Democrat, but moved into the Free Soil Party in the 1840s and subsequently the Republican Party. A moderate, he is famous for being the sponsor of an amendment shortly after the outbreak of the Mexican-American war (1846) proposing that any new treaties won from Mexico would be closed to slavery. The Wilmot Proviso passed the House but failed in the Senate. The failure of the proviso had major political repercussions. The Democratic party explicitly opposed the Proviso and ran in 1848 on a platform of popular sovereignty. A new party – the Free Soil Party – was formed in support of the proviso. Wilmot joined this party, and later the new Republican Party.

53. Lewis Cass (1782-1866)
A Michigan solider and politician who is primarily famous for running for president in 1848 under the banner of popular sovereignty to determine the fate of slavery in new territories. The main idea of popular sovereignty is the argument that the people in a territory, not Congress, should get to decide the all-important issue of whether that territory would organized as a free or a slave state. Cass lost the election to General Zachary Taylor.

54. Daniel Webster (1782-1852)
A giant of the Senate, Daniel Webster was a Massachusetts politician and a Whig who stood for modernization, strong national government, banking and industry, and against the western and southern farmers and slaveowners who formed the base of Jacksonian Democracy. A skilled lawyer, Webster argued more than 200 cases in front of the Supreme Court and through his mastery of constitutional law influenced both the thinking of many Supreme Court justices and jurisprudence more generally. In the Senate, he represented the interests of northern manufacturers and their support for tariffs, but also sought to maintain the stability of the Union through compromise with the South. Indeed, he disappointed many of his constituents by supporting the Compromise of 1850, which, among other things, provided for a Fugitive Slave Law that compelled federal officials to return runaway slaves.

55. William Seward (1801-1872)
A governor and senator from New York, Seward was a leader of the Republican Party who contended for the nomination in 1860 but lost out to the more conciliatory Lincoln. He loyally served as Lincoln's Secretary of State during the Civil War, and led the purchase of Alaska from Russia in 1867.

56. Stephen Douglas (1813-1861)
A US Senator who attempted to hold the center between North and South in the 1850s, Douglas strongly believed that popular sovereignty could provide the solution to the sectional crisis. Douglas is primarily responsible for the Compromise of 1850, which provided some breathing room, but he reopened the slavery issue with the Kansas-Nebraska Act of 1854, which brought popular sovereignty into a territory in which slavery had previously been banned. Douglas's position was badly eroded by the *Dred Scott* decision, which denied citizenship to any person of African descent, slave or free, and explicitly prevented Congress from banning slavery in any of the territories. The Democratic Party split over the issue in 1860, and Douglas was nominated by the Northern Democrats. He died shortly after the Civil War began, after staunchly rallying people to the Union cause.

57. Harriet Beecher Stowe
Author of *Uncle Tom's Cabin*, an account of life under slavery for African-Americans. Stowe came from a family of famous Protestant ministers and became a staunch abolitionist. *Uncle Tom's Cabin* was the best-selling novel of the nineteenth century, and helped fuel the abolitionist cause.

58. Charles Sumner (1811-1874)
A leading Radical Republican from Massachusetts, Sumner was beaten nearly to death by Representative Preston Brooks in 1856 on the Senate floor in a foreshadowing of the violence of the Civil War. After recovering from his wounds, Sumner returned to the Senate and then, with Thaddeus Stevens, lead Radical Reconstruction of the South. Sumner was in favor of equal political and civil rights for freed blacks and indeed for all people – he fought to change immigration and naturalization laws that favored whites.

59. James Buchanan (1791-1868)
The fifteenth president of the United States (1856-1860), Buchanan is most famous for presiding over the secession of the South. Upon taking office in 1856, he worked hard to placate the South, but only succeeded in alienating both the South and the North.

60. Abraham Lincoln (1809-1865)
The sixteenth president of the United States (1860-1865), Lincoln is generally rated as the greatest president in American history due to his leadership during the Civil War, which consumed the entirety of his five years in office. A young Whig lawyer and politician from Illinois, Lincoln stood for free soil and free labor. Despite being less experienced than Republican rivals like William Seward and Salmon Chase, Lincoln proved to be an extremely effective party and national leader during the war, holding the Union effort together with moral authority and political skill. He delivered some of the greatest speeches in American history, including the Gettysburg Address and the Second Inaugural Address. His death made the difficult task of Reconstruction even more challenging.

61. Jefferson Davis (1808-1889)
The President of the Confederate States of America during the Civil War, Davis was a soldier and politician who served in Mexican-American war and as a Senator for Mississippi. Davis could neither lead the Confederacy to victory, economic success, nor diplomatic recognition, although he was dealt a difficult hand without an active party organization in the South. He was captured by the Union Army in 1865 and charged with treason. He was not tried, however, and quietly lived out his life in Mississippi.

62. George McClellan (1826-1885)
McClellan was the leader of the Union Army from 1861-1862 and spent a great deal of time and energy organizing and equipping the Army, often to the frustration of Abraham Lincoln, who wished that McClellan would spend less time organizing and more time fighting. After the failure of the Peninsular Campaign of 1862 and the bloody stalemate of Antietam, Lincoln dismissed McClellan, who responded by running against Lincoln in the election of 1864, on a Democratic platform of negotiation with the Confederacy.

63. Robert E. Lee (1807-1870)
A distinguished soldier and graduate of the United States Military Academy at West Point, Lee served in the Mexican-American War and, choosing loyalty to his home state of Virginia versus the United States, refused Lincoln's offer of command of the Union Army. He took over the command of various Confederate armies early in the war and

won a number of victories over larger and better-equipped Union armies. However, he was unable to make an progress invading the North and could not hold off the Union Army in 1864 and 1865.

64. William T. Sherman (1820-1891)
A general in the Union Army, Sherman served under Ulysses S. Grant in Vicksburg, Mississippi and Tennessee. He was then given command of a larger army that conquered Georgia from the west, culminating in the capture of the city of Atlanta.

65. Ulysses S. Grant (1822-1885)
The eighteenth president of the United States (1868-76), Grant led the Union Army to victory in the Civil War. Grant's determination and willingness to fight allowed him to split the Confederacy geographically with victory at Vicksburg in 1863, and his success in the Overland Campaign of 1864 allowed the Union army to end the war in 1865. Grant served two terms as President, in which major achievements – a push to guarantee civil rights to blacks in the south, the suppression of the Ku Klux Klan – were married to corruption scandals and a struggling economy. At the end of Grant's second term, southerners and northerners opposed to his policies had taken over both Congress and the White House, ending Reconstruction.

66. John Wilkes Booth (1838-1865)
A famous actor who assassinated Abraham Lincoln at Ford's Theater in Washington, DC on April 14, 1865. Booth was part of a broader conspiracy to decapitate the government. He escaped but was eventually tracked down and was shot while resisting arrest.

67. Oliver O. Howard (1830-1909)
Known as the "Christian general," for his religious piety, Howard was a Union Army general who ran the Freedmen's Bureau from 1865-1871. The Bureau was responsible for providing education, agricultural training, and social services to freed slaves. He also served as the president of Howard University, a university for freed slaves, from 1867-73.

68. Andrew Johnson (1808-1875)
The seventeenth president of the United States, Johnson was placed on a Republican-Union joint ticket with Lincoln for the election of 1864 given his status as a pro-slavery but pro-Union Tennessean. After Lincoln's assassination, Johnson found himself in a very difficult situation as his sympathy and desire for reconciliation with the South were not matched by the Radical Republican desire to provide freed slaves with civil and political rights. Johnson's refusal to sign a Civil Rights Bill providing citizenship to African-Americans was overridden by the Republicans in Congress, and eventually relations between the President and Republicans in Congress deteriorated to the point where Johnson became the first president in US history to be impeached. He was acquitted in the Senate by a single vote.

69. Thaddeus Stevens (1792-1868)
A Republican congressman from Pennsylvania, Stevens was perhaps the most powerful and dedicated Radical Republican leader. Committed to delivering racial justice for African-Americans, Stevens used the military power of the Union Army to force the South to recognize the civil and political rights of African Americans. He died in 1868, and requested burial in a nonracial cemetery, a gesture worthy of his political and social vision.

70. Nathan Bedford Forrest (1821-1877)
Forrest was a self-made planter and slaveowner who worked his way up to the rank of lieutenant-general during the Civil War. Establishing a reputation as a ruthless and effective warrior, he did not give up the political battle after the surrender of the Confederacy, emerging as a leader of the Ku Klux Klan, an organization dedicated to maintaining white supremacy through force and terror.

71. Rutherford Hayes (1822-1893)
The nineteenth president of the United States (1877-1881), Hayes, a Republican, narrowly won election over Samuel Tilden (he lost the popular vote and barely scraped through in the electoral college thanks to some disputed electoral votes). Although he believed in equal treatment for the races and improvement through education, the narrow circumstances of his election and a consequent political deal cut with the Democrats resulted in the end of Reconstruction and the removal of federal troops from Southern capitals.

72. Andrew Carnegie (1835-1919)
A Scottish immigrant, Carnegie worked his way up from the factory floor to become a major industrialist in the steel industry, combining a number of steel companies to form US Steel. After selling his company to J.P. Morgan in 1901 for nearly $500 million, Carnegie became a major philanthropist, funding libraries, museums, peace institutes, schools, and the arts.

73. John D. Rockefeller (1839-1937)
Rockefeller was an industrialist who built the Standard Oil Company, the first and perhaps greatest of all the industrial monopolies of the nineteenth century. Rockefeller used a range of business practices, some ethical, some less so, in order to build his monopoly, and in the process became the richest man in the world, and the world's first billionaire.

74. Thomas Edison (1847-1931)
Perhaps the most prominent scientific figure in American history, Edison developed the phonograph, motion picture camera, light bulb, and much more in his laboratory at Menlo Park, NJ. His scientific credentials – Edison held over one thousand patents – were matched by his business acumen, as he pioneered the industrial lab, a combination of mass production techniques with rigorous scientific experimentation.

75. George Pullman (1831-1897)
Pullman was a successful inventor and industrialist who developed the Pullman sleeping car, a kind of luxury train cabin marketed to the upper and upper middle classes. He also built his own city, Pullman (now a part of Chicago), which he ran as a benevolent despot, sometimes more benevolent (supplying parks, good housing stock for a decent price, churches and theaters), and sometimes more despotic (no independent press, public speeches, town meetings). Despite (or perhaps because of) his efforts, his workers went on strike in 1894, a strike that was violently broken up by federal troops sent by President Grover Cleveland.

76. Eugene V. Debs (1855-1926)
Debs was a labor leader who helped found the Industrial Workers of the World and ran unsuccessfully for the Presidency several times. Starting off as a member of the Democratic party, Debs helped form the American Railway Union, the nation's first industrial union, which was instrumental in organizing the Pullman strike. Debs was imprisoned (not for the last time) as a result of not obeying an injunction to call off the strike. Educating himself about socialism in prison, Debs attempted to organize a socialist workers' party but never failed to win more than a few percent of the vote. He was sent back to prison in 1918 for violating the 1917 Espionage Act.

77. Jane Addams (1860-1935)
Jane Addams was a Progressive reformer who, through her work in Chicago's Hull House, attempted to help struggling immigrants deal with the challenges imposed by industrialization and urbanization. Hull House was designed to provide decent living conditions, education, and instruction in American mores and citizenship. Addams was a leader in the women's suffrage movement, and used her experience cleaning up the cities to support her argument for giving women the right to vote. She also fought for issues of better public health, world peace, and meeting the needs of poor children. In 1931 she received the Nobel Prize for Peace.

78. Walter Rauschenbusch (1861-1918)
A Baptist pastor, Rauschenbusch was a leader of the Social Gospel movement which sought to bring activist Christianity to urban areas. The main principle of the Social Gospel movement was that individual salvation and sin was intrinsically connected to social sin, and that it was therefore incumbent on good Christians to do everything they could to bring the Gospel, schools, healthcare and more to the cities. Rauschenbusch argued that too much emphasis had been placed on the individual sinner and not enough on sinful social structures that prevented people from flourishing.

79. Anthony Comstock (1844-1915)
A US Postal Service Inspector, Comstock is famous for his social work in favor of morality, particularly his formation of the New York Society for the Suppression of Vice. In 1873, he managed to get Congress to pass the Comstock Law, which made it a crime to deliver or transport "obscene, lewd, or lascivious" material. Included under this broad heading was public health information relating to contraception and sexually transmitted diseases.

80. W.E.B. Du Bois (1868-1963)
One of the great intellectuals in American history, Du Bois was a sociologist and civil rights activist who became the first African American to earn a PhD from Harvard. Du Bois' academic work on crime, the law, Jim Crow, and urban life, among other subjects, was informed by his deep concern with the lives of African-Americans in a nation governed by legal or de facto segregation. He criticized prevailing accounts of Reconstruction and the supposed criminality of African-Americans by collecting data that demonstrated the white racial bias brought to these supposedly impartial studies. He helped to found the National Association for the Advancement of Colored People (NAACP). He died just one year before the signing into law of the Civil Rights Act, which delivered the equal treatment before the law that Du Bois had spent his life fighting for.

81. William McKinley (1843-1901)
The twenty-fifth president (1897-1901), McKinley was a Republican dedicated to defending the interests of American business at home and abroad. A key plank in that mission involved maintaining the gold standard, which kept inflation at a low level while pushing many small farmers in the West close to bankruptcy. The defeat of Spain in the Spanish-American war led to the acquisition of substantial American dependencies in the form of Cuba and the Philippines.

82. William Jennings Bryan (1860-1925)
Bryan was a Democratic politician who ran three times for president, losing each time. He supported both popular democracy and religious humanitarianism, and as such opposed Gilded Age economics and overseas adventurism. Bryan carried out an active campaign for President in 1896, delivering over 500 speeches around the country in favor of Free Silver (i.e., higher inflation through an expanded money supply based on silver as well as gold), anti-imperialism, and trust-busting. He was famously on the side of prosecution during the Scopes trial over the teaching of evolution.

83. Josiah Strong (1847-1916)
A Protestant minister and leader of the Social Gospel movement, Strong viewed Protestantism as a key tool for ameliorating the ills caused by industrialization and urbanization. He took a strong view on both race and religion, arguing that Anglo-Saxon Protestantism was a superior religious and social system that should be used to 'uplift' other races.

84. Alfred Thayer Mahan (1840-1914)
Admiral and naval strategist who argued that America needed to build up its naval power in order to become a great power. His book influenced not just the United States but other nations, and helped contribute to the great naval buildup that preceded World War I.

85. Theodore Roosevelt (1858-1919)
The twenty-sixth president, Roosevelt enjoyed major achievements in both domestic and foreign policy. On the domestic front, he was an activist and Progressive president who favored conservation, the regulation of businesses, and a "Square Deal" for the average working person. He pushed America towards becoming a major international

power by building up its navy, intervening in Latin America (the Roosevelt Corollary announced America's intention to act as an 'international policeman' in Latin America), and pressing the interests of the business community overseas. After retiring from the Presidency in 1908, Roosevelt passed on the mantle of leadership to his chosen successor Robert Taft. Unhappy with Taft's unwillingness to take on activist and Progressive positions, Roosevelt formed a third party, the Progressive, or Bull Moose Party, but by splitting the Republican vote, both he and Taft lost to the Democrat Woodrow Wilson in 1912.

86. John Hay (1838-1905)
An American diplomat who served as Secretary of State in the McKinley and Roosevelt administrations, Hay is best known for the Open Door policy, which sought to defend US interests in China by allowing all the several powers who had designs on China to share access rather than each trying to dominate and exclude the other. Although he managed to gain agreement in principle, each of the foreign powers continued to try to dominate different regions of China, culminating in the Japanese invasion of Manchuria in the 1930s.

87. William Howard Taft (1857-1930)
The twenty-seventh president of the United States (1909-1913), Taft also served as Chief Justice of the Supreme Court (1921-1930). Taft was not a skillful enough politician to satisfy both the Progressive and conservative elements of the Republican party, and ended up disappointing both wings of the party. Although he retained the nomination in 1912, he lost reelection to Woodrow Wilson and in fact finished third behind Theodore Roosevelt.

88. Henry Cabot Lodge (1850-1924)
A Republican senator from Massachusetts, Lodge served as Senate majority leader and thorn in the side of President Woodrow Wilson. He led the opposition to Wilson's Treaty of Versailles, which included US membership in the League of Nations. Lodge feared both presidential encroachment on the right to declare war and international encroachment on the sovereignty of the United States government. Despite Wilson's efforts to defend the treaty by taking the issue directly to the American people, Congress rejected the treaty and the United States did not join the League of Nations.

89. Woodrow Wilson (1856-1924)
One of the first academic political scientists, Wilson wrote important works on both Congress and the Presidency, arguing in his later work that the Presidency, as the only nationally elected office, must take on greater power vis-à-vis the other branches in order to do the work of a rapidly industrializing and modernizing nation. He became president of Princeton University in 1902, Governor of New Jersey in 1911, and the twenty-eighth President of the United States in 1912. Harboring both Progressive and conservative sympathies, Wilson was extremely successful in passing legislation: his legislative achievements include the Federal Reserve, the Federal Trade Commission, the Clayton Antitrust Act, the Federal Farm Loan Tax and an income tax. Despite winning re-election on the premise of keeping the United States out of World War I,

Wilson found himself pushed into war in 1917 by the unrestricted submarine warfare of Germany.

90. John Dewey (1859-1952)
A great American intellectual, Dewey was both a philosopher and a social reformer, which was fitting in that his philosophy of Pragmatism stressed the linking of practice and theory. Dewey believed that public education and civic reform were crucially important in equipping the citizenry with the information and habits necessary to achieve democracy's full potential. He was a strong believer in the scientific method and in scientific experimentation to improve society.

91. Booker T. Washington (1856-1914)
An African-American leader, Booker T. Washington was a former slave who grew up in the Jim Crow South. Recognizing that the battle over Reconstruction was lost, Washington advocated an accommodationist posture towards segregation and advised his fellow blacks to work their way up through grindingly hard work and educational cultivation. He disagreed with the more confrontational stance of the NAACP, arguing that the best way for blacks to prosper given the political realities was through "industry, thrift, intelligence, and property."

92. Warren G. Harding (1865-1923)
The twenty-ninth president of the United States, Harding was a compromise choice in the election of 1920. He pledged to focus the country away from Europe and back towards the domestic economy and the interests of American industrialists. He won 60% of the popular votes but quickly ran into trouble due to political corruption in his administration, specifically the placement of friends and associates in financially beneficial positions. The Teapot Dome Scandal, in which Harding Cabinet members were found guilty of giving away oil leases at below-market rates in return for kickbacks, enmeshed the administration in a sensational political scandal. Harding did have a number of positive achievements, however, including a halving of the unemployment rate, acceptance of African-American civil rights, and a child welfare program.

93. Calvin Coolidge (1872-1933)
The thirtieth president of the United States, Coolidge was a pro-business Republican who served as Vice President under Harding and won the presidency in the election of 1924. A staunch pro-business advocate. Coolidge favored a free-market approach to economic regulation, saying in 1925 that "the chief business of the American people is business." Coolidge had a relatively progressive record on civil rights, and in 1924 signed the Indian Citizenship Act which made all Native Americans full US citizens who could nonetheless retain tribal and cultural rights.

94. Herbert Hoover (1874-1964)
The thirty-first president of the United States (1928-1932), Hoover appeared well-qualified for the job, with successful experience in engineering, business and government. However, his free-market ideology made it difficult for him to respond to the full weight of the Great Depression, although he certainly tried with the

coordination of volunteer poor relief, public works programs, and tax increases. He lost badly to Franklin Roosevelt in the 1932 election.

95. Clarence Darrow (1857-1938)
A famous lawyer who is best known for conducting the defense in the Scopes trial. John Scopes, a Tennessee science teacher, was on trial for violating the Butler Act, which outlawed the teaching of any non-Biblical account of creation in public schools. Although Scopes lost the case, Darrow became famous partly through his withering cross-examination of William Jennings Bryan, who served as a witness for the prosecution.

96. Margaret Sanger (1879-1966)
Margaret Sanger was a women's rights activist who fought for sex education and family planning. She coined the term 'birth control' and opened the first birth control clinic in the United States. Sanger was placed on trial in 1916 for distributing information about contraception; she gained a great deal of public sympathy and attention for her cause as a result of the trial. She founded the American Birth Control League, which became the Planned Parenthood Federation of America.

97. Franklin D. Roosevelt (1882-1945)
The standard against which all modern presidents are measured, FDR's two main achievements were victory over the Great Depression at home and over the Axis Powers in World War II. In some ways, the two achievements were closely linked as America did not fully pull out of the depression until war mobilization began in 1940. However, Roosevelt's New Deal went a long way to restoring confidence in the economy and stabilized the financial system, agriculture, and industry. Programs like Social Security provided many Americans with financial security in their old age for the first time. Roosevelt's steady leadership and wise diplomacy prepared the country sufficiently well for a long struggle against both Germany and Japan.

98. Harry Hopkins (1890-1946)
One of FDR's main advisors, Hopkins created and ran a number of major New Deal programs, including the Works Progress Administration. During World War II, he ran the Lend-Lease program, which supplied weapons, food and equipment to Britain and the Soviet Union, allowing their war efforts to continue during some very difficult periods. The Works Progress Administration hired out-of-work people to build and repair public infrastructure, including roads, parks, and bridges.

99. Francis Townsend (1867-1960)
A doctor and public health officer who became an old-age retirement activist, Townsend developed a retirement insurance annuity plan called the Townsend Plan, which became the core idea behind the Roosevelt administration's Social Security plan.

100. Huey Long (1893-1935)
A Democratic Governor and Senator from Louisiana, Long became nationally prominent for his left-wing economic program, which advocated significant wealth redistribution and federal spending on schools, public works and old age pensions.

Something of a demagogue (one who stirs up the masses for political gain), Long was accused by critics of his dictatorial control over Louisiana politics. His assassination in 1935 ended his aspirations for the presidency.

101. John L Lewis (1880-1969)
A major labor leader who served as the president of the United Mine Workers of America from 1920-1960. Lewis helped found the Congress of Industrial Organizations (CIO), a pan-industry union group, and later took the Mine Workers into the American Federation of Labor (AFL). Lewis was a sometime partner, sometime critic of the Roosevelt administration, helping FDR to victory in 1936 but calling nationwide coal strikes in the middle of the war effort.

102. John Maynard Keynes (1883-1946)
Perhaps the greatest economist of the twentieth century, Keynes provided a macroeconomic explanation of the causes of the Great Depression and also provided recommendations for its resolution. The Depression, he argued, was caused by a lack of aggregate demand in the economy brought on by the financial crisis and the resulting retrenchment of industry. Contrary to orthodox opinion, which held that the economy would reflate on its own accord through the operation of supply and demand, Keynes argued that the economy could settle into an equilibrium at low levels of output and employment. The only thing that could shock the economy back to a more acceptable equilibrium was an infusion of government deficit spending, the more the better. Although Keynes became famous with the publication of his *General Theory of Employment, Interest and Money* (1936), politicians on both sides of the Atlantic were reluctant to follow his logic and inject a sum of money into the economy large enough to restore employment to normal levels. Keynes enjoyed vindication with the buildup to war, in which virtually all the industrial economies returned to full employment as a result of heavy government spending.

103. Frances Perkins (1880-1965)
Perkins was the first female Cabinet officer, serving as FDR's Secretary of Labor for twelve years. She participated in the formation of a number of key pieces of legislation, including a minimum-wage law and the Social Security Act of 1935.

104. Harry Truman (1884-1972)
The thirty-third President of the United States (1945-53), Truman became President upon the death of Franklin Roosevelt less than three months into his fourth and final term. Immediately upon entering office, Truman was confronted with the existence of the atom bomb and forced to decide whether or not to use it to end the war in Japan. This baptism of fire was just the beginning of a number of difficult foreign policy challenges, as the start of the Cold War presented a variety of difficulties in Europe and Asia. Truman developed the Marshall Plan to help war-torn Western Europe back on its feet, and announced the Truman Doctrine designed to contain communism. He led a coalition of nations into the Korean War (1950-53), which proved to be a difficult and dispiriting conflict. Although he had won reelection against the odds in 1948, Truman's low approval ratings in 1952 persuaded him to retire.

105. Joseph P. McCarthy (1908-1957)
The prince of American demagogues, McCarthy was a relatively unknown Wisconsin Republic politician who made a career by capitalizing on Cold War fears of Communist infiltration. After making his name on the national stage with a 1950 speech that claimed that the State Department was deeply infiltrated by Communists, McCarthy gained authority to investigate a range of American institutions, both inside and outside the Truman administration. Incoming president Eisenhower failed to confront McCarthy, who upon his own reelection in 1952 proceeded to wreck the careers of a number of innocent Americans by accusing them of being Communists. McCarthy was only stopped when he took on the US Army, where his failure to identify communists left him exposed to increasing public negativity. Edward R. Murrow's news exposé on McCarthy finished the job, and McCarthy's political career from that point on was moribund. He was censured by the Senate in 1954 and died a few years later, a broken man.

106. George F. Kennan (1904-2005)
An American diplomat who, in the famous "Long Telegram" articulated a strategy of containment for dealing with the Soviet Union. Kennan argued that the Soviet Union was an aggressive and expansionary power who should be contained with American arms and economic power but not confronted directly on the battlefield. He believed that the internal contradictions of Soviet communism would eventually bring down the system. His strategy of containment was adopted, more or less, as official US policy for the next half-century.

107. Dwight D. Eisenhower (1890-1969)
The thirty-fourth president of the United States, Dwight Eisenhower was also the Supreme Commander of the Allied Forces in Europe during World War II. Eisenhower served two successful terms, in which he kept the United States out of any large conflicts and maintained prosperity at home. His major program at home was the creation of an Interstate Highway System that transformed the physical mobility of individual Americans.

108. Douglas MacArthur (1880-1964)
A highly decorated soldier over a nearly half-century career, MacArthur was placed in charge of the United States Forces in the Far East during World War II. He led the long and difficult effort to win first the Pacific islands and then surround the Japanese home islands. His victory over Japan made him an American hero, and he acted as viceroy with near-dictatorial powers over Japan from 1945-1951. He led the US forces in Korea, but his ill-fated decision to pursue the North Korean Army near the Yalu River border with China resulted in the entry of the Chinese army into the war and the eventual dismissal of MacArthur by Truman for insubordination.

109. Rosa Parks (1913-2005)
A civil rights icon, Rosa Parks became famous for refusing to give up her seat on a Montgomery, Alabama bus. . A trained activist, Parks's act of civil disobedience was part of the broader Montgomery Bus Boycott. She served as secretary and receptionist to John Conyers, an African-American member of congress.

110. John F. Kennedy (1917-1963)
The thirty-fifth president of the United States, John F. Kennedy was a war hero and son of financier and former SEC Chairman Joseph P. Kennedy. Kennedy and his wife Jackie brought glamour to the White House, but his tenure was cut tragically short by his assassination in November 1963. During his brief term, Kennedy articulated his political program, the New Frontier, which stressed the willingness of the United States to bear economic and political burdens in the broader cause of freedom. The Cuban Missile Crisis nearly resulted in a cataclysmic nuclear war; fortunately, back-channel communications were able to resolve the conflict while allowing both sides to save face.

111. Lyndon Johnson (1908-1973)
The thirty-sixth president of the United States (1963-1968), Lyndon Johnson had an extremely eventful five years in office. On the domestic front, he used his mastery of the Senate and a wave of sympathy for his martyred predecessor to pass the Civil Rights Act (1964), which guaranteed equal rights and treatment under the law for African Americans and all minorities. In 1965, Johnson passed the Voting Rights Act, which guaranteed African-Americans the right to vote. The same year, Johnson signed an Immigration Reform Act that opened US immigration in large numbers to non-European nations. These three major acts were only a part of his legislative legacy, however: Johnson's Great Society programs aimed to reduce economic risk through Medicare and Medicaid, which provided health care to the old and the poor; federal aid to education; and a War on Poverty that created a range of social welfare programs. Johnson's domestic legislative achievements as president are rivaled only by the New Deal. Foreign policy proved to be a far more difficult matter because of Vietnam. Inheriting a small war from Kennedy, Johnson followed the lead of Kennedy advisers such as Robert McNamara and Dean Rusk into a massive but drawn-out escalation, which failed to win the war and cost the lives of over 50,000 American soldiers. Vietnam tore through the social fabric of the country and also damaged the economy through high inflation, putting Johnson's Great Society at risk. Deeply discouraged by the war, Johnson abandoned his reelection campaign after a tough result in the Democratic New Hampshire primary.

112. Robert McNamara (1916-2009)
A Harvard-trained MBA, McNamara served as president of Ford Motor Company prior to becoming the Secretary of Defense under Kennedy and Johnson. Quantitatively motivated, McNamara aimed to win the Vietnam war through his mastery of operations and management. He succeeded only in escalating the conflict and increasing its casualties. McNamara resigned in 1967 and went to the World Bank, which some attributed to his desire to atone for his actions in Vietnam.

113. Martin Luther King, Jr. (1929-1968)
A civil-rights activist and probably the greatest American social movement leader of the twentieth century, King used nonviolent civil disobedience techniques pioneered by Gandhi and prescribed by the Bible to draw attention to the injustice of Southern segregation and racial domination. After leading the Montgomery Bus Boycott in 1955, King continued to raise money and organize the movement to push allies in Congress and the President into forcing the South to comply with Brown v. Board of Education and existing civil rights laws. King's "I Have a Dream" speech, delivered at the National Mall in 1963, helped to push national opinion towards a strong Civil Rights Act in 1964 and the Voting Rights Act in 1965. King was assassinated in 1968, which sparked numerous inner-city riots and national mourning.

114. Malcolm X (1925-1965)
A civil-rights leader and political agitator, Malcolm X from the start took a harder line on race relations than the conciliatory Martin Luther King. A member of the Nation of Islam at a young age, Malcolm X's powerful oratory and charisma propelled him quickly into its leadership class. He advocated the separation of the white and black races, and

115. Earl Warren (1891-1974)
The 14th Chief Justice of the United States, Earl Warren was already an accomplished politician upon being appointed to the Court, having served as the Governor of California. Despite being nominated by Dwight Eisenhower, Warren developed a liberal jurisprudence that sought to strengthen (and in some cases find) personal individual liberties in the constitution.

116. Betty Friedan (1921-2006)
The author of the *Feminist Mystique* (1963), Friedan directly challenged the cult of domesticity that had gained renewed strength during the 1950s. She argued that women could not reach their full potential without being allowed to flourish in the public and economic as well as the domestic sphere. The *Feminist Mystique* served as a guidebook for the women's movement of the 1960s.

117. Richard Nixon (1913-1994)
The thirty-seventh president of the United States, Nixon had previously served a Vice President under Dwight Eisenhower before narrowly losing the election of 1960 to Kennedy. He ran successfully in 1968 on a platform of having a "secret plan" to resolve the Vietnam War. A Republican working with a Democratic Congress, Nixon passed a number of relatively liberal economic and social-welfare programs, including the enforcement of desegregation in southern schools and the Environmental Protection Agency (EPA). He also scored a major foreign policy coup by opening up relations with Communist China. However, his policy to escalate and expand the Vietnam War in the hopes of negotiating a better outcome divided the country. He won a landslide reelection in 1972 but ran into deep trouble with revelations that his political associates had broken into Democratic Party headquarters. It turned out that the conspiracy ran all the way up to Nixon's inner

circle, and in 1974 Nixon faced a sure threat of impeachment. Upon conferring with the Senate and realizing that the votes to avoid a conviction were not there, he resigned the office of the presidency on August 9, 1974.

118. Henry Kissinger (1923-)
Perhaps the most influential and powerful Secretary of State since the 1950s, Kissinger served both as Secretary and National Security Adviser for Presidents Nixon and Ford. His main theory of foreign relations was *Realpolitik*, which held that the United States must be practical and cognizant of basic power politics rather than idealistic, with the implication that it could deal with any power, no matter how ideologically repugnant. Kissinger achieved a great deal by working out agreements with the Soviet Union and Communist China. He ended the war in Vietnam, but at the price of expanding the war to Laos and Cambodia, resulting in many deaths.

119. Gerald Ford (1913-2006)
The thirty-eighth president of the United States (1973-76), Ford took the office upon the resignation of Richard Nixon and damaged his political prospects by issuing a full pardon to Nixon for Watergate. Presiding over a weak economy, he was uncertain whether to run for reelection, but upon deciding to go for it barely won an intra-party challenge from Ronald Reagan. He was narrowly defeated by Jimmy Carter in 1976.

120. Jimmy Carter (1924-)
The thirty-ninth president of the United States (1976-1980), Carter's presidency featured a new emphasis on human rights overseas and a difficult economy at home. He had to face down an intra-party challenge from Ted Kennedy and lost his re-election to Ronald Reagan.

121. Barry Goldwater (1909-1998)
The political godfather of modern conservatism, Goldwater was a Senator from Arizona who lost the 1964 presidential election to Lyndon Johnson in a landslide. Goldwater had something of a last laugh, however, as the limited government principles that he espoused came to dominate American politics by the 1980s.

122. Ronald Reagan (1911-2004)
The fortieth president of the United States (1980-1988), Reagan led a conservative revolution that transformed American politics. Arguing that "government is not the solution to our problem, government is the problem," he slashed marginal tax rates, deregulated many industries, and reduced the money supply to constrain inflation. He presided over many years of strong economic growth, but also large and growing deficits, as the tax cuts and increased spending pushed the US government into a structural deficit. The ascension of Mikhail Gorbachev provided an opening that led to a new relationship with the Soviet Union, and, just after the departure of Reagan from the Oval Office, the fall of the Berlin Wall and the end of the Cold War.

References

Bach, Mark and Betsy Fitzgerald. 2005. *AP US History: An Apex Learning Guide.* New York: Simon & Schuster.

BEA. 2012. "NIPA Tables - Historical Tables." edited by B. o. E. Analysis.

Brown, Dee. 1970. *Bury My Heart at Wounded Knee: An Indian History of the American west.* New York: Holt, Rhinehart & Winston.

Bureau of Labor Statistics. "Labor Force Statistics."

Coen, Robert. 1973. "Labor Force and Unemployment in the 1920's and 1930's: A Re-examination Based on Postwar Experience." *The Review of Economics and Statistics* 55:46-55.

Deitch, Jo-Anne (editor). 2001. *A Nation of Inventors: Researching American History.* Carlisle, MA: Discovery Enterprises.

Divine, Robert A., T.H Breen, George M. Fredrickson, R. Hal Williams, Ariela J. Gross, and H.W. Brands. 2007. *America: Past and Present.* New York: Pearson.

Faust, Drew Gilpin. 2008. *This Republic of Suffering: Death and the American Civil War.* New York: Alfred A. Knopf.

Goodwin, Doris Kearns. 2005. *Team of Rivals: The Political Genius of Abraham Lincoln.* New York: Simon & Schuster.

Horton, James. 2012. "Race and the American Constitution: A Struggle toward National Ideals." *Gilder Lehrman Center.*

Neustadt, Richard. 1960. *Presidential Power and the Modern Presidents.* New York: Free Press.

Romer, Christina. 1986. "Is the Stabilization of the Postwar Economy a Figment of the Data?" *The American Economic Review* 76:314-334.

Shapiro, Fred. R. (editor). 2006. *Yale Book of Quotations.* New Haven: Yale University Press.

Skowronek, Stephen. 1993. *The Politics Presidents Make: Leadership from John Adams to Bill Clinton.* Cambridge, MA: Harvard University Press.

Stout, Harry S. 2006. *Upon the Altar of the Nation: A Moral History of the Civil War.* New York: Penguin Books.

US Census Bureau. 1949. *Historical Statistics of the United States: 1789-1945.* Washington: US Government Printing Office.

—. 1975. *Historical Statistics of the United States: Colonial Times to 1970.* Washington: US Government Publishing Office.

US Office of Personnel Management. 2012. "Historical Tables - Total Government Employment Since 1962."